W9-DIL-068

Border Crossings

GLOBAL ENCOUNTERS: STUDIES IN COMPARATIVE POLITICAL THEORY
Series Editor: Fred Dallmayr, University of Notre Dame

This series seeks to inaugurate a new field of inquiry and intellectual concern: that of comparative political theory as an inquiry proceeding not from the citadel of a global hegemony but through cross-cultural dialogue and critical interaction. By opening the discourse of political theory—today largely dominated by American and European intellectuals—to voices from across the global spectrum, we hope to contribute to a richer, multifaceted mode of theorizing as well as to a deeper, cross-cultural awareness of the requirements of global justice.

INTERNATIONAL ADVISORY BOARD
Shlomo Avineri, Hebrew University (Israel)
Gerhold K. Becker, Hong Kong Baptist University (China)
J. A. Camirelli, La Trobe University (Australia)
D. P. Chattopadhyaya, Centre for Studies in Civilisations, Delhi (India)
David Crocker, University of Maryland (United States)
Ahmet Davutoglu, Marmara University (Turkey)
Eliot Deutsch, University of Hawaii (United States)
Chaibong Hahm, Yonsei University, Seoul (Korea)
Paulin J. Hountondji, University of Bénin (Bénin)
Hwa Yol Jung, Moravian College (United States)
Raphael de Kadt, University of Natal (South Africa)
Hong-woo Kim, Seoul National University, Seoul (Korea)
Thomas Leithäuser, University of Bremen (Germany)
Jitendra Mohanty, Temple University (United States)
Amena Mohsin, Dhaka University (Bangladesh)
Chandra Muzaffer, Just World Trust, Kuala Lumpur (Malaysia)
Ashis Nandy, Centre for the Study of Developing Societies, Delhi (India)
Kazuhiko Okuda, International University of Japan, Niigata
Thomas Pantham, M.S. University of Baroda (India)
Bhikhu Parekh, University of Hull (United Kingdom)
Chaiwat Satha-anand, Thammasat University, Bangkok (Thailand)
Abdulkarim Soroush, Academy of Philosophy, Tehran (Iran)
Jesse Freire de Souza, University of Brasilia (Brazil)
Charles Taylor, McGill University (Canada)
Tu Weiming, Harvard University (United States)

Border Crossings: Toward a Comparative Political Theory, edited by Fred Dallmayr

Forthcoming:
Gandhi and Self-Government, edited by Anthony J. Parel
Race, Ethnicity, and Reconciliation: A Multicultural and Comparative Dialogue, edited by Willuam E. Van Vugt

Border Crossings

Toward a Comparative Political Theory

Fred Dallmayr

LEXINGTON BOOKS
Lanham • Boulder • New York • Oxford

LEXINGTON BOOKS

Published in the United States of America
by Lexington Books
4720 Boston Way, Lanham, Maryland 20706

12 Hid's Copse Road
Cumnor Hill, Oxford OX2 9JJ, England

Copyright © 1999 by Lexington Books

All rights reserved. No part of this publication may be reproduced,
stored in a retrieval system, or transmitted in any form or by any
means, electronic, mechanical, photocopying, recording, or otherwise,
without the prior permission of the publisher.

British Library Cataloguing in Publication Information Available

Library of Congress Cataloging-in-Publication Data

Dallmayr, Fred R. (Fred Reinhard), 1928–
  Border crossings : toward a comparative political theory / Fred R. Dallmayr.
    p.   cm. — (Global encounters)
  Includes bibliographical references and index.
  ISBN 0-7391-0042-4 (cloth : alk. paper). — ISBN 0-7391-0043-2 (pbk. : alk.
paper)
    1. Political science. 2. Political science—Philosophy. 3. International
relations—Methodology. 4. Comparative government. I. Title. II. Series.
JA66.D34   1999
320.5—dc21   99-33088
                                                                 CIP

Printed in the United States of America

♾™ The paper used in this publication meets the minimum requirements of American
National Standard for Information Sciences—Permanence of Paper for Printed Library
Materials, ANSI/NISO Z39.48–1992.

To all people seeking global justice and peace.

Contents

Acknowledgments

The editor wishes to thank Stephen M. Wrinn, editorial director of Lexington Books, for his willingness to endorse both the present volume and the new series, *Global Encounters: Studies in Comparative Political Theory*. Whereas most publishers are content to replicate established mainstream paradigms, Wrinn had the foresight and courage to support a new and relatively uncharted field of endeavor whose significance for the emerging cosmopolis is bound to be considerable. Thanks also go to Serena J. Leigh, the acquisitions editor for Lexington Books, and to the entire production staff, whose assistance was greatly appreciated. A special vote of thanks is due to Cheryl Reed, whose help in putting the entire manuscript into proper, camera-ready shape was invaluable.

The editor also expresses gratitude for a number of permissions to reprint. Chapters 1, 2, 5, 7, 8, and 10 are revised versions of essays which appeared in the Special Issue on "Non-Western Political Thought" of *The Review of Politics*, vol. 59 (Summer 1997), while chapter 9 appeared in *The Review of Politics*, vol. 60 (Fall 1997). The essays are published here with the permission of the general editor of *The Review of Politics*. Chapter 3 is a revised version of an essay first published in *Case Western Reserve Journal of International Law*, vol. 24 (1992); the essay appears here with the permission of the Journal. Chapter 6 was first published in the *Journal of Peace Research*, vol. 43 (1997), and is reprinted here with the permission of Sage Publications Ltd., London, UK.

Introduction:

Toward a Comparative Political Theory

Fred Dallmayr

The present volume seeks to inaugurate or help launch a new field of academic inquiry as well as of general intellectual concerns: the field of comparative political theory or philosophy. The impulse behind this initiative is a transformation which profoundly shapes our waning century and millennium: the emergence of (what some have called) the "global village," involving the steadily intensifying interaction among previously more or less segregated civilizations or cultures. Carried forward by a seemingly inexorable momentum, this transformation is both exhilarating and deeply perplexing or frustrating. One of the sources of perplexity has to do with the prevailing "babel of tongues"—evident in the fact that the emerging global community is so far marked by noncommunication. To be sure, there is no shortage of information channels, but whatever channels exist tend to be either strategically tilted or narrowly monolingual or monocultural in character. Differently phrased: the prevalent global discourse is a discourse of the market and, to some extent, a discourse of science, technology, and the media. What is lacking is a discourse about deeper existential and practical-moral concerns: a discourse about the meaning structure of the global village, about proper modes of living and sharing together, or about what Aristotle called the "good life." To this extent, our time is suffering from a global "culture lag": a lag of human understanding behind the immensity of technological change.[1]

In contemporary academia, comparative political theory or philosophy is either completely nonexistent or at best an embryonic and marginalized type of endeavor.[2] As practiced in most Western universities, the study of political theory or philosophy involves basically the rehearsal of the "canon" of Western political thought from Plato to Marx or Nietzsche—with occasional recent concessions to stands of feminism and multiculturalism as found in Western societies. Only rarely are practitioners of political thought willing (and professionally encouraged) to transgress the canon, and thereby the cultural boundaries of North America and Europe, in the direction of genuine comparative investigations. On the face of it, this assertion seems to be belied by the presence of a well-established subdiscipline in Western political science: the field of "comparative politics"; however, that field is not simply synonymous or congruent with political theorizing. As cultivated by mainstream practitioners, comparative politics is either empirical-descriptive in character or else governed by stylized or formal models of analysis—approaches which rarely question their own premises or assumptions. From the vantage of political theorizing, what is most dubious about these models or approaches is their unabashed derivation from key features of modern Western politics, including the structures of the secular nation-state with its accent on proceduralism, separated powers, and the bifurcation of public and private domains.

In large measure, reliance on these structures permits the comparativist or comparative political scientist to assume the stance of a global overseer or universal spectator whose task consists basically of assessing the relative distance or proximity of given societies to the established global yardstick. Here the political theorist must part company. Faithful to the Platonic motto of "wondering" (*thaumazein*), the reflective theorist in the global village must shun spectatorial allures and adopt the more modest stance of participant in the search for truth: by opening mind and heart to the puzzling diversity of human experiences and traditions—and also to the possibility of jeopardizing cherished preconceptions or beliefs. In more concrete terms, the Western practitioner of political theory/philosophy must relinquish the role of universal teacher (buttressed by Western hegemony) and be content with that of fellow student in a cross-cultural learning experience. In the inspired and inspiring words of Raimundo Panikkar, comparative philosophy might better be termed an "imparative" discipline— where "imparative" (from Latin *imparare*) denotes a learning endeavor and by no means a commanding or "imperative" enterprise. Whatever general "truth" can be found in the global village emerges here not through unilateral fiat but only through mutual interrogation, contestation, and lateral engagement.[3]

While inaugurating a new field, the present volume cannot hope (and does not claim) to be comprehensive or to convey a sense of the broad spectrum of that field. Properly pursued, comparative political theorizing would need to be genuinely global in character, by ranging from Europe and the Americas to Africa, Asia, and Australasia. Considerations of feasibility and limitations of space dictated that the focus be narrowed to a segment (still quite immense) of the global cultural fabric: the segment comprising the Islamic world, the Indian subcontinent, and the Far East. Using different geographical vocabulary, the volume presents an "Asian" focus, proceeding basically from West Asia to South and East Asia. In speaking of an Asian focus, one point needs to be made clear at the very outset: the contributors to this volume in no way subscribe to the notion of an Asian "essence" or the assumption of an "essential" or unbridgeable gulf between West and non-West. Such an assumption would fly in the face both of anti-essentialist trends in contemporary philosophy and (more importantly) of the evidence of historical experience. As history teaches, every culture involves a complex process of sedimentation, accretion, and transformation, a process which at all times involved a certain measure of cross-cultural learning (though not to the degree of today). At the same time, the denial of essential or invariant differences between cultures does not amount to an endorsement of essential sameness or nondistinction. Although propagated by "one world" and "end of history" formulas, the ideology of global sameness—typically of neoliberal vintage—ignores the reality of diverse historical-cultural trajectories and also the effects of profound asymmetries in the global distribution of wealth and power. In light of these factors, comparative political theorizing has to steer a difficult path between global uniformity and radical cultural difference, or between indiscriminate "assimilation" and discriminatory "separation" (to use the terms employed by Iris Marion Young).[4] This precarious path is indicated by the title of this volume, *Border Crossings*.

In large measure, "border crossings," or interactions between Western and "non-Western" societies and cultures, revolve today around issues of modernization and development or, more broadly phrased, around the normative status and acceptability of Western "modernity"—meaning by the latter term a welter of ideas and practices deriving from the European Enlightenment. As a corollary, political theorizing in the non-Western world today involves in large part the (avowed or unavowed) effort to respond to Western modernity, with responses varying from summary rejection to various forms of accommodation and syncretism. In her opening essay, Roxanne L. Euben addresses this theme of challenge and response, which today is a topic of truly global or cross-cultural significance. As Euben persuasively shows, the topic forms a mainstay of contemporary intellectual discussions around the globe, although its impact is probably most intensely or agonizingly experienced in the non-Western world and particularly in the context of Islamic civilization. To highlight the varying assessment of modernity by Islamic thinkers, Euben's essay offers a comparison between the relatively modernizing stance of Muhammad 'Abduh, a chief spokesman of Islamic reformism in the last century, and the more radical and uncompromising posture of Sayyid Qutb (d. 1966) for whom modernity basically denotes willful ignorance (*jahiliyya*) and whose indictment of that ignorance extends from modern rationalist epistemology to the secular nation-state with its structural accessories. Drawing on loosely parallel developments in Western thought critiquing the Enlightenment legacy, Euben raises the question to which extent critical responses to modernity can usefully be labeled premodern, anti-modern, or postmodern—suggesting as a preferred interpretation the notion of a "dialectical" mixture of perspectives both in the Western and the Islamic contexts.

The next several essays deal with a variety of "Islamic" topics—whose significance, however, transcend again narrowly regional confines. Nancy J. Hirschmann's essay concentrates on the symbolic meaning and political import of "veiling," an issue frequently and hotly debated by feminists in the West and the East. In these debates, the practice of veiling often functions as a kind of litmus test of modernity, with approval of the practice being equated with submission to a pre- or antimodern patriarchy and its rejection with endorsement of a modern, Western-style conception of individual freedom. For Hirschmann, the situation is much more complex and nuanced; stated in Foucauldian vocabulary, she seeks to extract veiling from the simple "blackmail of the Enlightenment" with its neat bifurcation of pro- and antimodern attitudes. In her presentation, veiling isn't always or necessarily repressive of freedom, nor is unveiling or open display by itself a synonym or warrant of free agency. Expressed in philosophical terms, freedom as a universal principle needs to be correlated or reconciled with the "veiling" function of cultural situatedness. Drawing on prominent studies of Muslim society—chiefly Abu-Lughod's study of Arab Bedouin women and MacLeod's work on women in Cairo—Hirschmann finds that veiling serves very different functions and obeys different protocols depending on social context; above all, veiling plays a complex role in either promoting or thwarting women's freedom and political agency. As she writes, used as an instrument of repression, veiling practices lend support to "claims about the universal appeal of Enlightenment conceptions," and especially about "Western understandings of freedom." In other contexts or situations, however, veiling may show the inadequacy or limitations of these Western conceptions, manifest in their neglect of the importance of cultural membership in the very constitution of autonomy and individual agency.

In discussions about Islamic civilization no issue stands out more prominently today than the question of the compatibility or incompatibility of Islamic teachings with the demands of modern democracy (as practiced especially in the West). In her essay, Azizah Y. al-Hibri clarifies many issues and debunks many prejudices or biases prevalent in this area. Basically, the essay focuses on two central aspects or principles of modern democracy: first, the principle of popular sovereignty manifest in the people's ability to elect their government and in the requirement that laws reflect the consent of the governed; and secondly, the (liberal) principle of separation of powers. Despite frequent assertions that Islam rejects popular rule (in favor of God's sovereignty), al-Hibri convincingly demonstrates that Islamic history offers no examples of "claims to rule of divine right, least of all by the Prophet." Both the messenger of God and his successors (or caliphs) were typically endorsed by a kind of covenant called "*bay'ah*" through which people expressed their support and allegiance to a ruler. In addition, there was a method of succession called "*istikhlaf*," which also involved extensive consultation. Regarding government by the consent of the governed, al-Hibri points to the Islamic tradition of *shura* in politics, where *shura* means the practice of consultation between rulers and relevant groups representing public concerns; flexibly interpreted and adjusted to modern needs, she argues, *shura* could be applied to "all those matters that are viewed today as the proper subject of consultation whether by parliament, cabinet, leadership of the armed forces or the supreme court of the land." The supremacy of Islamic law in politics might even be conducive to separate powers and checks and balances. Without being synonymous with the Western model, Islamic politics can thus contribute to democratic thinking and practice, or at least to a process of mutual learning and contestation.

The following essay by Ahmet Davutoglu shifts the accent from constitutional principles to practical politics in Muslim societies during the twentieth century. According to Davutoglu, Muslim politics during this century moved through four distinctive phases, with each phase corresponding to roughly a quarter century and being marked by a distinctive mode of confrontation with Western colonialism and modernity. The first phase, in his account, was a period of semicolonial dependency coupled with the upsurge of strong Islamic anticolonial and reformist movements. Guided by the Ottoman state (the seat of the caliphate), Muslim politics aimed both at the revival of Islamic traditions and the restructuring of social and political institutions; Western science and Islamic culture combined were seen as harbingers of a distinctly Muslim modernity. The dismantling of the Ottoman state ushered in a phase of deepened colonial dependency during which most Muslim societies were placed under direct economic and political tutelage. Following a series of anticolonial struggles the third phase saw the emergence of Western-style Muslim nation-states, all of which were caught up at the time in the pressures of the international Cold War. Like their Western counterparts, Islamic states were exposed to the process of secularization and the impact of nationalist and socialist ideologies—an impact which paradoxically fueled countervailing tendencies of re-Islamization or a "return to the roots." These latter tendencies resurfaced strongly during the last phase of Muslim politics, a period characterized, in Davutoglu's view, by "civilizational revival," "political confrontation," and "reactive cooperation" with Western modernity. As he writes, the dominant feature of Muslim politics at the close of the millennium is the tension between Islamic revival and continued responsiveness to modern life-forms, a tension which only "sincere civilization dialogue" will be able to bridge.

Both al-Hibri and Davutoglu deal mainly with the Sunni tradition in Islam. Manochehr Dorraj moves attention further to the East and particularly to the heartland of Shi'ism: Iran. In a sense, Dorraj's essay takes up the theme of veiling again, but now under dramatic and even tragic auspices: the tradition of martyrdom in Iranian political culture. As presented by Dorraj, veiling takes the form of the shroud placed over the bodies of martyrs who died in the service of a higher religious or mythical cause, a shroud separating mundane-sensual concerns from transcendental or spiritual aspirations. To a considerable extent, fascination with martyrdom or self-sacrifice was already deeply embedded in pre-Islamic Persian culture, as is evident in the somber tales of Firdowsi's *Shahnameh*. After the arrival of Islam, the fascination with self-sacrifice was deepened and became a veritable hallmark of Shi'ite spirituality in Iran, drawing inspiration from the exemplary sacrificial deaths of Ali and Imam Husayn. Throughout the centuries, the spirit of martyrdom was kept alive and nurtured by the memory of these exemplary leaders and also by the activities of radical Shi'ite movements (including the extremist sect of Ismai'ilis known as "Assassins"). In our time, this fascination reached a new peak in the Iranian revolution led by Khomeini, when thousands of Muslims sought and found martyrdom in the struggle against the Shah's regime. As Dorraj notes, devotion to sacrifice can also be exploited by designing leaders for strategic or power-political purposes—an example being the immolation of huge waves of Iranian soldiers in the war against Iraq. Attentive to this ambivalence, Dorraj explores both the "symbolic" and the "utilitarian" dimensions of martyrdom in Iranian politics, reaching the conclusion that often it is not the substantive program of a movement that attracts the public but rather the "sincerity of its advocates," with sincerity being measured by the degree of sacrifice.

Continuing the journey eastward, the next two essays focus on cultural-political dimensions of the Indian subcontinent broadly speaking (comprising both present-day Pakistan and India). In his contribution, Robert C. Johansen offers the unique case study of a large Muslim community—the tribal community of the Pashtuns—who inhabit what today is northwestern Pakistan (formerly the North-West Frontier Province of British India). In many ways, Johansen's discussion provides a supplement and contrast to Dorraj's account of Iranian culture: while in the latter case, self-sacrifice was often accompanied by a readiness to sacrifice opponents, the behavior of the Pashtuns exhibited a more thoroughgoing commitment to nonviolence, that is, a willingness to suffer *without* inflicting violence in turn. This commitment was all the more surprising given the long-standing role of belligerence, blood feuds, and martial skills in Pashtun history. As Johansen indicates, the turn to nonviolence was chiefly due to the influence of an exemplary Muslim leader, Abdul Ghaffar Khan, who himself was profoundly inspired by the political practices of Mahatma Gandhi. Although severely tested by the brutality of the colonial masters, Ghaffar Khan managed to instill in his followers (the "Servants of God") the courage and tenacity of nonviolent resistance—akin to Gandhian *satyagraha*—as a path pointing beyond revenge toward ethical and political transformation. Despite the widespread association of Islam with warfare (a misrepresentation of *jihad*), Ghaffar Khan resolutely upheld Islam as a religion of peace—where peace extends to the relations between Muslims, Hindus, and others. Like Gandhi, he had to pay the price for his convictions, spending roughly thirty years of his life in jail (first under British, then Pakistani authorities). In the words of Johansen, despite a "multitude of humiliations and deprivations," Ghaffar Khan and his followers "stood by" their commitment to nonviolent science, tolerance, and reconciliation of creeds and races.

Tolerance and reconciliation are also central to Thomas Pantham's discussion of "secularism" in the context of post-independence India. As Pantham shows, secularism comes in many shapes and forms; accordingly, the relation between secular politics and religion varies greatly in different societies. The constitutional regime of post-independence India has tried to steer a course between theocracy (elevating Hinduism to state religion) and a rigid "wall of separation" principle, opting instead for a kind of differential entwinement involving a policy of equal support of all religions (*sarva dharma samabhava*). Basically, the Indian constitution enjoins the state to be "equally tolerant" of all religions, a maxim which requires, on the part of the state, sensitivity for religious concerns and, on the part of religious communities, respect for civil rules of the game. Pantham takes issue with several leading Indian social theorists who construe India's constitutional regime as too closely patterned on the modern Western model. In the view of these theorists, Indian secularism—inspired largely by Jawaharlal Nehru—is either antireligious by disdaining premodern modes of folk-religion (Ashis Nandy), inappropriate for the Indian subcontinent (T. N. Madan), or else inherently inconsistent in both its conception and its application (Partha Chatterjee). For Pantham, the distance between Nehruvian politics and Gandhian *satyagraha* (religiously motivated "truth force") is not as great as is frequently claimed. In a hopeful vein—and in the face of recent communal upheavals—he presents Indian constitutionalism as an attempt to secure modern citizenship "without requiring people to become irreligious or antireligious." Accordingly, the *relative* autonomy of religion and politics is here used for reconstructing "both the religious traditions and the modern state."

The next three essays deal with issues arising in the context of East Asian traditions, respectively the traditions of Confucianism, Buddhism, and Taoism. Among these cultural legacies, Confucianism stands out as most prominent because of its long-standing role in the formative training of political or governmental leadership in East Asia. In our century, many intellectuals and social theorists both in the West and in Asia have indicted Confucianism for being an engine of feudal repression or of an antimodern and antidemocratic type of authoritarianism. Other observers, by contrast, have credited Confucian teachings with providing important impulses for rapid modernization (especially among the "Asian tigers"). In his essay, Russell Arben Fox sorts out these conflicting arguments, pleading for a more nuanced assessment: although acknowledging the danger of repressive manipulation, he finds in classical Confucian teachings also the potential for liberating reform, and especially for the transformative reconstruction of a liberal democracy suffused with ethical responsibility and solidarity. On a more concrete level, L. H. M. Ling and Chih-yu Shih investigate the political and ideological scene in postcolonial Taiwan, with special attention to the relation between Confucianism and liberal democracy. In their view, Taiwanese politics today exhibits an extremely complex and hybrid confluence of global forces and local (Confucian) traditions, a hybridity which resists explanation either by the model of "conversion" (to Western liberalism) or that of xenophobic retreat (into "Asian-style" democracy). According to Ling and Shih, political life in Taiwan stretches across three contending normative domains: liberal political institutions, Confucian rationales for legitimacy, and Taiwanese nationalist sensibilities. Instead of being a cause of dismay, hybridity signals for them the prospect of vibrant and open-ended politics.

Although perhaps less directly influential in public life, both Buddhist and Taoist teachings have frequently provided important stimuli for political thought and action. In our century, versions of both Nichiren and Zen Buddhism have left their imprint on Japanese political life. Yoko Arisaka's essay focuses specifically on the political implications of the teachings of Kitaro Nishida, the founder of modern Japanese philosophy and a leading figure in the so-called "Kyoto School," which aimed to build a bridge between Zen Buddhism and modern Western philosophy. Like other members of the Kyoto School, Nishida has often been accused of being a spokesman, or at least an accomplice, of Japanese wartime nationalism and imperialism; by contract, other interpreters have seized upon certain "universalist" principles in his writings in an effort to ward off charges of nationalist particularism. For Arisaka, both readings are excessively simplistic. Rejecting in her own way the "blackmail of the Enlightenment," she finds universalism and particularism too closely enmeshed or contaminated to permit a neat political bifurcation: at a closer look, particularism may sometimes be repressive and sometimes liberating, just as universalist principles may harbor emancipatory effects or else a complicity with hegemonic domination. The liberating potential of particularism (or the refusal of universalist abstractions) is vividly illustrated by the tradition of Taoism, especially as it has operated in the Chinese context. On the part of Western observers, Taoism has frequently been downgraded as a mystical, quietistic philosophy tied to particular natural surroundings but completely irrelevant to serious moral and political debate. In his contribution, John J. Clarke takes issue with this judgment and boldly sketches the contours of a distinctly "Taoist politics." As he observes, not only have professional sinologists began to relocate Taoist traditions more firmly at the heart of Chinese history, but Western thinkers from a variety of disciplines have increasingly come to invoke Taoist teachings in a search for moral, political, and ecological transformation. Thus, in the face of technological triumphalism, Taoist wisdom may hold out an alternative vision or "an other way."

In his concluding essay, Hwa Yol Jung links the search for alternative visions—that is, the transgression of Eurocentric or Western-centered perspectives—directly with the fate of political theory/philosophy in our time and in the dawning twenty-first century. In Jung's account, despite its universalist pretensions Western modernity was vitiated or tarnished by its close connection with Eurocentrism and the elitist devaluation of non-Western cultures. By "deconstructing" this Eurocentric mindset, contemporary "postmodernism" opens the path to a more genuine global discourse emerging out of multiple "border crossings" between societies and cultures. Jung follows Maurice Merleau-Ponty in the endeavor to find "lateral universals" bypassing both uniformity and incommensurability;[5] the task facing political theory/philosophy today, he holds, is to chart a course beyond "faceless universalism" as well as "ethnic chauvinism" in the direction of a pluralistic cosmopolis. In his essay, Jung illustrates this path by pointing to certain features of Chinese thought, especially its contributions to the overcoming of the mind/body dualism (leading to a recovery of the "body politic") and to a strengthening of ecological awareness or "green thought" (including "gyn/ecology"). In Jung's words, what is required in an age of cosmopolitics is not merely the discovery of "a Plato, an Aristotle, a Machiavelli, a Descartes, a Kant, or a Hegel in the non-Western world" but also the engagement with "a Confucius, a Mencius, a Nishida, a Watsuji, a Hu, a Tagore, or a Radhakrishnan in the West." In pursuit of lateral universals, globalization emerges thus as "a matter of confluence, of mutual influence in the recognition of what Mikhail Bakhtin calls 'heteroglossia,' which makes linguistic and cultural dialogization (com)possible." In its limited way, the present volume seeks to make a contribution to this kind of cosmopolis and cosmopolitics—both on the theoretical and the practical-political level. Beyond purely academic concerns, theorizing in a comparative—or better, "imparative"—vein may well be conducive to deeper cross-cultural sympathy and hence to peace in the global village.

Notes

1. To be sure, there have been significant efforts of cross-cultural understanding, carried forward chiefly by anthropologists or ethnologists and, to some extent, by theologians and students of religion. In the latter camp, one must take note of successive meetings of the Parliament of the World's Religious and of the many attempts to promote Muslim-Christian, Buddhist-Christian, etc. forms of dialogue. However, these efforts have on the whole not spilled over into the domain of political thought.

2. Presently, there are virtually no general texts in this field. For exceptions see *Comparative Political Philosophy: Studies under the Upas Tree*, Anthony J. Parel and Ronald C. Keith, eds. (Newbury Park, CA: Sage, 1992), and *Political Discourse: Explorations in Indian and Western Political Thought*, Bhikhu Parekh and Thomas Pantham, eds. (Newbury Park, CA: Sage, 1987).

3. See Raimundo Panikkar, "What is Comparative Philosophy Comparing?" in *Interpreting Across Boundaries: New Essays in Comparative Philosophy*, Gerald J. Larson and Eliot Deutsch, eds. (Princeton: Princeton University Press, 1988), 116-136, esp. 127-129. The same essay proposes the method of "diatopical hermeneutics" defined in these terms (130): "Diatopical hermeneutics is the required method of interpretation when the distance to overcome, needed for any understanding, is not just a distance within one single culture . . . or a temporal one . . . but rather a distance between two (or more) cultures, which have independently developed in different spaces (*topoi*) their own methods of philosophizing and ways of reaching intelligibility along with their

proper categories." For a similar proposal, under the label "hermeneutics of difference," see Fred Dallmayr, *Beyond Orientalism: Essays on Cross-Cultural Encounter* (Albany, N.Y.: State University of New York Press, 1996), 39-62. For the interlacing of universal truth and contextually situated dialogue, see also Kenneth L. Schmitz, "The Unity of Human Natural and the Diversity of Cultures" in *Relations Between Cultures*, George F. McLean and John Kromkowski, eds. (Washington, D.C.: Council for Research in Values and Philosophy, 1991), 305-322.

4. See Iris Marion Young, "Together in Difference: Transforming the Logic of Group Political Conflict," in *The Rights of Minority Cultures*, Will Kymlicka, ed. (Oxford: Oxford University Press, 1995), 155-176.

5. For the notion of "lateral universals," see Maurice Merleau-Ponty, "From Mauss to Claude Lévi-Strauss," in *Signs*, Richard C. McCleary, trans. (Evanston, IL: Northwestern University Press, 1964), 119-120.

1

Mapping Modernities, "Islamic" and "Western"[1]

Roxanne L. Euben

Introduction

The steadily increasing appeal of Islamic fundamentalist ideas in the Middle East has often been characterized as a premodern, antimodern or, more recently, as a postmodern phenomenon. Such terminology reflects a consensus that both the substance and appeal of Islamic fundamentalist political thought are usefully defined and understood in terms of a profound relationship to something called "modernity"; it is simply the nature of that relationship that is contested. Some have argued, for example, that fundamentalism represents the last gasp of atavistic impulses and archaic commitments associated with premodern—implicitly European—forms of community and social organization, commitments increasingly untenable in the face of modern processes such as the globalization of capitalism, the spread of technology, and the pressures of liberalization.[2] Others argue that fundamentalists' commitment to the authority of absolute truths over both public and private spheres expresses no less than a rejection of the processes and ideas constitutive of the modern (implicitly Western) condition, one that at the very least "sees in the expansion of scientific knowledge a technological transformation of a society that pluralizes options both for learning and living."[3] Still others suggest that the fragmentation of social and political ideas characteristic of postmodernism is to some degree causally linked to ethnic and religious revival. Given the conclusion that "modernism does not provide any longer the basis for human meaning and species survival,"[4] fundamentalism thus represents an essentially postmodern "attempt to resolve how to live in a world of radical doubt."[5]

Designations of premodern, antimodern and postmodern have taken shape against the backdrop of Western experiences and evaluations of modernity. Crucial to that experience is the linkage of what it means to be modern to what have been referred to as *modernist* "value orientations," orientations reflective of and committed to "the ascendance of reason, science and statist forms of social organization as they emerged in Europe during the thirteenth to seventeenth centuries" and a "basic secularism, finding meaning in the combination of materialist and scientific developments that made knowledge the equivalent of what an earlier age had regarded as salvation."[6] Thus "premodern," "antimodern," and "postmodern" not only connote historical periods but delineate normative orientations toward such initially Western ideas and commitments. For example, as "premodern" is implicitly parasitic on a teleological view of history derived from Western experiences, to claim that fundamentalism is premodern is to position it as an archaism resistant to the forces of progress. The argument that fundamentalism is antimodern is often linked to the claim that fundamentalism and modernity are incommensurable. Such claims of incommensurability often overdetermine the equation of political Islam and threat and, at their worst, seem designed to provide a new "menace" in a post-Cold War world where older polarities no longer hold sway. Finally, to claim fundamentalism is postmodern is to assimilate it into an ongoing critique of modernity we in "the West" both recognize and in which we participate.

Yet despite these culturally and historically specific origins, it is still the case that the terminology of modernity may be usefully invoked to make sense of Islamic fundamentalism. This is not because modernity reflects inevitably universal commitments and processes but rather because the colonialism, imperialism and now globalization have entailed the *universalization* of processes and ideas that marked the Western experience of modernization such that they have come to frame non-Western experiences of the contemporary world as well;[7] as Bruce Lawrence rightly points out, "[b]ecause modernity is global, so is fundamentalism."[8] Determining the nature of the relationship between Islamic fundamentalist political thought and modernity, however, requires an examination of the particular experiences associated with modernity in a postcolonial, Islamic context. More particularly, before we can ask whether Islamic fundamentalist thought is premodern, antimodern or postmodern, we need to ask a prior question: What are Islamic understandings and experiences of modernity, and what, precisely, about modernity is pernicious, from an Islamic fundamentalist point of view? What might these understandings tell us about the relationship of fundamentalist political thought to modernity, and the usefulness of the terminology of modernity in both Western and non-Western cultural contexts?

A brief digression is necessary here, for just as there are "modernities" that must be specified, the deployment of "fundamentalism" cross-culturally requires explanation, particularly because the term arose in connection with the early twentieth-century American Protestant movement that called for religion based on a literal interpretation of the Bible. In the context of a history of Western colonialism and imperialism, the application of a specifically Western and Christian term to the Islamic world is rightly suspect.[9] However, the Western origins of such terms as "nationalism" and "socialism" have not limited their usefulness in other cultural contexts. More importantly, the word "fundamentalism" is useful across cultures inasmuch as it evokes a concern with fundamentals, origins, foundations. I employ "fundamentalism," then, to refer to contemporary religio-political movements that attempt to return to the scriptural foundations of the community, excavating and reinterpreting these foundations for application to the contemporary social and political world. It is, as John O. Voll describes it in relation to Sunni fundamentalism, "the reaffirmation of foundational principles and the effort to reshape society in terms of those reaffirmed fundamentals."[10] This understanding emphasizes the "this-worldly" orientation of such endeavors: fundamentalism is not defined by, in Max Weber's terms, an "other-worldly" orientation in which salvation requires withdrawal from worldly affairs. It is a movement in which salvation is possible only through participation in the world, or more precisely "within the institutions of the world, but in opposition to them."[11]

This definition also limits the discussion of fundamentalist movements to those that are part of scriptural religious traditions where the "fundamentals" in dispute are located in sacred foundational texts, whether it be the Torah, New Testament or Qur'an.[12] While origins have always been a contested source of legitimacy for many communities, the radicalism of fundamentalists lies not only in their conviction that textual authority is guaranteed by its divine author—for in this Muslims, for example, generally agree—but also that the essential core of the sacred text is clear and not subject to interpretation. On the contrary, it is human interpretation that introduces the fallible into the words of the divine. Fundamentalists thus tend to reject the authority of past religious commentaries and textual interpretations in favor of what the text "really says," thereby denying that determining what the text "really says" is itself an act of interpretation. Central to "fundamentalism," then—and what distinguishes it from other perspectives critical of the modern condition—is the antihermeneutic claim that certain truths about the nature and purpose of community life are absolute and self-evident. If we take such "truths" and the debates that attend them in the public sphere to be the stuff of politics, a crucial implication of this definition is that fundamentalism can be considered profoundly antipolitical.

Voll's definition captures the dynamics of revivalist movements throughout time; yet the final feature I want to emphasize here is the extent to which fundamentalism is a response to a particular set of dilemmas associated with the modern world. In this sense, one might be tempted to use the word "reactive," as does Martin E. Marty, for example, when he argues that fundamentalists' "essential feature is not that they are reactionary but that they are reactive: They 'fight back' . . . in the name of God or the sacred against modernity, relativism and pluralism."[13] Yet fundamentalists are not only a reaction against modernity but an expression of it.[14] It is thus perhaps more accurate to say that fundamentalists are profoundly critical of as well as constituted by assumptions regarding the requirements of modernity and modern politics.

With this definition of fundamentalism in mind, in this chapter I seek to explore questions about the relationship of Islamic fundamentalist political thought to modernity through a tripartite comparison about modernity across history and culture. The first comparison is across time: I contrast the critique of modernity formulated by one of the most influential twentieth-century Islamic fundamentalist thinkers with the attempt by a prominent Islamic "modernist" of the nineteenth century to define modernity as consistent with the truths of Islam. More specifically, I argue that Islamic "modernism" as exemplified by the nineteenth-century Egyptian thinker Muhammad 'Abduh (d. 1905) entails a commitment to the revitalization of Islam in the face of European ascendence, a revival that consists, in part, in casting Islam as the "religion of reason." By contrast, I analyze Sayyid Qutb's (d. 1966) critique of modernity as a condition of *jahiliyya*, that is, a global pathology of the modern world that can be traced to the substitution of confidence in human reason for the divine truths necessary for living and living well.[15] This critique entails a dismissal of 'Abduh's attempt to make Islam into the religion of reason as an apologia for Western dominance, and the argument that the vitality of Islamic *umma* (community) and the revealed truths that sustain it require instead a repudiation of Western, rationalist ways of knowing and thus organizing the world.

These are by no means the only significant voices in modern Islamic political thought, nor is this comparison the only one worth pursuing to illuminate the diversity of Islamic responses to a modernity associated with Western colonialism and imperialism. But Qutb's quarrel with 'Abduh's "modernism" in particular provides unique insight into both a significant version of Islamic modernism and an influential fundamentalist critique of modernity. As these perspectives are not necessarily familiar to Western students of politics, I spend some time in this chapter conveying the texture of their arguments. Such arguments reveal that, for both 'Abduh and Qutb, the problematic of modernity entails rearming Islam in the face of the ascendence of Western power and the concomitant invasion of modernist assumptions about the inherent opposition between religion and the modern, rationalist world. Yet the fact that Qutb and 'Abduh disagree significantly demonstrates that, despite Qutb's claim to be in possession of the one true understanding of what it means to be a Muslim in the modern world, there are and always have been voices who reject the particular oppositions that define Qutb's fundamentalist thought. That is, there are voices who find, for example, no inherent incompatibility between Islam and parliamentary democracy, reason and scripture, cultural authenticity and rationalism.

This lends force to the contention that, even or especially within the paradigm of Islamic revival, there are other ways of perceiving the same challenges posed by European hegemony and modernity, and perhaps most importantly, other ways of meeting those challenges.

In the last part of this essay, I conclude with a second, briefer comparison, this time a cross-cultural one. In particular, I argue that Qutb's characterization of modernity as a condition of crisis, decay, and loss is mirrored in many contemporary Western critiques of modernity and modern rationalism in particular. From postmodernist critiques of rationalist discourse to so-called "communitarian" concerns about the impoverishment of meaning to Christian fundamentalist diatribes against the moral anemia of secular humanism, there are a diversity of Western voices expressing similar concerns about the legacy of post-Enlightenment rationalism and shared anxieties that the rationalist foundations of modern political and moral life may have failed to sustain us in some crucial ways. In showing that there are radically different voices from *within* "the West" increasingly critical of the modern condition in general and the legacy of post-Enlightenment rationalism in particular, this parallel reveals the ways in which "the modern West" is itself riven by disagreements, and characterized by ambivalences toward, modernity. This challenges the often implicit equation of the "modern condition" with the "Western condition"; it also undermines the opposition between "Islam" and "the West" by suggesting that there is at times a common critique of modernity at work across cultures despite crucial differences in the ways modernity has been experienced and defined.[16]

Questions about the relationship between modernity and fundamentalism in many ways point beyond arguments that can be made here. Nevertheless, these comparisons at the very least challenge explanations of Islamic fundamentalism that portray the current purchase of Islamist ideas as the resistance of a static and essentially premodern "Islamic essence" to the imperatives of modernity; it makes little sense to characterize as premodern a phenomenon parasitic upon and profoundly engaged with modernity. Moreover, I argue that it is not particularly illuminating to characterize Islamic fundamentalist political thought such as Qutb's as antimodern unless we are willing to call all critiques of modernity antimodern. On the contrary, both of these comparisons reveal only a glimpse of the diversity of understandings of what it means to be modern within and across cultures, including the sense in which to live in the modern world may by definition entail serious criticisms of and ambivalences toward modernity. This means that Islamic fundamentalist political thought such as Qutb's is part of an ongoing and multivocal critique of modernity and rationalism in particular, a critique which "Westerners" not only recognize but participate in. Yet I also want to suggest that it cannot be helpfully seen as postmodern either, inasmuch as the Islamist insistence on absolute foundations is antithetical to the antifoundationalism characteristic of postmodernism. Ultimately, the comparisons here suggest that these critiques of the modern condition, both Western and Islamic, are perhaps best understood in terms of a dialectical relationship to modernity, one that entails not the negation of modernity but an attempt to simultaneously abolish, transcend, preserve, and transform it.

Muhammad 'Abduh's "Modernism": Islam as the Religion of Reason

The light of this Glorious Book which used to be followed by science no matter where it went, East or West, must inevitably return to its full splendor and rend the veils of error. It will return to its original place in the hearts of Muslims, and will take shelter there. Science will follow it, for it is its only friend, its sole support.[17]

Writing in the mid-nineteenth century, Muhammad 'Abduh was part of a generation of Muslim thinkers for whom the problem of modernity posed itself in terms of the tensions between Western power and the decline of the *umma* (Islamic community); the need to adapt to the seemingly inexorable advance of Western technology, science and military strength; and the danger to Islam of the assumption that the march into modernity required the secularization of the public sphere. More particularly, 'Abduh is one of the best known Islamist "modernists," a term that refers to a strand of nineteenth-century Islamic thought that posited a golden age in the earliest generations in Islamic history and sought to simultaneously revive and reform Islam in its image as a bulwark against the encroachments of Western imperialist and colonialist power upon a decaying Islamic community.[18] 'Abduh's argument that rationalism is not only compatible with Islamic teachings but is actually enjoined by such teachings when rightly understood provides a window into a particularly significant version of Islamic "modernism." 'Abduh's thought delineates the contours of an Islamic experience of modernity and underscores the ways in which his modernism consisted in a reformulation of both Islam and modernity rather than an uncomplicated embrace of ideas and processes constitutive of what we in the West identify as modernity.[19] This "modernism" and the Islamic experience of modernity that informs it are a central part of the fundamentalist perspective I outline in the next section.[20]

Against those who argue, on the one hand, that modernity renders Islam obsolete, and those who insist, on the other, that the threat of the modern West requires inflexible allegiance to Islamic traditions, 'Abduh seeks to affirm not only the relevance but the authority of revealed law in the modern world. He does so by arguing that modern reason and its fruits are a universal inheritance consistent with, and supportive of, Islamic truths rightly interpreted. In his most famous work, *Risalat al-Tawhid [The Theology of Unity]*,[21] 'Abduh invokes Qur'anic passages and the example of the Prophet Muhammad to challenge those who have argued that history of Islamic practices reveals an essential enmity between Islam and the exercise of critical reason. 'Abduh insists that the Islam we see around us is but a debased version of the true Islam—the "real" Islam has never ceased to exhort Muslims to exercise their reason. Indeed, close examination and right interpretation of the texts reveal that Islam was the "first religion to address human reason, prompting it to examine the entire universe, and giving it free rein to delve into its innermost secrets as far as it is able. It did not impose any conditions upon reason other than that of maintaining the faith."[22]

According to 'Abduh, Islam properly understood starts from the premise that reason is a feature of human nature, and human nature is created by God. Consequently, reason is no less a gift from God than is revelation.[23] As both revelation and reason are divine creations, a contradiction between the laws of God expressed in the Qur'an and traditions and those of God embodied in the functioning of nature accessible through reason is an impossibility.[24] For 'Abduh, then, rational religion, which is to say the *Islamic* religion, is one where belief is both consistent with and premised upon the laws of existence and the nature of the universe, rather than antithetical to them; the inherent rationality of such laws makes reason not only an appropriate but necessary means by which human beings may study them.[25] As 'Abduh notes, "God has sent down two books: one created, which is nature, and one revealed, which is the Qur'an. The latter leads us to investigate the former by means of the intelligence which was given to us. He who obeys, will become blessed; he who turns away, goes towards destruction."[26] Thus as it is a logical impossibility for Islam to be opposed to reason, it cannot be antithetical to the fruits of human reason, the discoveries of modern science. On the contrary, 'Abduh argues that the Qur'an and traditions encourage the pursuit of knowledge of the material world as the means necessary for survival and well-being. Indeed, he argues that Islam actually anticipates sciences such as modern astronomy and studies of the earth's resources, and prefigures much of the educational, economic, and political institutions necessary for growth and strength in the modern world. Such a claim underlies his attempt to reinterpret Islamic concepts in terms of Western ideas and vice-versa, linking, for example, *maslaha* (reform in the interests of the community) to utilitarianism, *shura* (the principle of consultation) to parliamentary democracy, and *ijma'* (consensus) to public opinion.[27]

Arguing that Islam properly understood is *rational* in these ways enables 'Abduh to argue that Islam is both constitutive of modern truths and their final judge, while at the same time problematizing the equation of rationalism and the West, modernity and westernization. In the work of a subsequent generation of Egyptian intellectuals, 'Abduh's delicate if dubious balance between the authority of reason and revealed truth is used to reach conclusions 'Abduh himself would not have endorsed: that science, rather than Islam, is the measure of real civilization, that Islam is peripheral to political and social matters, and that the territorial unit of nation takes precedence over Islamic identity.[28] But for 'Abduh, adapting to modernity need not require westernization; the use of reason in interpreting the Qur'an initiates not the marginalization of Islam but an indigenous path to modernity that will free Muslims from blind imitation both to Western models of secular society and to tradition-bound views of Islam. This is because the Qur'anic exhortation to reason about the world precludes the uncritical acceptance of dogma (*taqlid*, or blind imitation) on the authority of tradition, or the submission to logical impossibilities or contradictions against the clear weight of sense-evidence.[29] Reason for 'Abduh thus means the exercise of critical judgment on the basis of logical and empirical proof; it is defined in opposition to blind authority to all inherited truths. Yet unlike the *philosophes* of the French Enlightenment, reason is not posed in opposition to faith in divine truths, but in fact is the means to reach them.[30]

'Abduh's confidence that the methods and conclusions of reason will affirm the truths of Islam properly understood underlies his startling suggestion that when confronted with a part of the divine text or prophetic sayings that do not immediately conform to the dictates of reason, it is the text, not reason, that can and should be adjusted to effect reconciliation. Thus, although 'Abduh endorses the view that the teachings of the Qur'an and traditions differ with regard to matters of worship (*'ibadat*) on the one hand, and social relations (*mu'amalat*) on the other, on certain occasions, 'Abduh argues that reason may be required to reinterpret revealed law where it is explicit, as well as when revealed law is silent or unclear on particulars. Consequently, 'Abduh encourages *ijtihad* (independent interpretation) provided it is always exercised with a view to harmony with Islamic law generally, and is engaged in only by those with the requisite knowledge and intellectual acuity. Such adjustment by way of reasoned reinterpretation is the necessary means by which to arrive at the "true" meaning of the passage in question: "[i]f there comes something which seems contradictory, it is necessary for reason to believe that the apparent meaning is not the meaning intended. It has the freedom after that to engage in interpretation guided by the rest of the text, or to entrust it to God and His omniscience."[31] Similarly, 'Abduh contends that "[i]f anything appears in the doctrine [which would compromise the supremacy of the divine by equating God to other creatures], it is necessary to dismiss this apparent sense, either by referring it to God for knowledge of its real meaning with the faith that the apparent meaning is not intended, or by interpretation based on a reasonable approximation."[32] 'Abduh's argument here reflects, in Kerr's words, the assumption that "a rational explanation exists although man has not discovered it."[33]

However, 'Abduh is always alert to the dangers of unchecked reason to religious truths. As a result, he celebrates not only the relevance and role of reason in the "true Islam," but carefully delineates its limits. In every passage where 'Abduh extols the rationalism of Islam, he concludes with a crucial, if vague qualification: the imperatives of reason must be in conformity with Islamic law, its exercise guided by the aim of maintaining rather than undermining faith. Therefore, while 'Abduh exhorts believers to exercise their critical faculties in accordance with Qur'anic injunctions, he also admonishes rationalists to attend to the limits of rational inquiry. 'Abduh cautions repeatedly that reason cannot transgress its own limits: human faculties can never compass the unknowable, for example, God's essence and the essences of nature and human nature more generally. Such things are by definition beyond human comprehension; pursuit of the unknowable is not only fruitless but transgressive of the precepts of faith.[34]

The authority of the truths contained in the Qur'an and the traditions is thus established by way of both reason and revelation. Reason confirms some truths directly, others indirectly, by way of the Prophet's authority. Still others flow from the authority of God whose existence—but not essence—can be established rationally. Reason and revelation are not in conflict because they do not command distinct spheres of knowledge and action; they simply represent two ways of knowing the same set of truths. Reason is the human faculty which enables human beings to distinguish between true and false beliefs, and by which they may obtain awareness, if not full understanding, of the divine truths necessary for living and living well. Islamic revelation is necessary because, although congruent with reason, only revealed truths can persuade without appeal to reason, and provide the authority and rhetoric necessary to bring those not given to reflection to right belief. Islamic revelation thus leads the reasonable to affirm the inaccessible, and the unreflective to believe the necessary.[35] Furthermore, as reason can never really know the essence of the afterlife or its characteristics, it is revelation, not reason, that provides us with the knowledge of the punishments and rewards of the afterlife; contemplation of such possibilities provide the impetus to not only acknowledge but adhere to the precepts of divine law. As Kerr aptly puts it, for 'Abduh, "reason can tell men *what* they should or should not do, and revelation tells them the most compelling reason *why* they should or should not do it [emphasis in the original]."[36]

Sayyid Qutb's "Fundamentalism": Modernity as "Jahiliyya"

In contrast to 'Abduh's attempt to reconcile Islam with what he takes to be the rational imperatives of modernity, Sayyid Qutb offers a critique of modernity as *jahiliyya*, a kind of global pathology in which modern Western rationalist epistemology is both axial principle and underlying cosmology.[37] I concentrate on Qutb as the Egyptian thinker whose systematic analysis of Islam, modernity, and political action has shaped the commitments of a generation of Sunni fundamentalists—from spokesmen for the Islamic Salvation Front in Algeria to Sheikh Omar abdel-Rahman of Egypt, the cleric convicted of "seditious conspiracy" in connection with the bombing of the World Trade Center.[38] While Qutb's perspective cannot be taken as representative of "the Islamic fundamentalist worldview," it is nevertheless the case his arguments arise out of a widely shared experience whereby modernization and modern political thought were intimately intertwined with the experience of power and colonial domination. The breadth of this experience suggests that Qutb's perspective is

neither unique nor idiosyncratic, but that it lends insight into a broader indictment of modernity common to many varieties of Islamic fundamentalisms,
despite significant political, juridical, and historical differences.[39]

Qutb argues that the regimes of the modern West and those that imitate them
in the East are corrupt. We can see the signs of this corruption everywhere in
the visible world, he argues, but such political corruption is just a symptom of
a deeper crisis, a crisis in the values of the modern world that Qutb calls
jahiliyya. *Jahiliyya* is a term taken directly from the Qur'an; in its original
Qur'anic usage, *jahiliyya* meant simple ignorance of a divine truth that had not
yet been revealed by the Prophet. As used by Qutb (and by Abu al-Ala
Mawdudi, the Pakistani jurist from whom he liberally borrowed), however,
jahiliyya becomes an epithet rather than a period in Islamic history. Modern
jahiliyya describes a society that has willfully rejected a truth that has already
been revealed to the world. Human arrogance thus distinguishes modern from
ancient *jahiliyya*: the modern *jahili* society has rejected God's authority because
it has refused to accept divine authority over political as well as moral
conduct.[40]

This rejection is evident in the domination of politics by human, or
"man-made" sovereignty, for "man-made" sovereignty by definition assumes
men have the right to create values, to legislate rules for collective behavior, and
the authority to define how life is to be lived. (I deliberately use the term
"man-made" rather than "human" because this is true to Qutb's intention: for
Qutb there is no question that power and politics are a male preserve.) In this
definition, all modern forms of sovereignty, nationalist, socialist, or liberal, are
jahili.

Qutb is not only intent on criticizing modernity; central to his project is
curing its defining pathology. The first stage of the cure requires self-
knowledge, for part of the crisis is the fact that we are unable to see the cause
or the extent of the damage. In a point that resembles the charge of "false
consciousness," Qutb insists that we do not even know we need help because we
have defined prosperity in terms of material, scientific, and technological
achievement. But the only really prosperous community, Qutb insists, is the
moral one. Once we perceive our moral sickness we will recognize simultaneously that human values are empty and human knowledge is inherently
limited. Conversely, since God created the universe only He knows the nature
of truth and the purpose of humankind. Thus recognizing these limits must
inevitably lead to a rejection of any human authority and submission to divine
authority in all spheres of life. For Qutb, then, legitimate sovereignty is divine
sovereignty, that is, the rule of Islamic Law—the collection of prohibitions and
regulations derived from the Qur'an and the Sunnah, all the accumulated
traditions, practices, and sayings of the Prophet Muhammad—over almost all
aspects of human existence. Since Islamic Law regulates everything from
principles of administration and justice to rituals of washing, it governs as a
whole what is often divided into "public" and "private." This means that

government becomes a matter of administration only, because legislation has already been established by God; it means that the economy is regulated by the ends of the community; and it means that all actions explicitly banned or condoned in Islamic Law automatically become the law of the state.

I would like to suggest that Qutb's critique of modern sovereignty not only entails a rejection of secularism but a critique of and rebuttal to modern Western rationalist epistemology. Qutb rejects the argument that the privatization of religion makes the public space morally neutral; on the contrary, Qutb argues, this simply replaces God's morality with secularist morality—or what he often calls *ersatz* religion. So *jahili* authority is, finally, secular authority. But Qutb's target is not just secularism; he is ultimately concerned with the rationalist epistemology that justifies secularist power. By modern rationalism I mean the assumption that truths about the world can be reached by way of human faculties, in particular through methods that give us access to things as they really are. Such rationalism takes human comprehension as the determinant not only of how we come to know the world, but also what constitutes legitimate knowledge; this definition of knowledge has, over time, legitimated human mastery over nature and human nature. Although there are numerous "rational-isms" in the history of Western political thought, this particular formulation of rationalism is usually associated with the European Enlightenment.[41] When Qutb rejects human sovereignty, he is rejecting precisely this human-centered theory of knowledge.

It is important to note that what I am calling a challenge to rationalist epistemology is not a challenge to scientific knowledge and technology; indeed, Qutb regards the latter as absolutely vital to the survival of the community and insists that pursuit of technical and applied knowledge is separable from the cosmology that underlies and justifies it. Rather, what is challenged here is Western rationalist *epistemology*. This is clear when Qutb argues that the danger to our moral existence can be traced to philosophy, for it is modern Western philosophy that has linked men and women's ability to reach the truth through reason to an explicit repudiation of the authority of divine metaphysical truths over both the public and moral realms. Here reason becomes at once a method and justification for the completeness of human knowledge: it not only determines how—in what language, through what method—human beings may come to know the world but also defines what is worth knowing in terms of what is knowable to human beings. As a result, for Qutb, what we now take as worthwhile knowledge is only knowledge of worldly phenomena; we have ceased to even acknowledge the unseen world, the source of real Truth.

The result of such rationalist epistemology is not only a truncated concept of the world, but a robust justification of the right of humans to govern without divine intervention. Such justification at once represents the usurpation of God's rightful authority and signals the eclipse of the truths which contain the meanings for which human beings by nature yearn: answers to the basic questions of human existence, that is, why we are born, how we should live, and why we die.[42] For Qutb, this threat to meaning is far from abstract: in the Islamic world at least, military defeats, political disunity, corruption and poverty are the concrete results. This is why liberalism, socialism, Marxism and Arab nationalism all look disturbingly similar to Qutb; they are all instances of human sovereignty justified by a rationalist worldview. This is why Qutb insists on calling them all by just one name, *jahiliyya*. Of course, he's not just rejecting rationalism, he is actually offering an antidote to it: his insistence on divine sovereignty as arbiter of not only religious but political and social life is an affirmation of a distinctively nonrationalist theory of knowledge, one where God, not humans, can know and thus rule the world.

It is thus my contention that Qutb's critique of modernity as a condition of *jahiliyya* is a direct repudiation of rationalist ways of defining and organizing the world, a protest lodged not only against Western power and its proxies, but against an epistemology that defines what is knowledge and worth knowing in terms of human comprehension rather than by reference to divine (although never fully knowable) truths about human nature and purposes, truths necessary for both community and meaning itself.[43] Importantly, such a repudiation entails a critique of Islamic "modernists," such as Muhammad 'Abduh, who had offered a very different response to and reinterpretation of modernity a century earlier. In Qutb's view, 'Abduh's argument that the revitalization of the Islamic community requires recognizing that Islam is the religion of reason exemplifies the worst sort of *jahiliyya*, the corruption that comes from Muslims being all too willing to accommodate the moral, philosophical and epistemological bankruptcy of the modern West and its drive to destroy Islamic imperatives. Originally the result of European colonialism and imperialism, *jahiliyya* is now the defining characteristic of Egyptian culture, and Qutb argues that it is precisely when the threat to Islam comes from within that the danger is the greatest.

Thus, Qutb explicitly rejects Islamic modernism as an apologia for Western dominance, arguing that it is essentially defensive, an attempt to justify the rationality and modernity of Islam both against the obscurantism of Islamic scholars and attacks from Western and Eastern secularists.[44] The underlying premise and implication of such apologetics, Qutb argues, is that Islam is on trial because it is somehow "guilty," and therefore in need of justification.

> He who feels a need to defend, justify and apologize is not capable of presenting Islam. Rather, he is one who lives in *jahiliyya*, a life that is hollow, full of contradictions, defects and flaws. This is one who, in fact, wants to search for justifications of *jahiliyya*. These are the people who attack Islam, forcing some of its adherents—who are ignorant of its true nature—to defend it, as if Islam somehow stood accused, in need of defending itself, like a prisoner on trial.[45]

This defensive posture is one not of strength and certainty but of powerlessness; for Qutb, Islamic modernism is a prescription for further decay rather than renewal. For in deeming Islam in need of justification, Qutb argues, "modernists" have inadvertently acquiesced to the given terms of debate, thereby deepening and exacerbating the subservience of Islam to Western power.

Qutb contends that this subservience is reinforced by the "modernist" emphasis on the importance of reason in Islam and the concomitant compatibility of modernity and Islam, rationality and revealed law. For while Qutb does not eschew the exercise and importance of human reason for understanding aspects of the world, he insists that such faculties are by definition subsidiary to the authority of the divine, which alone has access to the deepest truths about human nature and purposes. Consequently, Qutb is disturbed by what he takes to be the modernist assumption that reason and scripture are equally important for knowledge and guidance when it is self-evidently true that:

> [Divine revelation] came down to be a source which human reason must consult, to be the standard in terms of which all judgments, knowledge and concepts of human reason are evaluated, and to correct the deficiencies and distortions produced by reason. There is, no doubt, congruence and harmony between the two but on this basis alone: the absolute supremacy of divine revelation over human reason, not a posited equality or commensurability between them.[46]

Like 'Abduh, Qutb assumes that the Qur'an encourages the exercise of reason and both allows and prefigures the development of such modern developments as technology. But central to Qutb's political thought is the argument that proper recognition of divine authority requires using reason to see the substantial limits of human insight into the most important secrets of the universe. More particularly, reason reaches its limits when confronted with the most significant questions of all: questions of moral judgment, human purpose and the divine plan for all creatures and things in the universe. Thus Qutb admits a role for *ijtihad* (independent interpretation), but its exercise is strictly delimited; it is necessary to clarify that which is unclear, apply what is general to specific historical circumstances, and compensate for what remains unsaid. While 'Abduh, too, is attentive to the limits of human capacities to know the world, by encouraging rational reinterpretation of revealed law when necessary, 'Abduh inadvertently grants reason an extraordinarily wide scope. Reason now operates to *define* as well as *elaborate* the meaning of scripture; it involves the creation—as well as reflection and clarification—of scriptural meaning. Qutb and 'Abduh agree that Islamic law and the laws of nature are both expressions of the divine laws, but Qutb insists that reinterpretation of scripture to accord with the dictates of reason will destroy both the substance of and authority behind revealed truths, truths which, by definition, are beyond human comprehension and interpretation. For both, modernity and the European ascendence that defines it necessitates a revival of Islam; yet for Qutb, such revival turns on the recognition of the ways in which rationalist epistemology erodes divine authority, expresses and accelerates Western power and inhibits the establishment of a legitimate social system.

"The Rage Against Reason"

Qutb's quarrel with 'Abduh provides insight into a significant version of Islamic modernism and a highly influential Islamic fundamentalist critique of "modernity" and, in so doing, illuminates the contours of key Islamic experiences of modernity. How might this comparison illuminate the more general questions I have posed regarding the relationship of Islamic fundamentalist political thought to modernity and the usefulness of the terminology of modernity to understand it? From this discussion it is clear that as fundamentalist political thought is both embedded in and engaged with "the modern condition," it makes little sense to understand it as premodern in either a chronological or substantive sense. Indeed, despite Qutb's insistence that 'Abduh and "modernists" like him are insufficiently attentive to the necessary purity of Islam, Qutb's own work betrays the stamp of unacknowledged modern, Western influences. This is because Qutb's critique of modernity ensures that his project is profoundly engaged with and influenced by such distinctively modern phenomena as Enlightenment philosophy, Marxism, socialism, and liberalism.

Thus, Qutb's indictment of modern *jahiliyya* and his version of a purified Islamic worldview are not the expression of some kind of unadulterated Islamic thought, but rather reflect the interaction of Qutb's version of Islamic thought with the contemporary world, a world where colonialism and the influence of modern Western political thought has set the terms of debates even for those, such as Qutb, who have sought to critique such influence. This is not to say that all non-Westerners are condemned to be, as Partha Chatterjee puts it, "perpetual consumers of modernity" because Europe and the Americas are "the only true subjects of history."[47] Rather it is the case because those in the postcolonial world must choose their "site of autonomy" from a "position of subordination."[48] Inasmuch as Qutb's Islamic fundamentalist political thought is in these ways both a product of modernity and one of its fiercest critics, it cannot be understood as premodern.[49]

Might we more logically infer that in rejecting the central epistemological premises of modernity, fundamentalist political thought such as Qutb's is, with all the appropriate caveats, essentially antimodern? The corollary to this conclusion is that we are witnessing a contest between two incommensurate ways of knowing the world, a contest between "Islamic knowledge" and "modern secular knowledge," the former expressing fundamentalists' yearning for meaning and unwillingness to live in a world of radical doubt, the latter expressing the Western ability to cope with a world in which human beings create their own knowledge and employ such knowledge to create a way of being at home in the world. Along these lines, Bassam Tibi argues that Islamic fundamentalists represent a specifically Islamic form of knowledge that is fundamentally incompatible with modern knowledge, and he concludes that the Islamist attempt to decouple modern sciences from modern secular knowledge will result in a fall back into an era of "flat-earthism" if the politics of the Islamization of knowledge becomes the authoritative source for determining the relationship between the contemporary culture of the Middle East and the place of sciences as an expression of modern secular knowledge in it. At the turn of the twentieth century, we are living in an age of the global confrontation between secular cultural modernity and religious culture. The challenge of Islamic fundamentalism has a most prominent place in this confrontation.[50]

This conclusion is supported by the fact that Islamic fundamentalists explicitly view history and modern politics as a Manichean clash between two incommensurate ways of seeing the world. Indeed, Islamists such as Qutb understand the movement's meaning and purpose in part in terms of a challenge to what they take to be Western, rationalist epistemological assumptions about the world. History thus becomes defined by a battle between the forces of light and darkness—where Islam becomes the light penetrating Western darkness, a reading that curiously mirrors post-Cold War narratives in which the West is stalked by an old foe in a new "green" (the color of Islam) guise. Yet it is also the case that this challenge is posed from within "the modern West" itself. Such a challenge is perhaps most evident among Christian fundamentalists in the United States who argue that the Enlightenment's vilification of religion has culminated in the moral impoverishment of secular humanism, a cosmology that underlies and ultimately unites both socialist and individualist ways of understanding and organizing the world.[51] As Gilles Kepel argues, Islamic, Christian, and Jewish fundamentalisms are all "at one in rejecting a secularism that they trace back to the philosophy of the Enlightenment. They regard the vainglorious emancipation of reason from faith as the prime cause of all the ills of the twentieth century. . . ."[52] Such rejection is expressed in a common repudiation of the generation of "modernists" that preceded and shaped them, that is, those who all too readily accepted the interpenetration of rationalism and technology, secularism and science. Like Islamic fundamentalists such as Qutb, many Christian fundamentalists are intent on driving a wedge between the fruits of modernity, such as technology and science, and the modern rationalist cosmology and methodology they regard as pernicious to the authority of the divine in modern life.[53]

But the critique of rationalism from within "the modern West" is not just the purview of "fundamentalists." The anxieties about the limits of rationalism also emerge in what Richard Bernstein has called "the rage against reason," an increasingly insistent critique of the costs of modern rationalism from a variety of political and intellectual perspectives.[54] This brings me to the second comparison of this essay, a comparison across cultures. Despite the unfamiliar language of *jahiliyya* and the distinctiveness of the colonial experience of modernity, Qutb's characterization of modernity as a pathology defined by the rationalist erosion of the truths necessary for living and living well is mirrored in several contemporary Western critiques of modernity, perspectives that express the anxiety that the rationalist foundations of modern political and moral life may have failed to sustain us in some crucial ways. That is, several Western political theorists with disparate political and theoretical sensibilities have argued that the modern condition is constituted by a degeneration of meaning, a process variously traced to the rupture with tradition, the dual rejection of theology and teleology inaugurated by Enlightenment rationalism, and the subsequent diminishment of meaning—in authority, morality, and community—that rejection is said to entail.[55]

For example, in *After Virtue*, Alasdair MacIntyre argues that modern morality is powerless to guide us in action or endow life with meaning.[56] This is because we can no longer turn to absolute standards of right and wrong to adjudicate between such opinions. Modern moral debate, MacIntyre argues, consists of inconclusive and interminable exchanges of positions that come down to a battle of opinions that are only justifiable in terms of the language of individual preferences and needs.[57] MacIntyre calls this condition of moral paralysis emotivism; in *The Ethics of Authenticity*, Charles Taylor calls it moral subjectivism.[58] Whatever its name, Taylor and MacIntyre suggest that the current state of moral discourse is connected with the advance of rationalism in the modern world.[59] For while transcendent frameworks such as divine law had purportedly given life its meaning, and moral judgments the power of truth in the past, modern rationalism has eroded these frameworks because it is built on the insistence that all knowledge is obtained through reason. Such an insistence entails the separation of fact from value, for within the older theological and teleological frameworks, MacIntyre avers, the project of ethics was defined by the attempt to move from the "is" to the "ought," from "man-as-he-happens-to-be" to "man-as-he-could-be-if-he-realized-his-essential-nature."[60] Since divine law, for example, cannot be established rationally, it cannot be taken as true. But having rejected such teleological frameworks in the attempt to ground morality anew in the imperatives of reason, Enlightenment theorists could no longer address the ends of moral action. In this way, rationalism has eroded the force of all such transcendent frameworks in a development Taylor calls a "narrowing of horizons" and a "flattening of our lives" to capture how our lives are now poorer in meaning. As MacIntyre argues:

> The explanation of action is increasingly held to be a matter of laying bare the physiological and physical mechanisms which underlie action; and, when Kant recognizes that there is a deep incompatibility between any account of action which recognizes the role of moral imperatives in governing action and any such mechanical type of explanation, he is compelled to the conclusion that actions obeying and embodying moral imperatives must be from the standpoint of science inexplicable and unintelligible.[61]

Importantly, this loss is not just a matter of resolving academic arguments: in losing the resources to reach any definitive conclusions about our values, MacIntyre argues that we have also lost resources that enable us to give meaning to our lives. Such a crisis of meaning is simultaneously a crisis of authority because rationalism has gutted such transcendent standards of their force and meaning and, as Arendt puts it, without the self-evident experiences and truths that constituted a common world and common language, political authority has simply vanished from the modern world.[62] In *Habits of the Heart*, Robert Bellah *et al.*, similarly argue that the atrophy of a shared moral discourse has pushed the American ideal of individualism into a kind of solipsism.[63] That is, the rationalist erosion of shared ends has fractured once participatory democratic communities into groups that cohere only around patterns of consumption. Bellah echoes Taylor and MacIntyre in arguing that the rationalist project has plunged us not only into moral impotence but also into social atomism. Capturing a sentiment expressed by all three theorists, MacIntyre suggest that when "doing your own thing" supersedes demands that transcend the self, fellow citizens stand in relation to one another as strangers, as though shipwrecked together on an uninhabited island.[64]

These critiques become the occasions for quite different prescriptions to redeem the human condition: while Taylor calls for a reactivation of the moral traditions actuating modern individualism, MacIntyre insists that individualism and its modern liberal justifications are at variance with the richer and ultimately more substantial tradition of Aristotelian virtues, and Bellah insists that only democratic participation in communities of memory inhibit the slide toward administrative despotism. Yet it is particularly striking that these voices share a critique of modernity as a condition of crisis and paralysis occasioned by the rationalist rejection of foundations that transcend human existence and power. Contrary to Enlightenment aspirations of opening up the world to new forms of knowledge, experience, and politics, in these critiques there is a sense that the organizing principle of modernity is not enlargement but foreclosure. Here emerges the anxiety that the achievements of rationalization may have been bought at too high a price, and that rationalism has been the midwife not of maturity but crisis. It is not Max Weber's wary appreciation of rationalism reflected here but rather his bleak cautionary note regarding the iron cage, his worry that modern reason would eventually, like Mars, devour its own progeny. It is, as Thomas Spragens calls it, "the irony of liberal reason": the very ideals which "liberal reason" had initially served are themselves destroyed in the inexorable purge of value from fact.[65] This construction of modernity thus reflects a vision of history that opposes itself to the optimism of Enlightenment philosophy of history; modernity is not a teleological ascent from the darkness of superstition to the freedom of enlightenment. On the contrary, the defining feature of modern history seems to be the relatively rapid decay of precisely these ideals through the inexorable advance of atomism, disintegration, meaninglessness, and even, or perhaps especially, the return of chaos and the irrational.[66]

My point in this necessarily abbreviated discussion is not that these critiques of modernity are *right*, nor does this parallel presuppose that these critics of modern rationalism agree with each other, or with Qutb, on the cure for modern malaise. Indeed, Taylor and MacIntyre's emphasis on meanings embedded in social practices is radically different from my description of "fundamentalism" as a form of antihermeneutic scriptural absolutism that is in some senses profoundly antipolitical. Moreover, as criticisms have accompanied modernity from the start—from the Romantic reaction to the Enlightenment, to writers such as Moser and de Bonald who decried the moral decay and civic unrest that had accompanied such modern processes as specialization, commercialization, and industrialization—this particular comparison is not exhaustive or exclusive of others.[67] Indeed, the sheer abundance and diversity of voices that today emphasize what is lost in the modern, rationalized world make any one account of this perspective incomplete. The virtue of this contrast is that it takes its cue from Qutb's own concerns about the limits of modern rationalism, and furthermore shows that such critiques come from contemporary philosophers as well as from medieval theologians, theorists of "irrationalism," and Christian fundamentalists. Just these few voices may be taken to illustrate, in a necessarily limited fashion, the lineaments of Western ambivalences and indictments of modern rationalism.

Ultimately I want to argue that this discussion illuminates some of the ways in which "the West" is itself riven with disagreements and ambivalences about modernity and rationalism; such critiques provide a glance at how the West has reevaluated its "modern Self," how disparate voices have united in interrogating the premises and assumptions that have framed Western intellectual thought since the Enlightenment. Such disagreements *within* Western culture belie characterizations of a coherent West better able to cope with doubt, with a human-centered universe, with radical uncertainty than others.[68] While many if not most of the ideas and assumptions constitutive of a rationalist, secular humanist vision of modernity originated in the West, the opposition between this vision *as* the West and an Islamic East simply does not easily map onto the sheer religiosity of American culture, the growth of religious revivalism in American politics, and the critiques of rationalism among scholars in the Western academy. Nor does it capture the diversity of reactions to "Western modernity" among Islamic thinkers only touched upon here, the selective embrace of the fruits of modern progress among Islamic fundamentalists, and the cultural syncretism evident in both 'Abduh's and Qutb's arguments about the relationship between Islam and modernity.

Such complications cut across the categories and oppositions that underlie both "Western" and "fundamentalist" conclusions of incommensurability. The suggestion here, then, is that Islamic fundamentalist ideas such as Qutb's and the sensibility they express are not premodern, although they often draw upon and reinterpret ideals located in a golden past. And although such Islamic funda-mentalist political thought coheres around a critique of many central epistemo-logical assumptions many take to be constitutive of post-Enlightenment modernity, it must be understood as modern, both in the historical sense and in the sense in which it is profoundly engaged with the processes and ideas we associate with both modernity and "modernism." Furthermore, as disparate Western voices continue to express similar anxieties about modernity and the costs of post-Enlightenment rationalism in particular, it is not particularly illuminating to argue that fundamentalists such as Qutb are antimodernists, unless we are willing to call all critics of modernity antimodern. Positioning all such critiques as the antithesis of modernity misses the opportunity to engage them as serious—if at times disturbing—interlocutors on the modern condition, voices contesting not only the value but the very definition of modernity in Western and non-Western contexts.

Could the arguments advanced here thus suggest a different conclusion? Could they sustain the claim that fundamentalist political thought such as Qutb's is not an irreducible "Other" but is perhaps a recognizable expression of the postmodern critique of modernity, a critique which we not only recognize but in which we clearly participate? Given the diverse and at times contradictory understandings of postmodernism, to begin to answer this requires an elaboration of what it could possibly mean to call fundamentalism a postmodern phenomenon. It could be argued, for example, that both fundamentalism and postmodernism of quite different stripes are reactions to modernity, and critical of the Enlightenment legacy in particular.[69] Both emphasize the schizophrenic dimension of contemporary life, describing a world marked by disjunction and discontinuity, "a landscape in the manner of Bosch, composed of an infinitude of fragments, pieces. . . ."[70] Malcolm Bull suggests that fundamentalists and postmodernists share a globalized frame of reference and an exaggerated sense of crisis; an ambiguous and symbiotic relationship to modernity in that neither pretends that modernity never existed, and neither seek a simple return to the past; a selective reappropriation of the past; a mixing of high and low cultures; and a dismissal of the need for any justificatory meta-discourse.[71] As an "attempt to resolve how to live in a world of radical doubt,"[72] then, fundamentalism can thus be understood as a zealously antimodern type of postmodernism.[73]

Yet while this fundamentalist political thought might be regarded as postmodern in the historical sense of being literally "after modernity," and while it is indeed part of an increasingly common rebuttal to the ideas and assumptions taken as constitutive of "modernity," it is not, I think, useful to understand it as postmodern inasmuch as postmodernism is associated, at the very least, with a radical suspicion of foundationalism and of all notions of truth. This is so despite the fact that the critique of the Enlightenment at the center of postmodernism has issued in, on the one hand, the insistence that the crucial "lesson in paganism" is "the need to be godless in things political,"[74] and on the other, a reassessment of religiosity and spirituality as experiences forced into the shadows of obscurity by the ascent of modern rationalism.[75] As I have argued, central to Islamic fundamentalism, and fundamentalism more generally, is an antihermeneutic embrace of scriptural absolutism; as Bassam Tibi rightly argues, "[t]he fundamentalist yearning for the absolute introduces a concept of absolutism in human knowledge, definitely not a postmodern idea."[76]

The antihermeneutic foundationalism central to fundamentalist political thought is thus incompatible with the postmodern suspicion of foundations. Western critics of modernity, like postmodernists, emphasize the dark side of rationalism, and insist we attend to what the post-Enlightenment vision of modernity has excluded and precluded. Contrary to postmodernists, however, voices such as Taylor and MacIntyre, along with Qutb, contend that there are or can be bases on which to reestablish "foundational" meanings necessary for living and living well; they thus seek an overarching moral unity to overcome the fragmentation of knowledge seen to characterize the contemporary world.[77] Yet like postmodernism, fundamentalists' paradoxical relationship to modernity represents an attempt to move beyond modernity in a way that is simultaneously parasitic upon it. Perhaps, then, the Western and Islamist critiques of modernity explored here are best characterized as an attempt to simultaneously abolish, transcend, preserve, and transform modernity; in short, to borrow from Shlomo Avineri (and Hegel), these perspectives represent a dialectical *Aufhebung* of modernity rather than an a priori negation of it.[78] What this means is that the resistance to a world of radical doubt, and the "yearning for meaning" such resistance is said to produce, cannot be explained away as the inability of certain personalities, groups or cultures to "cope" with the imperatives of modernity. Rather it reflects an increasingly vocal and transcultural contestation of the so-called imperatives of modern life in the name of multiple modernities.

Notes

1. For a more extensive version of some of these arguments, see Roxanne L. Euben, *Enemy in the Mirror: Islamic Fundamentalism and the Limits of Modern Rationalism* (Princeton, NJ: Princeton University Press, forthcoming).

2. This is implicit in Francis Fukuyama's "The End of History?" *National Interest* 16 (Summer 1989): 3-18; and *The End of History and the Last Man* (New York: Free Press, 1992).

3. Bruce Lawrence, *Defenders of God* (San Francisco: Harper & Row, 1989), 232.

4. Richard Falk, "Religion and Politics: Verging on the Postmodern," *Alternatives* 8 (1988): 380.

5. Akbar Ahmed, *Postmodernism and Islam: Predicament and Promise* (London: Routledge, 1992), 13.

6. Falk, "Religion and Politics," 379. Lawrence rightly insists on differentiating between "modernity" from "modernism," arguing that the former encompasses the processes associated with modernization, including but not limited to the "increasing bureaucratization and rationalization as well as technical capacity and global exchange," the latter signaling the "search for individual autonomy driven by a set of socially encoded values emphasizing change over continuity; quantity over quality; efficient production, power, and profit over sympathy for traditional values or vocations, in both the public and private spheres." Lawrence, *Defenders of God*, 27. "Modernism" is thus

the ideology of the "objective, structural givens" that constitute "modernity."

7. "Modernization" here does not refer to outdated and thoroughly discredited versions of modernization theory. Rather it should be taken as referring to, in Ira M. Lapidus' words, "processes of centralization of state power and the development of commercialized or capitalist economies which entail the social and cultural changes we call modernity," Lapidus, "Islamic Revival and Modernity: The Contemporary Movements and the Historical Paradigms," *Journal of the Economic and Social History of the Orient* 40 (1997): 444n1.

8. Lawrence, *Defenders of God*, 3.

9. Indeed, there is no word for fundamentalism in Arabic: the closest word in Arabic, *usuliyya*, was coined specifically to approximate the English "fundamentalism" (*usul* can be translated to mean fundamentals, or roots). For a powerfully argued case against the use of "fundamentalism" to describe Islamic revival, see Riffat Hassan's "The Burgeoning of Islamic Fundamentalism; toward an Understanding of the Phenomenon," in *The Fundamentalist Phenomenon*, Norman J. Cohen, ed. (Michigan: William B. Eerdmans Co., 1991), 151-71.

10. John O. Voll, "Fundamentalism in the Sunni Arab World: Egypt and the Sudan," in *Fundamentalisms Observed*, Martin E. Marty and R. Scott Appleby, eds. (Chicago: University of Chicago Press, 1991), 347.

11. Weber's distinction between "this worldly" and "other worldly" orientations rests upon the requirements for salvation. In "world-rejecting asceticism," participation in worldly affairs may lead to alienation from God, so salvation requires withdrawal from the "world." In "inner-worldly asceticism," salvation is achieved through participation in the world, or more precisely, "within the institutions of the world, but in opposition to them . . . the world is presented to the religious virtuoso as his responsibility." Weber, *The Sociology of Religion*, trans. Ephraim Fischoff (Boston: Beacon Press, 1964), 166.

12. Of course, as Martin Marty and R. Scott Appleby note, sacred texts do not play "the same constitutive role in South Asian and Far Eastern traditions as they do in the Abrahamic faiths." Yet it is all the more striking that in their study on comparative fundamentalism they find that at least four of the six South Asian or Far Eastern "fundamentalist-like movements . . . do in fact privilege a sacred text and presume to draw certain fundamentals—beliefs and behaviors—from it." *Fundamentalisms Observed*, 820. This is part of why the editors of "The Fundamentalism Project" find the term "fundamentalism" fruitful although not without controversy (they list several persuasive reasons for the comparative usefulness of the term on viii-ix).

13. Martin E. Marty, "Explaining the Rise of Fundamentalism," in *The Chronicle of Higher Education*, October 28, 1992, A56.

14. Here I agree with Lapidus's arguments in "Islamic Revival and Modernity: The Contemporary Movements and the Historical Paradigms," *Journal of the Economic and Social History of the Orient* 40 (1997): 444. Olivier Roy concurs when he argues that "[r]ather than a reaction against the modernization of Muslim societies, Islamism is a product of it." Roy, *The Failure of Political Islam* (Cambridge, MA: Harvard University Press, 1994), 50.

15. Qutb's political thought is, of course, only one perspective among many that today travel under the rubric of "Islamist political thought." Even during his lifetime, Qutb's militant version of Islamism competed with the more gradualist approach of Hasan Ismail Hudaybi, *Du'ah la Qudat* (Cairo: Dar al-Tabi'a wa al-Nashr al-Islamiyya, 1977). There

are today "reformist" wings of Islamism, such as the Muslim Brotherhood, which stress the power of the word, as opposed to so-called "radicals" who emphasize the power of the sword.

16. I place these categories within quotation marks to signal the ways in which both Islamist and Islamic modernist thought are culturally syncretic perspectives, complex and eclectic amalgamations of Western ideas and reinterpreted Islamic traditions, and that the "West" is itself riven with disagreements, and characterized by concerns and ambivalences and a diversity of experiences that undermine any single coherent identity.

17. 'Abduh, *Al-Islam wa al-Nasraniyyah [Islam and Christianity]*, 149. All translations are from the original Arabic.

18. Islamic "modernism" has often been referred to as Islamic reformism, or by the Arabic term *salafiyya*—a word deriving from the Arabic root meaning "predecessors" or "forebears." Yet Lapidus persuasively argues that there is a difference between Islamic modernism and Islamic reformism: Islamic reformism should be identified with the *ulama*; Islamic modernism should be associated with Muslim elites and intelligentsias. Lapidus, *A History of Islamic Societies* (Cambridge: Cambridge University Press, 1988), 560-570.

19. This is why I place "modernism" within quotation marks.

20. As my analysis of 'Abduh is delimited by my focus on this contrast, this discussion does not include an analysis of 'Abduh's life and thought in full, nor does it aspire to be an account of Islamic "modernism." In addition, it is worth emphasizing the fact that while 'Abduh is almost universally acknowledged as one of the most influential thinkers in this tradition, his work neither exhausts nor fully represents it. For fuller treatments of 'Abduh's life and/or work see, for example, Albert Hourani, *Arabic Thought in the Liberal Age: 1798-1939* (Cambridge: Cambridge University Press, 1983); Malcolm H. Kerr, *Islamic Reform: The Political and Legal Theories of Muhammad 'Abduh and Rashid Rida* (Berkeley: University of California Press, 1966); and Elie Kedourie, *Afghani and 'Abduh: An Essay on Religious Unbelief and Political Activism in Modern Islam* (London: Frank Cass & Co., 1966).

21. This is a collection of lectures on theology 'Abduh had originally delivered during his years in Beirut; they were revised and given again at Al-Azhar, Egypt's preeminent mosque and university. The lectures were then compiled by his student Rashid Rida and published as *Risalat al-Tawhid [The Theology of Unity]* in 1897.

22. *Risalat al-Tawhid*, (Cairo, 1966), 176.

23. *Risalat al-Tawhid*, 143.

24. *Risalat al-Tawhid*, 83.

25. *Risalat al-Tawhid*, 20.

26. Muhammad 'Abduh, *Al-Manar*, vii, 292, cited in Charles C. Adams, *Islam and Modernism in Egypt* (New York: Russell & Russell, 1968), 136.

27. Hourani, *Arabic Thought in the Liberal Age*, 144.

28. See Hourani's chapter on "'Abduh's Disciples: Islam and Modern Civilization" in *Arabic Thought in the Liberal Age*, 161-92, for an illuminating discussion of the successors to 'Abduh's reformism.

29. *Risalat al-Tawhid*, 143-45.

30. *Risalat al-Tawhid*, 26-32, 122.

31. *Risalat*, 122.

32. *Risalat*, 181.

33. Malcolm Kerr, *Islamic Reform*, 110.

34. *Risalat*, 55. 'Abduh argues that there are levels of knowing, or kinds of truths, some of which are accessible to human understanding, others of which are entirely inaccessible, and those which require confirmation by an authority other than reason. For example, reason can lead us to belief in the existence of God, an understanding of some of his attributes, awareness of the afterlife, distinctions between good and evil, and the authority of prophecy. Reason can thus lead us to accept the authority of revelation whose truths are therefore consistent with the products of rational inquiry. Such revelation—disclosed by the Prophet whose authority has been established by reason—provides the means to accept truths which reason cannot reach.

35. 'Abduh sees in human nature wide variations in intellectual ability and concludes that most people are either deficient in, or are incapable of fully exercising, their reason; while the elite may after long reflection respond to the authority of rational argumentation, the limited intelligence of most requires the deployment of myths and examples designed to speak to emotion, fear, tradition, and that which is familiar. *Risalat*, 118-19. Thus while some truths cannot be known by reason at all, other limits upon reason are related to the defects in human nature.

36. Kerr, *Islamic Reform*, 127.

37. Qutb's formulation of *jahiliyya* has proven to be a powerful critical weapon for Islamic fundamentalists from Algeria to Egypt. It is primarily although not solely advanced in *Ma'alim fi-l Tariq [Signposts Along the Road]*, originally published in 1964, and *Al- Khasa'is al-Tasawwur al-Islami wa Muqawwamatihi [The Islamic Conception and Its Characteristics]*, originally published in 1960. Qutb's writings grew increasingly radical over time; these two books represent the final stage of his thought, one described by Muhammad Tawfiq Barakat as his distinctively "Islamist" phase (from the late 1940s on), as opposed to his earliest "liberal phase," and an interim phase where he began formulating moderate texts on Islamic thought. Barakat, *Sayyid Qutb, khulasat hayatihi, manhajahu fi al-haraka, al-naqd al-muwajah ilayhi* (Beirut, 1970), 11.

38. The remarkable impact of Qutb's ideas on the contemporary movement narrows but does not bridge the gap between Qutb's intent and how his arguments are disseminated, received, and reinterpreted. This discussion is not a substitute for such genealogy, nor is it intended as an analysis of Qutb's complete *oeuvre*. I approach Qutb's final stage of thought with a particular set of purposes. As a highly influential theorist of fundamentalism who was himself a part of the early fundamentalist movement in Egypt, Qutb's work is an opportunity to bridge the theory and practice divide: it is instructive on its own terms as a text of fundamentalist theory and symptomatically, as a guide to understanding the appeal of fundamentalist ideas in the modern world. For an account of Qutb's life and works, see Adnan A. Musallam, *The Formative Stages of Sayyid Qutb's Intellectual Career and His Emergence as an Islamic Da'iya: 1906-1952* (dissertation, Ann Arbor, University of Michigan, 1983). For an account of his entire body of political thought, see Ahmad S. Moussalli, *Radical Islamic Fundamentalism: The Ideological and Political Discourse of Sayyid Qutb* (Lebanon: American University of Beirut, 1992), Yvonne Haddad's "Sayyid Qutb: Ideologue of Islamic Revival," in *Voices of Resurgent Islam*, John Esposito, ed. (New York: Oxford University Press, 1983); and "The Qur'anic Justification for an Islamic Revolution: The View of Sayyid Qutb," in *The Middle East Journal*, 37, no. 1 (Winter 1983). See also Mahdi Fadl Allah, *Ma'a Sayyid Qutb fi fikrihi al-siyasi wa'l dini* [With Sayyid Qutb and His Political and Religious Thought] (Beirut, 1979).

39. While (Shi'ite) Iran is perhaps the best known example of Islamic fundamentalism to those in the West, many contemporary Islamic fundamentalist movements (e.g. in Jordan, Egypt, Saudi Arabia, Algeria, the Sudan, and the Occupied Territories) in the Middle East are Sunni. There are many differences among these movements, yet even John Esposito, who has insisted on the almost infinite variations of Islamic revival from context to context, acknowledges "recurrent themes" that make it possible to speak of a "revivalist worldview." Esposito, *The Islamic Threat: Myth or Reality?* (New York: Oxford University Press, 1992), 14-19.

40. Of course the problem of human hubris is not peculiarly modern. The Bible is replete with parables of human arrogance, and the very word recalls the ancient Greek belief that excess of hubris incites the gods' wrath. Qutb's critique here, however, centers on a particular form of hubris, that is, the claim that sovereignty is legitimate in part *by virtue* of the exclusion of divine authority. This is different from the theory (also illegitimate by Qutb's standards, but perhaps less essentially *modern*) that human sovereignty is legitimate insofar as it claims to be God's representative on earth. Qutb's complaint seems to be that this aggressively secular formulation of legitimacy is a peculiarly modern form of transgression, and is particularly widespread in the contemporary world.

41. In contrast to modern rationalism, for example, Greek rationalists tended to view reason as the means to discover and appreciate the order of nature underlying all things. Greek rationalism influenced Islamic philosophy and Qutb objects to the project of the Islamic philosophers as well. Yet in that context, Qutb's complaints have more to do with the way Islamic philosophers incorporated what was foreign to, and therefore corrupting of, Islam, than about the negation of divine authority.

42. *Al-Khasa'is al-Tasawwur al-Islami wa Muqawwamatihi*, 188-89.

43. Qutb's focus on epistemology here is not idiosyncratic. Ziauudin Sardar explicitly condemns what he terms as Western "epistemological imperialism." Sardar, *Islamic Futures: The Shape of Ideas to Come* (London: Mansell Publishers, Ltd., 1985), 85. Indeed, Syed M. N. al-Attas argues that the core of the threat from the West is primarily epistemological, and argues in response that "[t]he holy Qur'an is the complete and final revelation . . . and there is no other knowledge—except based upon it and pointing to it—that can guide and save man." Al-Attas, *Islam, Secularism and the Philosophy of the Future* (London: Mansell Publishers, Ltd., 1985), 127, 138.

44. Qutb, *Al-Khasa'is al-Tasawwur al-Islami wa Muqawwamatihi*, 17-20. In this book, Qutb singles 'Abduh out in his discussion of "modernism," as well as 'Abduh's student, Rashid Rida. Qutb's view in many ways continues to define the attitude of many contemporary Islamic fundamentalists toward Islamic "modernists" and all other thinkers seen as insufficiently attuned to challenges to Islamic authenticity.

45. *Ma'alim fi-l Tariq*, 159.

46. *Al-Khasa'is al-Tasawwur al-Islami wa Muqawwamatihi*, 20.

47. Partha Chatterjee, *The Nation and Its Fragments: Colonial and Postcolonial Histories* (Princeton: Princeton University Press, 1993), 5.

48. Chatterjee, *The Nation and Its Fragments*, 11.

49. Indeed, the classes most drawn to Islamic fundamentalism are themselves the product of such modern processes as urbanization, industrialization, and the expansion of educational opportunities. Studies of Islamic fundamentalism—and of Christian fundamentalism as well—note that the petite bourgeoisie is the class most consistently drawn to fundamentalist movements. See Michael Fischer, "Islam and the Revolt of the

Petit Bourgeoisie," *Daedalus* 3 (Winter 1982): 101-22; see also Gilles Kepel, *The Revenge of God: The Resurgence of Islam, Christianity and Judaism in the Modern World*, trans. Alan Braley (University Park, PA: Pennsylvania State University Press, 1994).

50. Bassam Tibi, "Culture and Knowledge: The Politics of Islamization of Knowledge as a Postmodern Project?" in *Theory, Culture and Society* 12 (1995): 20.

51. See, for example, Pat Robertson, *The New Millennium* in *The Collected Works of Pat Robertson* (New York: Inspirational Press, 1994), 50, 67; and George Marsden, *Fundamentalism and American Culture: The Shaping of Twentieth-Century Evangelicalism, 1870-1925* (Oxford: Oxford University Press, 1980).

52. Kepel, *The Revenge of God*, 192.

53. Marsden, *Fundamentalism and American Culture*, 148, 160, 166, 169.

54. Richard Bernstein, "The Rage Against Reason," *Philosophy and Literature* 10 (1986): 186-210.

55. This focus on the critique of modernity necessarily excludes those whom Taylor would call the "boosters" or supporters of modern culture. Charles Taylor, *The Ethics of Authenticity* (Cambridge, MA: Harvard University Press, 1992), 22. In keeping with the attempt to illuminate a perspective, I do not judge these views on intellectual and political grounds but rather use them to elaborate broader theoretical commonalities. For useful critiques and/or analyses of some of these positions and those of their opponents, see Amy Gutmann, "Communitarian Critics of Liberalism" *Philosophy and Public Affairs*, 14, no. 3 (Summer 1985), and Charles Taylor, "Cross Purposes: The Liberal-Communitarian Debate" in *Liberalism and the Moral Life* (Cambridge, MA: Harvard University Press, 1989).

56. Alasdair MacIntyre, *After Virtue* (Notre Dame: University of Notre Dame Press, 1984).

57. Of course, the presence of foundations or traditions that provide common standards to adjudicate between points of view does not end serious debates over interpretation; as centuries of scriptural commentary show, prior to the culture of emotivism real and often interminable debates over meaning and interpretation raged among those who supposedly shared a belief in common foundations.

58. Taylor, *The Ethics of Authenticity*.

59. Taylor, however, argues that the ethic of authenticity was originally actuated by a laudable concern for increased individual responsibility and the insistence, against utilitarian theory, that morality had a voice within, that "human beings are endowed with a moral sense, an intuitive feeling for what is right and wrong," Taylor, 26. By contrast, there is no nondebased form of emotivism for MacIntyre.

60. MacIntyre, *After Virtue*, 52.

61. MacIntyre, 82.

62. Hannah Arendt, "What Is Authority?" in *Between Past and Future* (New York: Penguin Books, 1968). Interestingly enough, Arendt's critique of modernity has issued a debate similar to the one about the relationship of fundamentalists to "modernity": while George Kateb argues that Arendt's critique is ultimately an expression of "antimodernist" nostalgia, Seyla Benhabib suggests that Arendt is a "reluctant modernist." Kateb, *Hannah Arendt: Politics, Conscience, Evil* (Totowa: Rowman and Allanheld, 1984), 183; Benhabib, *The Reluctant Modernism of Hannah Arendt* (Thousand Oaks, CA: Sage Publications, Inc., 1996). While Arendt does describe modernity in terms of loss, at the same time she often implies that it is for the same reason a moment

of great opportunity. Thus Arendt's critique of modernity cannot be reduced to a nostalgic yearning for an ancient past, nor does it issue in unrelieved pessimism. See Dana Villa, *Arendt and Heidegger: The Fate of the Political* (Princeton: Princeton University Press, 1996), 270.

63. Robert N. Bellah, Richard Madsen, William M. Sullivan, Ann Swidler, and Steven M. Tipton, *Habits of the Heart: Individualism and Commitment in American Life* (New York: Harper & Row Publishers, 1985).

64. MacIntyre, 250.

65. Spragens, *The Irony of Liberal Reason* (Chicago: The University of Chicago Press, 1981).

66. Such reevaluation comes from a variety of quarters, including the critique of rationalism and positivism from postmodernist and critical theorists. For example, in *Dialectic of Enlightenment*, Max Horkheimer and Theodor Adorno have argued that enlightenment is not characterized either by a teleological ascent to freedom or decay, but rather by a dialectical process whereby enlightenment returns to myth and back again. Horkheimer and Adorno suggest that modern bureaucracy in particular has given birth to its own peculiar forms of "irrationality" in a dialectical process they describe as a barbarous combination of myth and enlightenment. Max Horkheimer and Theodor W. Adorno, *Dialectic of Enlightenment*, trans. John Cumming (New York: Herder and Herder, 1972). The list of those who emphasize the darker side of modernity include an extraordinary variety of works, including Leo Strauss, *Natural Right and History* (Chicago: University of Chicago Press, 1953); Daniel Bell, *The Contradictions of Capitalism* (New York: Basic Books, Inc., 1976); John H. Schaar, *Legitimacy in the Modern State* (New Brunswick, NJ: Transaction Books, 1981); and Christopher Lasch, *The Culture of Narcissism: American Life in an Age of Diminishing Expectations* (New York: W.W. Norton & Company, 1991), to name but a few.

67. Indeed, Qutb's critique of modernity could be fruitfully contrasted with, for example, the work of Joseph de Maistre, and his engagement with the tension between reason and revealed truth could also be placed in the context of theological arguments about the place of rationalism in a divinely ordered cosmos engaged in by such thinkers as St. Augustine and St. Thomas Aquinas.

68. Indeed, far from representing a civilization with homogeneous roots and clearly delineated historical and contemporary boundaries, it could easily be argued that "the West" is itself an amalgamation of multiple traditions—the Greek, Roman, Christian, and Judaic to name a few—and is today made up of citizens who embrace radically diverse ethnic, religious, and racial identities. Moreover, "the West" has been constantly influenced by and shaped in terms of other cultures and civilizations: perhaps the best case in point for the purposes of this paper is the fact that it was Islamic philosophers who preserved and then reintroduced crucial classical Greek texts to medieval Europe. Further complicating the category "West" is the fact that there are groups who live within "the West" yet identify themselves as "Third World," and scholars have come to point out the existence of colonial situations *within* "the West."

69. It is interesting to note that Michel Foucault found in the Iranian Revolution (at least through early 1979) a quasi-Dionysian uprising against Western imperialism and rationalization, and thrilled to what he took to be an Iranian challenge to global hegemony, a challenge that revealed "an intensity of courage." Foucault, "Is It Useless to Revolt?" *Le Monde*, May 1979.

70. Félix Guattari, *Chaosophy*, Sylvère Lotringer, ed. (New York: Semiotext[e], 1995), 87. Of course, for Guattari and Gilles Deleuze, schizophrenia is not a pathology to be overcome as it is for Qutb. On the contrary, "[t]he schizophrenic has a lightening-like access to you . . . He's in the position of a 'seer' . . . whereas individuals who are frozen in their logic, in their syntax, in their interests, are totally blind." *Chaosophy*, 92, and Deleuze and Guattari, *Anti-Oedipus: Capitalism and Schizophrenia* (New York: Viking Press, 1972).

71. Bull, "Who Was the First to Make a Pact with the Devil?" *London Review of Books*, May 14, 1992, 22-3.

72. Akbar S. Ahmed, *Postmodernism and Islam: Predicament and Promise* (London: Routledge, 1992), 13.

73. Falk, "Religion and Politics," 380.

74. Jean-François Lyotard, "Lessons in Paganism," Andrew Benjamin, ed., *The Lyotard Reader* (Oxford: Blackwell, 1989), 122-55.

75. Philippa Berry and Andrew Wernick, eds., *Shadow of Spirit: Postmodernism and Religion* (New York: Routledge, 1992).

76. Tibi, "Culture and Knowledge," 13.

77. However, William Connolly points out "momentary points of convergence" between communitarians such as Taylor, and "antiteleologists" such as Foucault. Connolly, "Beyond Good and Evil: The Ethical Sensibility of Michel Foucault," *Political Theory* 21(3): 370.

78. Personal correspondence, July 25, 1995. I am grateful to Professor Avineri for this point.

2

Eastern Veiling, Western Freedom?

Nancy J. Hirschmann

In many ways, the concept of "freedom" can be seen as decidedly Western. Emerging out of the Enlightenment, the discourse of "natural freedom," with its "natural rights" to life, "happiness," and a range of subsidiary rights such as economic welfare and self-determination, has become a defining feature of Western culture. As developed in Western political theory in particular, freedom is seen as a core defining value. In social contract theory, for instance, it is seen as a fundamental feature of human nature, the basis for an entire construction of government and state apparatus through the voluntary expression of consent. For continental philosophers like Kant and Hegel, it is defined significantly differently, as the expression of the true will or reason or spirit, but is no less central to what it means to be a human. By contrast, in non-Western cultures, other values such as community, kinship, or nation—all affiliative ideals of some kind—often seem to take priority of place in defining what a "human being" is. Indeed, one might start off with the assumption that the conception of agency at the heart of Western conceptions of freedom—the individual who is independent and alone, self-reliant and self-controlled—would not be worth exploring in Eastern contexts, where the notion of community is much more intricately woven into conceptions of the self, agency, and choice.

This does not mean that freedom is irrelevant in such cultures, however, but only that it is not the "obsessional core" that it is for the West. Indeed, though people from non-European races may have historically placed importance on securing greater "freedom" in their own cultures—particularly freedom *from* the forces of colonialism and imperialism—it can be argued that it is precisely *through* colonialism and imperialism that "freedom" has developed throughout the world as a specifically Western concept; as Orlando Patterson argues, does "freedom" need to be such a central concern without "oppression"?[1] Certainly, "the West" has not been the exclusive oppressor in history; nor has it exerted the kind of unified force implied by use of the term "the West." But the world-wide imperialism of the United States and Europe in the modern era may in part explain why their language and conceptual vocabularies seem to dominate in international debates over human rights, nationalism and sovereignty and markets and trade. For instance, the UN Charter for Human Rights, the 1985 Nairobi Forward-Looking Strategies for the Advancement of Women, and the convention adopted by the 1995 Beijing UN Conference on Women, all give a central role to the concept of women's "rights" conceptualized in individualist terms.[2]

Does such language support the Enlightenment claim for the naturalness of freedom and its essentialness to humanity? Or does it attest to the hegemonic power of the West? It may be a bit of both. As Leila Ahmed points out, "Western political ideas, technologies, and intellectual systems comprehensively permeate all societies. There is no extricating them, no return to a past of unadulterated cultural purity."[3] Yet at the same time, resistance to westerni-zation and cultural "pollution" plays an important political and intellectual role in the struggles of many non-Western societies to forge new political identities.

Sensitivity to cultural specificity is something that has concerned Western feminists in recent years, and it might seem to pose an ambiguous challenge to feminist theorists interested in freedom. Within a specifically Western context, a feminist approach to freedom would concern itself with whether women are as free as men, or systematically restrained by virtue of gender. Feminists maintain that practices such as domestic violence, sexual harassment, rape, and sexual discrimination in the workplace all restrict women more than men by virtue of sexist attitudes, practices, and beliefs. Beyond this, however, a feminist approach to freedom is also involved in identifying the ways in which apparently "natural" restrictions on women are not only socially constructed, but constructed through, by, and for the interests of men—i.e. patriarchy—such that women are "disciplined" to desire and "choose" the very things that they are limited to.[4] Thus a feminist analysis of freedom requires us to understand not only external limitations on women's ability to pursue what they want, but also the "internal" limitations on desire itself, the ways in which sexist cultural restrictions actually produce people who will support and perpetuate its power by wanting the "right" things.

Tricky as this is within the contexts with which Westerners are most familiar, it becomes even more problematic to analyze the social construction of women in non-Western contexts. This is so not only because a focus on freedom may not be centrally important to non-Western cultures, of which women are important members, but also because of the dubiousness of using "feminism," "women," and even "gender" as unqualified terms. The error which Western feminists commit all too frequently is to treat women in different cultures as if they were simply variations on a basic theme defined by white Western middle-class experience: if "freedom" has a potentially Western bias, "feminism" does as well. Women have been specifically and differently impacted by virtue of their locations in various classes, nationalities, ethnicities, and races. This makes talking about "women's" freedom or lack of freedom a daunting task, one subject to a considerable degree of ambiguity. Thus, at the same time that many Third World and international feminists have adopted such universalist concepts as human rights, they have also argued repeatedly that a genuine feminism must appeal to all women and attend to cultural contexts, practices, and experiences that would seem to run contrary to Western freedom and individualism, not to mention the universalism they presuppose.

If feminists are to be able to develop versions of concepts like "freedom," however, they must have at least the potential for quasi-universal applications; thus in order for a theory of freedom to be "feminist," this ambiguity needs to be addressed.[5] In this paper, I undertake this through an examination of veiling. Much debated by feminists in recent years,[6] veiling is an important practice to explore precisely because freedom and agency are central issues. Throughout the modern era, the West has tended to view Islam as a form of barbarism—fueled in contemporary times by popular antipathy toward terrorist bombings and hostage-taking—which is often seen as a source of women's inequality; the veil is seen as the ultimate symbol, if not tool, of this inequality. Yet many Islamic women not only seem to participate voluntarily in the practice, but defend it as well, indeed claiming it as a mark of resistance, agency, and cultural member-ship. By examining veiling as a multifaceted and complex practice, located within varying and complex contexts, I hope to reveal a different understanding of freedom based on women's lives that both incorporates many aspects of Western conceptualizations and simultaneously challenges others.

To this end, I define feminism very basically as a political and philosophical devotion to ending the oppression of people by virtue of gender and sex.[7] Recognizing that women are the primary, although not the only, victims of such oppression, feminism is a political value system that has at its heart the empowerment of women to direct their lives. Though this may seem individual-istic—and hence decidedly Western—such direction is always located within the context of community: feminism as I use it here does not insist on an abstract notion of choice, but rather demands that women be able to share in the power structures that control their circumstances, for instance in areas such as sexuality and reproduction, economics and employment, relationships and lifestyle. Such a focus on context entails attention to other aspects of identity such as ethnicity, culture, race, and class—since "women" belong to multiple identity categories and their "gender" and "sex" are defined in terms of these other categories as well—but what makes something "feminist" is its primary devotion to *women*, regardless of how that category is defined by and within different contexts.

I believe that this definition is not exclusively Western. At the same time, it should go without saying that I view both veiling and freedom through a Western feminist lens; though my goal in this paper is to transcend that lens, I am obviously limited by my social location and experience. But such limitation should not altogether forestall analysis and even critique; rather, it should serve as a caution to Western scholars of the need to be self-critical. To insist that Westerners cannot talk about non-Western practices is to advocate a self-defeating, helpless relativism.

From a feminist perspective, it is even worse than that, for it contributes to the worldwide disempowerment of women: without the ability to identify cross-cultural expressions of women's devaluation, political action for women is seriously disabled. This is not to ignore the potential bias of Western feminism; nor do I claim to present an "Eastern feminist perspective." But the argument offered by many non-Western critics that "feminism" is by definition a Western idea and movement, is counterindicated by the local and national activities of many women's groups to improve women's lives, as well as the vibrant inter-national feminist movement. To dismiss such feminists as "Westerners" in disguise because they *are* feminists is not only viciously circular, but expresses the epitome of patriarchy: to define culture, even "the East," in ways that systematically and by definitional fiat exclude the interests, concerns, and experiences of women. As my discussion will show, women are important constructors of culture, and they constantly struggle to engage this construction on their own terms. How they do this can be illuminating for the question of freedom.

Furthermore, it is vital to recognize that the history and practices of veiling vary widely from country to country in terms of style, ranging from flimsy, sheer-fabric robes, to head scarves, to dark and heavy full-length coverings of the entire face and body. Veiling also varies in terms of how the practice is carried out, again running the gamut from overt coercion (state-mandates and "cultural police" in Afghanistan, Iran, and Algeria) to modest social pressure with an overt emphasis on women's individual choice. Furthermore, many Muslim women do not veil at all. Thus to talk of "veiling in Islamic countries" is as difficult as it is to talk about "women" or "the Third World"; such universal categories deny significant variations and specificity. At the same time, however, such generalities can reveal the similarities that patriarchal systems and practices display, as well as the commonality of generic oppression, whatever specific forms it takes in particular cultures.

I will try to address this issue of reconciling the specific with the general by first considering the symbolic content of the veil in historical perspective and then focusing on two cultures in which veiling seems to be a very important practice to the women who engage in it. My goal in doing this is not to define "veiling" as a unified practice or to argue that underlying the differences in various forms of veiling is a "sameness" relating to patriarchal oppression. Rather I wish to illustrate theoretical points about freedom and agency, to explore how women express these within patriarchal contexts by looking at how these contexts work to set the parameters within which women maneuver. Thus I will not address more obviously—at least to Western eyes—oppressive contexts, such as Afghanistan or Iran.[8] For it is the women who choose veiling, defend it, and consider it vital to their self-identity that so challenge Western notions of freedom. I will not use the concept of freedom to understand veiling and to determine whether women who veil are free, however; rather I will use veiling as a touchstone to develop a complex understanding of agency, subjectivity, and freedom.

The Symbolic Meaning of "The Veil"

Despite the great cultural diversity in the practice of veiling, one thing that *is* fairly universal is Western reaction to it. Feminists as well as nonfeminists often assume that veiling is in and of itself an inherently oppressive practice. Many view it like domestic violence: just as staying with an abuser seems beyond the comprehension of many, so does "choosing" the veil. Women are seen as brainwashed or coerced, and the veil is seen as a key emblem of this oppression.

This reaction to veiling has a long history, and is hardly a product of contemporary feminism. In the nineteenth century, British imperialists viewed women's veiling as the ultimate symbol of Eastern backwardness. Colonial measures against veiling, moreover, were asserted in the name of women's rights; but Ahmed argues that this "feminism" emerged as part of a larger nineteenth-century discourse that asserted dominance of West over East. In this discourse, "the veil and segregation epitomized [women's] oppression, and . . . were the fundamental reasons for the general and comprehensive backwardness of Islamic societies. Only if these practices 'intrinsic' to Islam (and therefore Islam itself) were cast off could Muslim societies begin to move forward." Western discourse thus created a dichotomy—either one embraces Islam and women's oppression, or one throws it off and is free—but in the process, "feminism" became part of the colonialist effort to delegitimize Islam.[9]

At the same time, however, this focus solidified the veil's symbolic force, for abandoning the veil has come to be identified with westernization and imperialism. Women's adoption of the veil was thus an important symbol in the late twentieth century pro-Islamist revolutionary movements in countries such as Egypt, Morocco, and Iran. On the one hand, then, Western attempts to "liberate" women by removing the veil simply reinscribed women's bodies as symbols of culture rather than as individual agents; it replaced one form of social control with another. On the other hand, however, it provided women with a method and language of resistance and agency, not only by introducing Western concepts of individual rights and freedom, but also by demonstrating the frequent inadequacy of these to Eastern social-cultural contexts. Indeed, although Westerners often focus on men assaulting women who do not veil, in fact the first people in contemporary movements to use the veil as a symbol of resistance were Egyptian university women.[10]

Does this mean that the veil, seen by Westerners as a mark of oppression, is in fact a mark of agency? Not quite, for the veil's symbolic value also can be seen to entail the subjugation of women's subjectivity. This can hardly be blamed exclusively on the West; indeed, much as Ahmed argues that Westerners treated women as the embodiment of Islam as exotic other, Mohamad Tavakoli-Targhi argues that nineteenth-century Persian (Iranian) observers of Western culture engaged in constructions of Western women that were just as biased as the West's was of Eastern women. For Iranian men,

> women of the West were often a displacement and a simulacrum for Iranian women. The focus and reflection on European women resulted in the production of the veil as a woman's uniform and as a marker of cultural, political, and religious difference and identity. What was perceived to be an Islamic dress for women was a product of the cultural and political encounter with the West.[11]

The argument here is not the contemporary one that Iranians were forced into a reactive stance against Western imperialism; indeed, such a reading seriously downplays men's agency. The men Tavakoli-Targhi discusses had "two conflicting images of the West. . . . One was grounded in a positive notion of freedom anchored to the memories of the French Revolution and called for the educating and unveiling of Iranian women."[12] In this view, European women were seen as "more" virtuous than Islamic women precisely because of their "freedom," specifically in regard to women's education and ability to conduct reasoned discourse, which meant that they would not pose the threat of mystery that needs to be controlled.[13] At the same time, however, the freedom of European women was also seen as license, and therefore morally corrupt: as one late nineteenth-century Persian traveler put it, "the freedom granted to woman-kind in this country [England] is great, and mischief arising from this unreasonable toleration is most deplorable."[14]

This second view "was grounded in a negative notion of freedom constructed on the indecency and corruption of European women and sought to protect Iranian women and the nation of Islam from the malady of the deviant gaze."[15] The "indecency of European women," as a central emblem of Western freedom, laid the starting point for Persian constructions; but such reaction was determined more by these men's preexisting values and perspectives than by Western hegemony.[16] The West had good and bad to offer, and Persian men adopted what appealed to them and shunned what did not. What did not appeal to them were practices that threatened male power to determine Iranian culture; thus it was the latter view—of women's freedom as morally corrupt license—that dominated in the end, for it allowed men to claim the "positive" liberty of education for themselves while denying women "negative" freedom of access. But moreover, the veil became a potent symbol, not so much as a "negative" symbol of reaction against the West, but rather as a "positive" reaffirmation of

Eastern Islamic morality.

Contemporary Islamic movements take a less ambivalent view, of course, and the veil today is often seen as a symbol of resistance to the perceived "loss of cultural purity" that Western power and influence threatens. But the manner and form of such resistance has strong ties to these earlier, and more obviously gender biased, responses. Indeed, those earlier "antagonistic articulations of European women have remained the organizing elements of twentieth-century Iranian modernist and Islamicist political discourses. The Islamicization of Iran since 1979 was grounded in the rejection and condemnation of unveiled women as European dolls."[17]

The issue for feminists is thus less whether Western freedom is "good" or "bad," than it is who determines what is "good" and "bad" about the West and East. For even though many women have joined the movement to veil as a sign of protest, and Western feminists should support them in their choices, feminists must also note that the such choices exist within a historically constructed context wherein "unveiledness and sexual liberty of women were viewed as the cause of corruption and moral degeneration of Europe."[18] Just as Western men used the veil as a symbol in their own political battles of imperialism, so did and do Eastern Islamic men use the veil in a similar fashion of resistance: in neither case do women take part in constructing the framework within which decisions about dress take place, but rather are forced to respond in conflicting directions to frameworks constructed by men.

Even so, there is vast disagreement on the significance, status, and meaning of veiling among Eastern feminists, in part due to the extreme variations in the practice from country to country. Some, such as Fatima Mernissi, see veiling as largely oppressive:

> the veil can be interpreted as a symbol revealing a collective fantasy of the Muslim community; to make women disappear, to eliminate them from communal life, to relegate them to an easily controllable terrain, the home, to prevent them moving about, and to highlight their illegal position on male territory by means of a mask.[19]

Yet at the same time, she is critical of Westerners', including Western feminists', readings of the veil, in which "women's liberty . . . has been viewed almost exclusively as a religious problem" instead of econonomic and political.[20]

Other feminists see veiling as a clear example of resistance to westernization and the preservation of culture.[21] Valentine M. Moghadam points out that "Purdah provides the opportunity for perserving one's own identity and a certain stability in the face of external pressures," a point on which others such as Leila Ahmed agree. But Moghadam also argues that its value as a symbol of resistance has operated less for women per se and more to "strengthen the *men's* will to resist."[22] This is a theme echoed by Algerian Marie-Aimée Hélie-Lucas, who suggests that the supposed "need" for unity in nationalist movements means that women's needs often get subverted or ignored; "women who try to defend their rights in Muslim contexts are generally accused of importing a foreign ideology whenever they ask for more social justice"; and indeed, the very concept of "universal social justice" is disabled because "women accept the fundamentalist premises that in matters concerning the private sphere, universal is equated to being West-dominated."[23] Thus, although "to be the guardians of identity and culture is an honor in the fundamentalist discourse," in actual practice, "women are honored for as long as they keep culture and religion in the way they are told to do."[24]

Still others dismiss veiling as a minor issue compared to more pressing problems of women's education, poverty and economic dependence, violence against women, and health care for women and children.[25] Others point out that veiling is not a practice intrinsic to Islam, but rather emerged out of other Eastern (including semitic) cultures,[26] and others have even questioned its gendered character; since modesty is a requirement of Muslim men as well as women, men's bodies are expected to be covered by long sleeves and trousers, as well as headgear. Others point out that veiling is not universal even among Muslim women.

Such diverse views suggest that the veil is *both* a marker of autonomy, individuality, and identity, *and* a marker of inequality and sexist oppression. In the two ethnographic studies I focus on here, this ambiguity is revealed not simply between different veiling contexts, however, but within particular cultural settings. The reason for this may be the unsettling effects of Western "penetration"; or it may be an inevitable tension between individualism and cultural identity. But I believe that it may indicate a different notion of freedom altogether that shares certain elements of Western conceptions, but introduces others quite different.

Autonomy and Freedom in Context of Community

Leila Abu-Lughod's study of Arab Bedouin culture offers one such picture of freedom. "Autonomy or freedom is the standard by which status is measured and social hierarchy determined. . . . Equality is nothing other than equality of autonomy—that is, equality of freedom from domination by or dependence on others."[27] Freedom is defined in terms of "the strength to stand alone and freedom from domination," and "is won through tough assertiveness, fearlessness, and pride" as well as "through self-control" over the "passions" (87), echoing many Western themes of freedom from external control (found in so-called "negative liberty" theorists such as Hobbes and Locke) and freedom as the triumph of the will over the self (found in so-called "positive liberty" theorists such as Rousseau and Hegel).[28]

Yet this notion of freedom also diverges from Western notions. The concept of "honor" is central to Bedouin identity, and although individual autonomy within tribes is important to the concept of honor, "maximization of unit autonomy"—independence *among* tribes—is also vital, as "Each tribal segment is theoretically equal to every other through opposition" (79). Thus on the one hand the honorable man "stands alone and fears nothing" for "fear of anyone or anything implies that it has control over one" (88); yet on the other hand, honor is also measured by obedience, both by the ability of the obeyed to secure the obedience of the obeyer, and by the willingness of the obeyer to give his or her obedience freely. Tribal status and autonomy are closely tied to individual status and autonomy, and tribal autonomy and honor can be upheld only if members respect hierarchy. There is thus a catch-22: to be free, one must obey, but one must give that obedience freely in order to assert one's independence. The honorable individual must be strong and independent, yet also enmeshed in hierarchical family relationships, wherein the higher up one is, the more honor one has.

Women's obedience, too, must be seen as choice; "people pity a woman who seems to obey her husband because she has no choice" because of poverty, for instance, or because she has no male kin to protect her (105). Although women exhort each other to obedience, however, and chastise women who violate tribal norms, they also seem to be proud of "willful" women; that is, women who do not necessarily flaunt tribal customs and authority but get around them through self-assertion. For instance, a woman who walks out on her husband declaring that she is "lonely" for her family, when in fact she is angry with him for ignoring her, makes a strong assertion of autonomy but does so in ways that maintain images of connectedness, honor to the family of origin, and respect for hierarchical authority. Such actions *seem* to express norms of deference and dependence while actually challenging them; for everyone in the tribe knows the "real" reason why the woman has acted this way, even though such a reason may not be offered into public discourse.

Veiling and women's seclusion are seen as an expression of this independence. Women view their segregation as a source of pride and honor; it signifies that they do not need the company of men, and declares their independence (46). Given that "self-mastery" is also key to honor, including "physical stoicism" (for example, not admitting to pain [90]), the veil, as a mark of modesty, indicates deference but also autonomy, in the way that it "masks" not just the body but "the 'natural' needs and passions" (115). The veil thus serves as a statement that the wearer is intent on preserving herself as separate from others, emotionally and psychologically as well as physically; it is a tangible marker of separateness and independence.

Thus veiling is an instrument of agency and freedom for Bedouin women. Yet at the same time, such values are defined within patriarchal parameters. Though women "share with their providers the same ideals for self-image and social reputation . . . the situations in which they can realize these ideals, in particular those of independence and assertiveness, are circumscribed" (111). As Abu-Lughod notes, the strong ideological relation between honor and modesty "serves to rationalize social inequality and the control some have over the lives of others . . . if honor derives from virtues associated with autonomy, then there are many, most notably women, who because of their physical, social, and economic dependence are handicapped in their efforts to realize these ideals" (33). Autonomy operates within particular structures and parameters set by community, but men have historically set and defined these cultural norms.

Even so, Abu-Lughod notes some gaps in the practice that women create for themselves: for example, a woman who marries an older man decides not to veil for anyone younger than him, and then declares that in fact everyone is younger; another woman declares she does not have to veil because she is so very virtuous (164). But the question of how much leeway most women really have—why these two women's decisions are accepted, how some can get away with it, and why all women don't try to make such claims—is hazy because of the fact that such acts of resistance operate within normative parameters which women may support through their actions, but have not created. Thus, although the freedom/honor duality is a catch-22 for men too, women are particularly caught: if they do not defend these rules and norms they are seen as weak and immoral, but by defending them, their autonomy is often compromised. Thus, women claim to admire men who can "control all their dependents and beat their wives when the wives do stupid things" (89). And though women may be praised for their strength when they go against community norms, such rebellion is limited by patriarchal values; for instance, premarital sex results in ostracism, not admiration.

Given that sex is seen as a particularly dangerous area in which the self can be lost to dependence on another, both men and women who express eagerness for sex are scorned for weakness (154). But this weighs more heavily on women than men, whose sexuality is at least acknowledged by practices such as polygamy, and allowed freer expression. Abu-Lughod cites an example of a man putting his head in his wife's lap while she is sitting with other women: unlike the man, the woman is visibly embarrassed by his expression of sexual affection, and the other women approve of such a reaction. Yet she cannot refuse him because he is her husband. This resistance/submission motif is prominent. For instance, girls traditionally cry when they learn they are to be married: "The good bride screams when the groom comes near her and tries to fight him off. She is admired for her unwillingness to talk to the groom" (154). Such resistance, however, may not extend to a refusal to marry: "as a good woman she should not resist a marriage arranged by her brothers, as this would constitute defiance" (215).

Thus, "the more women are able to deny their sexuality, the more honorable they are" (153). The veil—including the seclusion of women—is a convenient and powerful way to accomplish this, for it is a way to "avoid" men's attention and to "screen" women from men, both literally and symbolically. But such denial occurs "behind the veil" as well, i.e. among women, who seem to be the harshest critics of women who express sexual desire. Women encourage negative and dismissive attitudes about sex among themselves, and women who are perceived to want sex are scorned as weak. And while women whose husbands ignore them sexually are culturally allowed to "run away" to their homes of origin in anger, such anger is seen as justified only by the husband's violation of Islamic norms of honor and respect (for instance, by failing to "rotate" his wives, i.e. sleeping with each of them in sequential order). A wife who is ignored by her husband in favor of a newer wife suffers an insult to the respect she is owed by virtue of her seniority; the point is that it is honor and status, rather than sexual pleasure, that is discursively allowed as the justification for such anger.[29]

This formula basically forbids women's sexual agency. Women have no way to express their sexuality, or at best can express it only in ways defined by men.[30] Such patriarchal eroticization of women's waiting and indirect expression is, however, "perverse," because under this code of honor, women become dependent on men for sexual favor, in direct contradiction to its alleged intent to assert and maintain their independence and autonomy.

Of course, as many feminists will argue, Bedouin women may be no different, or at least no less free, than Western women in this sense. Indeed, many aspects that Abu-Lughod describes—particularly that modesty be voluntary rather than coerced (165), the definition of women's sexuality in terms of resistance to men's advances, and viewing women who are sexual initiators as dangerous to the very fabric of society—sound just like Rousseau's prescriptions for women in the *Emile*. It may be that the "differences" in this system allow Westerners to see the tensions and contradictions that we are blind to in our own culture, but that hardly makes this system qualitatively "worse" or "less free" than our own.

Thus, the point of this discussion is not to pity Bedouin women for a repressed sexuality, but rather to highlight the ways in which women's agency, resistance, and freedom can be understood only by their location in a context where the control of women by men is a relevant aspect. And while the emphasis on choice and self-direction again may seem to impose Western standards, these ideals are in fact internal to this particular Bedouin system as well; the question is whether their realization by men requires their denial to women. Though Abu-Lughod rightly asserts that "veiling is both voluntary and situational . . . an act undertaken by women to express their virtue in encounters with particular categories of men" (159), the fact of cultural sanction in a closed community also means this choice is to some significant degree coerced. If "respectability achieved through embodiment of the code's virtues is isomorphic with self-respect," then "by framing ideals as values, in moral terms, it guarantees that individuals will desire to do what perpetuates the system, thus obviating the need for overt violence or force" (238). But this is exactly how social control works, through the colonization of desire and will, as Foucault argues. And as he notes, it *is* a kind of violence, because it not only coerces individuals, but redefines such coercion as freedom and choice thereby denying individuals the ability to see the control they are subject to, and making them the instruments of their own oppression.[31]

Accommodation or Protest? Cairene Negotiations

Thus the question of women's freedom in Abu-Lughod's study is highly ambiguous, and such ambiguity can be used by women to great advantage. Similarly, Arlene MacLeod theorizes ambiguity as a strategy that women in contemporary Cairo utilize to cope with restrictive contexts. What she calls "accommodating protest" is an "ambiguous pattern . . . of women, who seem to both struggle in a conscious and active way against their inequality, yet who also seem to accept, and even support their own subordination."[32] Although proclaiming that Cairene women "are not passive victims, and they quite actively argue their case and seek to widen their opportunities when the chance is offered," MacLeod acknowledges that women's activity is "a form of influence or manipulation within constraints which differs from the powers exercised by the dominant groups" (41). Rather than having power over the terms of customs like veiling that set the parameters to individual choice, women instead maneuver within male-defined terms to negotiate their preferences, make their choices, or assert their identity.

To Western eyes, the situation in Cairo may appear different from Abu-Lughod's Bedouins, for Western dress has become a fairly common part of the cultural landscape and offers many women an apparently wide range of choices. In fact MacLeod reports that most women took to the veil by choice, and that the majority of women viewed veiling favorably (105). Echoing Western notions, many of the women she studied expressed strong sentiments of individual autonomy and choice founded on deeply held conviction, such as one who claimed "that putting on this dress is an important personal decision, and that it is wrong to take such a move lightly; without the proper feelings inside, it would be wrong to veil" (109).

Within such a context of choice, however, the notion of the subject is different from the dominant Western notion; like Abu-Lughod, MacLeod documents a different understanding of "individual agency" that is located in community and cultural membership. "Emphasizing being Muslim provides a sense of belonging to a specific group and also a sense of continuity and security in what have become controversial cultural decisions" (110). This location in community is important to individual identity but does not invoke the communitarian nightmare of the selfless soul; rather, individuals exist *within* social contexts, and the veil helps women express this "dual" location.

Thus, in direct contrast to Western stereotypes, the veil can help *forestall* patriarchal expressions of women's subservience. As the visceral reminder of a woman's location in relationship—not only in kinship relations (101), but in the larger "community" of Islam—the veil allows women entry into the working world by protecting women from sexual harassment and visibly demanding respect from a woman's husband, men in the office, and even on the street (133).[33] Veiling also "sets women off as a unique group, creating a strong feeling of gender identity for both sexes, which even overrides to some extent the very strong class boundaries." Such gender identification "works two ways, both locking women out from certain opportunities" but also "binding women together to create strong female ties and women's community built on important social, economic, and emotional networks" (100-101).

Women's community is particularly important in the workplace, as one of the major strictures that women attempt to resist via the veil is economic. MacLeod highlights the fact that many women, particularly of the middle- and lower-middle classes, work outside the home. This is generally out of economic necessity rather than for Western bourgeois ideals of career fulfillment—MacLeod notes that most women have low paying clerical jobs without opportunities for advancement—but women nevertheless value the economic independence and "freedom of movement" (71) such work affords.

Yet work puts them in an ambiguous position vis-à-vis Islam, which frowns on married women working outside the home, since it "detracts" from their family responsibilities. The veil is an important instrument in negotiating this ambiguity, because it allows women to enter the public sphere of work while at the same time making a clear statement that they are "good" women, i.e. attentive to the tenets of Islam, not "westernized." As one woman notes, "'It says to everyone that I am trying to be a good wife and a good mother. The *higab* is the dress of Muslim women, and it shows that I am a Muslim woman'" (120). The veil helps solidify community among women within the work world by presenting a visible marker of the shared cross-pressures that Islamic married working women face between economic need and traditional Islamic norms.

Thus on this reading, the veil is a "protest" less against the West—except in the indirect sense that being a "good woman, wife and mother" requires that one be a "good Muslim," which cannot really be done in Western clothes[34]—than against Islamic forms of patriarchy, such as strictures against women's wage work and subservience to men in the family. "The *higab* voices the protest that many women dare not voice directly to their husbands, and perhaps that many cannot articulate completely even to themselves" (133). The veil can be seen as a tool of women's agency in that it allows women to negotiate the strictures of patriarchal custom to gain what they want, to assert their independence, to claim their own identity. Thus, MacLeod maintains, "veiling . . . does more as a symbol than express women's dilemma; the *higab* also serves to resolve women's conflict. The new veils enable women to regain control and create a new self-image, offering in symbolic fashion a partial resolution of the pressures women experience at the intersection of competing subcultural ideologies" (120).

And yet at the same time, such control may be somewhat illusory; for instance, one woman who emphasized the importance of having "the proper feelings inside" before making the personal choice to veil, later told MacLeod privately "that she had no intention of putting on this dress and was very comfortable with her current skirts and blouses" but that she "avoided making these comments to her colleagues. Instead, she confronted them within the prevailing ethos of appropriate behavior" by emphasizing that she did not "yet" have the appropriate feeling, thus leaving open the assumption that, eventually, she *would* have this feeling and adopt the veil. Indeed, MacLeod notes that regardless of whether they want to take veil, "few are willing to criticize the idea of veiling" and "few are willing to argue that their religion or cultural traditions are in some way wrong" (115).

As was the case in Abu-Lughod's study, such responses reflect the hegemony of the dominant patriarchal construction. Indeed, "Women are not responding primarily to male pressure, but to an internalized feeling that they wish to make this accommodation to the traditional ideals of woman's identity and proper role" (140). Thus, when women claim the veil protects them from harassment, "Rather than placing the blame . . . onto men, women accommodate by altering their dress to fit the prevailing norm that men should not be tempted by women." Similarly, using the veil to allay a husband's jealousy means that "the necessity to change is placed not on men, but on women who accommodate to the norm of women's proper behavior by adopting dress which will avoid improper comments" (107).[35]

Thus many of these women fail to bring a critical political perspective to bear on their experiences, resulting in problematic constructions of them; as one woman says, "Today I can come and go as I please. I ask Mohammed but he almost always says of course I can go" (71). Such constructions trap women more deeply in repressive contexts by simultaneously blinding them to their entrapment. For instance, many women view the veil as a form of fashion, which may on one hand undercut Western charges of oppression, but on the other robs veiling of its political significance (139). Indeed, many of these women are very critical of those who take on more extreme forms of dress for political purposes, indicating not only the divisive effects of class differences among women (the fact that one woman "goes too far" in her veiling is attributed to the fact that "her family comes from the village" [111]) but how the constructions of class and gender work together to disempower women, who apparently feel threatened by using the veil to make overtly political statements.

Women's sexuality is similarly depoliticized. Women have a double "nature": as wife and mother, the virtuous center of family, and as sexual temptress who threatens the very fabric of that same family. In this, "Veiling and seclusion are examples of society's check on women's unruly nature . . . women cannot be trusted, so they must be controlled by outside forces" (83). The naturalization of men's and women's relations to each other, the sexual division of labor in the family, and visions of sexuality that posit women as temptress and men as helpless prey, all set parameters on the very possibilities of free action that women cannot determine. Again, Western political theorists are likely to be reminded of Rousseau, and as in Rousseau, this naturalization goes beyond sexuality to the structure of the family and the sexual division of labor. But in those areas as well, women's agency is circumscribed by its patriarchal framework.

Eastern Veiling, Western Freedom?

What can these analyses of veiling tell us about Western understandings of freedom? On the one hand, it might lend support to claims about the universal appeal of Enlightenment conceptions. Both MacLeod's and Abu-Lughod's accounts reveal many parallels to Western ideals of freedom: control over the self, the absence of external restraints, the importance of individuals, and the relation between individual and community. On the other hand, however, it suggests that Western conceptions of freedom are inadequate, for these two contexts reveal powerful differences from Western freedom in the importance that honor, obedience, and cultural membership have to autonomy and the free "self." In contrast to Western individualist political theories of freedom, the picture of the subject portrayed here is one located in contexts of kinship and community, cultural traditions, social structures, and relations. Within such a context, the formation of desire and the ability to act on desire become part of a single process rather than discrete moments. The richer, more complex understanding of agency and subjectivity this yields is much more amenable to feminist theories of freedom, which must inevitably involve analysis not just of whether the choosing subject can act on her choices, but how that subject and her choices are constructed in the first place.[36]

This could be taken to suggest that Westerners should focus on the less dominant, but nevertheless insistent so-called "positive liberty" dimensions of their own tradition; theorists from Rousseau and Hegel to Charles Taylor all argue for the importance of community to freedom.[37] But most of its variants cannot accommodate the strong individualism found in the two cultures discussed here. Nor do they capture the notion that agency must be seen as complex, multi-layered, and most importantly contextual. Moreover, such a conclusion would ignore what is most signficant in the above analysis, namely that women can act within parameters determined by social power structures, and indeed may be criticized for not protecting their autonomy in those terms, but do not participate in the creation of those terms even though they may often support them. This in turn hampers women's ability to challenge the framework: MacLeod's office workers may be aware that gender relations are unfair, but they cannot articulate this to men even in their own homes, let alone in the political arena; and Abu-Lughod's Bedouin women would consider it a mark of dishonor, and thereby unfreedom, to challenge the hierarchy of familial agnation. To say that women veil as a way to reconcile work with traditional values, or independence with honor, may recognize women's active agency, but circumvents a larger question: is it a mark of freedom to uphold traditional values or codes when these oppress women?

This is hardly a uniquely Eastern problem. Nor is it simply a problem for women; as the discussion has indicated, the ability of individual men to challenge cultural norms is often hampered as well. But it must also be recognized that men as a group are not only the creators, but the enforcers of these norms, and that the norms themselves allow to men more power, choice, and freedom of movement than they do to women. This greater freedom gives men as a social entity more power to challenge and change the norms, just as it does in the West: in cultures as diverse in their readings of the Qu'ran as Iran, Afghanistan, and Egypt, men have the power to interpret the religious texts, and it is in these interpretations that the conditions of women's and men's lives are determined.[38]

The expression of this power differential through veiling reveals important insights about the gendered character of freedom. For instance, it suggests that not just the West's colonization of the East, but men's colonization of women needs to be confronted. To take women and the veil as symbols of tribal or national identity, or of cultural and religious norms, as the political discourse of the veil often does, subverts the gendered dimensions of veiling. This results in a paradox: for women's ability to choose their practices is key to freedom; yet the fact that women choose the veil does not *of itself* make it a free action, or even a protest. Indeed, it could be a sign of the closed circularity of women's political disempowerment and colonization. For instance, Leila Ahmed points out that the majority of women in Egypt favor the return of *shari'ah*, or religious law, without fully understanding how it would change their daily lives;[39] such lack of understanding is in part required by women's frequently inferior education in many cultures, as well as their socialization to respect hierarchy and not become politically knowledgeable. If a "good Muslim woman" belongs in the home, then part of that construction is to be disinterested in politics and to trust in men as their political representatives. But such trust can become a trap for women, who then are systematically left out of the process of formulating the framework within which their agency can be expressed.

Thus the *act of choosing* is necessary but not sufficient for freedom. What is also needed is the ability to *formulate choices*, and this requires the ability to have meaningful power in the construction of contexts: for instance, developing a new religious code that provides the moral security and certainty these women seek, without the gender repression they fear and oppose. Such a code would obviously have to derive from a reading of the Qur'an that differs from the one that tends to dominate in many Muslim cultures, but one which some feminists have suggested.[40]

This does not make veiling uniquely oppressive, of course; indeed, the need to attend to contexts within which choices are made should make Westerners wonder whether the veil is any more oppressive (or any less liberating) than Western miniskirts or blue jeans. Rather, precisely because it challenges Western assumptions about what women "should" choose, veiling illustrates how power operates in all contexts. If, as Foucault maintains, "wherever there is power, there is resistance," then wherever there is resistance to such overarching, hegemonic, and diffuse power systems such as patriarchal gender construction, the resister is inevitably reinscribed within the existing framework of power relations. Women who utilize the veil to express agency subvert the practice by turning its norms against itself, but also reinforce its underlying power structure; they may "negotiate" patriarchal restrictions, but they also feed into and support them. Hence the lines between agency, choice, and resistance on the one hand, and oppression, domination, and coercion on the other, become blurred: what looks like oppression may in fact be resistance, and what looks like free choice and agency may in fact be oppression. Indeed, it is often the case that resistance and agency are *simultaneously* an expression or illustration of oppression.

This might yield a rather depressing conclusion for feminists concerned with freedom, for it would seem to offer no way out of current patriarchal contexts. But a feminist notion of freedom at least requires recognition of this dynamic, and in such recognition lies a potential response. "Third world" feminists like Chandra Mohanty have argued precisely that all feminists need to develop complex understandings of agency, resistance and oppression that can counteract Western and masculinist misinterpretations of oppression as agency and agency as oppression.[41] This involves the effort to critically evaluate women's choices, and the criteria for determining freedom must take into account the powerful effects of individual construction by social norms. But moreover, women must be able to question those norms, to challenge not only practices but the contexts in which those practices are formed and take meaning. Because we are constructed by patriarchal contexts, women must engage in a constant struggle to be aware of the implications of their actions, for such awareness is the foundation for change.

Questioning, of course, does not necessarily entail rejection. But it is the *possibility* of change that is key to freedom. By putting contexts on the table to consider their patriarchal aspects and demanding that women be able to participate in reconfiguring those contexts, feminists are able to point out that, whatever else veiling may achieve—and that may be significant—it nevertheless supports male dominance, and is at least *in part* a symbol of women's lack of freedom. Indeed, as both Ahmed and Tavakoli-Targhi suggest, it even supports Western imperialism by reinscribing Western definitions and dichotomies onto Eastern practices in a reactive manner.[42] This raises serious questions about Islamic male militants' embrace of the veil in countries such as Iran and Afghanistan: if it is not as revolutionarily powerful as they claim, then why is it seen as such an important symbol? Could it be that the oppression of women is at least as important a goal, and that "revolution" is really about certain men's desire for power?

Feminists concerned with freedom must strive to question and challenge the social construction of women and men through institutional, cultural, and relational practices, customs, and meanings. A feminist perspective can help us recognize that many women's lack of freedom stems not from Islam itself, but from the *use and interpretation* of Islam to feed into and support overtly political agendas and purposes, which are in turn developed by and for men and serve patriarchal interests, just as Western men have used supposedly gender-neutral value systems such as liberalism and Christianity. Thus veiling itself is not the source of women's lack of freedom; but since veiling may be used as a tool within some patriarchal contexts to exercise generic restraint, it merits feminist attention and questioning.

But at the same time, if attention to context is key to freedom, what about Foucault's claim that the more one resists one's context, the more one will be reinscribed in its terms of power? Feminist theorists such as Maria Lugones and Vicky Spelman have suggested that various kinds of "dialogue"—between "East" and "West," "North" and "South," industrialized, "post-industrial," and "developing" nations and cultures—can help feminists overcome cultural blinders and thus develop more thoroughgoing and inclusive critiques.[43] I believe their suggestion has a great deal of potential for the issues under consideration here. External, or cross-cultural critique, by operating from a *different* cultural context, can provide insight into how social construction operates in that context as well as in our own, and can suggest modes of resistance. Of course, such a critique, precisely *because* it is external, is necessarily incomplete, and often incorrect: it is always developed through the lenses of our own contexts. But that is why dialogue is so important. Through a "back and forth" we may be able to operate *within* our cultures—which is necessary to change them—through the benefit of "outside" perspectives—which are necessary to seeing what *needs* to be changed.

Calls for cross-cultural dialogue may seem naive given the history of such efforts, where Westerners say "do it our way" and refuse to attend authentically to other cultures. But imperialism is self-defeating for Western feminists: indeed, external critique from non-Western contexts may enable Western feminists to see the power to which we are blind in our own practices, but which operates no less completely. Westerners must realize that more comprehensive understandings of our own experiences—including the way we dress and its significance for Western women's freedom—cannot occur without such cross-cultural attention. Women's freedom and unfreedom take different forms in different contexts; but to avoid the trap of cultural relativism, it is crucial that feminists from all contexts be able to make critical evaluations of different kinds of freedom and oppression, and not simply abandon analysis to the tyranny of an indeterminate "difference." Without any critical evaluation of what's good or bad about "our" way and "their" way, there can be no feminist account of freedom, because the terms of "cultural difference" are all too often defined by and in the interests of men who have political power. In order to break out of the vicious circularity of such cultural constructions of difference, feminists need to develop a way to make critical comparisons that attend to differences in context. Such a strategy can help sharpen our critical edges, and facilitate our understanding not only of "the other," but of ourselves as well.

Notes

Thanks to Cornell University for a study leave, and to Thomas Callaghy for providing me with access to the Univeristy of Pennsylvania library, that enabled me to write this paper. Thanks also to Anne Norton, Deborah Harrold, and several anonymous reviewers for their thoughts and comments on this project.

1. Orlando Patterson, *Freedom: Freedom in the Making of Western Culture* (New York: Basic Books, 1991).

2. See Stanlie M. James, "Challenging Patriarchal Privilege Through the Development of International Human Rights," *Women's Studies International Forum* 17 (1994): 563-78.

3. Leila Ahmed, *Women and Gender in Islam* (New Haven: Yale University Press, 1992), 236.

4. Diana Coole, "Constructing and Deconstructing Liberty: A Feminist and Poststructuralist Analysis," *Political Studies*, 51 (1993): 83-95.

5. On the "quasi-universal" in feminism, see Nancy Fraser and Linda Nicholson, "Feminism Without Philosophy: An Encounter Between Feminism and Postmodernism," in *Feminism/Postmodernism*, Linda Nicholson, ed. (New York: Routledge, 1990).

6. A complete list of such debates is impossible, but perhaps most significant for this paper is the degree to which this debate has taken place within Western political theory. For instance, see Anna Elisabetta Galeotti, "Citizenship and Equality: The Place for Toleration," *Political Theory*, 21 (1993): 585-605; and Norma Moruzzi, "A Problem with Headscarves: Contemporary Complexities of Political and Social Identity;" Galeotti, "A Problem with Theory: A Rejoinder to Moruzzi;" and Moruzzi, "Response to Galeotti," all in *Political Theory*, 22 (1994): 653-79.

7. I follow bell hooks here, who argues that to define feminism as women's equality with men traps feminism within a discourse that is not only masculinist—because men become the neutral standard used to evaluate women's experience, thus erasing gender difference—but racist and classist as well—to which "men" do such feminists want to be equal? Poor African-American men? Or wealthy white men? She maintains that a truly inclusive feminism should be defined as a struggle dedicated to "ending sexist oppression." See *Feminist Theory: From Margin to Center* (Boston: South End Press, 1984).

8. For a discussion of veiling under the Taliban in Afghanistan, as well as the unveiling ordered by the Shah in Iran, see my article, "Western Feminism, Eastern Veiling, and the Question of Free Agency," *Constellations: An International Journal of Critical and Democratic Theory*, 5, no. 3 (1998): 345-368.

9. Ahmed, *Women and Gender*, 152, 150.

10. *Women and Gender*, 220.

11. Mohamad Tavakoli-Targhi, "Women of the West Imagined: The *Farangi* Other and the Emergence of the Woman Question in Iran," in *Identity Politics and Women: Cultural Reassertions and Feminisms in International Perspective*, Valentine M. Moghadam, ed. (Boulder: Westview Press, 1994), 98.

12. "Women of the West Imagined," 99. It should be noted here that "positive" and "negative" conceptions of freedom do not draw on Berlin's notion of freedom as self-control versus freedom as absence of external obstacles (although those conceptions

do have a loose relationship to her use of the terms here), but rather to the normative use of the terms, i.e. "good" and "bad." Isaiah Berlin, "Two Concepts of Liberty" in Berlin, *Four Essays on Liberty* (New York: Oxford University Press, 1971).

13. "Women of the West Imagined," 104.

14. "Women of the West Imagined," 102, 105.

15. "Women of the West Imagined," 99.

16. "Women of the West Imagined," 114.

17. "Women of the West Imagined," 99.

18. "Women of the West Imagined," 110.

19. Fatima Mernissi, "Virginity and Patriarchy" in *Women and Islam*, Azizah al-Hibri, ed. (New York: Pergamon Press, 1982), 189.

20. Fatima Mernissi, *Beyond the Veil: Male-Female Dynamics in a Modern Muslim Society* (Bloomington: Indiana University Press, 1987), vii.

21. See particularly Ahmed, *Women and Gender*, and Margot Badran, "Gender Activism: Feminists and Islamists in Egypt," in *Gender and National Identity: Women and Politics in Muslim Societies*, Valentine M. Moghadam, ed. (Atlantic Highlands, NJ: Zed Books Ltd., 1994), esp. 203.

22. Valentine M. Moghadam, "Reform, Revolution, and Reaction: The Trajectory of the 'Woman Question' in Afganistan" in *Gender and National Identity*, 82. Her account also suggests that the heavier the veiling—the more covered women are, the stricter and more extensive the segregation—the more oppressed they are.

23. Marie-Aimée Hélie-Lucas, "The Preferential Symbol of Islamic Identity: Women in Muslim Personal Laws," in *Identity Politics and Women*, 399.

24. Hélie-Lucas, "The Preferential Symbol," 394.

25. See Ahmed, *Women and Gender*.

26. Hélie-Lucas, "The Preferential Symbol," 395.

27. Leila Abu-Lughod, *Veiled Sentiments: Honor and Poetry in a Bedouin Society* (Berkeley: University of California Press, 1986), 79. Subsequent references will be made in the text.

28. See Berlin, "Two Concepts of Liberty."

29. Reproduction is another justifiable motive, though it is related to status, which women gain by being the mothers of sons.

30. Throughout *Veiled Sentiments*, Abu-Lughod emphasizes Bedouins' stoicist association of strength with control over one's feelings. Yet she also devotes a significant portion of the book to a consideration of Bedouin poetry, which is the socially accepted form through which men and women alike may express the emotions and feelings that they are socially proscribed from expressing verbally to others; the idea is that poetry expresses the feelings of the writer by putting them into words at the same time it "veils" them by making this expression in abstract, symbolic, and artistic forms. Despite its important place in the culture, however, it seems rarely to effect concrete change. She offers one example of a man who responded to his wife after reading a poem that Abu-Lughod had transcribed; but the point of poetry is precisely that it is recited, not written, and the appropriate circle in which such recitations are acceptable does not usually result in change.

31. See Michel Foucault, *Discipline and Punish: The Birth of the Prison* (New York: Vintage Books, 1979), and *Power/Knowledge: Selected Interviews and Other Writings, 1972-1977*, Colin Gordon, ed. (New York: Pantheon Books, 1980).

32. Arlene Elowe MacLeod, *Accommodating Protest: Working Women, the New Veiling, and Change in Cairo* (New York: Columbia University Press, 1991), xiv. Subsequent references will be made in the text.

33. It is not clear whether the veil really does protect women from street harassment, or whether this is simply a rationalization. For instance, when a man tells MacLeod that a woman "walking alone" on the street is inviting sex, she mentioned that his sisters often walk alone coming home from work; he immediately replies "That is completely different!" (84). But there is no linking of this "difference" to the veil; it is not the case that the man was referring to *unveiled* women walking alone, nor did he assert that his sisters are not "inviting sex" simply because they are *veiled*. Rates of sexual assault vary from country to country, whether veiled or not, and low statistical findings of sexual assault could result from sexist standards of reporting and prosecution (for instance, in Iran a charge of rape requires verification from three male witnesses, virtually making rape a logical impossibility) as easily as it could from an actually low assault indicidence.

34. As one woman puts it, "Muslim women are careful about their reputation. Egypt is not like America! In America women are too free in their behavior. . . . This is not our way" (109).

35. MacLeod also asserts that "veiling allows women into the workplace by, in essence, removing the reminders of gender" (107), but unless she means sex—i.e. by hiding women's sexuality—then she would seem to contradict herself, since the veil is a distinct *mark* of gender, and indeed, would seem to reinscribe gender difference. If she means "sex," then I agree with her, because it is the desexualization of women that seems to lie at the heart of the veil's facilitation of women's movement in the public realm.

36. See Nancy J. Hirschmann, "Toward a Feminist Theory of Freedom," *Political Theory* 24 (1996): 46-67.

37. Charles Taylor, "What's Wrong with Negative Liberty?" in *The Idea of Freedom: Essays in Honor of Isaiah Berlin*, Alan Ryan, ed. (New York: Oxford University Press, 1979).

38. See Fatima Mernissi, *The Veil and the Male Elite* (New York: 1991).

39. Ahmed, *Women and Gender*, 226-8.

40. Ahmed, *Women and Gender,* 226-8: Ahmed suggests that the "misunderstandings" mentioned above, of the gender repression the reimposition of *shari'ah* would entail, stem precisely from Islam's tendency toward gender-equality. Indeed, she maintains that women's "misunderstandings" are less about Islam than about politics in the patriarchal state. Similarly, in *The Veil and the Male Elite*, Mernissi argues that patriarchy runs contrary to the tenets of Islam, and develops a reading of the Qur'an that is egalitarian in terms of gender.

41. Chandra Talpade Mohanty, "Under Western Eyes: Feminist Scholarship and Colonial Discourses," in *Third World Women and the Politics of Feminism*, Chandra Talpade Mohanty, Ann Russo, and Lourdes Torres, eds. (Indianapolis: Indiana University Press, 1991).

42. Ahmed, *Women and Gender*; Tavakoli-Targhi, "Women of the West Imagined."

43. Maria Lugones and Elizabeth V. Spelman, "Have We Got a Theory for You! Feminist Theory, Cultural Imperialism, and the Demand for the Women's Voice," *Women's Studies International Forum*, 6 (1983): 573-81.

3

Islamic Constitutionalism and the Concept of Democracy[1]

Azizah Y. al-Hibri

Introduction

Recent developments in the Muslim world have given a new and urgent impetus to popular demands for genuine democratic forms of government in the region. Among the major developments are those related to the Gulf War and its aftermath, the Algerian bloodbath, the rise of the tyrannical Taliban in Afghanistan, the heavy-handedness of the military in Turkey, and the upheavals resulting from the Southeast Asian crisis.[2] The demands for democracy have spurred a broad-based debate among Muslims. Two concerns are central to this debate. The first is that of determining the correct Islamic point of view on the subject. The second relates to the applicability of Western democratic principles in non-Western cultures (Muslim or otherwise). This article contributes to this important debate by analyzing the position of Islamic constitutionalism on democratic governance.

To render the analysis accessible to Western readers, it will be conducted from a Western constitutional vantage point. In other words, the article will study the Islamic system of governance in light of principles basic to Western democracies in general, and the United States in particular. This approach is being used solely for heuristic purposes. It is not meant to suggest that Western democratic principles provide the ultimate criteria in determining the democratic character of alternative systems of government. Indeed, some Muslim thinkers believe that, if fully developed, the democratic character of a modern Islamic system of government would surpass that of any existing Western system.[3]

In the predominantly secular world of Western democracies, the concern with the correct Islamic point of view may appear quaint. For, it seems that generally the Muslim World continues to lag behind the West in terms of its political development. More specifically, it has yet to fully undergo the secularization and democratization process experienced by the West in the past few centuries. This perception of the situation, however, is too parochial. The Muslim World is quite diverse, and each region is politically and culturally *sui generis*. Thus an expectation that the development of Muslim political systems will mimic the development of Western political systems ignores important historical facts.

For example, the Middle-Eastern region of the Muslim World is the birthplace of the three Abrahamic religions: Judaism, Christianity, and Islam. Other Muslim countries belong to regions which are the birthplace of other faiths, such as Hinduism and Buddhism. Thus, religion is taken very seriously by inhabitants of these regions, a fact which makes a broad acceptance of secularization very difficult. Moreover, the relation of religious institutions and the state in the Muslim World is unlike that experienced in Europe. For example, in Islam there is no clergy, and every qualified Muslim has the right to engage in religious interpretation (*ijtihad*). For this reason, no centrally organized religious institution ever developed that could challenge the ruler's authority.[4] As a result of this state of affairs, political regimes in Muslim countries tried repeatedly to extend their domination to religious leaders. When religious leaders resisted, they were often severely punished.[5] This fact has cast Muslim religious leaders, who relied on faith in their crises, as role models in the fight against despotism. For all these reasons, the most significant debates taking place in the Muslim World today are not about secularization versus promotion of Islamic forms of government. Rather, they are about the democratization of existing forms of government in a manner consistent with Islamic law. This is a process that, though informed by Western democratic experiences, is viewed as neither inherently Western nor secular.

Thus, the quest for the Islamic point of view on the subject of democratic governance is not a mere academic exercise. It addresses the concerns and could actually impact the actions of a large Muslim population in the Muslim World which takes the topic very seriously. With that in mind, this article will discuss select, basic principles of Islamic law relating to democratic governance, pointing out in the process certain areas of disagreement surrounding them in the literature and the grounds for such disagreements.

Part II of this essay presents a brief overview of Islamic law in order to provide a foundation for later discussion. The article then assesses the Islamic system of government in light of two major principles of Western democracies. They are (1) the principle that the will of the people shall be the basis of the authority of the government (Principle A) and (2) the principle of separation of powers (Principle B). In the case of Principle A, the discussion focuses on two topics: (a) the ability of the people to express their will in choosing a head of state and (b) whether the laws of the land rest on the consent of the people. Part III assesses the democratic character of the procedure for choosing the head of the Islamic state. Part IV examines the sources of Islamic law and studies the problem of combining the concept of democratic government with the concept of laws which embody the will of God. Principle B is assessed in Part V. Part VI summarizes the conclusions of this article.

Islamic Law: A Brief Overview

This section provides a brief introduction to Islamic jurisprudence in order to lay the groundwork for later discussion.

A. Basic Sources

The Qur'an

The basis of all Islamic law is the Qur'an, which is literally the word of God revealed to the Prophet Muhammad over a period of 22 years (610 A.D.- 632 A.D.) in Arabic, through the Angel Gabriel.[6] As the word of God, the Qur'an is immutable.[7] Since its revelation, the text of the Qur'an has not changed even in the minutest detail.[8]

The Qur'an is comprised of *surahs* (equivalent to chapters), which are in turn comprised of *ayahs* (equivalent to verses). The Qur'an contains two kinds of rules, general and specific; the general rules are far more numerous. The specific rules tend to deal with matters of worship or with matters relating to family, and commercial or criminal law.[9] Other matters, including those in the area of constitutional law, are governed by general rules.[10] Since general rules, by their very nature, require interpretation before they can be applied to a specific context, they are the sources of a fair amount of flexibility. Therefore, the Qur'an's predominant reliance on general rules was viewed by *mujtahids*[11] as an indication of divine mercy and a wish to facilitate for Muslims the practice of their religion throughout the ages.[12] This view was articulated in a major jurisprudential principle that is discussed in section B of this part.

The Sunnah

Another major source of Islamic jurisprudence is the *sunnah* of Prophet Muhammad. The *sunnah* is comprised of the *hadith* (reported sayings of the Prophet) and the Prophet's reported actions, and is used to supplement Qur'anic laws as well as to help interpret them.[13] Since the Prophet prohibited, in the early days of the revelation of the Qur'an, the recording of the *sunnah* in order to underline the status of the Qur'an as the only source of divine law, a significant part of the *sunnah* was not recorded until the ninth and tenth centuries during the 'Abbasid rule.[14] For this reason, it became necessary for Muslim scholars to develop, in connection with the *sunnah*, a sophisticated science of attribution in order to minimize the problems associated with hearsay.[15] As a result, claims regarding the sayings or behavior of the Prophet were divided into numerous categories including claims that were judged to be false, weak, truthful, or completely trustworthy.[16] All claims, however, were collected in books which discussed in detail why each claim was judged as it was. The final decision on these matters was left to the reader.

The fact that Muslim scholars, while stating their reasoned opinion, left the final decision regarding the *sunnah* to the Muslim reader is a manifestation of the Islamic belief that each Muslim is responsible directly to God for her or his own decisions and actions.[17] A Muslim may rely on the analysis of a scholar, or may discuss the matter at length with other Muslims, but in the final analysis, a Muslim has to take personal responsibility for her or his own actions. It is for this reason that Islam has no clergy mediating the relationship between God and humans. Islam has only *mujtahids*. Furthermore, the field of *ijtihad*, which is based on serious scholarship, is open to all qualified Muslims.[18]

Note that not all the utterances or actions of the Prophet constitute *sunnah*. Some were the utterances and actions of a mere layman. The Prophet was clear about this distinction and pointed it out on more than one occasion.[19] In situations requiring nonreligious expertise, he readily deferred to the experts.

There is another distinction which has been a greater source of confusion than the former one. Some of the *sunnah* of the Prophet dealt with specific situations relating to his epoch and his community and were applicable only within that narrow framework. Other parts of the *sunnah* were general and, thus, suitable for all times and places, as with many of the Qur'anic general rules. Obviously, failure to draw this distinction properly tended to result in an unnecessary rigidity of interpretation.[20] In practice, it has also resulted in significant differences of opinion.[21] *Ijtihad* addresses not only such basic matters as distinguishing between specific and general rules, but it goes further to derive from the general rules of the Qur'an and *sunnah* the Islamic laws best suited to the relevant epoch and community. Therefore, if *mujtahids* disagreed on the very basic scope of a rule derived from the *sunnah*, their difference permeated the whole body of jurisprudence which is based on that rule.

A high level of tolerance among *mujtahids* was fostered by the Qur'an and the *hadith*. In one instance, for example, the Prophet is reported to have said that a jurist who engaged in *ijtihad* and reached the correct conclusion would be considered as having done two good deeds; if, however, a jurist reached the wrong conclusion that jurist would be considered to have done one good deed.[22] The implication was that the attempt to discover the truth was in itself, regardless of the end result, praiseworthy. This saying, along with Qur'anic verses describing God's infinite knowledge and the limits of human knowledge,[23] encouraged humility, debate, and hard work among *mujtahids*.

Thus, the Prophet's encouragement of scholarship led to a variety of religious interpretations which, as stated earlier, were viewed as an expression of God's mercy upon the Muslims. This variety made it possible for each Muslim to adopt the jurisprudence which was best suited to her or his circumstances, beliefs, and needs. Indeed, many of these differences in interpretation resulted from the growth of Islam that reached distant countries and communities with different customs, needs, and circumstances and, hence, different points of view.[24]

A setback to Islamic thought, however, occurred around the tenth century when *Sunni* jurists increasingly discouraged *Sunni* scholars from engaging any further in the activity of unaffiliated *ijtihad* (i.e. *ijtihad* outside the scope of any of the existing schools of jurisprudence).[25] Instead, *Sunni* scholars were encouraged to confine their *ijtihad* within the boundaries of the established schools. The intention was to limit the uncontrolled proliferation of ideas, some of which, it was feared, were tainted with foreign influence. This policy undoubtably contributed to, if not significantly accelerated, the decline in intellectual activity that had begun to manifest itself during that time. Centuries passed before Muslims began to stir and assert their right to unfettered free thought in Islam.[26] Yet, in Islam *ijtihad* is not only a right but the duty of every qualified Muslim.[27]

Other Sources

Many treatises on Islamic law list other sources of *shari'ah*;[28] however, not everyone accepts these sources as legitimate.[29] The most established are consensus (*ijma'*) and reasoning by analogy (*qiyas*). None of these lesser sources will be discussed in this brief overview, although one may point out the democratic character of basing decisions on consensus.

B. Basic *Shari'ah* Principles

Muslim jurists have agreed upon a number of basic principles of *shari'ah*.

Change in Time, Place, and Circumstance

As already stated, a major principle of Islamic jurisprudence is that laws may change with the passage of time and the change of place or circumstances.[30] Properly understood, this principle permits a *mujtahid* to examine a specific *ayah* in light of both the attendant circumstances of its revelation as well as its meaning to determine the scope and significance of the *ayah* in general, or with respect to a specific situation at hand. A corollary of its principle is that a change in law is permitted whenever a custom on which such law is based changes.[31]

Necessity/Avoidance of Harm

This principle has also been stated in terms of choosing the lesser of two evils. Several Qur'anic *ayahs*, as well as the *hadith*, clearly permit what is prohibited in case of necessity or severe harm.[32] Some *ayahs* state that God will forgive anyone who breaks the law under duress.[33] A famous saying of the Prophet is that Islam is a religion of facilitation not complication.[34] For this reason the *Hanafis* (one school of Islamic thought), among others, permitted drinking alcohol and eating pork out of necessity.[35]

Cessation of Cause

Where an Islamic law applies to specific factual situations, the existence of the law itself is dependent on the continued existence of that factual situation.[36] For example, the Qur'an encouraged Muslims to give a certain group of Arabs, called "*al-Mu'allafatu Qulubuhum*," a share in the charitable donations paid by Muslims.[37] This group consisted of leaders of local communities who were either not Muslim or whose belief in Islam was weak. The share was assigned to them in order to bring them closer to Islam. But after the death of the Prophet, *Khalifah 'Umar Ibn al-Khattab* refused to continue the practice on the basis that it was predicated on Islam's initial weakness.[38] Since Islam had become strong, the *Khalifah 'Umar* concluded that the practice was no longer justifiable. Note that this reasoning was applied by *Khalifah 'Umar* to a practice based on explicit verses in the Qur'an which clearly encouraged such payments. This principle could be viewed as a corollary of that stated in subsection 1.

Public Interest

Islamic laws must accord with public interest. If they do not, they must be reexamined and reformulated. Furthermore, if public interest changes, Islamic laws must change accordingly.[39]

C. Approach to Change

Despite the fact that, from its dawn, Islam caused a clear change in the Arab Peninsula's religious life, it is not a religion of abrupt change. Islam itself professes to be a continuation of the teachings of Abraham, Moses, Jesus, and other prophets.[40] Islam also proclaims Prophet Muhammad as the last of these prophets. Furthermore, the God of Islam is the same God of Judaism and Christianity. (The Orientalist adherence to the Arab Word for God ("Allah"), which is used in the Arab world by Christians and Jews as well as Muslims to refer to "God," created much unnecessary confusion in this regard.)

The Qur'an was not revealed all at one time. Rather, it was revealed gradually in accordance with the needs and capabilities of society. For example, Arabs consumed substantial amounts of alcohol in pre-Islamic times. Hence, the Qur'anic prohibition of drinking alcohol was imposed gradually on them. First, the prohibition was only advisory, then it was made binding but only at the time of prayer. Later the prohibition became absolute.[41]

Gradualism is an important feature of Islamic law.[42] It applies to many aspects of Islamic life but not all. There was no gradualism, for example, in Islam's rejection of idol worship or the belief in more than one God.[43] These matters are so fundamentally inconsistent with Islam that a gradualist approach is inapplicable to them.

On the other hand, some jurists have discouraged an abrupt change in the system of government, even for a good cause, if it results in chaos and divisiveness among the Muslim people.[44] This position may reflect a preference by such jurists for maintaining the status quo, but the better view is that this position is the direct result of the application of the *shari'ah* principle, discussed *supra* in subsection 2, combined with the Qur'anic view of the good Muslim as someone who promotes the unity of the *ummah* (the Muslim community), a matter of primary value.[45] This suggests that the proper Islamic approach for democratizing institutions is one that builds consensus in the *ummah* for the desired change, rather than advocates it by the use of divisive force. On the other hand, the use of force may be excused if it is shown to be either unavoidable or the lesser of two evils.[46]

Western Democratic Principles and the Islamic Point of View

This article now examines the Islamic system of government in light of Principle A: the will of the people shall be the basis of the authority of the government. As previously stated, the will of the people is expressed in two major ways: first, through the people's choice of a head of state, and second, through the people's choice of a constitution. This section focuses first on the procedure for the choice of a head of the Muslim state.

Historically, the doctrine asserting that the will of the people was the basis of the authority of the government was formulated in the West as a response to monarchs who claimed to possess a divine right to rule. Despite an abundance of examples of authoritarian rule in the Arab and Muslim world, there is generally no history of claims to rule by divine right, least of all by the Prophet.[47] This messenger of God was chosen as the leader of the Muslims through the process of *bay'ah*. Many of his successors were selected in a similar fashion. As heads of an Islamic state, they ruled in accordance with the laws of God, not as his representatives on earth.

Since this process of *bay'ah* was used repeatedly for choosing heads of the Muslim state, it is necessary to examine this process with an eye to determining any democratic features it may have.

A. Bay'ah

The word "*bay'ah*" is derived from "bay'," which means "selling." As such it connotes a contract between someone who makes an offer and another who accepts it, the latter being the one engaged in *bay'ah*. In the case of political succession, *bay'ah* is the act of accepting and declaring allegiance to a potential ruler. *Bay'ah* takes place when one or more individuals inform another that they support his assumption of the leadership position and pledge their allegiance to him. In the past, this was usually done by visiting the potential leader, expressing allegiance face to face and shaking his hand as is traditionally done when concluding a sale. Hence, the use of the term *bay'ah*. Of course, no *bay'ah* is valid without the acceptance of the potential leader. If the majority of the people gave their support, the potential leader would ascend to the leadership position. In the days of the Prophet, for example, women sent a delegation to the Prophet to inform him of their support and allegiance to him.[48]

Historically, the process of the *bay'ah* of the *khalifah* came to consist of two stages. In the first stage certain individuals, referred to as "*Ahl al-Hal wa'l 'Aqd*" (those who can enter into a contract or dissolve it), engaged in extensive consultations to build a consensus and then gave the *bay'ah* to a potential *khalifah* they agreed upon. This choice was tantamount to a nomination and it carried great weight. In the second stage, the general public gave its *bay'ah* to the chosen candidate.[49]

Individuals engaging in consultations at the first stage had to meet certain requirements. Basically, they had to be just and had to possess the kind of knowledge which would enable them to make the best choice for *khalifah* in light of the requirements that such *khalifah* had to meet. They also had to be capable of making a wise choice in light of all the relevant circumstances at that time.[50] These requirements were sufficiently loose to qualify a large number of people. As a result, no limitations were placed on the number of individuals who could be considered part of *Ahl al-Hal wa'l 'Aqd* (hereinafter referred to as "Wise Ones"), nor were there any economic, racial, or gender-related requirements for obtaining such a status in society.[51]

Theoretically, therefore, in an Islamic nation-state of tens of millions of people, the number of Wise Ones (unless deliberately limited by the people or otherwise reduced by requiring additional qualifications) could run into the millions.[52] Among the Wise Ones would be members of various segments of society, including lawyers, doctors, engineers, teachers, farmers, workers, and homemakers. Each would provide a valuable perspective which would enrich the selection process. The mechanics of this process would be immensely facilitated by the use of the media and electronic voting and tallying. In addition, such Wise Ones may in turn decide to elect a limited number of the most qualified amongst them to choose a *khalifah*. The details of such process may vary from country to country, depending on the circumstances, customs and needs of each.

Historically, however, there was no general election of the Wise Ones to their preferred position. Indeed, there was no specific mechanism for selecting them or removing them. They were simply recognized in their society as the Wise Ones.[53] Originally, in the small community of the *Sahaba* and the early Muslims, such recognition was easily achieved. However, as Islam grew and Muslim communities proliferated, it became necessary to develop new ways for choosing the Wise Ones which could cope with the sheer size of the Muslim state, as well as its diverse communities.[54] This was not done. Instead, Islamic governance took a different direction.

B. Istikhlaf

There was another, less common form of choosing a head of the Islamic state, which existed during early Islam. It was that of *istikhlaf* (choosing one's own successor).[55] According to the *Sunni* view, the Prophet did not use this form.[56] After his death, Muslims chose his successor through *bay'ah*.[57] Some of the early Muslim rulers, however, did choose their own successors and this form of transfer of power later took root. Some jurists, however, arguing from early Islamic precedents, have approved of this method of succession only if *istikhlaf* was based on extensive consultation.[58]

While it is generally agreed that the *bay'ah* of the Wise Ones to a nominee must be followed by the *bay'ah* of the general public, there is some disagreement in the literature as to whether such a *bay'ah* is necessary after *istikhlaf*. The better view is that a *bay'ah* by the public is necessary after *istikhlaf*, because *istikhlaf* is merely a form of nomination, similar to that engaged in by the Wise Ones at the initial stage of the traditional process of *bay'ah*.[59] Some, however, have argued that *istikhlaf* does not require a *bay'ah* unless the nominee is a parent or child of the *khalifah*.[60] Still others have argued that a *bay'ah* after any *istikhlaf* is not necessary at all.[61] Some of these latter views were infected by outside political pressures exerted by dynastic rulers. Clearly, however, the democratic character of the process of choosing a head of state is at least partially related to whether the *bay'ah* of the general public (or its representatives) is viewed as necessary.

The variety of views on such an important topic should not be surprising. Since the Qur'an did not specify the mechanisms for the choice of a head of state, the task was left to the Muslims. A succession system, consistent with the teachings of the Qur'an, as interpreted with the help of the *sunnah*, was to be developed by Muslims in accordance with their times and circumstances and the other principles previously discussed in Section II(B) (henceforth referred to collectively as "*Shari'ah* Principles"). Given Islam's flexible approach to *ijtihad*, scholars formulated different proposals, each more suitable to the milieu and epoch in which the scholar lived. These various approaches reflected the political realities and pressures to which the scholars were subjected.[62] To the extent this diversity was the result of flexibility and the free exercise of *ijtihad* in the light of the Qur'an and *sunnah*, it was healthy.

C. Some Observations

The democratic character of a selection by the Wise Ones depends in part on the process through which the Wise Ones are chosen. If the Wise Ones are chosen by the people as such, whether directly or indirectly, then the group of Wise Ones would be no different than a democratically chosen nominating (election) body. There is no reason in Islam why the Wise Ones cannot be chosen, and historically the spontaneous recognition by the community of their status was tantamount to a vote of confidence. Today, more may be needed to familiarize a growing community with the qualifications of its members. But, in this age of the global village, the flow of such information should be easily attainable. Note that if the Wise Ones are democratically elected, then even if the *bay'ah* of the general public is dispensed with, the democratic character of the process will remain significant.

On the other hand, the democratic character of succession by *istikhlaf* depends on whether the nomination is followed by *bay'ah* and, in any case, whether the role being played by the *khalifah* is akin to that of a constitutional monarch or is more akin to that of an absolute one.[63] These matters are addressed in Part IV, which argues that there is no such thing as an absolute monarch in an Islamic state. It also discusses the separation of powers and the role of consultation in Islam.

Before concluding these observations, a brief comment about the applicability of the concept of *khalifah* to today's world is in order. A *khalifah* must meet several requirements that are very demanding. For example, the *khalifah* must be knowledgeable enough to engage in *ijtihad* and be a very wise and prudent political leader.[64] Very few people today would satisfy this combination of requirements, and if they did, it is unlikely that they would be the best *mujtahids* or the best political leaders. Furthermore, the *khalifah* is supposed to be the leader of the Muslim *ummah* and, at the present, the *ummah* is part of numerous nation-states. These facts, considered in light of the *Shari'ah* Principles, suggested to some the need to modify the concept of *khalifah* so as to make it applicable to nation-states and not to the *ummah* as a whole.[65] Others proposed revising the qualifications of the *khalifah* so as to make them more realistic.[66] In exchange, the system of government was somewhat revised to provide additional support for the *khalifah*. For example, under such proposals one would require the *khalifah* to be pious but not necessarily a *mujtahid*. In exchange, the system of government would allow for a *majlis shura* (consultative council of *mujtahids*), whom the *khalifah* may or ought to consult when making certain decisions. Such an approach, its proponents argue, could be used to bolster democracy.

Compatibility of Divine Law
with a Democratic Form of Government

Democratic governments derive their legitimacy from the will of the people and rest legality on their consent. More specifically, in a democratic government, the elected representatives of the people enact the laws. In Islam, the laws derive their legitimacy from divine will. They have not been enacted by representatives of the people. Rather, they have been revealed to the Prophet through God's will. The contrast appears striking. In the one case, the people are subject to laws of their own making. In the other, the people are subject to another will, a divine will. The latter seems to be more akin to a totalitarian system than a democratic one. In this section it is argued that the contrast between democratic government and Islamic government is superficial and that a closer look results in a different conclusion.

Perhaps the best way to approach this problem is by studying more closely a specific system of democratic government, such as the democratic form of government in the United States. Our system is based on a constitution that is supplemented by laws and regulations promulgated by the legislative and executive branches of government. While the laws are enacted by the representatives of the people and the regulations are introduced by the executive branch to implement these laws, the Constitution has a different stature. The Constitution is that historical document on which the whole political system in the United States rests. It is superior to any law which may conflict with it, even though such laws may have been passed by a majority vote of the legislature.

Having described the United States political system this way, the "Antimajoritarian Difficulty," discussed by Lawrence Tribe, becomes more apparent.[67] In Tribe's words "[i]n its most basic form, the question . . . is why a nation that rests legality on the consent of the governed would choose to constitute its political life in terms of commitments to an original agreement—made by the people, binding on their children, and deliberately structured so as to be difficult to change."[68] A corollary question is: why have remarkable powers of judicial review been ceded by the system to federal judges, so as to permit them to invalidate as unconstitutional certain laws promulgated by the legislative branch?[69]

This is not the place to debate the antimajoritarian difficulty or judicial review. But these matters were mentioned in order to point out the fact that societies historically coalesce around some basic sets of deep values and beliefs that define them as a group. These sets of shared values and beliefs are usually memorialized in a most basic document, like the Constitution of the United States or the Magna Carta. As time passes, these documents are reinterpreted and supplemented to highlight an issue or resolve a problem. But through all the decades, the essential character of these documents remains the same and best reflects the values of the society that created it.

Therefore, in matters that relate to such deep beliefs and values, a majoritarian consent is not sought every year or every generation. Once given, it is assumed to be there unless the people clearly say otherwise. And when they do, such statements constitute challenges that can result in civil wars because they tear at the very fabric of society.[70] The case is no different in Islam. The Qur'an is the core of the Muslim's constitution.[71] It defines the very essence of the Muslim society for generations to come. Just like in the United States, the consent of the Muslim *ummah* was achieved at the outset, when the Islamic state was first established.

Since the Qur'an provides mostly general laws, a Muslim legislature needs to promulgate a multitude of laws in the process of governance, just as our legislature does. And, just as our legislature sometimes discovers, some of these promulgated laws may be "unconstitutional," i.e. they may run contrary to the Qur'an. The Muslims who would have the power of "judicial review" in the Muslim state would be those of a judicial *majlis shura*, referred to at the end of Part III.[72] Other *mujtahids* outside the *majlis*, like their American counterparts, i.e. the constitutional scholars, can contribute to the discussion.

This discussion should not be interpreted as suggesting the historical existence of a separate judicial branch in the Muslim state which reviews the actions of the legislature and executive branches. This is not the case. A discussion of the separation of powers will follow in Part V. All that is being suggested here is that such a structure can be adopted, if desired. Where the actual religious leadership of an Islamic nation or the *ummah* is vested in *majlis shura*, such a group can be regarded as the "Supreme Court" of the Muslim state, because it would provide the highest Islamic judgment as to whether a certain law is contrary to the Qur'an.[73] Is the *khalifah*, however, bound by the decisions of the *majlis*? This is also discussed in Part V.

One might point out an important difference between the U.S. Constitution and the Qur'an. The former can and has been amended. The latter cannot. The difference, however, is to a large extent semantical. The American Constitution has rarely been amended by introducing a later provision which superseded an earlier one. Rather, jurists have tended to resolve even the most substantial constitutional issues through reinterpretation, a process analogous to *ijtihad*. Amendments were generally used to enhance, clarify, and supplement constitutional principles. In this sense, the Qur'an has already been supplemented by the *sunnah* and can be further supplemented by legal scholars who see the need for articulating additional principles. As explained earlier, Islam is flexible, and part of its flexibility lies in the ability to interpret and supplement the Qur'an, in ways consistent with the Qur'an, to produce laws suitable to a certain epoch and society. While the additions will have the weight of constitutional laws, they will never, however, be confused with divine laws. This distinction should carry no legal significance; but from a religious point of view it is very significant in so far as it separates the inner sanctum of the Muslim's religious beliefs from the temporal cultural ones.

To summarize our response to the problem posed by this section, the Qur'an was consented to by the Muslim people when the Islamic state was established. As a result, it reflects not only Divine Law but the will of these people to abide by such law. This reduces the problem at hand to a variant of the "antimajoritarian difficulty" described by Lawrence Tribe and can thus be treated along the same lines. Furthermore, all laws that supplement the Qur'an have also either been consented to at the outset, as in the case of the *sunnah,* or are formulated by legislative bodies. Therefore, Islamic laws rest their legality on the consent of the *ummah* in the same sense that the United States laws rest their legality on the consent of the American people.

The result of the discussion of Principle A shows that the Islamic system of government is sufficiently flexible as to admit the most democratic structures. The discussion also shows that the flexibility of the Qur'an permits Muslims to choose from a variety of political systems ranging from monarchist to republican, depending on the needs, customs and other relevant circumstances of the community.[74] The discussion concludes by rejecting the notion that Islamic Divine Law does not rest on the consent of the Muslim people. But, to formulate final conclusions about the democratic character of the Muslim system of government, one still needs to examine such system in light of Principle B: the principle of the separation of powers.

The Principle of Separation of Powers

In the days of the Prophet, all legislative, executive and judicial powers rested with him.[75] This arrangement made sense during that period, since the Prophet was the Messenger of God. He was in charge of teaching Muslims the basic principles of Islam, and showing them how to act and live in accordance with these principles.

However, even the Prophet consulted his companions, though only in matters not relating to religion.[76] For, in matters of religion, he was the expert. In worldly matters, like those of agriculture or warfare, the Prophet consulted the experts.[77] He also repeatedly encouraged Muslims to do the same. Furthermore, the Prophet was in the habit of consulting with other Muslims, and at times followed the advice of Muslims even when he clearly disagreed with it.[78] Such was his respect for the consultative process that, in one instance, when the advice of his companions cost him the battle, he did not blame them.[79] This course of conduct by the Prophet established the importance of consultation (*shura*) in government as part of the *sunnah.*

After the death of the Prophet, *al-Khulafa' al-Rashidun* (the first four successors to the Prophet, also referred to as the Rightly Guided *khalifahs*) followed in the Prophet's footsteps to the greatest extent possible. Since the revelation of the Qur'an was completed before the Prophet's death, Muslims had to do their best to find the proper laws governing each new situation they encountered, based only on the teaching the Prophet left them and on common sense. If they erred, God would not intervene with a revelation to correct them. They were thus thrown into the world on their own. To minimize error, the *khalifahs* turned to *shura*. In matters of religion, other *mujtahids* were consulted. On other matters, the *khalifahs*, following the example of the Prophet, also relied on *shura* with the appropriate groups. Thus, *shura* was a hallmark of early Islamic governance.

We shall now turn to a discussion of the *Shura* Principle, in order to lay the foundation for assessing its democratic merit.

A. The Shura Principle

Shura represents one of the most basic principles of Islamic government. It is referred to twice in the Qur'an. The first *ayah* in the Qur'an about *shura* mentions it in the same sentence with two of the cornerstones of Islam, prayer and *Zakat*.[80] The *ayah* draws a picture of good Muslims as those who respond to their God, pray, reach their decisions by discussing matters amongst them in accordance with *shura* and pay (in *Zakat*) what God has given them.

In another passage, the Qur'an says:

> It is part of the Mercy of God that you deal gently with [your people]. Were you severe or harsh-hearted, they would have broken away from around you. So pass over [their faults] and ask for God's forgiveness for them and consult them in important matters. Then, when you have taken a decision, put your trust in God [and execute it], for God loves those who put their trust [in him].[81]

In this passage, the need for *shura* was communicated to the Prophet in an imperative form. Therefore, the need for the ruler to consult is not subject to interpretation in Islam.[82] What is subject to interpretation, however, is the range of matters requiring *shura,* the method of selecting those who provide *shura* and whether, once *shura* takes place, the ruler is bound to abide by the resulting advice. Different scholars have come up with different conclusions on these matters, depending on their own reading of the Qur'an and *sunnah* as well as their own experiences and circumstances in the country and epoch in which they lived.[83]

Range of Matters Covered by Shura Principle

Some *mujtahids* held that any matter, other than one covered by specific Qur'anic laws, is the proper subject of *shura*.[84] Others, based on their interpretation of sunnah, limited *shura* to military matters.[85] Still others argued that *shura* applied to "important matters" only.[86] Therefore, the scope of matters covered by the *Shura* Principle, though not the principle itself, is subject to *ijtihad*. As such, it is also subject to the rules used by the *mujtahids*, including those which permit flexibility in interpretation in accordance with the *Shari'ah* Principles.

This means that a *mujtahid* living in this epoch of democratic governance can define the range of matters which are covered by the *Shura* Principle liberally so as to include all those matters that are viewed today as the proper subject of consultation whether by parliament, cabinet, leadership of the armed forces, or the supreme court of the land. In other words, the *Shura* Principle could readily become applicable to all the different branches of democratic government and thus take different, more complex forms than it did in the early days of Islam. It also could become applicable to each branch of government at its various levels. This complexity, of course, is to be expected in the era of the technetronic society.

Whether Advice Resulting from Shura Is Binding

Scholars have also disagreed on this matter. Those who believe that advice resulting from *shura* is not binding argue that the Qur'an imposed on a ruler the duty to engage in *shura*, but it did not bind the ruler to follow the resulting advice.[87] The actual *ayah* says, "when you have taken a decision, put your trust in God [and execute it]."[88] The focus of dispute became the phrase "when you have taken a decision." Some concluded that such decisions need not conform to the advice received, but only be informed by it. Others disagreed.[89] The *sunnah* is not totally clear on the matter.[90]

Regardless of the dispute, two things are clear. First, the ruler in Islam does not have absolute power. The ruler's power is, at minimum, limited by the Qur'an and *sunnah*, some of which is quite specific and permits little room for interpretation. Second, depending on the subject matter for which *shura* is sought, it may well be advisable in some circumstances to permit the ruler to override the advice received or choose to be bound by it, as the case may be. This is already part of the practice in modern Western democracies where the president often has the right of veto in certain legislative matters and the right to consult his staff without necessarily abiding by the staff's advice on certain executive matters. Such flexibility could be accommodated in a system based on *shura*.

Qualifications and Selection of Those Who Provide Shura

In the days of the Prophet, those who provided *shura* (the "*Shura* People") were Wise Ones and ascended to their status by a natural process of recognition by the Muslims at large.[91] They ranged from wise heads of tribes to individuals who were first to adopt Islam and Madinah leaders who supported the Prophet when he left Makkah for Madinah in order to escape persecution.[92] Later, these were supplemented by astute politicians, experienced military leaders and religious scholars of note in the community.[93] Since then, the *mujtahids* have formulated the main qualities required in the *Shura* People.

For matters relating to religion, the *Shura* People must be *mujtahids*.[94] In other matters, they must be experts in the relevant field.[95] In both cases, however, rationality and Islamic morality (like honesty and truth) are basic prerequisites. Furthermore, no advice by the *Shura* People may contravene the laws of the Qur'an or *sunnah*.[96] Finally, according to *sunnah*, choosing the best qualified group for *shura* is a serious religious duty; not doing so to the best of one's abilities constitutes betrayal of God and fellow Muslims.[97]

For this reason, it is more important in today's complex and populous society to develop a more workable method of selection. Writers who view a *majlis shura* as tantamount to a parliament argue for a selection process based on general elections; others would leave it for the head of state to choose the providers of *shura*.[98] The expanded concept of *shura* discussed earlier would accommodate both views if it required, for example, the election of the legislative *majlis shura* but left to the head of state the freedom to appoint members of the judicial *majlis shura* (subject to confirmation by the legislative *majlis shura*) and choose personal advisers.

B. Checks and Balances in the Islamic State

As mentioned earlier, there is no separation of powers in the days of the Prophet. There was no fully articulated system for separation of powers later either, although such separation did occur and was a hallmark of the Islamic system of government.[99] Rather, it was always understood and agreed that the *khalifah* and the state were subject to the rule of the Qur'an and *sunnah* whose interpretation rested with the *mujtahids*. Furthermore, it was always understood and agreed that it was the duty of every Muslim to right wrongs even if the perpetrator was the *khalifah*.[100]

To emphasize his submission to the rule of the Qur'an and *sunnah*, *Khalifah* Abu Bakr said to Muslims in his first address after he became *khalifah*: "I have been given authority over you, but I'm not the best of you. If I do well help me, and if I do ill, then put me right."[101] In another instance, *Khalifah* 'Umar attempted to reduce the amount of "Mahr" (agreed upon amount of money or other gifts given by the prospective groom to his prospective bride as an indication of his serious matrimonial intentions). An old woman in the mosque, who understood correctly the role of Mahr in providing the prospective bride with a cushion for her own sole use in business or pleasure, objected by saying; "You shall not deprive us of what God gave us." *Khalifah* 'Umar backed down saying: "A woman is right and a man is wrong."[102]

The last story reflects three facts.[103] The first is about the *Khalifah* 'Umar; namely, that he continued to struggle (with different degrees of success) throughout his life against his strong pre-Islamic patriarchal upbringing. This struggle was greatly helped by the Prophet's extensive *sunnah* on the question of women.[104] The second, which is true of the first story as well, is that every

Muslim (regardless of class, race or sex) had a voice in the state. The third, also true of the first story, is that in matters of religion Islamic law prevails even if it is being used by an ordinary Muslim against the head of state. In fact, a Muslim has a duty to right a wrong and to state the truth. Unfortunately, this tradition was quickly lost with the rise of absolute monarchies during the Umayyad and 'Abbasid periods, and later even some of the greatest *mujtahids* were punished by the state for their religious views.[105] Such a development was clearly contrary to Islamic tradition insofar as Islam respected the human dignity of individuals and favored *ijtihad*.

The Islamic system of government was left by the Qur'an and *sunnah* to the Muslims to develop in accordance with (i) the dictates of their own epoch, customs and needs, and (ii) the few basic but flexible and democratic divine rules, but was never really fully developed. In fact, its development was seriously hampered by the increasing political and jurisprudential obstacles that faced *mujtahids*. This led Muslims to utilize older and sometimes outdated forms of political institutions for their system of government.

In modern times, however, many Muslim thinkers have reclaimed their right to free *ijtihad* and restudied the structure of the Islamic state. As a result, some have already argued that the notion of separation of powers is not only desirable but in fact already exists in a theoretical framework of the Muslim state as a fundamental principle.[106] In one such study, the author analogized the *Shura* People to a parliament and called for checks and balances. On the whole, such views have tended to restrict unnecessarily (and perhaps unintentionally) the scope of *shura* to a parliamentary form, since (as discussed earlier) the *Shura* Principle permeates all levels and branches of government.

The task of the modern *mujtahids,* therefore, is to develop a modern system of government, suitable to the needs and customs of their respective nation-states, which is based on a principle of *shura* in all the branches of such government, to the extent appropriate to each branch and among the branches, and which develops a system of checks and balances that preserves the democratic ideals propagated by the Prophet and his successors *al-Khulafa' al-Rashidun.*

Conclusion

Both the Muslim state, regardless of its particular form of government, and its head of state are subject to the rule of Islamic law, which is based on the Qur'an and *sunnah*. Islamic law rests on the consent of the Muslim people in the same way the American Constitution rests on the consent of the American people. The Qur'an does not attempt to articulate, except in certain specific cases, detailed rules to be followed in every country or epoch. Rather, the philosophy of the Qur'an is to establish certain basic principles which could then be used by Muslims to develop specific laws suitable for their epoch, customs, and needs.

With respect to developing a method for the selection of a head of state, different Muslims developed different methods. These methods depended in part on whether the system of government adopted was monarchist or not. In any case, the general view is that each method required first the selection of a nominee, whether by a group of people or the existing head of state, and then the acceptance of such nomination by the public at large.

Regardless of the form of government chosen, the Qur'an requires that the Muslim government be based on the principle of *shura* (consultation). This requirement, combined with the supremacy of Islamic law and the fact that the interpretation of such law rests with the *mujtahids*, points to a *de facto* if not *de jure* separation of powers. For this reason, this article concludes that attempts by Muslims to improve the democratic character of their various Muslim states, if properly undertaken, need not run afoul of the rule of Islamic law, but may in fact enhance it.

Notes

The author thanks Dr. Jamal Badawi, Chair, Islamic Information Foundation (Canada), the late Dr. Mahmoud Abu-Saud, former president of the American Muslim Council, and Professor John Paul Jones, T. C. Williams School of Law, for their valuable comments on earlier drafts of this article. The author also acknowledges the valuable assistance of Mr. Gamil Youssef, Librarian at the Oriental Division of the New York Public Library, for facilitating the research for this article.

1. This article appeared originally in *Case Western Reserve Journal of International Law*, vol. 24, no. 1 (1992), and is being republished with the journal's permission. The introduction has been updated and some minor revisions and corrections were made in the body of the article. The author notes that the inclusion in the footnotes of the less authoritative modern English secondary sources, as opposed the exclusive reliance on primary and classical Arabic sources, is designed to facilitate further reading on the subject by the English-speaking reader.

2. Least known among these are the events unfolding in Southeast Asia in connection with the "Anwar Ibrahim Affair." After the collapse of the Southeast Asian economies, including that of Malaysia, Anwar Ibrahim, the former finance minister of Malaysia, was expelled from office. He was then arrested and tortured on charges of engaging in prohibited sexual activity. News reports have alleged that these charges were manufactured and that Ibrahim's fall from grace related directly to his refusal to use the country's financial reserves in order to save cronies of the prime minister from financial ruin. See, e.g., "The Anwar Episode: An Analysis," *Commentary: International Movement for a Just World* (Malaysia), Special Issue, October 1998, esp. 2.

3. See, e.g., Tawfic al-Shawi, *Siyadat al-Shari'ah al-Islamiyyah fi Misr* (Cairo 1987), 118, 120, who expresses this point of view forcefully. Cf. Abd al-Razzaq al-Sanhuri, *Fiqh al-Khilafah wa Tatawwouruha* (1926, N. Sanhouri and T. Shawi, trans., Cairo 1989), 230 (argues that the Islamic system of government is quite similar to the system of government in the United States).

4. See, e.g., Hassan al-Turabi, "The Islamic State," in *Voices of Resurgent Islam*, John L. Esposito, ed. (New York: Oxford University Press, 1983). See also, Al-Sanhuri, *Fiqh al-Khilafah*, 71-72, 191-92. Al-Sanhuri points out that the *khalifah* has no power to absolve Muslims from their sins or to excommunicate them. It appears that Western media are not fully aware of these facts, because they keep referring to Iranian Muslim scholars as "clerics." Incidentally, *"khalifah"* means literally "successor." The *khalifah* (also referred to in English as "Caliph") is the successor of the Prophet, not of God.

5. See Abu Hamid al-Ghazali, *Ihya' 'Ulum ad-Din* [Reviving Religious Sciences] (Matba'at Mustafa al-Babi al-Halabi: Cairo, 1939), 33-4; Hassan az-Zein, *Al-Islam wa al-Fikr al-Mu'asser* (Dar al-Fikr al-Hadith: Beirut, 1997), 45-6; cf. also al-Ghazali, at 337-351 (providing instances where people who spoke out to the ruler directly were not punished); Ibn Khaldoun, *Al-Muqqadimah* [The Introduction] (Kitab al-Qalam: Beirut, reprint, 1978), 209; Ibrahim al-Wazir, *'Ala Masharif al-Qarn al-Khamis 'Ashar al-Hijra* (Dar al-Shuruq: Beirut 1989), 42. It is worth noting that every one of the founders of the four major schools of *Sunni* jurisprudence in existence today suffered at the hands of the political authorities.

6. Good sources in the English language for an introductory but substantive overview of Islam include the following: John L. Esposito, *Islam: The Straight Path* (New York: Oxford University Press, 1991); Seyyed Hossein Nasr, *Ideals and Realities of Islam* (London: Allen and Unwin, 1975); Fazlur Rahman, *Islam* (London: Weidenfeld, 1967).

7. Espositio, *Islam*, 20-21. See also Rahman, *Islam*, 32. For additional discussion on the Qur'an, see Nasr, *Ideas and Realities*, 41-66.

8. This is one reason why the Qur'an has served throughout the ages as a standard of the classical Arabic language. For more on this point, see e.g., Esposito, *Islam*, 21; Subhi Mahmassani, *Falsafat al-Tashri' fi al Islam*, 3rd ed. (Beirut, 1961), 146; Nasr, *Ideals and Realities*, 45; Subhi Al-Saleh, *Ma'alim al-Shari'ah al-Islamiyyah* (Beirut 1975), 79-110. See also Seyyed Hossein Nasr, *An Introduction to Islamic Cosmological Doctrines* (1964), 6-8 (discussing, among other things, the character of the Arabic language as a vehicle of both divine revelation and most of the Muslim sciences).

9. For a detailed discussion of this point, see Abd al-Hamid Mutawalli, *Mabadi' Nizam al-Hukm fi al-Islam*, 2nd ed. (Alexandria, 1974), 34-46. See also Esposito, *Islam*, 77-80.

10. Mutawalli, *Mabadi' Nizam*, 34; J. al-Suyuti, *Al-Itqan fi 'Ulum al-Qur'an* (fifteenth-century, M. Ibrahim, ed., reprint, Cairo 1967), 69.

11. This term literally means "those who study hard" or "those who exert themselves intellectually." It refers to any capable Muslim who engages seriously in the process of interpreting Islamic texts and Islamic law. Unfortunately, Western media sometimes confuses such Muslim scholars with religious practitioners who do not engage substantially in interpretation and who are usually referred to by such media as "clerics." The activity in which the *mujtahids* engage is called *"ijtihad."*

12. The Prophet always advocated the facilitation of the practice of religion, stating that the best of religious practices is the easiest. His wife, A'isha, stated that whenever he faced several choices, the Prophet always chose the easiest one unless it was religiously prohibited, in which case he was furthest from it. Zarruq al-Fassi, *Sharh Sahih al-Bukhari* (fifteenth century, I. Attiyah and M. Ali, eds., reprint, Cairo 1973), 149n3. Muslim scholars have often said that "Rahmat al-ummah fi ikhtilaf al a'immah." Literally, this means "mercy for the Muslim people is to be found in disagreements among its scholars." Mahmassani, *Falsafat*, 136n3, 481; Esposito, *Islam*, 85.

13. Esposito, *Islam*, 77; Mahmassani, *Falsafat*, 151. The *sunnah* also includes reports of the Prophet's silence or acquiescence in instances where such behavior is viewed as permissive.

14. Esposito, *Islam*, 81. According to the *hadith*, the Prophet said: "do not record my sayings and anyone who has recorded any of my statements other than Qur'an[ic reve-lations] should erase them." Muslim Ibn al-Hajjaj, *Al-Jami' al-Sahih* (ninth-century, reprint, Beirut n.d.), 229. There is, however, evidence of recordation of the *hadith* during the life of the Prophet. This fact lends credence to the view that the prohibition was temporary and related only to the earlier period of Qur'anic revelations.

15. See Esposito, *Islam*, 81; Rahman, *Islam*, 59; Mahmassani, *Falsafat*, 154-58. See also Diya' al-Din Nasr allah Ibn al-Athir, *Jami' al Usul fi Ahadith Al Rasul* (twelfth century, A. Arna'out, ed., reprint, Beirut, 1969), 544-606.

16. Subhi Mahmassani, *Al-Awda' al-Tashri'iyyah fi al-Duwal al-Arabiyyah*, 3rd ed. (Beirut, 1965), 148. See also Rahman, *Islam*, 60-64 (explaining why a minority of jurists rejected the *hadith* as a source and limited their *ijtihad* to the Qur'an).

17. Esposito, *Islam*, 28; Al-Turabi, "Islamic State," 248; Al-Qutb Tabliah, *Al-Islam wa Huquq al-Insan* (Cairo, 1976), 311 (compares Islamic and *Jahiliyyah* [pre-Islamic] views of responsibility). In *Jahiliyyah* the whole tribe was viewed as responsible for the individual's action. In contrast, while the Qur'an continued to recognize collective responsibility in certain instances, it emphasized the fact that each individual is responsible for her or his own actions. One famous *ayah* states, "no bearer of burdens can bear the burden of another" (VI:164). The Qur'an, however, also states that where someone misleads unwitting others away from God, such person shares their burden (XVI:25), the reason being that one ought to be responsible for the consequences of one's actions. Furthermore, the Qur'an cautions that God may inflict collective punishment in certain instances (VIII:25). In writing this article, the author referred to A. Yusuf Ali's translation of the Qur'an (1983), but the translation was often not adopted verbatim.

18. See, e.g., Noel Coulson, *A History of Islamic Law* (Edinburgh: University Press, 1964), 25; Al-Turabi, "Islamic State," 244. See also Al-Sanhuri, *Fiqh al-Khilafat*, 192.

19. On point is the following famous story about the Prophet. One day, he happened to pass by a group of people in Madinah who were pollinating palm trees. Upon finding out what they were doing, he opined that the trees would bear fruit with or without their help. The people stopped their activity. Subsequently, the palm trees did not bear fruit. When the Prophet passed by them later in the year, he saw the barren palm trees and inquired about them. On hearing what had happened he said "You are more knowledge-able in your worldly matters." Muslim, *Al-Jami'*, 95; Mutawalli, *Mabadi' Nizam*, 39n1, 39n3.

20. Mutawalli, *Mabadi' Nizam*, at 38n1, 38n3. For examples of flexibility of interpretation, See Mahmassani, *Falsafat*, 205-215.

21. Mahmassani, *Falsafat*, 205-15; Esposito, *Islam*, 77-78; Ibn Khaldun, *Al-Muqaddimah* (fourteenth century, reprint, Beirut 1978), 218.

22. Badr al-Din al-'Aini, *'Umdat al Qari fi Sharh Sahih al-Bukhari* (1434, reprint, Cairo, 1979), 66-67; Muslim, *Al-Jami'*, 131. The *hadith* refers to "*hakim*." This word is ambiguous. It means literally "one who rules." It could refer to a ruler or a jurist. The better view is that it refers to the latter.

23. See, e.g., Qur'an XIII:8-10; XXI:4; XXXI:34.

24. Esposito, *Islam*, 77. See also Mahmassani, *Falsafat*, 132-36 (arguing that such differences are also rooted in the different analytical methods used for interpretation).

25. Esposito, *Islam*, 84 (stating that as the consensus of scholars evolved, it served as a brake on further individual interpretations); Mahmassani, *Falsafat*, 183; Nasr, *Ideals and Realities*, 105. This development is often labeled as the "closing of the door of *ijtihad*." The label is not accurate because it suggests a complete bar to *ijtihad*. It was not. Many *Sunni* jurists, like Ibn Taymiyah, continued to engage in *ijtihad*; but intellectual activity was already on the decline for a variety of other reasons. Consequently, there were fewer outstanding *mujtahids*.

26. Esposito, *Islam*, 122; Nasr, *Ideals and Realities*, 117.

27. The Prophet said, "The best of religious practice is the easiest and the best worship is engaging in *Fiqh* [Islamic jurisprudence which is based on *ijtihad*]." Al-Fassi, *Sharh Sahih*, 149. See also Mahmassani, *Falsafat*, 185-88 (stating that the qualifications of a *mujtahid* include rationality, maturity, morality, piety, and knowledge of the literature, the facts, and the applicable modes of reasoning). It is worth noting that the *shi'i* view on some of the matters discussed in this article (like that of *ijtihad*) is different from the *Sunni* view. These differences, however, can not be discussed without delving into scholastic arguments that go well beyond the scope of this article. At this level of discussion, there are no significant differences between the two views that are worth focusing upon, nor do these differences alter the conclusions reached in this article. Nasr, *Ideals and Realities*, 105.

28. "*Shari'ah*" means the body of Islamic law. Originally, it referred only to Qur'anic, then *hadith*-based laws. Now, it is also used to refer to laws developed by Muslim jurists on the basis of at least two additional sources, namely, consensus and reasoning by analogy. See, e.g., Mutawalli, *Mabadi' Nizam*, 51-57.

29. See Rahman, *Islam*, 71-79. Mutawalli questions the usefulness of these two additional sources in today's Islamic community. Mutawalli, *Mabadi' Nizam*, 51-57. See also Mutawalli, *Mabadi' Nizam*, 78-79 (discussing reasons for rejecting the remaining sources). Cf. Al-Sanhuri, *Fiqh al-Khilafat*, 67-82 (arguing that *ijma'* is basic to modern Islamic democracies). For a good discussion on *ijma'*, see Al-Sanhuri, 68-82.

30. See, e.g., Coulson, *A History*, 49; Mahmassani, *Falsafat*, 201.

31. Esposito, *Islam*, 98-101 (providing an example for the interaction of Islam with local customs); Mahmassani, *Falsafat*, 200-01 and 214.

32. Qur'an VI:119 and 145; Muhammad Ibn al-Hasan al-Shaybani, *Sharh Kitab al-Siyar al-Kabir* (eighth century, S. Munajjid, ed., reprint, Cairo 1971), 1427; Mahmassani, *Al-Awda'*, 480, Mahmassani, *Falsafat*, 215-16. These sources define "necessity" narrowly, meaning to save one's life.

33. Qur'an XVI:115.

34. See Al-'Aini, *Umdat*, 45-46. See also Al-Fassi, *Sharh Sahih*, 12.

35. Al-Shaybani, *Sharh Kitab*, 1427.

36. Mahmassani, *Falsafat*, 201-02; Al-Sanhuri, *Fiqh al-Khilafat*, 258 (considering the implications of this principle for a deficient *khalifah*). A deficient *khalifah* is one who does not possess all the required qualifications for the office.

37. Quran IX:60.

38. Mahmassani, *Falsafat*, 207.

39. Mahmassani, *Al-Awda'*, 480.

40. In fact, the Qur'an asserts that Abraham was a Muslim (III:67). This is because Abraham yielded to the will of God and "Islam" means "to yield to divine will." For this and other reasons, Islam is viewed as a primordial religion, revealed by God at various stages of history through Abraham, Moses, Jesus, and other prophets before Muhammad.

Prophet Muhammad is viewed as having communicated the last stage of this revelation.

41. Qur'an, II:219; IV:43; V:90.

42. For a discussion of this principle, see Mutawalli, *Al-Islam* (Alexandria n.d.), 71-72.

43. Qur'an II:163; XXXI:13. The Prophet was a member of the powerful Quraysh tribe, although he belonged to a less powerful clan of that tribe. Quraysh, like most other tribes in the Arabian peninsula, worshiped hundreds of idols installed in *Ka'bah*, a cubic structure in Makkah which was built as a house of God by Abraham. When the Prophet began spreading his message he was forced to flee Makkah to Madinah. After the successful spread of Islam, he returned to Makkah with his supporters, fought the idol-worshippers and banished idols from the *Ka'bah*, which became once again the sacred House of God. Islam has five "pillars." Monotheism is the first among them.

44. See, e.g., Mutawalli, *Mabadi' Nizam*, 469-70; Al-Sanhuri, *Fiqh al-Khilafat*, 262 (arguing that under some circumstances Muslims may obey a deficient *khalifah* to avoid chaos); Muhammad F. al-Nabhan, *Nitham al-Hukm fi al-Islam* (Kuwait 1974), 528.

45. Qur'an III:103, 105. See also al-'Aini, *Umdat*, 262.

46. A more radical point of view was discussed by al-Nabhan, *Nitham al-Hukm*, 528 (noting that certain Muslim groups, basing their arguments on certain *ayahs* in the Qur'an, justified the removal of an unjust head of state by use of force in order to reestablish a just state).

47. A small minority argued at one point that the *khalifah* derives his authority from God's authority. But this group has been historically insignificant and the majority holds otherwise. For more on the minority view, see Mutawalli, *Mabadi' Nizam*, 185. See also al-Mawardi, *Al-Ahkam al-Sultaniyah* (eleventh century, reprint, Cairo 1983), 14.

48. This *bay'ah* was reported in the Qur'an LX:12.

49. Theoretically, *Ahl al-Hal wa'l 'Aqd* could reach an impasse or the general public could reject the nomination. However, because of the extensive efforts by *Ahl al-Hal wa'l 'Aqd* at consensus building and the small size of the Muslim community at that time, neither problem appeared, although a small faction, called thereafter "*al-Khawarij*," did reject one such nomination. The fact that the general public tended to accept the choice made by *Ahl al-Hal wa'l 'Aqd* led some jurists to argue that the choice was not a mere nomination but an actual election confirmed by the public. See, e.g., al-Nabhan, *Nitham al-Hukm*, 477. Al-Sanhuri divides the process into three stages, including an initial one where several candidates are nominated and considered by the Wise Ones; see *Fiqh al-Khilafat*, 141-42. But his discussion here is uncharacteristically confusing. It does appear, however, that the Muslim Brotherhood, a political movement that was formed in Egypt around the turn of the century, holds a view of this process similar to that of al-Sanhuri. For a more expanded discussion on the Muslim Brotherhood's views, see Richard P. Mitchell, *The Society of the Muslim Brothers* (1969), 245-250. Generally, the Muslim Brotherhood's views on democracy coincide with those of mainstream Muslim scholars.

50. See al-Mawardi, *Al-Akham*, 6; al-Sanhuri, *Fiqh al-Khilafat*, 136-37.

51. See generally al-Turabi, "Islamic State," 244. In an address during his farewell pilgrimage, the Prophet said: "All people are equal, as equal as the teeth of a comb. The only basis for preferring an Arab over a non-Arab, a white over a nonwhite or a male over a female is that of piety." Muhammad S. 'Awwa, *On the Political System of the Islamic State* (1980), 111. The Qur'an also states that God created humanity as male and female and of different nations and tribes so that people may meet and know each other, the most righteous amongst them being the most pious (XLIX:13).

52. See al-Turabi, "Islamic State," 244. Cf. Mutawalli, *Mabadi' Nizam*, 255-56 (disputing the claim that the Prophet at times asked the "people" for counsel. He argues that the Prophet could not have possibly asked for counsel from any one other than those who were capable of good advice, namely, the Wise Ones). I believe that Mutawalli's argument is elitist and that the Prophet was not. What is clear, however, from the literature is that the Prophet gave more weight to the views of some experienced Muslims from the *Sahaba* (companions of the Prophet) over others. It is reported that the Prophet once said to his companions 'Umar and Abu Bakr: "If you agree on an advice I would not overrule you," Abu Al-Fida Isma'il Ibn Kathir, *Tafsir* (fourteenth century, reprint, Beirut, 1966), 142-43. Tabliah, *Al-Islam*, 631, reports that A. al-Mawdudi, a Muslim scholar, holds the view that the *khalifah* was not free to consult at whim anyone he wished using arbitrary procedures. He was obligated to consult those who had the confidence of Muslims. This does not refute the position that the *khalifah* may consult the public at large. It only shows that if he does not and chooses to restrict his circle of advisers, they must be selected carefully and they must be Wise Ones.

53. Mutawalli, *Mabadi' Nizam*, 256-57.

54. Al-Turabi, "Islamic State," 246, 248.

55. See al-Mawardi, *Al-Akham*, 9. For a discussion of the various methods for choosing a *khalifah*, see Abu Abdullah al-Ansari al-Qurtubi, *Mukhtar Tafsir* (thirteenth century, T. Hakim, ed., Cairo, 1977), 56-61.

56. See, e.g., Javid Iqbal, "Democracy and the Modern Islamic State," in *Voices of Resurgent Islam*, 252 and 254. See also Esposito, *Islam*, 38; Sa'id Hawwa, *Al-Islam*, 3rd ed. (Beirut, 1981), 385; 'Awwa, *On the Political System*, 30-31.

57. Iqbal, "Democracy," 255, Esposito, *Islam*, 38; Hawwa, *Al-Islam*, 385.

58. Ahmad Ibn Muhammad Ibn-Hanbal, *Al-Musnad* (ninth century), 56, accompanied in the margin with Ali Ibn Abd al-Malik al-Muttaqi's *Muntakhab Kanz al-'Ummal fi Sunan al-Aqwal Wal Af'al* (sixteenth century, reprint, Beirut, 1969) (quoting *Khalifah* 'Umar that one who gives his *bay'ah* to a potential ruler without consulting the Muslims has no *bay'ah*). See, e.g., 'Awwa, *On the Political System*, 35-36 (arguing that consultation is essential in the process of choosing a head of state and that no ruler may be chosen without the will of the *ummah*. He also argues that the *ummah* may not be deprived of this basic right of choosing its head of state even under the pretense of preserving its unity).

59. See, e.g., Hawwa, *Al-Islam*, 364, 386-89; Mutawalli, *Mabadi' Nizam*, 203-06; al-Sanhuri, *Fiqh al-Khilafat*, 149-51.

60. Mutawalli, *Mabadi' Nizam*, 207; See also al-Mawardi, *Al-Akham*, 9, which argues that once a ruler designates his successor, then so long as the successor is neither his father nor son, the designation does not require confirmation by anyone, even the Wise Ones.

61. See, e.g., al-Mawardi, *Al-Akham*, 9. But this view is erroneous and is criticized at length by al-Sanhuri, *Fiqh al-Khilafat*, 149-51.

62. These views were sometimes influenced by pressure from the head of state. See, e.g., al-Sanhuri, *Fiqh al-Khilafat*, 63 (including n. 12). See also 'Awwa, *On the Political System*, 27.

63. Hawwa, *Al-Islam*, 366 (recounting the story of the *Khalifah* 'Umar, who inquired about the difference between a *khalifah* and a king. An unidentified individual responded that the difference between them lay in the fact that a *khalifah* takes only what is rightfully his and utilizes it only in the service of the truth. A king on the other hand, he

said, oppresses people, for he is unjust. He takes from anyone and gives to anyone, as he so chooses. The comparison appears to be drawn between a *khalifah* and an absolute monarch. The speaker rejected equating the two because the *khalifah* is bound by divine principles of truth and justice. An absolute monarch is not so bound). This story confirms our analysis in above (71-73).

64. Among the requirements listed are *ijtihad* (based on a good grasp of Islam, a sense of justice, physical fitness, wisdom in political and administrative matters, and courage). See al-Mawardi, *Al-Akham*, 6.

65. Iqbal, "Democracy," 255-57. Historically, there have been many instances where several *khalifahs* ruled different parts of the Muslim world. For example, while the Abbasids ruled in the East, the Umayyads ruled in Spain. The trend today is to reject this approach as having been instrumental in the ultimate weakening of the *khilafah* system (the system in which the *khalifah* is the head of state). However, if the concept of a single *khalifah* for all the Muslims is to be advocated today, the end result would be to enhance the *khalifah's* role as the religious leader of Muslims but diminish his political leadership role since Muslims inhabit many nation-states. His status would thus become similar to that of the pope. This would distort the true significance and function of the *khalifah*. On the other hand, permitting a coexistence of several *khalifahs*, while preserving the basic concept of *khilafah*, consecrates the fragmented state of the Muslim world. Those problems could probably be avoided today by forming a council of Muslim heads of state whose transitional function would be to work towards a unified Muslim community, in the fashion of the European Council. Such a council could even elect a *khalifah* as its leader. The relation between the *khalifah* and members of the council can be structured to respect the varied national interests of such members while giving supremacy to interests relating to the *ummah* as a whole.

66. See, e.g., Mutawalli, *Mabadi' Nizam*, 162-64. See also al-Sanhuri, *Fiqh al-Khilafat*, 128 (including n. 24) (discussing the views of some Hanafi jurists on this matter). The most radical proposal in this arena came from the *Khawarij*, in the early days of Islam. They proposed that the Muslim community rely totally in managing its affairs on mutual consultation and dispense altogether with the office of *khalifah*. The *Khawarij*, though, did not represent the mainstream point of view. Iqbal, "Democracy," 256.

67. Lawrence Tribe, *American Constitutional Law* (1978), 9.

68. *American Constitutional Law*, 9.

69. *American Constitutional Law*, 47-52.

70. While Lawrence Tribe refers to this point of view, he seems to reject it. He argues that constitutional changes could take place through "constitutional discourse and decision in political dialogue." *American Constitutional Law*, 13. Whether a proposed change to the Constitution is viewed as a challenge which plunges the country into civil war or is viewed as the subject of dialogue, depends to a great extent on a variety of its attendant circumstances, including the subject matter of this proposal. I suppose that a powerful movement for the repeal of the Thirteenth Amendment could result in a civil war. Few on the opposing side would find the proposal a suitable subject of constitutional discourse and decision in political dialogue. This same analysis applies to the discussion of the Qur'an as the constitution of the Muslim state, and the possibility of amending such constitution.

71. Al-Turabi, "Islamic State," 244. Al-Turabi extends the argument from the Qur'an to the whole of the *shari'ah*. However, where *shari'ah* is defined conservatively to include only those Islamic laws which are the direct, clear, and uncontroversial consequences of Qur'anic passages, or uncontroverted and unambiguous parts of the *hadith*, the extension is reasonable. However, where *shari'ah* is defined liberally to include laws based on other sources, the extension is unwarranted.

72. Muslim scholars seem to think of *majlis shura* as being analogous to a parliament. See, al-Turabi, "Islamic State," 245; Tabliah, *Al-Islam*, 633; Mutawalli, *Mabadi' Nizam*, 251; but cf. Iqbal, "Democracy," 259 (suggesting that a committee of *'ulama* or scholars supervise legislative activity). This is a result of the fact that the Islamic *majlis shura* had many functions, reflected in its constitution as a body of experts belonging to fields ranging from religion and engineering to art. One could develop the notion of *majlis shura* and refine it further by calling for several bodies of *shura*, each having a different function. The judiciary *majlis shura* would be analogous to the Supreme Court, the legislative branch would be analogous to the parliament, and the executive branch would be analogous to an executive council. Once such an approach is accepted, the relationship of each *majlis* to the other needs to be addressed. It has been argued that complete independence of the judiciary must be insured in accordance with the Qur'an and *sunnah*. See Iqbal, "Democracy," 258.

73. This structure of course may not detract from the right of each Muslim to engage in *ijtihad* and follow her or his own religious conclusion. The relationship, however, between such individual and the state, as represented by the judicial *majlis shura*, must be explored further to deal with cases of fundamental disagreements between them.

74. See, e.g., 'Awwa, *On the Political System*, 64 (for others sharing this point of view).

75. Mutawalli, *Mabadi' Nizam*, 223. See also Coulson, *A History*, 11; Mahmassani, *Al-Awda'*, 93.

76. For example, before the battle of Badr, a fighter named al-Habbab ibn al-Jamouh gave the Prophet advice as to the best location to be occupied by the Muslim armies. Al-Habbab, however gave his advice only after he ascertained that the original location proposed by the Prophet was not the result of divine revelation. The Prophet followed the fighter's advice. Abd al-Malik Ibn Hisham, *Al-Sirah al-Nabawiyyah* (ninth century, M. Sirjani, ed., reprint, Cairo, 1978), 192-93.

77. See Ibn Hisham, *Al-Sirah*, 193 (recounting the story of Sa'd bin Ma'az, who was one of those who gave the Prophet military advice). See also the story of the battle of Khandaq, which recounts that the Prophet abandoned his proposal of seeking peace with the enemy, after two of his expert fighters advised against it.

78. E.g., in one instance the Prophet was not inclined to go out and meet the Quraysh armies which had amassed at the outskirts of Madinah. But many Muslims insisted that it was best to meet them than to wait for them in town. Despite this disagreement, the Prophet abided by the majority view. He went out and engaged in the battle of Uhud, in which the Muslims were defeated. This incident has been reported extensively. Ibn Hisham, *Al-Sirah*, 6; Tabliah, *Al-Islam*, 627-28; Mutawalli, *Mabadi' Nizam*, 242.

79. See Ibn Hisham, *Al-Sirah*, 6; Mutawalli, *Mabadi' Nizam*, 244n3; Tabliah, *Al-Islam*, 623-24.

80. *Zakat* is best analogized to a tax paid solely for charitable purposes. In the past, *zakat* was paid by Muslims to the treasury of the Muslim state in order to support the needy. Today, Muslims often pay their *zakat* money directly to the poor. The translated text of the *ayah* is as follows: "And those who answer the call of their Lord and establish regular prayer, who conduct their affairs by mutual consultation, and who spend out of what we have bestowed upon them [are true believers]." Qur'an XLII:38.

81. Qur'an III:159.

82. Indeed, early *mujtahids* concluded that a ruler who abandons *shura* must be removed. See, 'Awwa, *On the Political System*, 90; al-Qurtubi, *Mukhtar Tafsir*, 261 (citing Ibn Attiyah, who said that it is the duty of Muslims to remove a *khalifah* who does not engage in *shura*).

83. Al-Sanhuri, *Fiqh al-Khilafat*, 224-26; Tabliah, *Al-Islam*, 633-36, 642. For a detailed discussion of this matter, see Mutawalli, *Mabadi' Nizam*, 247-50.

84. See, e.g., al-Turabi, "Islamic State," 245; Tabliah, *Al-Islam*, 625, 637.

85. Mutawalli, *Mabadi' Nizam*, 252-54; Tabliah, *Al-Islam*, 625.

86. Mutawalli, *Mabadi' Nizam*, 253-54.

87. See, e.g., Iqbal, "Democracy," 253; Al-Qurtubi, *Mukhtar Tafsir*, 262-63. See also Ibn Kathir, *Tafsir*, 142-43.

88. Qur'an, III:159.

89. 'Awwa, *On the Political System*, 93-97 (arguing that such advice is binding in all matters subject to *shura*. He argues further that those who take the opposite view relying on certain historical precedents have seriously misunderstood these precedents). See also Tabliah, *Al-Islam*, 643; Mutawalli, *Mabadi' Nizam*, 243-44.

90. This is consistent with the argument that in Islam there is no class of clergy which constitutes a final authority on certain matters.

91. Tabliah, *Al-Islam*, 630-31; Mutawalli, *Mabadi' Nizam*, 257.

92. Tabliah, *Al-Islam*, 630; Mutawalli, *Mabadi' Nizam*, 257.

93. Tabliah, *Al-Islam*, 630-31; Mutawalli, *Mabadi' Nizam*, 257.

94. Tabliah, *Al-Islam*, 631; Mutawalli, *Mabadi' Nizam*, 255.

95. Tabliah, *Al-Islam*, 634; Al-Turabi, "Islamic State," 245.

96. 'Awwa, *On the Political System*, 89; Tabliah, *Al-Islam*, 629-31.

97. Tabliah, *Al-Islam*, 632 (referring to a *hadith* by the Prophet stating that anyone who brings to power an unsuitable ruler betrays God, the Prophet and all believers).

98. Nevertheless, those selected must be Wise Ones.

99. See al-Sanhuri, *Fiqh al-Khilafat*, 65, 204-225 (describing the existing separation of powers and arguing that judges also derive their power from the *ummah*, not the appointing *khalifah*). Al-Sanhuri provides precedents which illustrate the independence of judges and the ability of the people (including non-Muslims) to sue the *khalifah*, 213, 228. See also al-Nabhan, *Nitham al-Hukm*, 39 (arguing that the *khalifah* had solely executive tasks).

100. Qur'an, III:110 (stating that Muslims enjoin what is right and forbid what is wrong). See also 'Awwa, *On the Political System*, 114.

101. 'Awwa, *On the Political System*, 115; Al-Muttaqi, *Muntakhab*, 161.

102. Al-Ghazali, *Ihya 'Ulum*, 50; Mutawalli, *Mabadi' Nizam*, 260 (stating "a woman is right and 'Umar is wrong").

103. The story also illustrates that, in those days, women prayed in mosques and participated in public debate.

104. The status of *Jahiliyyah* women depended mostly on the tribe to which they belonged. On the whole, such status steadily eroded as the Arab peninsula became increasingly subject to surrounding patriarchal Byzantine and Persian influences. The Prophet attempted to stem the tide and reverse it. See Azizah al-Hibri, "A Study of Islamic Herstory," in *Women and Islam*, Azizah al-Hibri, ed. (New York: Routledge, 1982), 207; see also al-Sanhuri, *Fiqh al-Khilafat*, 136-37.

105. One example of such creeping intolerance comes from the days of *Abbasid Khalifah* al-Ma'mun, who persecuted the leading mujtahid Ibn Hanbal for disagreeing with him on the philosophical question of whether the Qur'an was created by God or, as the word of God, was eternal.

106. See, e.g., al-Sanhuri, *Fiqh al-Khilafat*, 65, 219 (stating that the principle of separation of powers is fundamental to the Islamic system of government, agreeing that *shura* permeates all branches of government and pointing out that the *khalifah*, in any case, has no legislative powers and no religious ones either. Cf. Mutawalli, *Mabadi' Nizam*, 236-38 (arguing that the *khalifah* system was not based on the concept of separation of powers because the checks and balances relied upon in the early days were internal, springing from piety and the Muslim ethics). With the introduction of monarchies, the internal checks and balances eroded. For this reason, Mutawalli argues that a modern system of *khilafah*, which incorporates the principle of separation of powers, may be worth considering in light of the present practices and circumstances. Mutawalli also points out that the *khilafah* system should not be considered a basic principle of Islam. It is, rather, a political system developed by Muslims in light of Islamic law. As such, it is open to modification in light of the *Shari'ah* Principles. I add that, while it may be true that the specific *khilafah* system known today is not basic to Islam, certain features of it, like *shura*, the office of the *khalifah*, and the supremacy of the Qur'an are. Furthermore, in denying the separation of powers in the Islamic state, Mutawalli appears to have confused theory with practice.

4

Rewriting Contemporary Muslim Politics: A Twentieth-Century Periodization

Ahmet Davutoglu

Introduction: Civilizational Challenge and Politics

The developments and transformations in the theoretical and practical agenda of the politics of the Muslim World in this century may provide us with significant clues to make projections for the twenty-first century. The aim of this essay is to develop a framework for the periodization of Muslim politics in this century from the perspective of the political, cultural, and economic conditions and their correlation with the changes in political imagination and thought. The general characteristics of each period and their relevance to the formation of political understanding will be analyzed in order to show the elements of consistency in the dialectic of continuity and change.

Islamic civilization had to face three significant civilizational challenges throughout history: namely Crusaders, Mongol invasion, and the colonial expansion of Western civilization. Crusaders had a limited objective to conquer Holy Lands, although they aimed at destroying Muslim lands on their way to Jerusalem. Despite its aggressive rhetoric and brutal military practice, the challenge of Crusaders was a more defensive one in the sense of cultural and political relations between Islamic and Christian worlds. Crusaders had to withdraw from the Muslim lands after being impressed by the supremacy of

Islamic civilization in all fields of this confrontation.

The Mongol invasion was like a whirlwind which destroyed physical and written legacies of Islamic civilization. The main spiritual, intellectual, and cultural parameters of the Islamic civilization, however, continued to survive even stronger than before. The peak of the Islamic civilization in the sixteenth century and the rise to dominance of Ottomans in Europe and the Middle East, Safavids in Iran, Uzbeks in Central Asia, and Baburs in India, signaled a strong response to this Mongol invasion.

These two challenges were military threats. Therefore they did not create a civilizational crisis in the Muslim World. Contrary to these earlier threats the European challenge in the modern era and its political consequence in the form of colonialism was a total challenge in all spheres of civilizational confrontation. Therefore, it created a comprehensive civilizational crisis in the Muslim World.

The basic parameters of the traditional civilizations, including Islamic civilization, have been dissolved and reshaped by the comprehensive influence of modern Western civilization. A disharmony emerged between the surviving substance of traditional civilizations and the political and economic institutions which were created by the Leviathan of the colonial political system and of the rising world economy. The modernist expectation that the new institutional framework would necessarily transform the traditional self-perception and mentality of the Islamic civilization, however, did not come true. On the contrary, there is a rise of self-confidence in all traditional civilizations on the eve of a new millennium.

This dilemma of civilizational transformation and its relation with modernity still require sustained investigation. A systematic periodization of the theoretical and practical agenda of Muslim politics in this century is necessary to understand its dynamic character and direction of change. Such a framework of periodization may also be a guideline to analyze the consistencies, continuities and discontinuities of this comprehensive civilizational challenge and its transformation in the long run.

The transformations of the Muslim World in the twentieth century can be analyzed in four different phases, each of which belongs to almost one-quarter of the century: (1) the era of semi-colonial dependency in the first quarter till the end of the First World War; (2) the interwar period of absolute colonial dependency; (3) the period of the formation of nation-states from anticolonial revolutions until the establishment of the Organization of Islamic Conference (OIC) in 1969; (4) the era of civilizational revival, political confrontation and reactive cooperation in the post-OIC period. Each of these historical phases marks a different relationship with the existing international system and dominant power centers.

The Periodization of Muslim Politics
in the Twentieth Century

Semi-Colonial Dependency and Pan-Islamic Anti-Colonialism

There was a continuity between the nineteenth century and the first quarter of this century in terms of the theoretical and practical issues of Muslim policy. The international context of colonialism determined the basic parameters of Muslim politics in this period. The basic characteristic of the international status of the Muslim World in this first phase (1900-1924) was a combination of semi-colonial and colonial structures. The Ottoman state, the center of Muslim politics due to the Caliphate, was under the threat of disintegration by the colonial powers while other Muslim countries had already been colonized.

The economic counterpart of this political situation was the semicolonial Ottoman economy, on one hand, and direct economic colonialism in the rest of the Muslim World, on the other. Colonial powers were controlling the Ottoman economy through fiscal and financial policies that were organized by *Duyun-i Umumiye*. Direct colonial dependency was the main characteristic of the political economy of the other Muslim lands. The center-periphery dependency in colonial economic structure established special economic structures in the Muslim lands to transfer economic resources of the colonized countries to the colonizing centers.

Sultan Abdulhamid II (1876-1909) was aware of the close interdependency between these two economic and political realities. He realized that the survival of the Ottoman state was only possible by marshalling these two realities against the colonial international system. The Caliphate played a central role in this relationship as a symbolic and institutional instrument of legitimacy to implement policies for the socio-political integration of the Muslim communities within the territories of the Ottoman state and for the political mobilization of Muslim masses against colonial powers.

Therefore, his policy of Pan-Islamism had both idealistic and realistic dimensions.[1] This policy was seen as a strategic remedy for the survival of the Ottoman Caliphate consistent with the traditional ideals and institutions of the Islamic civilization. There were two objectives of this strategic choice: one was related to the international resistance against colonialism; the other was related to the internal socio-political integration.

Islamic legacy has provided a strong identity and force of social integration for the anticolonial movements throughout the nineteenth century and the beginning of this century. Muridism under the mystic-political charismatic leadership of Syhah Shamil in Caucasia against the Russians, Caliphate movement in India and *Mahdi* movement in Sudan against the British, *Sarekat Islam* in Indonesia against the Dutch, Ahmad al-Hiba and Ibn Abd al-Karim's anticolonial resistance in Morocco against French colonialism, originated from this attempt for civilizational survival. So the Muslim World, from the Far East in Indonesia to the Far West in Morocco, was under the influence of a wave of anticolonial movements against almost all colonial powers at the turn of this century. Traditional values and symbols of Islamic civilization were the backbone of this struggle.

Two examples from Indonesia and Morocco may clarify the Islamic background of this collective anticolonial spirit. Deliar Noer describes the situation in Indonesia at the turn of this century as follows:

> There was thus a challenge from the West, i.e. from the Dutch and Christianity, felt by the Indonesian Muslims; a challenge which they had to face and respond to by every means if they wanted to survive. . . . The Indonesians called the Dutch "satans," "kapir londa" (Dutch kafir), words which not only indicate hatred but also the opinion that they were enemies of Islam and the Muslims. The prejudice against Dutch clothes and schools among many of the Muslims at the turn of the century can be explained from this attitude.[2]

The same feelings and thoughts might be found in the writings of al-Kattani from Morocco:

> They (Europeans) go to the Muslim lands in every direction. They turn toward them from every side. They see no opportunity in Islam without seizing it. . . . There are no limits to all this, so that of the Islamic *umma* that numbers some 300 million people, only about a third now remains (in 1908) free and independent.[3]

The collective anticolonial spirit led to a belief of common fate among the Muslim societies in different parts of the globe. Two strong anticolonial voices from Istanbul and Lahore, Mehmet Akif and Muhammad Iqbal, expressed this feeling of survival and common fate through poetry. Iqbal's poems on Ottoman resistance in Libya and the Balkans, and Mehmet Akif's poems on the defense of Gallipoli and on several issues of the Muslim World, reflected Muslim perception of this civilizational challenge in the poetic literature. The Ottoman state was the last resisting independent political center against colonialism at the turn of this century and this was the reason for the natural connection between survival of the Ottoman state and colonized Muslim lands. Therefore, mass movements in the colonized Muslim lands, like the Caliphate movement in India, supported the Ottoman state during the First World War and Turkish War of Liberation under the leadership of Mustafa Kemal:

> Of course, Turkey and the Caliphate were matters of pivotal significance around which the entire Khilafat campaign turned, for political opinion among Muslim elites (secular no less than religious) was increasingly devoted to the Caliphate as a free institution and the Caliph as a free agent. . . . Azad, the ideologue of the Khilafat movement, maintained that all Muslims owed political loyalty to the Caliph. . . . The response of India's Muslims to these Pan-Islamic appeals was very generous: in 1921-2, a total of 36.5 lakhs of rupees (about US $1,180,000 at that time) were collected (of which only 19 lakhs, however, were transferred to Turkey).[4]

The second objective of this Pan-Islamic policy was synchronizing the attempt of integration among Muslim masses within the Ottoman state and the process of the political, social, and economic reformation. Both Sultan Abdulhamid and his opponents among the circle of Young Turks agreed on this synchronization between pro-Islamic rhetoric of the political legitimacy and reformation of the system.

The strengthening of the administrative and military structure through pragmatic bureaucratic reforms was the instrument of this objective. Therefore structural/bureaucratic political reforms and Islamic rhetoric were two distinctive aspects of Muslim politics resulting in eclectic approaches to political theory and practice. Sultan Abdulhamid, who tried to synthesize and synchronize these two aspects, tried to reconcile the idea of Pan-Islamism with the reforms of the educational system.[5] There is an interesting parallel between Ottoman and Indian Muslim experiences from this perspective. Aligarh College established by Sayyid Ahmad Khan in 1881 and transformed into a university in 1920, and Osmania university founded by the Nizam of the Deccan, Osman Ali Khan in Hyderabad, had similar functions in India during this phase.[6]

The main objective of these policies was to create a new generation equipped with Western sciences and Islamic culture. There was no significant disagreement between Sultan Abdulhamid and his opponents from this perspective.[7] His opponents were also stressing that Islamic principles and reformation of the Ottoman state do not conflict. Mizanc Murad, one of his opponents among the intellectual leaders of Young Turks, mentioned these two aspects as fundamental principles of a new reformation:

1. The Moslem religion is not the direct cause of the weakness of the Ottoman Empire; no more does it constitute an obstacle to its recovery; 2. the population is young, vigorous, temperate, devout; 3. the governmental organism demands a radical transformation; 4. the reconstituted government must have a solid constitutional support.[8]

The harmonization of Islamic values with Western science and the synchronization of Islamic traditional structures with institutional reforms have been the basic arguments of the Islamicists[9] in the process of civilizational challenge of modernization. This is one of the elements of continuity in the responses to this civilizational challenge of westernization, which had officially started with the declaration of Tanzimat Rescript in 1839.[10] Due to this factor of continuity, a radical elimination of the elements of Islamic political culture and institutions was not part of the political agenda of the Muslim World during the first quarter of this century. On the contrary, their efficient survival with the support of new institutions was accepted as an essential policy for the survival of the Ottoman state. Even the pro-Western leaders of Ittihad Terakkî were very much aware of this phenomenon.

This reconciliatory attempt inspired the forerunners of Islamic political theory of this period. Al-Afghani's influence on the idea of Islamic unity as well as on the nationalistic tendencies in the Muslim World,[11] Khayruddin Tunusi's attempts to create bureaucratic reforms within the framework of the Islamic approach,[12] Mehmed Akif's and Said Nursi's[13] Islamic opposition against Sultan Abdulhamid to establish a more participatory political practice of constitutionalism, the Islamic political remedies of Saîd Halim Pafla, who was the prime minister of the government of Ittihad Terakki[14]—all are examples of these reconciliatory and eclectic attempts to find a solution for the survival of the Islamic political order against the colonial international system.[15]

In spite of the institutional westernization, the conceptual and theoretical framework of Islamic policy was still carrying a traditional character. The classical core concepts of Islamic political thought such as *Dar al-Islam, Jihad, Khilafat, Shura, Bayah* continued to be the basic parameters of the political imagination of an individual Muslim. They also continued to have a functional role in the socio-political culture of Muslim society and in the political rhetoric of legitimacy of the governing elites as well as in the mobilization of Muslim masses against colonial forces. The mobilization of the Muslim masses for extensive wars from 1911 to 1923 in all regions of the Ottoman state and anti-colonial movements in different parts of the Muslim World could be achieved through this socio-cultural and socio-political link. Declaration of *jihad* against Western powers and colonial rulers was a common practice in several parts of the Muslim World.[16] The Islamic and nationalistic tendencies developed side by side during this struggle against Western colonialism.

The Balkan Wars and the First World War ended this era. After the defeat in the Balkan Wars, the Ottomans lost their European lands—except a small portion, Eastern Thrace. The Muslim World has been imagined as an Asia-African phenomenon throughout the century especially after the withdrawal of the Ottomans from the Balkans, until the reemergence of the Muslim Eurasian countries in the last decade of this century. Therefore, even authentic European Muslim nations, such as Albanians and Bosnians, have been represented as the alien elements in their own lands during the crisis in the region in the last decade of this century.

Absolute Colonial Dependency:
The End of Traditional Muslim Politics

The period which started with the abolition of the Caliphate in 1924[17] and continued till the anticolonial revolutions after World War Two, was an era in which Muslim masses experienced the most radical changes throughout the history of Islamic civilization. It was the most critical historical period in terms of Islamic identity, socialization of Islamic institutions, and economic periph-eralization of the Muslim World. Almost all traditional concepts and institutions have been marginalized by the political and economic practices of the western-ization-oriented elite.

The basic character of international relations during this period was determined by two significant phenomena: the replacement of religion by the systematization of ideologies and the consolidation of the colonial political structures. Colonial Western powers controlled almost all non-Western countries through the monopolization of the international system and the establishment of the psychological and ideological foundations of the colonial mentality.

The end of the Ottoman Caliphate after the First World War made the Muslim World purely an Asia-African civilizational entity of the colonial system rather than a part of the European system. Apart from three countries—Turkey, Iran and Afghanistan—the whole Muslim World was under colonial administration during this second phase (1924-1947). Among these three, Iran and Afghanistan had semicolonial economic and political structures under British and Russian influence, while the new political elite in Turkey was implementing a radical policy of westernization in order to be a part of the Western world.[18]

Each Muslim colony became part of a different colonial system during this phase. This metropolis specified resource-production processes, fiscal and financial policies, priorities of economic planning, and mentality of public administration. Colonized societies did not have any political will to govern their own resources. Therefore it was impossible to speak of an independent non-Western political economy in this era.

The use of raw materials and resources was planned according to the needs of the colonial structure. The financial blocs of British pound and French franc divided the world economy into two categorically separated financial entities. Economic planning in colonized countries was based on the assumption that this colonial structure had an eternal character and each colonial system had its own economic integrity specified by colonial administration. This assumption created regional alienation among the colonized lands, which were separately linked to different colonial centers according to the economic needs and priorities of each colonial center. This intracolonial dependency prevented any rational relation among the colonized Muslim lands.

For example, in North Africa, Egypt, Libya, and Algeria were under different colonial administrations—respectively, British, Italian and French—having conflicting economic plans for the region. The same was true for the Middle East, divided by French and British colonial hegemonies. British, Dutch, and French colonial administrations in Southeast Asia created different political economies which did not have direct regional links among each other. Dutch administration governed the Indonesian islands according to the needs of their colonial system, while British colonial administration changed even the demographic structure of Malay peninsula for its own economic plans. Division of Borneo into two different political and economic zones did not have any regional justification except different colonial backgrounds. The historical economic zone of the Indian Ocean from East Africa to Bengal and from Yemen to Malacca, which goes back to thirteenth century, was fractured by the Western colonial system in order to achieve colonial center-periphery dependency at the expense of regional alienation. This intraregional alienation among Muslim societies is still one of the major barriers for the regional economic cooperation attempts.

The end of the Caliphate was consistent with the internal structure of this world system in this phase. The Caliphate as a political institution continued to survive throughout Islamic history until this century, except for some period of crisis as in the case of Mongol invasion in the thirteenth century. The end of the Caliphate in this phase showed two interconnected marginalizations of the Muslim policy in political affairs: first in the international system and second in the Muslim World itself.

So, the end of the Caliphate was the end of the Islamic world system as an alternative to Western colonialism. It also created an ambiguity related to the concept of *Dar al-Islam*, which had served as an alternative political order throughout the centuries.[19] This meant the loss of the most significant centers of resistance against colonialism as an oppressive international system, and against modernism as an ideological, theoretical, and institutional rival. The relationship of economic and political dependency between the Eurocentric colonial system and the Asia-African Muslim societies and lands reached its peak during this phase. So, for the first time in its history, the Muslim World became a peripheral element in world politics. This peripheralization created a psycho-social tension among Muslims because of the irreconcilability between the strong theoretical self-perception and the weak international status.

The other aspect of marginalization was in the internal structure of Muslim societies. The role of Islam in political and daily life was eroded during this period. The central position of authentic Islamic institutions was replaced by the newly adopted institutions of modernity established by the colonial and secular elites. The radical change in the educational systems during this colonial era became instrumental for the establishment of an intermediary elite between the colonial centers and the colonized societies, especially during the neocolonial era of the third stage. The emergence of this intermediary elite has guaranteed the continuation of the colonial influence.

This new international context has influenced the theoretical framework and discussions related to Muslim politics. Islamic political theory in this phase might be analyzed under two aspects. The first aspect was the emergence of attempts to interpret the end of the Caliphate and the new political structuralization.[20] The basic trends on this issue were reflected in three approaches developed by three significant personalities: (1) the denial of the political message of Islam, which was the foundational backbone of the institution of Caliphate (The arguments of this approach were best formulated by Ali Abd ur-Razik in his *Usul al-Hukm*,[21] which tried to eliminate the contradiction by denying the historical theory and practice of the Caliphate as a political institution); (2) the theoretical frameworks for the reformation of the political institutions (The best example of this approach was Rashid Rida's book *Al-Khilafah*,[22] which provides a synthesis of traditional and modern elements to restructure the institution of the Caliphate); (3) the evaluation of Muslim policy within a general philosophical/theoretical framework which emphasizes the reconstruction of Islamic thought as a whole. Iqbal's reinterpretation of the role of *Ijma* (consensus) in establishing a republican spirit in his masterpiece, *The Reconstruction of Religious Thought in Islam*, is the best example of this approach:

> The growth of republican spirit, and the gradual formation of legislative assemblies in Muslim lands constitutes a great step in advance. The transfer of the power of *Ijtihad* (interpretation) from individual representatives of schools to a Muslim legislative assembly which, in view of the growth of opposing sects, is the only possible form *Ijma* can take in modern times, will secure contributions to legal discussion from laymen who happen to possess a keen insight into affairs.[23]

The second aspect is the absence of an organic relationship between the state and its Islamic social functions. Such an organic relationship was a common socio-political practice throughout Islamic history. The emergence of Islamic social groups to fill this vacuum in Islamic activities is an outcome of this aspect. For the first time in history, the Muslim masses faced the problem of fulfilling Islamic responsibilities without the support of the state. In many countries they even had to perform Islamic duties in spite of the political power of the state, which created a socio-political confrontation. They took over the responsibility of *jihad* against the colonial powers, a role supposed to be performed by the political authority of the Caliphate. They also started to function as social network to fulfill same Islamic responsibilities, such as the collection and distribution of *zakat*. They also became the centers of the popular Islamic opposition against the secular elite who were trying to achieve a radical civilizational transformation through marginalizing Islam in the daily life of the Muslims. The *Ikhwan al-Muslimin* in Egypt, the *Jamaat al-Islami* in Pakistan, and the *Nur* movement in Turkey were established during this era. These movements established new and alternative channels in the social life of the Muslim masses in order to protect the central role of religion in social life.

The basic political question of this era was how to develop a new theoretical and conceptual framework after the peripheralization of the traditional concepts and institutions and thus to overcome the problems of marginalization in political practice. After the end of the Caliphate, the Muslim masses entered into direct confrontation against the colonial forces. The colonial masters had assumed that these were the last gasps of Islamic civilization against the irresistible forces of modernism and colonialism. The strong self-perception among Muslim masses, however, became the main psychological impetus for the revival of the Islamic identity in the subsequent phases.

Post-Colonial Phase: Formation of Muslim Nation-States

The basic characteristic of the third phase after the anticolonial revolutions was the formation of Muslim nation-states in a bipolar international system of the Cold War. This was one of the most radical changes in the history of Muslim societies. These nation-states did not emerge in a vacuum. Four significant interacting forces determined the characteristics of these nation-states: traditional political culture, the process of modernization, the colonial heritage, and the existing international order of bipolarity. The most vital question in the formation of nation-states was the question of legitimacy. The contradictions among these interacting forces transformed this question into a crisis which effected theoretical and practical issues of Muslim politics in this phase.

The Muslim World had to adopt basic parameters of the Westphalian nation-state system during this phase. It was, however, difficult to reconcile the territorial identity and its segmented counterparts with the traditional political imagination of the Muslim masses, which was based on the universal consciousness of being one *Ummah*. From this perspective, the inconsistency between the imagination of *Dar al-Islam* and the world system based on the nation-states was clear. *Dar al-Islam* theoretically implies an independent and consistent world order in theory and practice. Therefore, it was not an element of the nation-state system, but rather an alternative to it because of the coexistence of different political authorities[24] and autonomous *dhimmî* groups.

So there was a plurality within unity in *Dar al-Islam*. This tradition conflicted with the unifying characteristic of the nation-state. The Ottoman *millet system* was the last example of this traditional political order. The rivalry between the Ottoman millet system and the European Westphalian system continued until the disintegration of the Ottoman Empire. In fact, the disintegration of the Ottoman Empire was a consequence of the nationalistic tendencies under the impact of the French revolution.

This irreconcilability created new dynamic tendencies in theory and practice. Two main trends emerged as a response to this crisis. The first trend was based on a secular nationalism, which tried to minimize the role of traditional/Islamic concepts and values in the process of political legitimation. The leaders of this trend tried to create a new national identity and culture, a territorial political system and a nationalistic economy in order to justify their authority over the territories which were, in fact, reflecting colonial zones of influence rather than real historical and geographical entities. Their main political agenda was how to legitimize and preserve the territorial integrity of the *de facto* political entities that emerged after the end of the colonial hegemony. The pseudo-sovereignty of the interstate system led these political elites to form either control-based totalitarian states or traditional kingdoms in the Muslim World. Cultural and economic policies were only adequate tools for this objective:

> It is not only outside observers, but also the leaders of the Middle Eastern states themselves that see their tasks in terms of engineering, architecture, blueprints and the like. They are designing new societies, and the state is that collection of agencies that will enable them to build what they have designed. Ideologies vary but not the

perceived need for state intervention. And no state in the region has been able to pass up the exercise of elaborating a national plan.[25]

The second trend, on the other hand, tried to reconceptualize and resystematize the Muslim policy in order to produce an alternative state model. The core concepts of the traditional political order, such as *Dar al Islam* and millet system, were replaced by the Islamic counterparts of the modern political system, such as *Islamic state*.[26] The central position of the concept of *Islamic state* during this period reflected the need to reconceptualize Islamic polity in a new framework.[27]

The new literature and its political rhetoric developed by Mawdudî in India and Pakistan,[28] Sayyid Qutb in Egypt,[29] Allal al-Fasi in Morocco,[30] and Ali Shariatî in Iran[31] was a consequence of this process of reinterpretation of Western political theories and institutions from an Islamic perspective. There was no theoretical and practical base for such a conceptualization in traditional Islamic polity before the impact of the colonial era when Islamic world order was still functioning as a consistent world system. It was impossible to imagine a non-Islamic state or political authority in traditional politics due to the legitimizing role of the Islamic value system. Therefore, *Dar al-Islam* as a basic concept of traditional Islamic polity was used to describe the geographical area under Islamic political authority which enables the implementation of the norms of Islamic law.

These two approaches reflected two trends in the formation of the political and cultural elite in Muslim societies. Struggle among these elites has been one of the factors of internal disputes in the third and fourth phases. The nation-state idea has been taken over mainly by the Western-oriented secularist elite because traditional Muslim masses avoided the colonial educational structures during the second stage. The colonial masters also preferred to deliver the political authority to this prototype of leadership as they would be instrumental in continuing the colonial links within a neocolonial framework.

A change in the formation of the political and cultural elite of the second trend, on the other hand, started to be observed especially in the later part of this phase. A new prototype of intellectual leadership emerged from among the graduates of the new schools which differs from the classical leadership of *ulama* in the first two phases. So the traditional leadership of *ulama* has been replaced by Muslim intellectuals who had a Western way of education.[32] These new leaders were doctors, engineers and social scientists who tried to reformulate Islamic theory in a new form of consistent systematization. This was called the ideologization of Islam by Western analysts of Islamic revivalism. In fact, it was a natural response that might be seen in all social, political, and intellectual movements, which were marginalized in domestic and international politics.

This crisis of legitimacy necessitated a new definition of the relationship between religion and politics. Three different approaches emerged in this regard.

The first is the use of religious identity, symbols, and values as the backbone of the political legitimacy. The best example of this approach was the establishment of Pakistan as an Islamic state. Jinnah's two-nation theory proposed a separate nationality for the Muslims in India who would be the people of the future state of Pakistan though they were linguistically and ethnically not very different from the other subgroups of the Indian subcontinent. So, the nationality defined for Pakistan had to based on Islamic identity. This religious/national identity specified the constitutional characteristic of the new state as an "Islamic state." The fact that the literature on Islamic states first emerged in Pakistan was an outcome of this practice. The same practice made Pakistan one of the champions of the Islamic solidarity in international politics: "Even as Pakistan entered into alliance relationships with the West, it regularly expressed a desire to cultivate its Islamic ties, reminding the Muslim World that Pakistan was the only modern state created exclusively in the name of Islam."[33]

The second approach in redefining the relation between religion and politics was using the symbols and values of religion as a secondary instrument for the process of political legitimacy. The best way of doing this was to make religion a part of the official secular ideology of the new nation-state. A striking example of this was the principle of Panca Sila (Five Principles), part of the tissue of the national state of Indonesia: (1) *kebangsaan*, nationalism; (2) *perikemanusiaan*, humanity or internationalism; (3) *jatan*, democracy or consultation; (4) *kerakkeadilan sosial*, social justice; and (5) *ke-tuhanan, orpengakuan ke-tuhanan Jang Maha-Esa*, faith in God. Van Nieuwenhuijze described this formulation of the state ideology as a process of "deconfessionalization" of the Muslim concepts and thought; "an attempt to take off the sharp edges of exclusivity, so as to avoid all points which according to an unwritten code make for interdenominational exchange of views."[34] This deconfessionalization has created a crisis of political legitimacy among the *santris*, devout followers of Islam, while *abangan*s, more syncretic elements, welcomed this approach.

Another way of using religion as a symbolic instrument of political legitimation was doing it through religious institutions and practices, such as taking *fatwa* from *ulama* for individual policies of the government. A good example of this case was Egypt where religious institutions such as *al-Azhar* in particular and *ulama* in general were taken under the tightening control of the political regime after the military coup in 1952. The Egyptian *ulama* became salaried employees of the state while the appointment of *Shaikh al Azhar* became the sole prerogative of the president of the republic. So, as Olsen underlines, *al-Azhar*, which has been a major channel of communication between Egypt and the Muslim World, became the leading interpreter and legitimizer of Nasser's revolution.[35]

The third approach was elimination or minimization of the role of religion in public life, especially in the process of political legitimation. This approach has been accepted mainly by Marxist regimes and in the countries under the influence of absolutist secularism. The best example of the radical elimination of the role of religion in public life was Enver Hodja's regime in Albania. The ultimate aim of this regime was to establish an atheist state and society where there would be no religious affiliation in any sense. Minimization of the role of religion in the process of political legitimation, on the other hand, has been observed in *Baath* regimes where secular Arab nationalism became the sole legitimizing ideology of the state. Islam did not have an independent value in this approach. It has been seen as a secondary outgrowth of Arabism, which was assumed to be an existing reality before the emergence of Islam.[36]

This question of legitimacy has effected economic structures of the Muslim World as well. As a consequence of the lack of rational economic mechanisms based on a real legitimacy, the distribution of the national economic resources became an issue of intra-elite power struggle among totalitarian bureaucracies or traditional ruling families during the formative era of many young nation-states. The absence of a real political and economic legitimacy and the weakness of the intermediary institutions between political elite and people has prevented the mobilization of the masses for the consistent long-term economic development programs.

This internal structure has deeply affected the regional and international policies of these new states, especially their political and economic preferences in the global environment of the international political economy. The economic, political and cultural structures of these new nation-states facilitated a new type of dependency on the dominant capitalistic world system, which determines interstate relations, as has been rightly underlined by Immanuel Wallerstein:

> The states are thus, we are arguing, created institutions reflecting the needs of class forces operating in the world economy. They are not however created in a void, but within the framework of an interstate system. This interstate system is, in fact, the framework within which the states are defined. It is the fact that the state of the capitalist world-economy exist within the framework of an interstate system that is the *differentia specifica* of the modern state, distinguishing it from other bureaucratic polities. This interstate system constitutes a set of constraints which limit the abilities of individual state machineries, even the strongest among them, to make decisions. The ideology of this system is sovereign equality, but the states are in fact neither sovereign nor equal.[37]

Three important interacting phenomena determined the political economy of the Muslim World in this phase. The same characteristics prevented rational and long-term intraregional and interregional economic cooperation among Muslim countries.

First, each country's predominant political preference of economic planning was to establish a self-sufficient economic structure, which was assumed to be the first and foremost prerequisite of the pseudo-sovereignty of the interstate system. Political elites preferred national investment policies within the given territorial integrity rather than regional economic cooperation, even if national investment was economically irrational. Import-substitution policies, which helped these countries develop their own industrial infrastructure, created closed economic systems which discouraged regional cooperation. The inefficiency of the protected national industries has negatively affected the results of import-substitution policies as well as the development of the rational alternative foreign policies based on a more open economic system.

Secondly, despite the political will to establish a self-sufficient national economic policy, the heritage of the colonial dependency of the previous phases continued to be the dominant characteristic of the foreign economic relations of the new independent states. The existing peripheral character of colonies continued to be effective even after the declaration of independence. The policy of transition led by colonial masters gave them a significant advantage to keep the relationship of dependency intact. The leaders of the new states had to continue main manufacturing and trading links with the colonial centers due to the lack of a technological infrastructure and organizational manpower.

Thirdly, the bipolar character of the international system during this era forced these countries to make an ultimate decision to be member or supporter of one of the main blocs. This political imposition had two very significant consequences: a new type of regional alienation and strict implementation of a specific economic system. Intrabloc trade and production relationships became another predominant preference of each country. The main argument for the justification of this intrabloc economic interdependency were regional security considerations against neighbors which were supposed to be partners of a rational economic cooperation. The best example of this alienation is the tense relationship between North and South Yemen throughout this phase. Ideological polarization destroyed the rational bridges to develop alternative planning based on economic rationality.

In short, despite the increasing grip of the Muslim societies on their economic resources and political administration after the anticolonial revolutions, the theoretical and practical agenda of the Muslim World had to face many problems related to the process of legitimacy in conformity with the formation of the nation-states.

Post-OIC Period: Civilizational Revival, Political Confrontation, and the Era of Reactive Cooperation

The first characteristic of this phase is the increasing tension between the power centers of the international system and several states and groups of states in the Muslim World. The first indication of this tension emerged in Palestine after the Israeli occupation in 1967. The Palestinian crisis, which has been presented as an Israeli-Arab conflict, became a common Islamic issue especially after *Masjid al-Aqsa* in Jerusalem under Israeli occupation was attacked in 1969. Similarly, the tension over Cyprus between Turkey and Greece, the question of Kashmir between Pakistan and India, and the issue of Mindanao in the Philippines created a common response in the Muslim World in the 1970s because of the sufferings of Muslim minorities and double-standards against Muslim countries.

Three significant events in the late 1970s and '80s have accelerated this tension between some countries of the Muslim World and leading powers of the international system: the Iranian revolution against the United States, *jihad* in Afghanistan against Soviet Union, and the *Intifada* in Palestine against Israel. The Iranian revolution came as a shock to American regional and global foreign policy, while *jihad* in Afghanistan became a shattering blow to the Soviet Union, which led to the end of this superpower. *Intifada* as a civil movement of resistance, on the other hand, became much more successful than the violent methods implemented by PLO in 1960s and 1970s, to force Israel to make concessions in Palestine.

This confrontational tension has been accelerated in the post-Cold War era. Muslims are being presented as an incongruous element of and a new threat to international order by Western analysts and decision makers, especially during the Gulf crisis. At the same time, the feeling of insecurity has spread among Muslim masses in relation to the functioning of the international system because of the double standards in international affairs in early years of post-Cold War era:

> The *Intifada* has been called a terrorist activity while mass rebellions in East Europe have been declared as the victory of freedom. There was no serious response against the Soviet military intervention in Azarbaijan in January 1990 when hundreds of Azaris were killed while all Western powers reacted against the Soviet intervention in the Baltic Republics. The international organizations which are very sensitive to the rights of small minorities in Muslim countries, did not respond against the sufferings of the Muslim minorities in India, the former Yugoslavia, Bulgaria, Kashmir, Burma [etc.] The atomic powers in some Muslim countries like Pakistan and Kazakhistan have been declared dangers to international peace when such weapons have been accepted as the internal affairs of other states such as Israel and India. Muslims who make up about 25% of the world's population, have no permanent member in the Security Council and all appeals from the Muslim World are being vetoed by one of the permanent members.[38]

This confrontational tension and Muslim perception of insecurity in international relations reached its peak during the Bosnian crisis when there was no international intervention despite ethnic cleansing, war crimes, the use of barbaric tortures against Muslim women, and the killing of a quarter of a million innocent Muslims. The Muslim masses have lost their confidence in the international system as a neutral problem solver after this experience, which created a wave of anti-West sentiment in the Muslim World similar to the anti-colonial reactions in the nineteenth century.

The prejudicial approach of the power centers in the international system influenced even the most secular groups of the Muslim societies during this period. They realized that the marginalization of the Muslim countries in the international system continued in spite of their pro-Western policies. So the elites and masses of the Muslim World started to think that the prejudicial and confrontational Western approach against the Muslim World continues despite the humanistic slogans of the collective security system of the United Nations.

The second characteristic of this phase is the reactive cooperation and solidarity among the Muslim countries. These political pressures and oppressions coming from the power centers in relation to the political problems of the Muslim World—such as in the cases of Palestine, Cyprus, Afghanistan, and Bosnia—accelerated the impetus of this cooperative approach, despite different and conflicting interests of the individual countries. This confrontational relation between systemic powers of international politics and the Muslim World during this phase in the last quarter of this century has created a sense of solidarity in the Muslim World.

The first indication of these reactive cooperation attempts was the establishment of the Organization of Islamic Conference. The First Islamic Summit Conference in 1969, convened as a gesture of Islamic unity in reaction to the profanation of Masjid al-Aqsa, became a turning point in this period and reflected this psycho-political change. So, for the first time since the end of Caliphate, the existing political elites of the Muslim World realized that they needed to cooperate to strengthen the international position of the Muslim World in general and individual states in particular. The objectives of OIC as declared in Article II of its charter reflect this fact very clearly.[39]

This reaction against the prejudicial behavior of the power centers of the international system brought about the need for the institutionalization of Islamic solidarity in several fields of international relations, including economic and cultural cooperation.[40] The OIC has been transformed from a consultative forum to a more organized cooperation system during this phase, especially after the General Agreement for Economic, Technical and Commercial Cooperation was signed by the member countries.

The rise of solidarity in common issues and internal disputes among Muslim countries are two sides of the same coin in Muslim politics during this phase. Civil wars in Lebanon, Afghanistan and Algeria, the long and destructive war between Iran and Iraq, the Gulf War as a result of Iraqi invasion of Kuwait, and several small-size tensions among neighboring Muslim countries resulted in loss of confidence in these attempts for solidarity. These internal disputes have wasted scarce resources of the Muslim countries.

The reactive character of political solidarity, on the other hand, did prevent the development of a rational and efficient conflict resolution mechanism. Therefore, OIC was not able to play a positive and efficient role in resolving the crises among Muslim countries. It was more functional in the crises where individual Muslim countries have common or closer stands, such as in Mindanao and Bosnia. The Muslim World still lacks a rational, efficient, and operational mechanism of conflict resolution.

The third aspect of this phase is the changing character of the economic structure of the Islamic World and its relation with the world economy. The basic economic force of the Muslim World in the 1970s was oil reserves and its use for political purposes. Many other regional, subregional, and sector-based attempts for economic cooperation among Muslim countries emerged during this phase. Some of them were established merely by Muslim countries, such as RCD/ECO, while others were run mainly by Muslim countries, such as OPEC. The reactive and exclusive character of some of these policies brought about advantages for the Western financial system at the expense of very negative consequences for some other Muslim and Third World countries. Western bankers found alternative ways to benefit from these policies through transferring petrodollars from oil-producing Muslim countries to non-oil-producing Muslim countries: "London and New York bankers voluntarily [and for a profit] became risk-bearing intermediaries for transferring the oil money from one group of developing countries—the oil exporters—to another—the non-oil-producing, capital starved, less developed countries [LDC's] of the Third World."[41]

The axis of the economic dynamism changed in the 1980s after OPEC and oil-producing countries lost their power in the world economy. The new axis emerged in Southeast Asia after the rise of Asian tigers. Malaysia and Indonesia were presented as the new rising stars of the East and the Muslim World. This economic dynamism has been presented as an indication of the rise of Islamic revival by Anwar Ibrahim, one of the leaders of these two phenomena, economic growth and Islamic revival in Southeast Asia: "The wave of Islamic revivalism that began with the anti-imperialist struggles of the previous century has gained further momentum in our time among Muslims in Southeast Asia."[42] The economic crisis in East Asia in 1997 and its political consequences both in Indonesia and Malaysia, however, have disappointed these expectations.

The fourth aspect of this phase is the dynamic change in internal sociopolitical structures of the Muslim societies and the impact on the relations between religion and politics. There has been a rise of democratic demands especially in the 1980s and 1990s. These demands for a more participatory political system necessarily resulted in the increase of the role of Islamic values and institutions in the political system. The sociological forces of modernity, such as mobilization of masses due to socio-economic change and urbanization, intensification and spread of social communication, radical social transformations and crisis of identity, resulted in a rapid socialization of religious and traditional values in modern forms. These changes have synchronized the demands for the processes of democratization and Islamization. A process of democratization naturally leads to a reflection of social values in the political system enabling socio-cultural mass movements to influence political structures.

Since Islam has been the fundamental force of social integration in the Muslim societies, this natural process of democracy has created a tension between secular political/bureaucratic elites and popular Islamic socio-cultural forces.

This is why the demands for democratization have been presented by the secular elite as a threat to the established system of nation-states which were formed mainly after the anticolonial revolutions in the third phase. They started to think they have to make a choice between the official secular/nationalistic ideology and Islamic values on the one hand, and totalitarianism and democracy on the other, in order to protect the established system of the state.

Their choice for the official state ideology has been legitimized by an untested assumption that Islam and democracy can not coexist. Such an assumption has been utilized to stop the process of democratization in order to protect the political system against the "fundamentalist threat." This rhetoric of legitimacy has been supported by the new conceptual framework and theoretical analysis developed by Western academics, especially after Islam has been declared the new threat to international order. The best example of this case is Algeria, which has been going through one of the most destructive civil wars in our century.

The fifth aspect of this phase is the emergence of a new literature on Islam and its revival, both in Western and Islamic academia. This is not the place to attempt a comprehensive review of the literature developed in last two decades, but consideration may be given to some points so as to underline the fundamental issues of theoretical aspects of Muslim politics at the end of this century.

A spate of books appeared in the 1980s on Islamic revivalism.[43] There is a significant difference between the wave of orientalistic studies in the nineteenth century and this new wave of studies on Islam in the last quarter of this century, despite the fundamental element of continuity in the sense of the objectives of orientalism as a strategic instrument for domination over the non-West.[44] The change of international context and its impact on the focal concern of these studies, however, resulted in a change in content, methodology, conceptual framework, and objectives of these two waves.

Two significant differences might be mentioned as examples of this change. First, there was a Eurocentric self-pride of the rise of Western colonialism in the first wave of orientalistic studies while the rise of the Islamic revival as a non-Western challenge created a feeling of annoyance in the second. The widespread prejudicial assumption that Islamic revivalism might become an international threat is the basic cause of the lack of originality, comprehensiveness, and objectivity of much of the contemporary researches on Islam. This assumption is the origin of the second difference related to the concentration of these studies. Islamic studies in the second wave became mainly a subject of international politics in the 1980s, while the orientalistic studies concentrated more on the legacy of the non-Western civilizations in the first wave in the nineteenth century. This difference has affected the methodology as well. The contemporary studies on Islam are products of the methodology of social sciences, while classical orientalistic studies originated from philosophical, historical, and theological analysis.

The positive dimension of this new wave is the weakening of the Eurocentric monologic approach after "the rise of a global arena in which non-Western cultures and societies are increasingly active participants in shaping the future of the world," as it has been described by Fred Dallmayr:

> Orientalist monologue in our century has given way to an incipient dialogue making room for the participation of intellectuals and writers from the (formerly) colonized world. Reflecting on the story of Western encounters with non-Western modes of thought, Wilfred Cantwell Smith hails this fledgling dialogue as an important new phase in cultural relations. . . . While the nineteenth century was a time of immense encyclopedic, but one-sided, erudition about other cultures, our century inaugurates a phase where "those other peoples themselves" are present. . . .[45]

The rise in Islamic-oriented literature in this phase, especially after the late 1970s is a reflection of this presence. The theoretical discussions on Islamic education[46] and science[47] prove that the questions of the challenge of modernity in the nineteenth century and during the first phase of this century are still among fundamental issues of civilizational challenge in the Muslim World on the eve of the twenty-first century. Those who write on Islamic economics try to be more operational while studies on Islamic sociology and psychology concentrate on the methodological issues. The question of economic development and its achievement within an Islamic framework has been the fundamental issue of Islamic economics:

> A major challenge confronts the world of Islam: the challenge of re-constructing its economy in a way that is commensurate with its world role, ideological, political and economical. What does this demand: economic development with a view to "catch up" with the industrialized countries of the West . . . our primary concern is not with the "catching up" ideology. Instead, our objective is to discern the nature and ethos of economic development in an Islamic framework.[48]

The fundamental objective of many of these studies is integration of the Islamic value system and legacy with the Western social sciences. This process has been called Islamization of knowledge in general and Islamization of social sciences in particular. Ismail al-Faruqi, one of the leading scholars of this process, defines this attempt comparatively as follows:

> The West claims that its social sciences are scientific because they are neutral; that they deliberately avoid human judgement and preference; that they treat the facts as facts and leave them to speak for themselves. This is a vain claim. For there is no theoretical perception of any fact without perception of its axiological nature and relations. . . . Islamization of the social sciences must endeavor to show the relation of the reality studied to that aspect or part of the divine pattern pertinent to it. Since the divine pattern is the norm reality ought to actualize, the analysis of what is should never lose sight of what ought to be.[49]

The rise of Islamic self-consciousness has been seen by Muslim thinkers as an ultimate way of a liberation from slavery in every sense. Naqib al-Attas, another influential scholar during this phase, has declared Islamization as "the liberation of man first from magical, mythological, animistic, national-cultural tradition, and then from secular control over his reason and his language."[50] Alija Izzetbegovic, president of Bosnia-Herzegovina and an outstanding Muslim thinker as well, correlated Islamic ontological consciousness to a framework of humanism:

> "Man is a product of his environment"—this basic postulate of materialism served as the starting point of all subsequent inhuman theories in law and sociology, and of the practice of manipulating human beings, which in our time reached monstrous proportions during the time of Nazism and Stalinism. All other similar seductive theories of society's priority over individuals, of man's obligation to serve society, and so forth, belong here as well. Man must not serve anybody; he must not be a means. Everything must serve man and man must serve God only. This is the ultimate meaning of humanism.[51]

The Muslim World on the Eve of a New Millennium: Civilization Revival versus Geopolitical Exclusion

Three significant new dimensions relating to the Muslim World, which became very influential especially in the post-Soviet era, should be mentioned. The first dimension is directly related to the concept and geographical image of the concept of the Muslim World itself. The concept of the Muslim World in the first phase of this transformation referred to the Ottoman state in its last agony as the Sick Man of Europe and other colonized Muslim lands.

The concept of Muslim World was used as a mere Afro-Asian colonial phenomenon in the second phase of this century. John Mott's foreword to his book *The Moslem World of Today* reflects this Eurocentric approach related to the concept of the Muslim World: "Moslem world of today is markedly different from that of yesterday. . . . Almost every Moslem land—in Africa, in Western, Central and Southern Asia, and in the East Indies—is ablaze with new national and social aspirations and ambitions."[52]

The Muslim World in the third phase meant a collection of the conflicting individual states lacking internal cooperation and coordination. The religious Near-Eastern question around the rhetoric of the Sick Man of Europe, which was used for the Balkans in late nineteenth century, began to be used for the Middle East in this third phase, after the establishment of Israel as a Jewish state in Muslim political environment. The Muslim World has been identified with the Middle Eastern question during this phase because of the fact that the main confrontation between systemic forces and the Muslim World has been in Palestine during this era.

The geographical meaning of the concept of the Muslim World changed again in the post-Soviet era after the reemergence of the Euro-Asian component of the

Muslim World. The reemergence of the Muslim rimland after the end of the bi-polar Cold War meant a radical change relating to the image of the Asia-African Muslim World. The Euro-Asian component of the Muslim World came to be an important factor in international relations. The Muslim World began to be seen as an Euro-Asian entity as well as an Asia-African entity after the emergence of the new republics in Central Asia, Caucasia, and the Balkans. This might be seen as the decolonization process of the Euro-Asian Muslim nations.

Another significant change in the concept of the Muslim World is the increasing demographic proportion of Muslim masses in Western countries, such as Algerians in France, Pakistanis in Britain, and Turks in Germany. This demographic factor is in fact a reflection of the colonial spheres of influence in the second phase of this century, except for Turkish migration to Europe. About a third of the world's Muslim population today live as minorities in non-Muslim majority countries. So the concept of the Muslim World today does not only reflect a geographical zone, but comprises a demographic factor in non-Muslim majority countries. Therefore, a new interdependency emerged between Muslim countries in the traditional geographical zone of the Muslim World and demo-graphic extensions of them in other parts of the world.

There are significant geopolitical, geoeconomic, and geocultural consequences of this change in the concept of the Muslim World. The geography of OIC-member countries in the fourth phase, especially after the emergence of the Euroasian component, has proven that the most significant geopolitical and geostrategic zone of the world from northern Caucasia to Tanzania in a north-south direction and from Morocco to Indonesia in a west-east direction—called rimland by Spykman—is populated by Muslim countries and communities. For example, eight out of the sixteen strategically most important choke points (the Suez Canal; Bab el-Mandeb, or the exit from the Red Sea; the Strait of Hormuz, or the exit from the Persian Gulf; the Strait of Malacca; the Sunda Strait, between Sumatra and Java; the Lombok Strait, between Bali and Mataram; and Bosphorus and Dardanelles, as exits from the Black Sea) are under full control of Muslim countries while one of them (the Strait of Gibraltar) is separating a Muslim (Morocco) and European (Spain) state. This means that almost all choke points in Eurasia (except the English Channel and the Danish Straits) as the keys of the rimland are under the control of the Muslim countries.[53]

A similar change might be observed in the geoeconomics of the Muslim World. From the perspective of geoeconomics, the Muslim World has been seen as the arena of the colonial competition in the first phase while it has been the object of an absolute partition in the second phase. The fundamental character-istic of the third phase was the establishment of national economic entities on one hand, and the significance of oil in international economics on the other.

The fundamental question in the last phase has been the integration process in the global economic system. The rise of East Asian economies, Turkish application for full membership of European Union, the process of privatization in several Muslim countries, and the distribution channels of the geoeconomic resources of the Muslim World—such as oil, natural gas, and strategic minerals of Central Asia and the Middle East—are several aspects of this process. It is difficult to say that this process goes smoothly. The fact is that systemic forces of the world economy want to have a geostrategic control over the Muslim World without seeing them as partners within the existing system of international political economy. The rejection of Turkey's application to the European Union, although Turkey has been of one the main contributors to the success of NATO throughout the Cold War, is a striking example of this.

The geopolitical, geostrategic, and geoeconomic significance of the Muslim World is among the fundamental reasons why regional and international conflicts have intensified in the Muslim World in the last decade of this century. It is also the main factor for the geopolitical exclusion of the Muslim World after being declared a threat to international peace in the post-Soviet era. Such a geopolitical exclusion cannot be consistent with the idea of international law and the concept of world order, as has been rightly stated by Richard Falk:

> Can international law be extended to serve as an effective vehicle for achieving equitable inter-civilizational participation in world order structures and processes without eroding its achievements in regulating state-society relations by way of protecting individual human rights? Perhaps I can best clarify my point of departure by reference to what might be called the geopolitics of exclusion, both with respect to the dynamics of global governance and those substantive and symbolic issues that seem to be of greatest concern to the Islamic world.[54]

The geopolitics of exclusion is a counterpart of the second important new dimension, namely, the rising confrontational approach of some circles in Western power centers. Creating an image of the Muslim World as the new threat in the post-Cold War era—as is done in Fukuyama's *The End of History*[55] and in Samuel Huntington's "Clash of Civilizations"[56]—reflects this confrontational approach. As Francine Friedman writes: "Many analysts, of course, point to the Bosnian Muslims as an anomaly in the middle of Christian Europe and imply that the collapse of Communism meant that other threats to European stability—such as the menace of Muslim radicalism—needed to be dealt with."[57] Such an exclusionist approach paved the way for ethnic cleansing in Bosnia. Serbian forces used the rhetoric of an imaginary Islamic threat to legitimize their barbaric actions against innocent women and children.

The third significant new dimension is the revival of the cultural and social parameters of Islamic civilization. There is a radical change in the theoretical and practical agenda of the Muslim World, especially in comparison with the second phase. Islam's strong self-perception has been restored, replacing the psycho-political crisis of the colonial era. The civilizational parameters of Islamic civilization, which were imagined to be in the process of annihilation or assimilation during the second phase,[58] showed a process of revival especially in the last two decades of this century. The collapse of socialism and crisis in the modernist paradigm provided new elements in this reanimation of the Islamic civilizational parameters and new forms of psychological, intellectual, social, economic, and political dynamism.

A new geoculture is emerging in the Muslim World. The fundamental characteristic of this new geoculture might be summarized as plurality within unity. The unifying element of the culture of the Muslim World is the civilizational revival and its universal parameters as response to modernity. There has been a two-sided relation between geocultural revival and geopolitical exclusion. Geocultural revival of Islamic civilization has been misused by the theoreticians of geopolitical exclusion by presenting it as a visible indicator of an anti-Western strategic threat while, on the other hand, geopolitical exclusion has accelerated this process of the geocultural revitalization of Islamic self-perception, especially in the regions where the survival of national identity has been attached to the religious identity. The following statement of a Bosnian soldier reflects this psychology:

> I never thought of myself as a Muslim. I never went to mosque. I am European like you. I do not want the Arab world to help us, I want Europe to help us. But now, I do have to think of myself as a Muslim, not in a religious way, but as a member of a people. Now we are faced with obliteration, I have to understand what is about me and my people they wish to obliterate.[59]

Conclusion

Von Grünebaum asks a historic question in his article on the persistence and continuity of the basic elements of Islamic civilization:

> Nations come and go. Empires rise and fall. But Islam persists and continues to include the nomads and the settlers, the builders of civilizations within Islam and those that destroy them. What then are the factors that keep together as one *ummah* those many people that, consciously or not, are inclined to maintain their individuality while cultivating their tie with universal Islam as their most precious spiritual possession?[60]

This question has a special significance for both historical analysis and futuristic projections. Historically it is true that Islamic civilization was able to produce a universal system of being-knowledge-value paradigm,[61] a consistent normative foundation for a way of life, similar forms of a civilizational substance in the sense of aesthetics shared by all Muslim nations from Far East to Far West, from Euroasia to Subsaharan Africa. Similar philosophical trends emerged in Central Asia and in Andalusia (Spain) during the rise of classical Islamic thought. Similar architectural forms were developed to reflect the same cultural substance in several cities established by different nations of the Islamic civilization.

The main factor of the universality of the Islamic civilization is the ontological consciousness which directly shapes individual human life regardless of ethnic and regional origin. Common cultural and political responses to colonialism and modernity in different parts of the Muslim World are the very indicators of this consciousness. The rise of Islamic identity and its socio-cultural reflections in the lands of the atheistic former Soviet Union confirms the impact of this onto-logical consciousness.

This ontological consciousness will continue to be the common ground of the universal substance of Islamic civilization. The being-knowledge-value paradigm based on this consciousness may produce a new approach challenging the assumptions of the modernist paradigm. The revival of Islamic civilization should not be evaluated from a perspective of strategic pragmatism, which creates an intracivilizational and intercivilizational conflict. Despite the sufferings of Muslims in several parts of the globe (i.e. Bosnia, Kosovo, Palestine) Islam has been declared the new threat in the post-Cold War era by the defenders of strategic pragmatism. This contradiction creates a feeling of insecurity among Muslim societies similar to the case of anticolonial responses at the beginning of this century. In spite of the crisis and the difficulties to develop an alternative civilizational axis, the civilizational vitality in the Muslim World will, in the long run, necessarily transform itself into a new theoretical framework which will be an asset for the whole human culture.

A real and sincere civilizational dialogue will ultimately create a productive civilizational interaction and synthesis between hegemonic Western civilization and reviving non-Western civilizational and cultural entities. The presence of different cultures is a precondition for such an era of dialogue because "in helping to maintain difference, cultural movements also carry a broader political significance: they prevent the monopolization of 'the political.'"[62] Thus, the theoretical and practical reflections of the cultural revival of non-Western civilizations should not be used to legitimize a rhetoric of threat. Rather, they should be seen as natural consequences of the plurality of human culture.

Notes

1. For several aspects of his policy of Pan-Islamism see his memoirs, *Abdulhamid'in Hatira Defteri*, Ismet Bozdag, ed. (Istanbul, 1975); Çetinsaya Gökhan, *Abdülhamid Döneminin ilk Yillarinda 'Islam Birligi' Hareketi (1876-1878)*, MA thesis, Ankara University, 1988; Cezmi Eraslan, *II. Abdülhamid ve Islam Birligi* (Istanbul, 1992); Nikki R. Keddie, "The Pan-Islamic Appeal: Afghani and Abdulhamid II," *Middle Eastern Studies*, 3 (1966): 46-67.

2. Deliar Noer, *The Modernist Muslim Movement in Indonesia 1900-1942* (London: Oxford University Press, 1973), 21, 29.

3. Muhammad bin Jafar Al-Kattani, *Nasihat ahl al-Islam: Tahlil Islami 'Ilmi li-'Awamil Suqut al-Dawla al-Islamiyya wa 'Awamil Nuhudiha* (Rabat: Maktabatal Badr, 1908) translated and cited by Henry Munson, *Religion and Power in Morocco* (New Haven: Yale University Press, 1993), 88-89.

4. Jacob M. Landau, *The Politics of Pan-Islam: Ideology and Organization* (Oxford: Clarendon Press, 1994), 206-7. For details of Pan-Islamic relations between Ottomans and Indian Muslims see Azmi Özcan, *Pan-Islamizm: Osmanli Devleti, Hindistan Müslümanlari ve Ingiltere (1877-1924)* (Istanbul: ISAM, 1992).

5. For these educational reforms during his reign and their impact on Ottoman-Turkish modernization see F. Mardin, "Religion and Secularism in Turkey," in *The Modern Middle East: A Reader*, Albert Hourani, Philip Khoury and Mary C. Wilson, eds. (London: I. B. Tauris, 1993), 358-363.

6. For this function of educational institutions in India and their role in Islamic modernism, see Fazlur Rahman, *Islam and Modernity: Transformation of an Intellectual Tradition* (Chicago: University of Chicago Press, 1982), 63-83.

7. For a comparison between the objectives of Sultan Abdulhamid's policy of Pan-Islamism and ideas of Young Turks, see Enver Ziya Karal, *Osmanli Tarihi*, vol. VIII (Ankara: Türk Tarih Kurumu, 1983), 543-550.

8. Mourad Bey, *La Force et la Faiblesse de la Turquie: Les Coupables et les Innocents* (Geneva, 1897), 58-59; English translation has been cited in Ernest Edmonds Ramsour, *The Young Turks: Prelude to the Revolution of 1908* (Princeton: Princeton University Press, 1957), 42-43.

9. Japanese success in integrating Western science and Japanese traditional values has been a point of reference for them. Abdurreflid Ibrahim, a leading Pan-Islamist and Ottoman envoy to Far East and Japan, played an intermediary role in exchanging experiences of these two non-Western societies. See Abdurreflid Ibrahim, 20. *Asrin Bafllarinda ilam Dünyasi ve Japonya'da Islamiyet*, 2 vols. (Istanbul, 1987).

10. The introductory part of the Tanzimat Rescript carries this characteristic. The aim of this new policy was described in this part as the restrengthening of the Islamic order and *Shariah*, which had been declared as the basic force behind the historical success of the Ottoman state. For the text of Tanzimat Rescript, see Enver Ziya Karal, *Osmanli Tarihi*, vol. V (Ankara: Türk Tarih Kurumu, 1983), 255-258.

11. Jacob Landau sees this characteristic as al-Afghani's greatest merit in the context of Pan-Islamism: "al-Afghani's greatest merit, in our context, was to have shown that, in his days at least, Pan-Islam and nationalism could be mutually complementary (he even toyed with the idea of a confederation of semi-autonomous Muslim states, with the Ottoman Sultan as their suzerain)." *The Politics of Pan-Islam*, 21.

12. Mardin underlines his effort to reconcile Western institutions and Islamic tradition: "For him the decline of the Ottoman empire was of interest for all Islamic nations and meant the establishment of European hegemony in lands where Islam had been once powerful. Thus his scheme was a proposal for the rejuvenation of Islamic states in general and focused on the Ottoman Empire only because the latter had been the leader of Islamic nations for centuries. His preponderantly Islamic approach was indicated by the title of the book, *Reforms Necessary to Islamic States*. . . . Actually, there was nothing in the Islamic creed which precluded Islamic states from taking over Western institutions. Indeed, the statement of the Prophet to the effect that science should be sought wherever it existed was indication of the latitude provided in this matter by Islam." *The Young Ottoman Movement: A Study in the Evolution of Turkish Political Thought in the Nineteenth Century*, Ph.D. thesis, Stanford University, 1958, 281, 283.

13. For his ideas on the unity of the Muslim World and reformation in political institutions see his books *Münazarat* (Istanbul: Envar, 1993) 28, 34, 39-40; *Sunuhat* (Istanbul: Sözler, 1977), 36-40; and *Divan-i Harb-i Örfi* (Istanbul: Sözler,1978), 41-50. For an adaptation of this periodization of the Muslim policy in the twentieth century to the life and thoughts of Said Nursi, see Davutoglu, "Bediuzzaman ve 20.Yüzyilda Islam Dünyasinin Siyasasi [Bediuzzaman and the Politics of the Muslim World in the Twentieth Century]," *Uluslararasi Bediuzzaman Sempozyumu III* (Istanbul: Yeni Asya 1996), 606-628.

14. His book on the crisis of the Muslim World, which was published first in 1918 (*Buhranlarimiz* [Our Crisis], Istanbul: Tercüman 1001 Temel Eser, no. 9, n.d.), has a critique of the westernization strategies as well.

15. For a collection of the works and arguments of the leading figures of Islamism during this phase see Ismail Kara, *Türkiye'de Islamcilik Düflüncesi*, 2 vols. (Istanbul: Kitabevi, 1997).

16. The Ottoman Sultan and leaders of Young Turks during the First World War, as well as nationalist leaders of Turkish army under the command of Mustafa Kemal in Anatolia during the War of Liberation, proclaimed *jihad* for the religious legitimacy of war against colonial forces.

17. John R. Mott, a Western observer of this period sees the end of the Caliphate as the most striking event of the process of change in the Muslim World: "The most remarkable event of all has been the abolition of the Caliphate.The effect of this startling development has been like dropping from its place the keystone of an arch of pan-Islamism. This weakening of the sense of solidarity and moral unity of the Muslim peoples will be felt increasingly." Mott, *The Moslem World of Today* (London: Hodder and Stoughton, 1925), vii.

18. As Mardin emphasizes, this cultural westernization was trying to "provide Turkish citizens with a new view of the world which would replace that of religion and religious culture." See Mardin, "Religion and Secularism in Turkey," 371.

19. Of course, the legalistic meaning of this term continued to survive.

20. For theoretical discussions on the institution of the Caliphate during the transitional period in Turkey (1922-1924), see Sami Erdem, "Cumhuriyet'e Geçifl Sürecinde Hilafet Teorisine Alternatif Yaklaflimlar: Seyyid Bey Örnegi (1922-1924)," *Divan-Ilmi Araftirmalar*, 2 (1996): 119-146.

21. See Abd ur-Raziq Ali, *Al-Islam wa Usul al-Hukm* (Beirut: 1966).

22. See Rashid Rida, *Al-Khilafah* (Cairo: Al-Zahra´ li'l-I'lam al-Arabia, 1988).

23. Muhammad Iqbal, *The Reconstruction of Religious Thought in Islam* (Lahore: Sh. Muhammad Ashraf, 1988), 173-74.

24. The emergence of many Muslim states in some historical periods because of the expansion of Islam or because of the political incapacity of the Caliph made it clear that *Dar al-Islam* is a politico-legal boundary beyond the power control of individual states. These individual states sometimes filled the political vacuum which arose as a result of the incapacity of the political center, as in the case of Salahaddin Ayyubi's struggle against the Crusaders. Sometimes they asked approval from the Caliph to legitimize their political power, as with the request of Seljuki Sultan Tugrul from the Abbasid Caliph or Indian Muslim ruler's request from Ottoman Caliph. However, none of them declared that *Dar al-Islam* was limited within the geographical area controlled by their states.

25. Alan Richards and John Waterbury, *A Political Economy of the Middle East* (Boulder: Westview Press, 1990), 186.

26. See my article "Devlet," *Türkiye Diyanet Vakfı Islam Ansiklopedisi* (Istanbul: Encylopedia of Islam), 8, (1994): 234-240.

27. The attempt to reconcile Islamic tradition with Western political institutions reached the point that Rousseau was declared a Muslim at heart by Ilyas Ahmad in his book *The Social Contract and the Islamic State* first published in Allahabad on the eve of this phase in 1944: "The resemblance of these first principles of the Islamic political edifice with Rousseau's political ideas does not end with the city state as the unit of a wider federation and his emphasis upon the rights of man—of life, liberty and property as also of equality, justice and fraternity. There is a third point still of greater significance. It is by making the social contract that he creates an Organic Community. In Islam also the Community has been made by the Social Contract. . . . Now if this was his belief (and in the absence of an open declaration by him of his acceptance of Islam) would it be going too far to suspect that Rousseau might have been a Muslim at heart?" *The Social Contract* (New Delhi: Kitab Bhavan, 1981), 140-141, 155-156.

28. For Mawdudi's ideas on the Islamic state and political system, see *Fundamentals of the Islamic Constitution* (Lahore, 1952), and *Islamic Law and Constitution*, trans., ed. Khurshid Ahmad (Lahore, 1955, 1960).

29. Ibrahim M. Abu-Rabi' relates Qutb's ideas on religion and state to Hegelian political philosophy: "Consciously or subconsciously, Qutb follows the Hegelian notion of the insoluble bond between religion and (theocratic) state. In an interesting piece on the relation of religion to the state, Hegel argues the case of monotheistic religions in his *Lectures on the Philosophy of Religion* and concludes that 'In a general sense, religion and the foundation of the State are one and the same; they are in their real essence identical.'" Ibrahim M. Abu-rabi', *Intellectual Origins of Islamic Resurgence in the Modern Arab World* (Albany: State University of New York Press, 1996), 155.

30. His argument that the prophets of Islam tried to eliminate "tyrants who put themselves in the place of gods and ensalve and oppress the people" reflects the rising rhetoric of Islamic political thought in this phase. See his book *Maqasid al-Shari'a al-Islamiyya ma Makarimuha* (Casablanca: Maktabat al-Wahda al-'Arabiyya, 1963), 205; cited in Henry Munson, *Religion and Power in Morocco*, 78.

31. Shariati's distinction beween Islamic state as an institution and Islamic movement shows the revolutionary character of his ideas: "Shariati, however, distinguished between an institution and a movement by stressing that the former is inert while the latter is dynamic. He criticized the establishment of on Islamic state—an institution—for its conduciveness to inertness and favored a dynamic Islamic order." See Mehran Tamadonfar, *The Islamic Polity and Political Leadership: Fundamentalism, Sectarianism and Pragmatism* (Boulder: Westview, 1989), 39.

32. For the analysis of this intellectual transformation in Turkey as a case study, see my article, "The Re-emergence of Islamic Thought in Turkey: Intellectual Transformation," *BRISMES Proceedings of the 1986 International Conference on Middle Eastern Studies* (London: Brismes, 1986), 229-239.

33. Shirin Thair-kheli, "In Search of an Identity," in *Islam in Foreign Policy*, Adee Dawisha, ed. (Cambridge: Cambridge University Press, 1983), 68.

34. C. A. O. Van Nieuwenhuijze, *Aspects of Islam in Post-Colonial Indonesia* (The Hague and Bandung: W. Van Hoeve, 1958), 180-181.

35. Gorm Rye Olsen, "Islam: What Is Its Political Significance? The Cases of Egypt and Saudi Arabia," in *Islam: State and Society*, Klaus Ferdinand and Mehdi Muzafferi, eds. (London: Curzon Press, 1988), 132.

36. Ibrahim Jum'a, "The Ideology of Arab Nationalism: The Authenticity of Arab Thought," in *Political and Social Thought in the Contemporary Middle East*, Kemal H. Karpet, ed. (London: Pall Mall Press, 1968), 48-52.

37. Immanuel Wallerstein, *The Politics of the World Economy* (Cambridge: Cambridge University Press, 1984), 33.

38. For a detailed analysis of this psychology of insecurity among Muslim masses, see my *Civilizational Transformation and the Muslim World* (Kuala Lumpur: Quill, 1994), 101-104.

39. "1. to promote Islamic solidarity among member-states; 2. to consolidate co-operation among member-states in economic, social, cultural, scientific and other fields of activities, and facilitate consultation among member-states in international organizations; 3. to endeavor to eliminate racial segregation and discrimination and to eradicate colonialism in all its forms; 4. to take necessary measures to support international peace and security founded on justice; 5. to coordinate efforts for the safeguard of the Holy Places and support of the struggle of the people of Palestine, and help them to regain their rights and liberate their land; 6. to strengthen the struggle of all Muslim peoples with a view to safeguarding their dignity, independence, and national rights; 7. to create a suitable atmosphere for the promotion of cooperation and understanding among member-states and other countries." Charter of Islamic Conference, in Abdullah Ahsan, *The Organization of Islamic Conference (An Introduction to an Islamic Political Institution)* (Herndon: IIIT, 1988), 128.

40. Many institutions, centers, committees, and commissions were established within the OIC-System during this phase in four different categories: (1) committee under the authority of the conference of kings and heads of the states and government, namely Standing Committee for Commercial and Economic Cooperation (COMCEC); (2) commission under the authority of Conference of Foreign Ministers, namely Islamic Commission for Economic, Cultural and Social Affairs (ICECSA); (3) Subsidiary organs of OIC linked to the General Secretariat, namely Statistical, Economic and Social Research and Training Center for Islamic Countries (SESRTCIC) in Ankara, Islamic Center for Vocational and Technical Training and Research (ICVTTR) in Dhaka, Islamic Center for Development of Trade (ICDT) in Casablanca, Islamic Foundation for Science, Technology and Development (IFSTAD) in Jeddah, and Islamic Civil Aviation Council (ICAC) in Tunis; (4) Independent Members of OIC-System, namely Islamic Development Bank (IDB) in Jeddah, Islamic Research and Training Institute (IRTI) in Jeddah, Islamic Chamber of Commerce, Industry and Commodity Exchange (ICCICE) in Karachi, International Association of Islamic Bank (IAIB) in Jeddah, Islamic Shipowners Association (ISA) in Jeddah, Islamic Telecommunications Union (ITU) in Karachi, and Islamic Cement Union (ICU) in Ankara. A detailed table of OIC-System might be found in *Economic Cooperation and Integration Among Islamic Countries*, prepared by V. Nienhaus for Islamic Research and Training Institute (Jeddah, 1987), 61.

41. J. Mauzegar, "Dealing With Debt," *Foreign Policy*, no. 68 (Fall 1987): 141.

42. Anwar Ibrahim, *The Asian Renaissance* (Kuala Lumpur: Times Books International, 1996), 124.

43. See *Voices of Resurgent Islam*, John Esposito, ed. (New York: Oxford University Press, 1983); E. Mortimer, *Faith and Power: The Politics of Islam* (London: Faber and Faber, 1982); D. Pipe, *In the Path of God: Islam and Political Power* (New York: Basic Books, 1983); M. Ruthven, *Islam in the World* (London: Penguin, 1984); E. Sivan, *Radical Islam* (New Haven: Yale University Press, 1985); R. Dekmejian, *Islam in*

Revolution: Fundamentalism in the Arab World (Syracuse: Syracuse University Press, 1985); and W. M. Watt, *Islamic Fundamentalism and Modernity* (London: Routledge, 1988).

44. For the role of orientalism in political domination, see the masterpiece of Edward Said on this topic, *Orientalism* (New York: Vintage Books, 1979).

45. Fred Dallmayr, *Beyond Orientalism: Essays on Cross-Cultural Encounter* (Albany: State University of New York Press, 1996), ix, 63.

46. Islamic Education Series on *Crisis in Muslim Education*; *Aims and Objectives of Islamic Education*; *Philosophy, Literature and Fine Arts*; *Curriculum and Teacher Education*; *Education and Society in the Muslim World*; and *Muslim Education in the Modern World*, published by King Abdulaziz University in late 1980s (General Editor: Syed Ali Ashraf, Jeddah), are among the first examples of these works.

47. One of the prominent Muslim scholars on Islamic science defines Islamic approach to modern science as follows: "What is positive in modern science can not be refuted by Islam because it is a knowledge corresponding to an aspect of reality. But what is completely unacceptable from the Islamic point of view is the positivism and relativism to which modern science lends itself because of its divorce from other forms of knowledge. . . . How can Islam allow knowledge of the particular to develop at the expense of knowledge of the Universal, to allow science in its modern sense to develop at the expense of wisdom, of *hikmah* or *sapientia* as was to happen in the West?" Seyyed Hossein Nasr, "Islam and Modern Science," in *Islam and Contemporary Society*, Salem Azzam, ed., (London: Longman and Islamic Council of Europe, 1982), 185.

48. Khurshid Ahmad, "Economic Development in an Islamic Framework," in *Islamic Perspectives: Studies in Honour of Sayyid Abul A'la Mawdudi*, Khurshid Ahmad and Zafar Ishaq Ansari, eds., (Leicester: The Islamic Foundation, 1979), 223.

49. Ismail R. al-Faruqi, "Islamizing the Social Sciences," in *Social and Natural Sciences: The Islamic Perspective*, Ismail R. al-Faruqi and Abdullah Omar Naseef, eds. (Jeddah: Hodder and Stoughton, 1981), 16-17.

50. Syed Muhammad Naquib al-Attas, *The Concept of Education in Islam: A Framework for an Islamic Philosophy of Education*, 2nd ed. (Kuala Lumpur: ISTAC, 1991), 45-46.

51. Alija Ali Izzetbegovic, *Islam between East and West* (Indianapolis: American Trust Publication, 1984,1989), 39-40.

52. Mott, *The Moslem World Today*, vii.

53. For a detailed analysis of the geopolitics of the Muslim World, see my article "The Clash of Interests: An Explanation of the World (Dis)Order," *Perceptions: Journal of International Affairs*, 2, no. 4, (December 1997-February 1998): 92-122.

54. Richard Falk, "False Universalism and the Geopolitics of Exclusion: The Case of Islam," *Third World Quarterly* 18, no. 1 (1997): 8.

55. "It is true that Islam constitutes a systematic and coherent ideology, just like liberalism and communism, with its own code of morality and doctrine of political and social justice. The appeal of Islam is potentially universal, reaching out to all men as men, and not just to members of a particular ethnic or national group. And Islam has indeed defeated liberal democracy in many parts of the Islamic world, posing a grave threat to liberal practices even in countries where it has not achieved political power directly. The end of the Cold War in Europe was followed immediately by a challenge to the West from Iraq, in which Islam was arguably a factor." Francis Fukuyama, *The End of History and the Last Man* (New York: Free Press, 1992), 45-46.

56. "A Confucian-Islamic military connection has thus come into being, designed to promote acquisition by its members of the weapons and weapons technologies needed to counter the military power of the West. . . . A new form of arms competition is thus occuring between Islamic-Confucian states and the West." Samuel Huntington, "The Clash of Civilizations," *Foreign Affairs* 72 (Summer 1993): 47.

57. Francine Friedman, "The Bosnian Muslim National Question," in *Religion and the War in Bosnia*, Paul Mowzes, ed. (Atlanta: Scholars Press, 1998), 1.

58. This was the term used by Arnold Toynbee for the surviving non-Western civilizations including Islamic civilization: "The ten survivors are our own Western Society, the main body of Orthodox Christendom in the Near East, its offshoot in Russia, the Islamic Society, the Hindu Society, the main body of the Far Eastern Society in China, its offshoot in Japan and the three arrested civilizations of the Polynesians, the Eskimos and the Nomads. If we look more closely at these ten survivors we observe that the Polynesian and Nomad societies are now in their last agonies and that seven out of the eight others are all, in different degrees, under threat of either annihilation or the assimilation by the eighth, namely our own civilization of the West." *A Study of History* (New York: Dell Publishing, 1981), I, 286.

59. Ed Vulliamy, *Seasons in Hell: Understanding Bosnia's War* (New York: St. Martin's Press,1994), 65; cited in Francine Friedman, *The Bosnian Muslims: Denial of a Nation* (Boulder: Westview, 1996), 224.

60. G. E. von Grünebaum, "Pluralism in the Islamic World." *Islamic Studies*, 5, no. 2 (1962): 50-51.

61. For a theoretical framework of this paradigm and its comparison with Western tradition, see my book, *Alternative Paradigms: The Impact of Islamic and Western Weltanschauungs on Political Theory* (Lanham, MD: University Press of America, 1994).

62. Fred Dallmayr, *Paths in the Global Village: Alternative Visions* (Lanham: Rowman & Littlefield, 1998), 294.

5

Symbolic and Utilitarian Value of a Tradition: Martyrdom in the Iranian Political Culture

Manochehr Dorraj

He who is in love never fears death. He fears neither punishment nor imprisonment. His heart is like a hungry wolf. The wolf does not fear the shepherd's cries.

Baba Taher

In the martyrdom of a candle flame is a luminous secret known best to that last tallest glimmer.

Forough Farokhzad

Introduction

Throughout the Iranian Revolution of 1979, many Shi'ite Muslims donned white gowns and marched in the streets, indicating a readiness to become martyrs for the Islamic cause. During the Iran-Iraq war, much of the world watched in amazement as thousands of Iranian youth voluntarily walked through Iraqi mine fields to clear a path for Iranian tanks and artillery divisions. Despite Iraq's superior fire power, Iran mobilized repeated human wave assaults on Iraq's fortified positions. These two events dramatize a significant symbolic component of Iranian political culture which has, so far, received little attention.

Throughout the history of Iran, martyrdom has been a recurring phenomenon to celebrate and safeguard the sacred boundaries, sublime values and exalted rituals by which the culture is sanctioned. The question of the persistence of martyrdom in the Shi'ite culture of Iran is a socio-historical one. Therefore, the first part of this paper delineates the sociological foundations and historical genealogy of martyrdom. Then the politicization and popularization of this ritual by religious and secular intellectual leaders throughout the 1960s and 1970s will be examined.

The tradition of martyrdom is by no means confined to the Islamic faith. Both Judaism and Christianity exalt martyrdom in the path of God as a noble act. Judaism, for example, is said to be a religion of martyrdom. It preaches that Jews, the chosen people of God, must be prepared to suffer and, if necessary, to die in order to safeguard and preserve their faith.[1] Christians are also taught to "confess and if need be to suffer for the name." The pious must carry the cross and the spirit it represents.[2] Indeed, Christians are told that the crucifixion of Christ was a corollary to the slaughter of other prophets: "The prophets, by their sufferings at the hands of the Jewish nation, had been witness of God's mercy and judgment and Jesus' sufferings would be continued in the lives of his followers."[3] Only through examples of martyrdom can the believers prove themselves worthy servants of God. Since all major religions, including Judaism, Christianity, and Islam, emerged as persecuted sects, they developed elaborate rituals not only to cope with repression and death associated with martyrdom but also to celebrate life.

Martyrdom is defined as a conscious attempt to embrace death for a personal or political cause. While it may appear as self-negation, as it would be demonstrated in the following pages, martyrdom is often an act of self-aggrandizement to affirm the time-honored tradition of the community. Loyalty to communal tradition strengthens the personal and the communal sense of honor and consolidates cultural vitality and historical continuity. Thus through martyrdom the community regenerates itself.

Martyrdom in Iranian Political Culture:
A Brief Overview

Two significant themes in pre-Islamic Iranian political culture directly influenced the development of a cult of martyrdom in Shi'ite Islam. Unlike the ancient Greeks, who believed that refinement of the human spirit is dependent on development of the body and thus encouraged sports and fine arts, the ancient Persians, for the most part, held that spiritual elevation is attainable only through an ascetic life. The individual who epitomized this outlook was Mani, one of the two major pre-Islamic prophets of Iran. Manichaenism synthesized elements of the philosophy of Eastern gnosis with Hindu stoicism and Christian unworldliness. Fasting, living ascetic lives, and self-castration were among the rituals that followers of Mani maintained.[4] Refinement of the soul was, for

Manichaians, possible only through self-denial and avoiding the pleasures of the flesh.

The second significant element contributing to pervasive celebration of martyrdom is the prevalence of tragedy in Iranian political culture. Before we proceed with a discussion of pervasiveness of tragedy in Iranian political culture, it is important to state the relation between tragedy and martyrdom. A culture in which art, literature, and popular myth are deeply imbued with tragedy, perceives of martyrdom as a dramatic expression of tragedy. In such social context, martyrdom is not an aberration but the manifestation of a culture of tragedy personified. It is a tragic fate. Seen in this dynamic relation, martyrdom is best understood when posited in historical context of recurring themes of tragedy in Iranian popular mythology and literature.

Firdowsi's (c.935-1020) *Shahnameh* (The Book of Kings), the great Iranian national epic, is replete with resonant tragic themes and stories: the tragedy of just and fair-minded Jamshid, brutally slain at the hand of the cruel and oppressive Zahhak; the tragedy of the murder of Iraj, the designated crown prince and the favored son of King Feraidun, by his older brothers Salm and Tur; and the most enduring tragedy, Sohrab's death at the hands of his father Rostam, the son of Zal, the mythical protector of Iranian monarchy, the great warrior and man of exceptional valor and virtue. This episode epitomizes the tragedy of filicide. Rostam, who faced the dilemma of killing his son or being killed by him, died a tragic death as well.[5] Tragedy surrounds the aura of another Rostam, the son of Farrokhzad who as the commander of Iranian forces under the last sasanid (224-651) ruler, Yazdgerd III, suffered humiliating defeat in the hands of invading Arab Muslim armies. Once a mighty empire with its proud people and civilization, Iran was subjugated, becoming a servant to its new Arab masters.

Tragedy is also the dominant theme in the life story of Siyavush, the son of King Kay Kavus. Siyavush was told by his father to attack Turan, the main rival of the ancient Persian empire ruled by Afrasyab. Siyavush refused to do so, and to escape his father's wrath he took refuge in Turan. Thus a great friendship and love emerged between the two men. Soon, however, Afrasyab suspected Siyavush of conspiring to overtake his empire and had him killed. Siyavush's death promulgated a cycle of revenge and bloodshed that devastated both Turan and Iran.[6] Afrasyab's murder of Siyavush accentuates the tragedy of murder of a beloved friend that triggers the death of thousands of innocent people. When the news of Siyavush's death reached his father, he lamented and said it was not Afrasiyab but rather he himself who killed his son. Thus, the tragedy of filicide is replicated. The tragedy continues with the death of Zarer, a devoted defender of the Zoroastrian faith. As Vishtasp, the holy king of the Zoroastrian church, is threatened by Arjasb, the king of the Chionites, for his conversion to the religion of Zoroaster, Zarer bravely volunteers to fight the mighty enemy Arjasb against extreme odds. Despite his valor, he is ruthlessly slain by Bidarafsh, Arjasb's brother. Zarer's death aroused much grief and lamentation in the

Zoroastrian community, over the years members of the community came together to partake in rituals to commemorate the death of their slain hero.[7] Thus,
in Firdowsi's *Shahnameh* there is a recurring tendency for episodes to end in
tragedy. Michael Hillman notes the uniqueness of Firdowsi's *Shahnameh* in the
context of literary epics:

> Although the literary epic tradition generally implies or represents nostalgia for a
> bygone heroic age, epics themselves generally recount the story of victory in the
> heroic age of the people or nation whose history the story represents. The Greeks
> defeat the Trojans in the *Iliad*. Odysseus returns home to Penelope in the *Odyssey*.
> The *Aeneid* celebrates the founding of Rome. Hope for humankind is the final
> message in *Paradise Lost*. The future holds promise for the Joads of America at
> the end of the *Grapes of Wrath*. But Firdowsi composed his *Shahnameh* as a
> national history culminating in disaster.[8]

Thus in "Immortalizing Defeat,"[9] *Shahnameh* has had a powerful impact on
the Iranian psyche through the ages: identification with defeat and tragedy.

Similar tragedies are repeated in the drama surrounding the deaths of the two
Shi'ite legends, Imam Ali (the first Shi'ite Imam) and his martyred son, Imam
Husayn. Ali was murdered by Ibn Muljam, a dissenting member of his own
camp, a Khariji'ite, while praying in the Mosque of Kufa. Husayn and his
family were brutally slain by perfidious Shimr in an unequal war. The conditions
of their deaths and their stoic attitudes toward it add to the drama of their ordeal
and its historical impact.

Shi'ites like to contrast the death of 'Umar (one of the four Sunni rightly
guided Caliphs) with that of Ali. When 'Umar was struck by his assassin [Firuz,
the Persian], he cried, "Grab that Magian who has killed me!" Ali, when struck
by his assassin, cried "Oh God, most fortunate am I!" The contrast is between
one who saw death as an end and one who saw it as the beginning of a return
to God.[10] Ali is quoted as saying: "Martyrdom has been my long-held dream.
He who dies in the path of God does not die, but rather is immortalized. More
than that he reaches perfection [Kamal] and becomes united with God."[11]

When the renowned poet Al-Farazdaq encouraged Imam Husayn not to go to
Karbala and risk his life fighting against overwhelming odds, Imam Husayn
answered:

> If the world be counted a thing precious, still the abode of God's reward (that is,
> paradise) is higher and more noble. And if bodies be made for death, then the
> death of a man by the sword in the way of God is the better choice. And if men's
> provisions be allotted by divine decree, then it is more worthy of a man not to run
> after worldly gain. And if wealth be gathered in order to be finally left behind,
> why should a man be tight-fisted with that which he would have to abandon.[12]

Martyrdom in the struggle against social injustice and oppression is said to be
the noblest of all causes. A Muslim's sincerity and devotion to the faith are

measured by his/her readiness to sacrifice his/her life for it.[13] Here again Imam Husayn provides the paradigmatic example for the Shi'ites. When he was advised by some companions to seek a compromise with the unjust and the impious Yazid, he responded:

> I shall go, for there is no shame in the death of a youth if he intends truthfulness and engages in the struggle as a Muslim . . . for then if I live I shall have no remorse and if I die I shall incur no blame. It is sufficient humiliation for you to live and be coerced.[14]

The enduring impact of Imam Husayn's martyrdom on the Shi'ite psyche and his exaltation as the lord of martyrs deserves closer scrutiny.

The Primordial Impact of the "Lord of Martyrs," Imam Husayn

The tragic martyrdom of Imam Husayn and the drama associated with it have a special place in the consciousness of Shi'ite Muslims. The martyrdom of Imam Husayn is perceived as a cosmic event to restore truth against falsehood and justice against oppression and to heal and redeem the community. According to Hamid Enayat, the significance of Imam Husayn's martyrdom must be understood on two levels: "First, in terms of a soteriology not dissimilar from the one invoked in the case of Christ's crucifixion: just as Christ sacrificed himself on the altar of the cross to redeem humanity, so did Husayn allow himself to be killed on the plain of Karbala to purify the Muslim community of sin; and second as an active factor vindicating the Shi'ite cause, contributing to its ultimate triumph."[15] Therefore, as a paradigmatic example, Imam Husayn represented both solace and comfort for all suffering souls, and became a role model for political action and militancy. The commemoration of the anniversary of his death in the Plains of Karbala in the month of Muharram in 680 became an established ritual when the Shi'ite dynasty of the Buyids popularized the ceremonies in the tenth century. The occasion marks the outburst of intense pent-up grief, weeping, lamentation, and self-flagellation. The introduction of Ta'ziyyah (a passion play) by the Shi'ite Safavid dynasty in the sixteenth century, combined with Rawzah Khani (recitation of the sufferings of holy martyrs) throughout much of the past history, symbolized a "submissive endurance of pain and suffering as the hallmark of all worthy souls."[16]

As Max Weber has observed, human beings are motivated by both ideal and material interests. "The most elementary forms of behavior motivated by religious or magical factors," wrote Weber, "are oriented toward this world. Religious behavior remains end-oriented, except that both the means and the ends become purely symbolic."[17] Seen in this context, salvation for a Shi'ite may be attained through grief and identification with the suffering and tragic faith of Imam Husayn. Hence, identification with Husayn's ennobling and dignified act of self-sacrifice safeguards one against the pitfall of wretchedness and cowardice that awaits the individual in every trial in life. As Imam Husayn redeemed the sins of his community through his suffering and martyrdom, those who weep for him and share his suffering would be rewarded (*sawab*) on the judgment day and those who do not must await the "awful punishment of strict justice with no mercy."[18] Thus, Imam Husayn is simultaneously the compassionate redeemer and the resolute judge, the healer and the avenger. Until very recently, however, Shi'ite scholars and theologians emphasized the healing and redeeming aspects of Imam Husayn's martyrdom.

As Enayat accurately asserts, the "passive and pietistic" aspect of Imam Husayn's behavior reflected in the orthodox Shi'ite writings on Karbala drama belies much of the contemporary politicized rendition of the drama as a defiant act of rebellion. The popular reference to Imam Husayn as a *Mazlum* has two connotations. First, it characterizes an individual who has been oppressed or sinned against. Second, it signifies an unwillingness, derived from a sense of noble generosity and forbearance, to act against others. To demonstrate the depoliticized connotation and the quiescent character of Imam Husayn's martyrdom in Shi'ite traditional sources, Enayat reminds us that the ritual of Ta'ziyah was used by both the Safavid and Qajar dynasties to ensure their hold over the masses.[19] Yet, the image of *mazlum* in Shi'ite tradition [as a person who has been violated, while evoking strong emotional response] also signifies passive acceptance of one's faith. Enayat's account is reaffirmed by Mahmoud Ayoub, who asserts:

> After the death of Imam Husayn, both the Imams and their followers lived in fear and had to propagate their teachings in secret. It was no longer easy to express their opposition to Umayyad and later Abbasid rule through armed struggle. The only vehicle was the secret, yet active, participation in the sufferings of Ahl Al-bayt through weeping and other means of remembrance.[20]

According to Sheikhoeleslami, the commemoration of Imam Husayn's death has a functional value for the faithful: it allows the participants in the ritual to deal with the "real anxieties men have about death. By bringing Husayn back to life every year, they feel a sense of victory over death. Indeed, in the aftermath of these rituals, the participants express a sense of well-being."[21] The concept of *ma'ad* (resurrection) also functions as a divine assurance that "the community will survive individually and collectively."[22] Hence, by believing in the return of the twelfth Shi'ite Imam, who is said to be in occultation, the oppressed maintained their chialiastic hope that justice would prevail some day and that the Mahdi would be the great avenger to punish the oppressor. If, in the orthodox account, the Shi'ite martyr represented the house of the prophet, the contemporary interpretation extends the privilege to any Shi'ite Muslim willing to die for the Islamic cause.

Only after World War II has the drama of Imam Husayn's martyrdom come to signify "combative vengefulness and a deliberate act of rebellion."[23] Throughout Islamic history, reenacting of the drama of Imam Husayn's martyrdom through elaborate rituals has exalted suffering and asceticism as necessary steps in spiritual refinement. This enduring impact is patently clear in Iran's modern political culture as well.

This glorification of noble suffering and the defiant embracing of death, the deliberate and conscious approbation of martyrdom, has profoundly influenced the Shi'ite collective consciousness throughout history.

Dialectics of Self-effacement and Self-aggrandizement

Some Western scholars have interpreted Firdowsi's *Shahnameh* as a celebration of defeat.[24] Others perceive the annual commemoration of Husayn's death in Murharram and Ashura ceremonies as another celebration of defeat.[25] The prominent role of tragedy in the Iranian collective unconscious and the celebration of defeats through the elaborate ritual of self-flagellation and intense lamentation has prompted Enayat to conclude that with the pre-Islamic myth of the Blood of Siyavush, as recorded in Firdowsi's *Shahnameh*, the religious hymns of the Alawite Ahl-i haqq describe how the supreme spirit of the perfect man transmigrated from Abel, through Jamshid, Iraj, and Siyavush, to Husayn.[26]

These rituals demonstrate a clear line of continuity between the pre-Islamic Iranian tradition and Islamic culture. Whereas the legend of Siyavush ensures justice for the oppressed, the legend of Husayn inspires faith in political justice.[27] To provide further evidence for this continuity, some refer to the Iranian affinity with Husayn. After Imam Husayn's martyrdom in the plains of Karbala in 680, many Iranians led by Mokhtar Thaqafi rebelled against the Umayyads in an attempt to avenge Husayn's murder.[28]

The primordial significance of tragedy in the Iranian collective psyche was further accentuated by the repeated historical defeats at the hands of the Greeks, Arabs, Mongols, Turks, Afghans, and Russians, to name a few. A nation that lives through tragedies gives expression to life through tragedy. Thus, the occurrence of historical calamities combined with long history of tyrannical rule have ensured the continuity of a tradition and its transmission through generations. In the pre-Islamic stoic tradition and Islamic asceticism, one can, for example, clearly discern elements of Mani's ascetic philosophy and its impact on the later development of Sufism in Iran. The exaltation of the suffering of Imam Husayn and the inexorable self-effacement of Sufi traditions in Islam are also linked. Al-Ghazali (d. 1111), who had a pronounced impact on medieval Islamic and Jewish religious thought, held that only in a stage of total negation of this world (*fana*) and total surrender of the self can one dedicate all his heart, soul, and love to God and become capable of seeking reunion with him. In Al-Ghazali's philosophy, for example, poverty is regarded as a crucial virtue (*zohd*) for rescuing the soul and a pious Sufi dervish (priest) must pursue a life of self-denial and spiritual refinement. This can occur in three stages: the dervish conserves his meager resources and does not attempt to increase or expand them; he learns to downgrade wealth, since he has learned not to suffer from deprivation; he becomes indifferent to both wealth and poverty.[29] Seen in this light, Sufi dervishes, like Buddhist monks and Franciscan Christians, believe that spiritual fulfillment is possible only through the negation of worldly pleasures and material pursuits. Since God is pure and innocent (*pak va ma'sum*) and man must reappear before him on judgment day, one must try to maintain one's purity and innocence so that one is worthy of appearance before God. Hence, hardship and deprivation are regarded as a gift of God to strengthen the spiritual and moral convictions of mankind because worldly pursuits are worthless compared to the glory that awaits the pious in reunion with God.[30]

This influence is also patently clear in the gnostic philosophy of such thirteenth-century mystics as Mowlawi, known in the West as Rumi (1207-1273), who perceived death as a stage in life that opens the gates to a higher state of existence and spiritual enrichment. Death begins a process in which the soul elevates itself to a morally superior state. In death, the human spirit, which is a part of divine spirit, will reunite with its beloved. Therefore, death must not be equated with annihilation or nothingness; rather, it is another stage in life's progression towards the ultimate purpose, which is unity with the divine, *Vahdat al-vujud*.[31] The path to perfection (*kamal*) is possible only if one negates worldly pleasures. In other words, self-purification and redemption can be attained only through living an ascetic life. Seen in this context, death is a natural outcome of living a life of self-denial. It is not an abrupt end, but a new beginning of the journey (*m'araj*) towards unity with God. As Rumi has put it:

From the inanimate I died and I became vegetation,
From vegetation I died and I became an animal,
From an animal I died and I became human.

I am not afraid of death; death has never made me lesser.
Once more I shall die as a human being,
And I shall fly as an angel;
Then once again I shall fly from the angelic,
and I will become something unimaginable.
I will become nothing, nothing, because the harp tells me:
"Unto him we shall return."[32]

This philosophical outlook on death casts a different light on martyrdom as a deliberate embracement of death. Gnostic self-effacement seems to be the dominant motif here. When present life has very little to offer, the hereafter becomes much more appealing. Through martyrdom one puts an honorable end to deprivations, frustrations, and sufferings and creates the possibility for a better tomorrow in heaven. Hence, the prevalence of stoicism in Iranian culture is not due to masochistic tendencies such as "love of death," as some have suggested; rather, it is a symptom of powerlessness and hopelessness. As Clifford Geertz has persuasively noted:

> The problem of suffering is, paradoxically, not how to avoid suffering but how to suffer, how to make of physical pain, personal loss, worldly defeat, or the helpless contemplation of others' agony something bearable, supportable—something, as we say, sufferable.[33]

By developing rituals of noble suffering, one builds a defense mechanism to confront repression and withstand it psychologically. Since all cultures develop elaborate rituals to deal with the existing social reality, the cult of martyrdom in the Iranian culture reflects the pervading atmosphere of political and cultural repression throughout its history.

This long tradition of political repression has not only created self-effacing rituals to cope with repression, but also has engendered many rebellious acts of self-aggrandisement to defy it. We witness the continuation of this tradition in Zayd's martyrdom (d. 740) in an unsuccessful attempt to avenge Imam Husayn's death, in the martyrdom of Mansur al-Hallaj (858-922), the renowned Sufi rebel who never denied his claim of divine incarnation in the face of torture and death, and in the murder of the great philosopher Suhrawardi (d. 1191) for his Isma'ili sympathies.[34]

The Ismai'ilis, the extremist Shi'ites known as the Assassins, lent a new vitality to the tradition of martyrdom from the eleventh through the thirteenth centuries. They were motivated by religious zeal to purify Islam and liberate it from usurpation of power by what they conceived to be illegitimate and corrupt rulers who deviated from the path of true Islam. They sought to set examples of self-sacrifice and strengthen the sense of commitment of their supporters and proselytise new members. Since martyrs were believed to have a special place in paradise, one could gain eternal salvation through martyrdom. They distinguished themselves by a massive campaign of assassinations of the Sunni leaders. Their campaign was particularly effective against the Turkish Seljugh Empire. The Ismai'ilis' belief in terror as a means for moral purification and the regeneration of collective faith had deep roots in gnostic philosophy and mysticism. Their egalitarianism was buttressed by an ascetic lifestyle, and their campaign of terror was accompanied by millenarian and chiliastic expectations of the return of the Mahdi. It was commonly believed among their ranks that their martyrdom would enhance the return of the Mahdi, thus making redemption possible. In their social philosophy martyrdom was perceived as a noble act of honor that would culminate in the ultimate goal of life, unity with God.[35]

As the Shi'ite sects became a persecuted and embittered minority, the ceremonies of Ashura and commemoration of Husayn's martyrdom assumed new significance. The celebration of Ashura rituals of lamentation and self-flagellation increasingly became an outlet for the expression of the pervading oppression in their own lives. Identification with Imam Husayn and his tragic fate enabled the Shi'ites to withstand their own suffering. For example, Fadl Allah Astarabadi (d. 1424), the leader of the Hurufyya movement (one of the extremist Shi'ite sects of the fifteenth century), on receiving the news of his execution in Shirvan, asserted: "The Husayn of the age am I, and each worthless foe a shimr and yazid. My life is a day of mourning, and Shirwan my Karbala."[36] Seen in this light, the theodicy of suffering projects martyrdom as a path to salvation:

> He who remembereth me, loveth me, and he who loveth me passionately desireth me; and him who passionately desireth me I passionately desire; and whom I passionately desire I slay; and of him whom I slay, I am the Blood-wil.[37]

The Ashura rituals were also used throughout history as instruments of cultural assimilation and mass mobilization. As alluded to earlier, the rituals of Ashura were present in Iran as early as the tenth century under the Shi'ite Buiyd dynasty. Shah Isma'il (1501-1524), the Safavid king, effectively used the legend of Imam Husayn to incite his soldiers against the Ottoman Turks in the sixteenth century: "We are Husayn's men, and this is our epoch. In devotion we are the slaves of the Imam; our name is 'zealot' and our title 'martyr.'"[38]

The ritual of Ashura also has a functional value: to instill a deeper Shi'ite identity in Iranians and to strengthen the communal bonds of solidarity and cultural loyalty. As Bronislaw Malinowski has aptly noted:

> The ceremonial of death, which ties the survivors to the body and rivets them to the place of death, the beliefs in the existence of the spirit, in its beneficent influences or malevolent intentions, in the duties of a series of commemorative or sacrificial ceremonies—in all this religion counteracts the centrifugal forces of fear, dismay, demoralization and provides the most powerful means of integration of the group's shaken solidarity and of the re-establishment of its miracle.[39]

Hence, the fact that since 1694 only four Iranian monarchs survived either murder or forced abdication further indicates why no symbols and rituals of secular solidarity and secular nationalism binding the nation and the state developed. The lack of such symbols and rituals further explains the popularity of mass Shi'ite rituals and their resilience, appeal, and political vitality over the years.[40] Historically martyrs have been sacred symbols, comforting the sorrows and pains of the community. With the increasing politicization of Iranian polity after World War II, martyrdom assumed a new political cast, calling on the faithful to sacrifice themselves for the cause. A delineation of the salient features of the metamorphosis of Iranian political culture in this period reveals the broader social context in which this new and highly politicized interpretation unfolded.

The Preeminence of Populist Asceticism
in the Political Culture of Post-World War II

The Iranian political culture of the 1960s and 1970s, both religious and secular, experienced a profound populist metamorphosis, and Shi'ite asceticism assumed a new vitality and political dynamism. The autocratic absolutism of the Shah's regime reproduced itself in all societal institutions, thus driving political life underground and lending it a clandestine character. An ascetic populist culture among the committed members of the lay and secular intelligentsia developed in response to the dominant values of a society that espoused hedonism, consumerism, and materialism. Self-denial and an austere lifestyle, forbearance and self-sacrifice were among the constituent elements of this political culture.

This asceticism was present in the political thought of some of the leading Muslim traditionalist and modernist activists of this period. Navab Safavi, the founder of Fadayeen-i Islam, a Muslim traditionalsit organization that assassinated a number of intellectuals and politicians, preached asceticism and martyrdom to his followers. The lay intellectual Mehdi Bazargan, for example, sought the solution to Iran's economic dependence and backwardness in forbearance and stoicism. He asserted, "In order to free ourselves from Western domination, we must become self-sufficient. To become economically self-sufficient, we must accept deprivation and an austere life."[41] Hence, according to Shariati, "the world belongs to the one who has no house in this world and the wealth belongs to the one who has no wealth in this world."[42] Shariati also perceived "revolutionary self-making as a process that involves a revolutionary metamorphosis, a spiritual elevation. This is possible only through active engagement in improving the lives of the impoverished masses."[43] To arouse his audience, he drew upon the example of Imam Ali: "Ali was so full of love and compassion for his fellow men and women that when he would hear of the news of oppression or injustice done to those whose rights he could not defend, he would become outraged and would not sit still until he punished the oppressor."[44] The readiness of Ali and Husayn, the two paradigmatic figures of authority in Shi'ite Islam, to accept and even glorify death has a direct impact on the Shi'ite attitude toward death in general and martyrdom in particular. Ali, for example, is cited as having said, "I swear to God the son of Abi Taleb [Ali] is more attuned to death than a child is to his mother's breast."[45] The allusions to Ali as the avenger of the oppressed were intended to have reverberations for the intelligentsia. As Shariati observed, the intellectuals are susceptible to becoming lost in their subjectivity. Only by linking themselves to the masses, laboring with them, living like them, and experiencing their misery and deprivations can they fulfill their revolutionary responsibility.[46]

The secular intelligentsia also shared this populist assessment of the role of intellectuals and artists in society. Iran's leading post-World War II "committed" literary figures, from Nima Yushi'ij to Shamlu and Sa'edi, sensitively wrote about the pain and suffering of the impoverished masses. Ahmad Shamlu eloquently captures this spirit:

I write
for the prostitutes and the bare,
for the tubercular,
the destitute,
for those who, on the cold earth are hopeful
and for those who believe no more in heaven.
Let my blood spill and fill the gaps among the people.
Let our blood spill
and graft the suns
to the sleepy people.[47]

But even when "sleepy people" do not wake up and hear or comprehend his message, when the engaged artist realizes his loneliness, that he has "shouted in a vacuum," he concedes:

I am twice condemned to torture:
to live so
and to live so
among you
with you
whom I have loved for so long.[48]

In the Islamic gnostic philosophy of love, the individual, drawing upon his/her powers of reason and love, transcends a personal quest for spiritual self-fulfillment and reaches a state of love for all.[49] Seen in this light, not only is love of "the people" deeply rooted in gnostic philosophy, but martyrdom as a noble act of self-sacrifice in the path of ideals of the collectivity also finds its roots in the Islamic concept of gnostic love.

For Khosrow Golsorkhi, the secular populist writer of the 1960s and 1970s, and a martyr himself (d. 1973), the artist must bear pain, suffering, and torture because his goal is an exalted one. "The artist," writes Golsorkhi, "is a fighter who does not have modern technological tools at his disposal. He struggles with primitive means. But this struggle is in the realm of human values and ideals. Therefore, it is a sublime resurrection for an exalted cause."[50] Armed by their ideas, the populist intelligentsia drew strength and power from their political faith, faith in "the people."[51]

Like the Gnostics, the populist intelligentsia sought to liberate the "self" from the hollow material attachment of a corrupt world. While for the religious intelligentsia salvation could be attained by cleansing the self of the sinful dross of a profane world, the challenge for the secular populists was to overcome their "petit bourgeois" values. Only through such a transformation could one become a conscious and dedicated revolutionary capable of leading the liberation of the masses. Filled with "the love of the people," the populists went to the people to experience their pain and suffering, hoping to become one with them. The religious populists held that since to serve God was to serve his vice regent on earth, the people, then the path to God was made possible by love of "the people." For the secular populists, dissolution of the self in the masses was a necessary step to learn from them, to gain their trust, and to liberate them; only then could one fulfill his/her historical mission. Therefore, in sharing the suffering of the masses, both populists demonstrated their sincerity and the seriousness of their political commitment.[52]

The populists extolled as epic-making heroes those who had the physical and psychological capacity to withstand barbaric tortures; those victims who failed in this task were considered as the "treacherous betrayers of the people's cause." Many political prisoners, for example, used to refuse food and clothing that their parents brought them. The more a political prisoner refused to be comforted and suffered under torture without recanting or revealing organizational secrets, the more he/she was revered.

While their modern education rendered many of them suspicious of absolutes, in the face of the fragmentation and alienation of modern life, the intelligentsia still yearned for a unifying vision, for a monolithic ideology that would resolve the dilemma of moral choice and explain the problems of modern society. Heir to a glorious past that no longer existed and inspired by a future that could be realized only through the negation of perceived cultural malaise and moral degeneration of the present, the intelligentsia lived in a vacuum. To gather the fragmented pieces of its suspended existence in a repressive and increasingly bureaucratic society, the intelligentsia were in dire need of a cohesive holistic idea that would explain the cosmos and provide an orientation towards the here and beyond. If one could not realize this unifying vision in life, then through martyrdom such unity would become eternal. The pervading sense of spiritual hunger and the thirst for faith in a profane society was so intense among the alienated intelligentsia that self-sacrifice in the name of an ideal or ideology seemed like a small price for such exalted stature. In this context the holistic interpretations of Marxism and Islam, and their depiction of the descending utopia as a unitarian classless society in which oppression has ended and justice and virtue reign supreme, became intensely appealing to the committed intelligentsia.

Inspired by belief in progress and the creation of a new moral order, the populist intelligentsia began a crusade inspired by the suffering of the downtrodden, whose "noble virtues" were extolled as the force of social regeneration. Caught amidst a corrupt society, the populists elevated a romanticized image of the toiling people as the source of purity and virtue. In the suffering and misery of the poor, the populists found a sense of spiritual superiority and moral dignity that was lacking among the nobility. Objectively, the life of poverty, deprivation, and ignorance had dehumanized the poor, subjectively, their suffering had humanized them. In order to make them fully human, the populists aspired for a social revolution that would destroy the old order.

Perceiving history as a process of development guided by universal laws, the intelligentsia gave this Newtonian scientific theory a divine twist. If history is a continuous march of progress and development in which human beings can play a role, then to understand the logic of historical necessity is of paramount significance to the individual and his/her place in the chain of historical events. Since freedom is the realization of historical necessity, then to become aware of the unconscious process of historical development and to act accordingly is the most significant challenge to conscious and free men and women. Only then could the individual find his/her unique place in life and perform his/her unique mission. This nineteenth-century sense of mission, an idea attributed to the heroic age of European romanticism, became exceedingly appealing to the Iranian intelligentsia in the post-World War II era. The conviction became popular that the ineffable felicity of the future is possible only through the massive self-sacrifice of the present. This political eschatology portrayed martyrdom as a small necessary step on the path to the realization of the grand ideal of liberating humanity. Since the autocracy was deemed the embodiment of inequality and oppression, it was intrinsically evil and had to be destroyed. Intensely suspicious of any reforms initiated from above, the intelligentsia scorned gradualist and reformist tactics as either manifestations of a naive liberalism or a deliberate treacherous betrayal and deception of the masses. Only a full-fledged social revolution could provide a viable remedy to the misery and wretchedness of the masses. In realizing this goal, the populist intelligentsia lived a self-effacing life marked by a strict discipline, unswerving faith in the irrevolutionary ideal and an enormous capacity for self-sacrifice. Their faith in scientific progress and revolutionary change became the basis of their new political religion. In fulfilling their responsibilities towards the impoverished masses, in paying back their debt, these individuals totally sacrificed their personal lives and careers to their political cause.

Driven by a sense of moral revulsion against autocracy and their passion for social justice, the populist intelligentsia sought to regenerate the society morally and to create a new social order. Considering themselves the awakened conscience of their society and an instrument of liberation for the impoverished masses, they sought to avenge their suffering. They perceived of their own organizations embodying their sacred goals as the historical vehicles of social transformation and salvation. Inspired by their own sense of dignity and moral obligation, the committed populist intelligentsia believed that all human beings deserve to live a dignified life free of oppression, tyranny, and exploitation. Only such a sense of personal integrity could drive individuals to romantic embracement of their own deaths.

In the absence of free political parties and other channels of political participation, many individuals took the gigantic task of social transformation upon themselves. Convinced and elevated by their political faith, they perceived themselves as new apostles of change whose self-negation would give life to the mass movement. It was in this context that politicization and exaltation of martyrdom permeated the political atmosphere of the past four decades. During their trial by the Shah's regime, two political prisoners, one a Muslim and the other a Marxist, reveal the essence of this mindset: "The only thing we do not expect from you is justice. Between us stand only weapons. Therefore, we will bring you to justice with our most effective weapon, our blood."[53] The other prisoner also expressed his willingness to sacrifice himself for the cause in these words: "If it takes blood to awaken the people, let rivers flow from our veins."[54] Both prisoners were executed after their trials.

As individualists who sought self-aggrandizement, the power of faith enabled them to elevate themselves above the prohibitive material social obstacles that stood in the path of realizing their ideal. As Emile Durkheim has perceptively observed:

> The believer who has communicated with his God is not merely a man who sees new truths of which the unbeliever is ignorant; he is a man who is stronger. He feels within him more force, either to endure the trials of existence, or to conquer them. It is as though he were raised above the miseries of the world, because he is raised above his condition as a mere man. . . .[55]

Driven by their passionate embracement of their political faith, many dedicated revolutionaries conquered the fear of death and thus became imbued with a sense of invincibility. Their own death was no longer considered annihilation, rather a transhistorical migration to an elevated state of spiritual existence (*Me'araj*). A further analysis of the vicissitudes of this culture of martyrdom in the contemporary political culture of Iran reveals a remarkable continuity in the resiliency, sanctity and vitality of this time-honored sublime tradition.

Martyrdom in Contemporary Iranian Political Culture

Through the further study of the political writings of Muslim and secular intellectual leaders, it becomes patently clear that the concept of martyrdom has undergone a complete metamorphosis since World War II. For example, using Qura'nic traditions Ayatollah Taleqani (1911-1979), coleader of the 1979 Islamic revolution and one of the most revered clerics after World War II, deduced the word *shahid*, the martyr, from *shuhud*, the person who has witnessed the truth. Therefore, the martyr sacrifices his life with full consciousness. He "annihilates himself, like a drop in the ocean of truth."[56] By doing so he elevates himself above this lowly world and strengthens the faith. Ayatollah Mutahhari (1920-1979), one of the chief theoreticians of the Islamic Republic, defined *shahid* as the individual who sacrifices himself/herself consciously for a cause. The blood of the martyr is not wasted; it "infuses fresh blood into the veins of the society." He revitalizes his sense of zeal and commitment and immortalizes himself through exemplary self-sacrifice.[57] Repeated references are made to the two grand Shi'ite martyrs, Ali and Husayn, to legitimize this new interpretation. By linking the concepts of *jihad* (holy war) and martyrdom, Mutahhari opened up the possibility of systematic martyrdom that pervaded Iran during the war with Iraq.[58] He asserted, "The sacred cause that leads to *shahadat* or the giving of one's life has become a law in Islam. It is called *jihad*."[59] In the same vein, Ayatollah Khomeini (1902-1989) asserted that the martyr is "the heart of history and the blood of each martyr is like a bell which awakens the thousands."[60] Through martyrdom, a society strengthens its ties and revives itself spiritually. In this sense, martyrs are the conscience and the heroes of the community.

Perhaps the most politicized and systematic exposition of martyrdom was made by Ali Shari'ati (1933-1977), the intellectual precursor of the 1979 revolution and the hero of Muslim youth. For Shariati, one of the greatest and most revolutionary contributions of Islam to human society has been to instill a sense of devotion and sacrifice in the pursuit of justice.[61] Through martyrdom a society refines itself. By sacrificing the most precious possession (i.e., one's life), the individual also affirms his/her faith in the ideals of the collectivity and adds to the credibility and sanctity of this ideal. Shariati utilized the deep tradition of martyrdom in the Iranian culture to elevate the level of commitment and generate the spirit of militancy and self-sacrifice necessary in any successful political struggle. As he put it:

> In different ages, when the followers of a faith or idea seize power, they struggle to safeguard their rule. When events render them feeble and deprive them of all means of struggle, through martyrdom, they preserve life, movement, faith and power in their history. Martyrdom, in one word, is not an incident, it is an involvement. It is an imposed death on a hero, it is a tragedy, and in our culture it is life, it is a medal of honor. It is not a means, it is an end. It is genuine and elevating. It is a bridge to new heights. It is a great responsibility, it is a short-cut to elevate oneself above mankind. And it is a culture.[62]

Seen in this light, martyrdom is not a means, but a sacred end; it is the most dramatic statement about the power of faith. It is a defiant gesture renouncing the present order. It is self-actualization through negation. More than that, it is an act of self-aggrandizement that enables individuals to transcend time and be placed on the highest summit of history.

The "self-imposed death of a hero" is a dominant motif in some of the secular politicized literature of this period as well. In Samad Behrangi's (1939-1968) *Little Black Fish*, for example, a determined little fish defies the advice of a large school of older fish and other sea creatures and against extreme odds chooses to confront the mighty enemy, the fish eater, single-handedly. The little black fish is well aware of all the dangers on the path. It is also fully conscious of the possibility of death. But it willingly accepts the risks as a historical necessity for the emancipation of the collectivity.[63] The immense popularity of this story reflects the tragic aura and the romantic image surrounding the faith of the hero. The community accepts the loss of one of its most beloved members, the one who is the most devoted to the ideals of the collectivity, not only to safeguard its *raison d'etre* but also to elevate itself morally and spiritually. The story reenacts the ritual of the sacrificial lamb and this symbolic value is represented in Shi'ite Islam in human terms. If the blood cleanses the community of its sins and the meat provides food and nourishment, the martyr satisfies the collective spiritual hunger and enriches communal power and strength. Seen in this light, the community devours a part of itself to maintain its sanctity and pride, a concept clearly reminiscent of Durkheimian "altruistic suicide."

The burning desire for unity with the beloved, i.e. God, necessitates gnostic forbearance and noble suffering (*Sukhtan va Sakhtan*). Like candles that illuminate only by burning, martyrs bestow meaning on life through their self-sacrifice. The sanctity of tradition in Iranian culture has ensured historical continuity. Mowlawi's desire for unity with God, for example, is echoed in the works of Iran's finest poet of the 1960s, Forough Farokhzad (1935-1967), who longed to "sink in earth," to "plant" and immortalize herself.[64] Imam-i-Ali's concept of the martyr as an immortal omnipotent saint is replicated by martyred journalist/poet of the 1970s, Khosrow Golsorkhi's, depiction of the fallen hero of the community:

Your body is like the mountain of Damavand
Standing proud in infinite skies
The dagger of the enemy can never stab you in the back
Your body is all eyes
Your body is an ever growing forest standing tall
Hell fire can do you no harm.[65]

According to the literary critic, Reza Baraheni, the idea of martyrdom is one of the central motifs in the writings of Jalal Al-e Ahmad (1923-1969), Iran's renowned writer of the 1960s. Jalal "always spoke of martyrdom. He expected to become a martyr, but he didn't. I feel he wanted to be a living witness to martyrdom. And those who are put in the position of martyrdom possess charisma."[66] Likewise, another social critic, Leonardo Alishan, contends that after 1963 Ahmad Shamlu (b. 1925), one of the leading Iranian poets, "spoke of poets as prophets" and of both as martyrs.[67] Both critics hold that since intellectuals are the victims of political tyranny and the "philistine people" in much of the Third World, they identify with martyrs. After the emergence of guerrilla organizations that fought against autocracy in the 1970s, Shamlu, for example, wrote several poems glorifying those who "stand before the thunder" and "light the house" before "they die."[68]

Thus, in the secular culture, the religious metaphors reappear in a different cloak. The secular vision of the world does not preclude spiritual needs; to the contrary, it exacerbates them. To the extent that the individual loses his/her religious conviction as a cognitive moral map of the world, to borrow a phrase from Geertz, the feelings of emptiness instigate an even more intense soul searching. Hence, the preoccupation of the secular intelligentsia with making a career or pursuing art and literature is precisely geared to fill such a spiritual void. To compensate for the feelings of guilt that stem from one's encounter with an amoral world, the intelligentsia never overcame the psychological need for transcendence and deliverance.

As Weber has aptly noted, the abnegation of the world is facilitated for the faithful by taking refuge in the redemptive value of religion. "The rational aim of redemption religion," wrote Weber, "has been to secure for the saved a holy state, and thereby a habitat that assures salvation."[69] Through martyrdom, one purifies the self from past sins and becomes an immortal saint. Thus, death sanctioned through the sublime collective traditions of the community becomes a means to celebrate life and to strengthen and consolidate communal bonds.

Some Muslim opposition groups under the Shah, such as Mojahedin-iKhalq, considered Imam Husayn's martyrdom a focal point in human liberation and freedom. The example of Imam Husayn, in other words, is a transhistorical paradigm that shows the way to future generations.[70] The Mojahedin argued that human beings distinguish themselves from animals and become united with God only through self-sacrifice. Having accepted the necessity for "suffering and endurance," many members of these organizations died under torture without revealing organizational secrets.[71]

In the spirit of the myth of the blood of Siyavush, upon receiving the news of their execution, some of the guerrillas sang the song "from our blood carnations will grow," and they awaited their death with a hysteric sense of joy and jubilation. Others saw their death as a necessary drop in a flood that would ultimately cleanse the dross and "moral filth" by washing away the regime that promulgates it. The words of Reza Reza'i, one of the three brothers from the Mojaheedin-iKhalq organization who were executed by the Shah's regime, reveal the essence of this mindset. In a letter to his mother he wrote: "The blood of my brothers showed us the way. Like them I would also be most willing to sacrifice my life in the path of the oppressed people."[72] To provide an Islamic justification for their populist program, Mojahedin often utilized the euphemism coined by Shariati: to serve God one must serve His creatures, i.e. the people.

Driven by a sacred rage against the present order, the revolutionary guerrillas called for a moral revival of society. Thus, they saw their own death as a necessary sacrifice toward the sacred end, the descending utopia. Socialized through Shi'ism, they were heirs to the rich gnostic philosophical tradition of the past. As they became politicized, the dominant influences of self-effacement present in early childhood evolved into conscious emotive feelings of self-aggrandizement. It is methodologically wrong, however, to erect a wall mechanically separating the two concepts. They are interchangeably linked, and each evolves from the other and carries the germs of its antithesis.

The secular political groups also used martyrdom as an effective theme to instill a sense of self-sacrifice and devotion in their followers and the general public. While religious groups repeatedly referred to Imam Ali and Husayn as the source of inspiration, for the secular opposition, "people and their suffering" justified revolutionary struggle and self-sacrifice. The words of Shokralah Paknezhad (d. 1981), the leader of an organization known as "Palestine Group," captures the spirit of martyrdom among secular opposition:

> There are human beings who consciously rise for the people's cause in decisive historical moments. Standing at the crossroads of life and death, they willingly walk toward death, a death that is a testimony to the eternal living legends of the toiling masses and is a source of inspiration for other struggles yet to come.[73]

In the same vein, Karamat Allah Daneshiyan (a colleague of Khosrow Golsorkhi, who was executed with him in 1973), perceived martyrdom as a necessary sacrifice for the moral regeneration of society:

> The oppressed people of Iran have lost many of their heroic children in the path of struggle. This is a necessity dictated by the very nature of the struggle and the movement itself. Sacrifices, martyrdom and resistance will break the back of the enemy. It is absurd and naive to think that the children of the masses will constantly die and vanish in the process of revolutionary resurgence. Such an illusion can be entertained only by the enemies of the people. The movement will grow and become popular. The workers, the peasants and the oppressed will begin a new and a happy life. Martyrdom is the least precious gift we can offer for the victory of the masses. Each martyr's death is a window closed to evil. Each martyr's death is a window closed to lies, prostitution, poverty and hunger. And then a new window will open up, a window through which the light of life will shine. We must surrender to the glimmer of this light.[74]

This depiction of the martyr as the vanguard of the masses, who through his/her self-sacrifice will awaken them to the necessity of political struggle, was already evident in the writings of some of the leaders of the Marxist Fedayeian-i Khalq organization.[75] With the publication of Parviz Poyan and Mas'ud Ahmad Zadeh's theoretical treatise in defense of armed struggle, many guerrillas now saw themselves as a "spark" rekindling a wild fire that would burn the old system to ashes. They considered their own martyrdom a necessary step in the political awakening and historical march of the masses toward their ultimate and inevitable victory. Seized by a messianic sense of mission, they saw themselves as cadres of history, as the vanguard of humanity whose self-sacrifice would determine the course of the future.

Having witnessed the political apathy of the masses, political activists substituted their own willpower, determination and devotion for the societal antipathy toward politics. Seen in this light, the concept of rebirth present in the myth of the martyrdom of Siyavush appears in a new form. By negating self one gives life to the movement. The movement immortalizes the individual by preserving his/her ideals. The words of Bijan Jazani (d. 1975), one of the foremost leaders of Fedayeian and a martyr, reveals the essence of this mindset:

> The vanguard cannot mobilize the masses for revolution unless it takes the initiative in resistance and self-sacrifice. What inflames the cold steel of the masses is the burning glimmer of the vanguard. It is the self-sacrifice of the vanguard that ultimately engulfs the masses. This self-sacrifice and heroism are a direct outgrowth of the pain and suffering of the masses. It is the anger and hatred of the masses that burns through the vanguard. The revolutionary spirit of the vanguard is inspired by the material interest of the masses. Thus, it ultimately explodes their energy and potential.[76]

Politically speaking, in a society such as Iran in which severe mistrust pervades all aspects of social relationships, martyrdom has a utilitarian value as well. It is not so much the political program of an organization or a group that attracts the public; rather, it is the sincerity of its advocates. Their willingness to sacrifice themselves for the cause becomes the focal point of attention. Given the high rate of illiteracy and the popularity of traditional values among the laity, the determining political factor in the number of supporters is not so much dependent on novel or profound political ideas as it is on the number of martyrs. Since political sincerity is measured by the degree of self-sacrifice, martyrs become political capital, an asset for legitimacy and credibility. No organization can grow substantially without any primitive accumulation of martyrs. Therefore, it is not accidental that all political groups that enjoyed any measure of popular support throughout the 1960s and 1970s were organizations that not only had a history of political struggle but also shared "the honor of martyrdom," proudly displaying the long list of their fallen comrades.

Throughout the revolution of 1979, the clergy, as custodians of the Shi'ite faith, used the tradition of martyrdom to mobilize millions against the Shah's regime. As some of the demonstrators were shot by the security forces, the clergy effectively employed the tradition of commemorating the deceased on the seventh and the fortieth days after their death to mobilize even larger numbers of people. Thus, as the number of martyrs grew, so did the number of anti-Shah demonstrators.[77] Since its ascendance, the Islamic Republic has used the postrevolutionary systematic martyrdom that occurred during its eight-year war with Iraq to maintain a permanent state of mass mobilization and to ward off criticism by presenting itself as "the guardian of the honor and blood of martyrs."

If prior to the revolution martyrs were to be rewarded in the hereafter, after the revolution there were worldly inducements for martyrdom as well. A "Foundation of Martyrs" was established. The families of the martyrs were given preferential treatment in receiving coupons for food subsidies, entrance to universities and job placement in governmental bureaucracies. Large numbers of urban poor, peasantry, and lower-middle classes volunteered for the war with Iraq, thinking that if they died, heaven awaited them and financial security and

honor awaited the family members they had left behind. This worldly induce-
ment so prevalent during the war years that the statement below represents a
typical attempt on the part of governmental officials to maintain the religious
sanctity that was historically associated with the aura of martyrs and martyrdom:

> He drank the sweet syrup of martyrdom, but left a heavy burden on our shoulders
> to safeguard his pure blood and forbid those who may use his innocent blood as a
> bridge to reach a position or get ahead.[78]

While rituals, rites and symbols have social functions, once practiced, they
develop a dynamism and a life of their own which binds the continued existence
of the community to the vitality of traditions. Commenting on the political
significance of the rituals of Ashura in Iran, Sheikholeslami asserts:

> The commemoration of the deceased emphasizes the historical continuity of the
> community, and the social sentiment which the ritual arouses is more than
> sufficient to compensate for the death, i.e. the breach of solidarity. All these
> mourning rituals are associated with commensality which brings the community
> together, and the partaking of the food in particular brings life, contrasted with
> death, into a clearer focus.[79]

Only in this dialectical juxtaposition of life and death can we fully grasp the
meaning of martyrdom, not as annihilation but as a conscious act celebrating
life. In the final analysis only something as profound and complex as life itself
can explain the voluntary and romantic embracement of death. In the deliberate
act of self-sacrifice one makes the most powerful statement about life and its
meaning. With the sense of Socratic calm as they face their death, the martyrs
echoed a popular poem of the time: "the bird shall die, but flying is eternal."
The martyr may die, but martyrdom is eternal.

Conclusion

"Of all sources of religion," wrote Malinowski, "the supreme and final crisis
of life—death—is of the greatest importance."[80] Death threatens the very
foundations of human existence. The dual response of fear and awe evoked by
death, creates emotionally ambivalent feelings of a will to survive—a further
attachment to life—and an affection toward the deceased that engenders a
compulsion to be united with him. This powerful motif in the human geist,
touching the very heart and soul of the community, has been effectively used for
political purposes throughout Iranian history. Martyrdom not only has been used
to sanction certain political ends, but also maintain communal solidarity and
loyalty. Historically, the integrative power of such symbols has been significant
in inculcating a sense of identity and culturally assimilating and politically
mobilizing the populace. The remarkable resonance of this tradition in secular
political culture is indicative of the vitality of religious symbols in post-

traditional societies and also partially explains the defensive nature of secular ideologies in the Middle East in the post-colonial era. This analysis also suggests why the secular opposition failed so badly in the Iranian Revolution of 1979.

Notes

1. See W. H. C. Frend, *Martyrdom and Persecution in the Early Church* (New York: New York University Press, 1967), 22.

2. Frend, *Martyrdom*, 58.

3. Frend, *Martyrdom*, 61.

4. See Naseh Nateq, *Bahsi Dar Bareh-e Zendegani Mani Va Paym-e Ou* [A Discussion of Mani's Life and Message] (Teheran: Kavian Publisher, 1978), 49-85. Although Manichaenism never became all-pervasive throughout Iran, its intellectual impact was distinct and powerful.

5. Firdowisi, *The Epic of the Kings: Shah-nameh the National Epic of Persia*, ed. Ehsan Yarshater, trans. Reuben Levy (Chicago: The University of Chicago Press, 1967). Rostam was killed in 637 after his armies were defeated by 'Umar's forces in the battle of Qadasyyia.

6. Shahrukh Miskub, *Sug-i Siyavush: Dar Marg va Rastakhiz* (Mourning for Siyavush: on death and resurrection) (Teheran: Kharazmi Publishing House, 1975). The death of Siyavush inspired a cult of mourning that lasted until the tenth century. A significant myth associated with this cult depicts Siyavush as a divine martyred saint whose death generates new life. According to legend, from Siyavush's blood grew a herb called "the blood of Siyavush." Thus, the death of Siyavush is followed by a rebirth and the martyred hero becomes immortal.

7. Ehsan Yarshter, "Ta'ziyeh and Pre-Islamic Mourning Rites in Iran," in *T'ziyeh Ritual and Drama in Iran*, Peter Chelkowski, ed. (New York: New York University Press and Soroud Press, 1979), 89-90.

8. Michael C. Hillman, *Iranian Culture: A Persianist View* (Lanham and London: University Press of America, 1990) 14, 15.

9. Hillman, *Iranian Culture*, 15.

10. Michael Fischer, *Iran, From Religious Dispute to Revolution* (Cambridge, MA: Harvard University Press, 1980), 16.

11. Muhammad Ray Shahri, *Shahadat Dar Nahj Albalaqeh* [Martyrdom in the Nahj Albalaqeh] (Qum: Yaser Publishers, n.d.), 9, 41, 50.

12. Mahmoud Ayoub, *Redemption Suffering in Islam: A Study of Devotional Aspects of Ashura in Twelver Shi'ism* (New York: Mouton Publishers, 1978), 242.

13. The legacy of this asceticism and the virtue of noble suffering goes back to Prophet Muhammad. The prophet was told, "The Lord wishes to try thee with three things to test thy patience. The first was hunger and privation, as he was to give all that he possessed to the poor. The second trial was the persecution and calumnies which Muhammad had to suffer at the hands of the hypocrites and the wounds inflicted upon him. The third trial was the persecution and wrong his family was destined to suffer after him." The Imams, the descendants of the prophet, "were from the beginning destined by God to drain the cup of suffering and martyrdom and to play a decisive role in human salvation and judgement. To a large extent, the intercessory prerogative of the Imams is dependent upon their patient endurance of privation, rejection and persecution. Indeed, Shi'i piety

has insisted, in many cases with little or no evidence, that all the Imams were martyred." In Shi'ite devotional piety "the house of sorrow" represents "the community of suffering,which is basically the twelve Imams, the prophet and his daughter. Into this community, the pious devotees of the Imams can enter through their participation in the suffering of the Holy Family." See Ayoub, *Redemption Suffering*, 16, 198-199.

14. Ayoub, *Redemption Suffering*, 108.

15. Hamid Enayat, *Modern Islamic Political Thought* (Austin: The University of Texas Press, 1982), 183.

16. Enayat, *Modern Islamic Political Thought*.

17. Max Weber, *The Sociology of Religion* (Boston: Beacon Press, 1963), 6-7.

18. Ayoub, *Redemption Suffering*, 232.

19. Enayat, *Modern Islamic Political Thought*, 183-184.

20. Ayoub, *Redemption Suffering*, 143.

21. Ali Reza Sheikholeslami, "From Religious Accommodation to Religious Revolution: the Transformation of Shi'ism in Iran," in *The State, Religion and Ethnic Politics: Afghanistan, Iran and Pakistan*, Ali Banuazizi and Myron Weiner, eds. (Syracuse: Syracuse University Press, 1986), 229.

22. *The State, Religion and Ethnic Politics*, 229.

23. This new interpretation became popular not only among Shi'ites in Iran, but also Muslim and secular intellectuals in Egypt and other parts of the Sunni world depicted Imam Husayn as a heroic rebel who fought consciously against oppression to set an example for the posterity. See Enayat, *Modern Islamic Political Thought*, 184-188.

24. See, for example, G. E. Von Grunebaum, "Ferdausi's Concept of History," in *Islam, Essays in the Nature and Growth of a Cultural Tradition* (New York: Barnes & Noble, 1961), 168-184. See also Michael Hillman, *Iranian Culture*, 14, 15.

25. Edward Mortimer, *Faith and Power* (New York: Vintage Books, 1982), 31-120.

26. Enayat, *Modern Islamic Political Thought*, 181.

27. *Modern Islamic Political Thought*, 181.

28. Abdol Rafie's Haqiqat, *Tarikh-i Nehzat hay-i Fekr-i Iranian* [The History of Iranian Intellectual Thought] (Teheran: Mo'alefan Publishers, 1976), 116-117.

29. I. P. Petroshevsky, *Islam dar Iran* [Islam in Iran] (Tehran: Payam Publication House, 1971), 352-355.

30. *Islam dar Iran*, 370-371, 398.

31. Ali Asghar Halabi, *Shinakht-i Irfan va Arifan-i Irani* [The Study of Persian Gnosis and Gnostic Philosophers] (Teheran: Zavar Publication, 1981). For a discussion of Rumi's philosophy and poetry, see *Ghozideh-i ghazaliat-i shams* (A selection of Poetry of Mowlana Jalal-al Din Mohammad of Balkh] (Tehran: Sherkati-i Sahami-ye Ketabhay-i Jibi, 1984). See also *Te Ruins of the Heart: Selected Lyrics of Poetry of Jelaludin Rumi*, trans. Edmund Helminski (Threshold Book, 1981). Other philosophers, such as Ummar Khayyam, are considered by some to be the intellectual precursors of modern exitentialism, whose social philosophy consists of rebellion against the absurdity of death and fatalism.

32. *Mathnawi* (vol. 111.111.3901-07) as cited by Mehdi Abedi and Gary Legenhausen, *Jihad and Shahadat: Struggle and Martrydom in Islam* (Houston: The Institute for Research and Islamic Studies, 1986), 67-68.

33. Clifford Geertz, *The Interpretation of Cultures* (New York: Basic Books, 1973), 104.

34. Martyrdom has also been used by numerous Shi'ite sects throughout history to proselyte and to seize political power. For a comprehensive study of use of individual terrorism in Islam, see David C. Rapaport, "Fear and Trembling: Terrorism in Three Religious Traditions," in the *American Political Science Review*, 78, no. 3 (1984): 658-677, especially 664-668.

35. Bernard Lewis, *Origins of Ismai'ils* (Cambridge: Cambridge University Press, 1940), and *The Assassins: A Radical Sect in Islam* (London: Nicholson and Weidenfeld, 1967).

36. E. G. Brown, "Future Notes on the Literature of the Hurufis and Their Connection with the Bektashi Order of Dervishes," as cited by S. A. Arjomand in *The Shadow of God and the Hidden Imam* (Chicago: The University of Chicago Press, 1984), 73.

37. Arjomand, *The Shadow of God*, 73.

38. Roy Mottaheden, *The Mantle of the Prophet* (New York: Simon and Schuster, 1985), 173. The annual observance of Husayn's martyrdom engendered a drama and a theatrical passion play known as *Ta'Ziyeh*. While having deep roots in pre-Islamic Iranian tradition, it was systematically developed only in the sixteenth century during the Safavid rule.

39. Bronislaw Malinowski, *Magic, Science and Religion* (Boston: Beacon Press, 1948), 33-35.

40. Sheikholeslami, "From Religious Accommodation," 230.

41. Mehdi Bazargan, *Sirr-i aghab oftadegy-i Mellal-i Muslman* [The Secret Behind the Backwardness of Muslim Nations] (Houston: Center for Book Distribution, 1977), 51.

42. Ali Shariati, *Abuzar* (Abudhar), Collected Works, vol. 3 (n.d., n.p.), 105.

43. Ali Shariati, *Khod sazi'i inghilabi* [Revolution Self-making] (Tehran: Hossienieh Ershad, 1977), vol. 2, 133.

44. *Khod sazi'i*, 89.

45. See, for example, *Negahi Be Ali* [A Look at Ali], by Mohammada Taqi Ja'fari (Tehran: Jahan Ara Publishers, n.d.), 115.

46. *Negahi Be Ali*, 163-177.

47. Leonardo Alishan, "Ahmah Shmlu: a Rebel Poet in Search of an Audience," *Iranian Studies*, 18, nos. 2-5 (Spring-Autumn, 1985): 380.

48. "Ahmad Shmlu," 385.

49. Aligholi Biani, *Manteq-i Ishq-i Irfani* [The Logic of Gnostic Love] (Tehran: Inteshar Publishing Company, 1985), 162.

50. *Ferdowsi*, Monday, December 5, 1978, 26.

51. For a study of Iranian populism see Manochehr Dorraj, *From Zarathustra to Khomeini: Populism and Dissent in Iran* (Boulder, Co.: Lynne Rienner Publishers, 1990).

52. Dorraj, *From Zarathustra to Khomeini*, 109-150.

53. *Zendegy Nameh va Modafe'at-i Mojahed-i Shahid Saeed Mohsen* [The Life Story and the Trial Defenses of the Martyred Mojaheed Saeed Mohsen], published by Iran's Freedom Movement Abroad, 1976, 16.

54. See *Salrooz-i shahdat-i Roofagha Pooyan, Sadequi nejad, Pirvandiri* [The Commemoration of the Martyrdom of Our Comrades] (Pooyan, Sadeqi Nejad and Pirvandiri), published by Cherik Hay-i Fdayee-Khalq (n.d.), 7.

55. Emile Durkheim, *The Elementary Forms of the Religious Life: A Study in Religious Sociology* (Glencoe, IL: Free Press, 1947), 416.

56. Abedi and Legenhausen, *Jihad and Shahadat*, 67-68.

57. *Jihad and Shahadat*, 136. This concept of martyrdom is pervasive among Sunni theoreticians as well. Sayyid Qutb, one of the leaders of the Muslim Brotherhood in Egypt, for example, echoed the same theme when he asserted that the Mujahid (one who strives to realize God's will; soldier willing to lay down his life for the cause of God) does not die. "All the people die; he is a martyr. He departs this world to the Garden while his opponent goes to the fire." Sayyid Qutb, *Maalim fi al Tariq* (Cairo: Maktabat Wahbah, 1964; English translation: Milestones, Cedar Rapids, Iowa: University Publishing Company, n.d.), 226, as cited by Yvonne Haddad "Sayyid Qutb: Ideologue of Islamic Revival," in *Voices of Resurgent Islam*, John L. Esposito, ed. (London: Oxford University Press, 1983).

58. During the Iran-Iraqi War the leaders and the publicists of the Islamic Republic made a special effort to further popularize the idea of martyrdom and enhance mass mobilization. Basing his comments on Imam Ali's advice to Mohammad Hanifeh, Hojal Al Islam Ali Akbar Nategh Noori, the former minister of the interior, proclaimed to graduating Gendarmeri students: "Fear is the main reason for defeat. If human beings were not afraid of death and surrendered totally to God's will, they would never surrender to degradation and humiliation. So far as our nation was tied to the past system and had its eyes focused on worldly gains, it was afraid of death and would commit any disgraceful act to escape. But since the day that our nation has come under a leadership modeled after the prophet, the leadership of Imam Khomeini, and stepped in the Imam's path, it has grown immensely and has overcome the fear of death. Death in God's path is no longer regarded as death but martyrdom" (*Jumhury-i Islami*, January 4, 1982, 2). In the same spirit Mr. Chamran, the former commander of the armed forces, addressed the troops at the Iraqi front, drawing upon the example of Ali Shariati: "Ali Shariati, like Ibrahim, sacrificed all of himself for the love of God thus he became all light. As the candle illuminates only when it burns and melts, Shariati consciously burned to illuminate others. All his life, he anxiously awaited martyrdom" (*Kayhan Havai*, June 20, 1990, 19).

59. Abedi and Legehausen, *Jihad and Shadadat*, 129.

60. *Iran Times*, November 16, 1982, 12.

61. Ali Shariati, *Eqbal, Ma'mar Tajdid Bana-ye Tafakkor-e Islamic* [Eqbal, the Architect of the Renewal of Islamic Thought] (Teheran: Forough Publications, 1973), 29.

62. Ali Shariati, *Shahadat* [Martyrdom] (Tehran: Husaynieh Irshad, 1971), 68.

63. Samad Behrangi, *Mahi Siayah-i Kouchoulou* [The Little Black Fish] (Teheran: Kanon-i Parvaresh-i Fekryi Koodakan, 1972).

64. Ahmad Karimi-Hakkak, *An Anthology of Modern Persian Poetry* (Boulder, CO: Westview Press, 1978), 137-159.

65. Khosrow Golsorkhi, "Tau" (You), reprinted in *Payam*, a publication of the *Iranian Student Association*, vol. 12 (1974), 58.

66. *Jalal Az Didgaheh Doctour Reza Brahani* [Jalal in Dr Reza Brahani's Pespective] in *Mi'ad ba Jalal* [Rendezvous with Jalal], Mirzad Jahani, ed. (Teheran: Ravaq Publishers, 1983), 102.

67. For analysis of politics in the poetics of Ahmad Shamlu, see Alishan, "Ahmad Shmlu," 375-422.

68. "Ahmad Shmlu," 409.

69. H. H. Gerth and C. Wright Mills, *From Max Weber: Essays in Sociology* (New York: Oxford University Press, 1979), 327.

70. See for example *Ashora Falsaphe-i Azadi* [Ashura, the Philosophy of Freedom] (Mojahadin Khalq, 1979). See also Ahmad Reza'i, *Rah-i Husayn* [Husayn's Path] (Teheran: Sahab Ketab, 1979).

71. See *Hamasay-e Yak Payedary-i Bozorg* [The Epic of a Great Resistance] (Mojahadin Khalq, n.d.), 38-43.

72. *Payam*, vol. 12 (1974), 30.

73. *The Defense of the Great Revolutionary Shokrallah Paknejad*, reproduced by the Association of Iranian Students in the United States, 1976, 2.

74. Reprinted in *Elm va Jam'a* [*Science and Society*], no. 15, 40.

75. For a description of these organizations see Ervand Abrahamian, "The Guerrilla Movement in Iran: 1963-1977," *Merip Reports*, no. 86 (1980).

76. Bijan Jazani, *Tarh'i jamea'h Shenasi va Mabani-i Strategy Jonbesh-i Enqelab-i Iran* [The Sociological Scheme and the Strategic Basis of Iranian Revolutionary Movement), vol. II, part 1 (Fedayeian Khalgh, 1978), 69.

77. There is a clear parallel here with Lebanese Shi'ites' increasing bid for political power in that country. As the Israeli invasion of Lebanon led to their concomitant confrontation with the hitherto subdued and submissive Shi'ite community in the south and as the number of Shi'ite causalties grew, so did their involvement in politics and their political power.

78. *Junhury-i Islami*, 10, Day, 1359, 5.

79. Sheikholeslami, "From Religious Accommodation," 229.

80. Malinowski, *Magic, Science and Religion*, 29.

6

Radical Islam and Nonviolence: A Case Study of Religious Empowerment and Constraint

Robert C. Johansen

Religious Traditions and the Choice of Violence or Nonviolence

Religious identities and religious legitimation of the use of military force often ignite the flames of collective violence, as indicated by events as diverse as Joshua's storming the walls of Jericho in the thirteenth century BCE, European crusades to plant a Christian flag in Jerusalem in the eleventh and twelfth centuries, and Saddam Hussein's effort to invoke Islamic *jihad* while conquering Kuwait in 1990. The unconscionable recent atrocities among Roman Catholics, Orthodox Christians, and Muslims in the former Yugoslavia have underscored the contemporary importance of religious traditions in fomenting violence, even among people who may not be personally religious. Hindus and Muslims have attacked each other in India, and even within notably pacific Buddhist traditions, monks have assassinated other monks in Sri Lanka. Examples of religious militancy can be found, to varying degrees, in every major religious tradition today.

Indeed, although political scientists and Western pundits in the past have been slow to recognize the importance of religious traditions in shaping human choices to use or to reject violent means to wage conflict, religion now may be taking center stage as a focal point for defining new security threats. In claiming that the clash of civilizations will replace the Cold War as the defining quality of future security conflicts, the well-known political realist, Samuel Huntington, has drawn special attention to religious traditions: "In the modern world, religion is a central, perhaps *the* central force that motivates and mobilizes people."[1] Religious activists are increasingly being "portrayed as the modern West's most formidable foes."[2]

To be sure, religion may define the identities of and mobilize more people than any other contemporary force, and its common-law marriage with nationalism produces especially fearful offspring. Yet religious traditions also may restrain violence and encourage people to transcend national and even religious boundaries to express solidarity with people of different traditions. Although few scholars have studied how religious traditions might contribute to international peace,[3] these traditions could play a powerful political role in promoting peace and nonviolent forms of conflict resolution, even in contexts where violence may seem fully justified and where deep-seated hostilities exist between people of different traditions. This case study demonstrates that militant religious traditions contain widely unrecognized ingredients for restraining the faithful from inflicting violence on people of other traditions even as the faithful engage in powerful political action to promote major change. The choice for believers is not limited to active religious violence, on the one hand, and inactive, otherworldly religious stagnation on the other. Nor is the choice limited to debates between religious fanaticism and secular liberalism. There is an additional path, marked by religious faithfulness, bold action for change, and nonviolent or antiviolent behavior. Religious values, if sensitively understood and implemented, can contribute more powerfully to peace than to war. Religious values can shape a more compassionate future than they have constructed a tolerant past.

If these positive consequences are to occur, however, political and religious leadership will need to avoid simplistic caricatures of all religious traditions, eschew exaggerated attributions of malevolent qualities to other traditions, acknowledge pluralism within all major religions, and understand that no tradition is a changeless entity. The failure during the Cold War of many in the West to acknowledge an evolutionary pluralism among communists and officials' tendency to misunderstand the nature of genuine threats to humanitarian values should remind us of the need to proceed more thoughtfully now, as should the ease with which some Western political leaders have described an Islamic threat as the national security sequel to earlier perceptions of the Soviet threat. NATO's Secretary General Willy Claes, for example, once said that "Islamic fundamentalism is at least as dangerous as Communism was."[4]

The case study presented here, drawn from the experiences of Pashtuns living in Northwest Frontier Province of colonial India, near what is now the Pakistani-Afghan border, stunningly informs us that Muslims living in traditional societies and engulfed by profoundly dehumanizing economic, political, and social conditions may develop the motivation, organization, and leadership to engage in bold political action aimed at self-determination, social and economic development, democratic political forms, and opposition to corruption while at the same time adhering to strictly nonviolent action despite violent provocation by their oppressors.

Purpose

The current rise of religious nationalisms that foment violence places an added responsibility on scholars to understand how religious affiliation and motivation influence peoples' choice of violent or nonviolent means in waging conflict. Case studies of political activists for whom religious faithfulness is important and yet who deliberately confine themselves to nonviolent means can be especially instructive. The present analysis is but one of many case studies that scholars might conduct as a contribution to world peace and justice. Studies that listen to the voices of those who are simultaneously committed to their religious faith and to legitimate national goals, while still inclined toward nonviolent, nonmilitary modes of action, have several merits.

First, they can provide an antidote to the oversimplifications and often inaccurate caricatures of Hinduism, Buddhism, and Islam that exist in the West. It is instructive to amplify the seldom heard voices of devout people who have chosen a nonviolent path in fulfilling their desire to be good Buddhists, Hindus, or Muslims. One need not claim that the historical threads examined in such cases represent a majority of people within the tradition, but only that, given our particular moment in world history, the selected threads are too important to ignore any longer. Whether or not one agrees with such minority views, they are views from which we have much to learn. If they are not studied and discussed, they appear not to exist.

Second, some religious threads that have been considered idiosyncratic or politically irrelevant in the past may have a new relevancy in this age of political interdependence, ecological fragility, economic disparity, and weapons of mass destruction. Certain behavior that a religious tradition assumed was acceptable in the past may no longer be legitimate in the present. For example, all of the major religious traditions have historically coexisted at some time with slavery, monarchy (or some form of kingship), patriarchy, and imperial empires—institutions that were once widely accepted by the faithful. Christian clergy, to take but one specific example, blessed the capture of Africans and their forced enslavement as they boarded ships in West Africa to embark for the New World. But today no major religious tradition condones slavery. Moreover, although most traditions still practice some discrimination against women, few explicitly condone patriarchy. We may speculate that gender equality will be supported increasingly in all traditions through the process of religious reinterpretation of ancient scriptures and the reconstruction of the tradition where necessary.[5]

Like the time-honored institutions of slavery, patriarchy, and divine-right monarchy, war is also an institution created by human beings. Because humans created it they can also abolish it, as they have those other institutions that religious authorities once blessed but whose successors relegated to the realm of illegitimacy and immorality. Although still controversial, a belief has taken root that Christian just-war doctrine inclines one toward nuclear pacifism, illustrating how time-honored beliefs justifying war may lead to new constraints on its legitimacy. In any case, a central question for our time is: What role will religious traditions play in helping to eliminate war?

Third, by highlighting promising threads in the world's larger religious tapestry, some of the faithful may be inclined, as they interpret their religious beliefs, to examine seldom-noticed threads of tolerance and compassion, and to give them and the accompanying possibility of peaceful change, new emphasis, and meaning. Conversations about such possibilities are important for people within every religious tradition, because today it often seems that those people who are most chauvinistic, intolerant, and violent succeed in making the claim that they also are the most faithful. Yet this case study lends support to the view that the most faithful in any tradition need not be the most violent. Similar studies by others might show that the fundamentals of a tradition are not found in hostility toward people of other traditions. Instead, the supreme test of one's faith might be how one treats the stranger in one's midst.

To understand religions' potential contribution to peace, and to maximize that contribution, we might remind ourselves that every generation reconstructs its religious tradition to fit its perceptions of contemporary conditions. Although the tradition's slate is never wiped clean, neither is the slate ever read from precisely the same angle by any new generation. Systems of belief and action are always subject to change; people frequently contest their meaning. This remains true whether or not reinterpretations of belief are conscious acts.

Gordon Kaufman has cogently explained that "the central theological ideas of God, humanity, and the world are—in a radical way not true of many other concepts—human imaginative constructs." As a result, people's thinking about religion "should become an activity of *deliberate* imaginative construction, carried out as self-consciously and responsibly as possible." To avoid the twin religious problems of irrelevancy or idolatry as the world changes, people "must always take a thoroughly critical stance toward received traditions, and they must never hesitate to undertake drastic reconstruction when it becomes clear that traditional practices or beliefs can contribute to dehumanization." Concepts of God "must be reconceived with attention to our modern understandings of ourselves and of the universe, and to our new consciousness of the destructiveness we humans have worked in the world as well as on our fellow humans."[6]

Even divinely revealed scriptures are communicated through words, yet the meaning of words may change, and words can never be the reality to which they refer, just as a map can never be the territory that it represents. Thus even if one believes, as many do in the Muslim, Christian, and Jewish traditions, that God has dictated or divinely inspired scriptures for the faithful to follow, their content, which can only be communicated through symbols, must rely upon human interpretation to apply them to ever-changing concrete realities. Moreover, in most traditions, God or reality is not fully knowable; such concepts extend beyond the limits of human comprehension. Hence religious people, regardless of their faith, have the opportunity—and the duty—to reflect on their systems of belief to determine whether their beliefs contribute maximally to understanding the meaning of life and to implementing their faith's highest values. As each generation reinterprets its tradition, it faces the question: What particular enhancements will contribute to human dignity and peacemaking in the future?

For scholars in one tradition to encourage people of other traditions to follow a nonviolent path if it would keep the latter in a position of economic, political, or military inferiority would of course be pernicious. Critics of analyses demonstrating the transformative power of nonviolence fear that such analyses may disarm those who otherwise might be justified in using violence to pursue their own liberation. In this case study I give attention to strategies of nonviolent direct action because I believe that they may prove in many contexts to be the most effective means for oppressed people to achieve justice and peace. But here I am not offering prescriptions for people of other cultural or religious traditions,[7] nor do I study nonviolence out of ignorance of the powerful forces arrayed against global justice and peace. To amplify the voices and report the experiences of nonviolent activists may be profoundly important for others to examine from within the same religious tradition; amplifying these voices also enables those outside the tradition to be better informed about how to relate to people in that tradition. If more people in the United States and Western Europe, for example, begin to appreciate the diverse strands of development that exist within Islam, they may become able to treat Muslims in ways that will avoid bringing the West's exaggerated fears of a worldwide Islamic threat closer to reality.

A Case Study from the Islamic Tradition

For many in the relatively wealthy societies of the West, Islam poses the most serious contemporary test of the hypothesis that the major religious traditions can contribute to world peace. For that reason, a case is presented here from the world of Islam, with concluding comments that suggest possible parallels in Hindu and Buddhist traditions. As indicated above, this study focuses on a social reform movement among some Pashtuns who inhabited the region around the town of Peshawar in what is now northwestern Pakistan. Although frequently characterized as a warlike people, a large number of these people took radical nonviolent action against both local authoritarianism and British imperialism in the 1920s, 1930s, and 1940s, courageously standing up to brutality without flinching and without inflicting counter violence despite enormous provocation. Their behavior was so remarkable as to be truly breathtaking, yet sufficiently understandable to be instructive in analysis of contemporary conflicts.

The Pashtuns' Commitment to Violence

The Pashtuns living in the Northwest Frontier Province of British India early in this century had established a long-standing reputation for being skilled in the arts of both war and interpersonal violence. Part of a loose confederation of approximately 60 tribes of varying size, inhabiting large areas of what have become northwestern Pakistan and Afghanistan, the Pashtuns today comprise one of the world's largest functioning tribal communities, with an estimated 14 million Pashtuns living in Pakistan and 7.5 million in Afghanistan.[8] The people inhabiting this region have for centuries lived astride the strategically important, ancient trade route connecting Europe, the Mediterranean world, and western Asia with civilizations in India and the East. They have suffered a tormented history filled with recurring invasions, conquests, and occupations.[9] In 1896 William Crooke wrote, "The true Pathan [Pashtun] is perhaps the most barbaric of all the races with which we are brought into contact." Pashtuns are "cruel, bloodthirsty and vindictive in the highest degree. . . ."[10]

The commander of British frontier forces there wrote in 1859 that it was necessary "to carry destruction, if not destitution, into the homes of some hundreds of families" because "with savage tribes, to whom there is no right but might, the only course open [to the British] as regards humanity as well as policy, is to make all suffer." Indeed, "if objection be taken to the nature of punishment inflicted as repugnant to civilization, the answer is that savages cannot be met and checked by civilized warfare, and that to spare their houses and crops would be to leave them unpunished and therefore, unrestrained. In short, civilized warfare is inapplicable."[11]

Because India was the greatest source of wealth in the British Empire and the Pashtuns inhabited the overland gateway to India through the Khyber Pass, the stakes in this region were extremely high. The British were determined to hold the region at almost any cost, as indicated in the more than 100 punitive military expeditions sent there during their colonial rule.[12] Frustrated at being unable to bring the Pashtuns into submission, the British claimed Pashtun resistance justified a "forward school" of imperial occupation. The local residents, however, fought persistently to maintain their independence, so fiercely resisting foreign intrusion that the British never succeeded in achieving stable control of their society.

In characterizing the Pashtuns as subhuman savages, uncivilized brutes, and treacherous murderers, the British no doubt expressed negative stereotypes commonplace in British imperial thinking, overlooking both positive Pashtun qualities and the likely causes of the pervasive violence.[13] Nonetheless, the Pashtuns' resistance to foreign occupation and their extraordinary martial skills remain well-known to this day. In addition to their independence and resistance to foreign invaders, they had developed a code of honor, Pashtunwali, for handling disputes over property, women, and personal injury that often resulted in blood feuds within and between their own families and clans. This code often required them to repay insult with injury; acts of revenge were an honorable duty and frequently inherited from generation to generation, causing many to die young.

Unlike the Hindu Indians of the plains, who had little experience in the use of weapons, the Pashtuns had easy access to firearms and were highly skilled in their use. They also had a well-established tradition of tribal organization that constituted a military confederacy. Nearly all men carried firearms and prized them highly. Wars were the normal business of the land, and resistance to all outsiders was an ancient way of life. The British strategy was periodically to send expeditions into Pashtun villages to beat, jail, or kill Pashtuns, sometimes by the thousands, because their fierce resistance prevented the British from completely controlling the region. As early as 1842, a forty-five-hundred-member British Army was completely exterminated, save one sole survivor who was allowed to return home to tell the story. The Pashtuns engaged in recurrent guerrilla warfare against the British for more than eighty years.

In selecting a case of nonviolent action from this cultural context, one is examining a difficult case in which the people and culture seemed unusually violent, in order to demonstrate that a militant group, displaying what today would be called "fundmentalist" tendencies bearing the fervor of religious nationalism (although led by a rare traditional leader), developed nonviolent strategies, pursued by a wide following, and achieved notable success. In calling this an extreme case, however, one should not forget that the violence expressed by people in this society, both against foreign invaders and others within their tribal system, was at least in part a product of being vicitimized by the violence of external invaders over many years. In some ways, those external societies that invaded Pashtun lands expressed more cruelty and violence than the Pashtuns who defended their home.

Arising from this tradition, Abdul Ghaffar Khan, a devout Muslim and son of a respected chieftain, felt a personal religious calling during his youth to serve God by uplifting his people through social reform and education. He was born in Utmanzai in 1890 and eventually became well-known as a reformer of enormous integrity, a man who listened to and understood his people. In 1910, opposed by the British and the local Muslim mullahs (who did not favor education and his social reforms), he established the first non-British school in his region. Later he walked from town to town and worked with uneducated villagers to build latrines, dig wells, teach hygine, and establish additional schools that were organized and taught by graduates of his original academy.[14]

By 1926 he began to press for social reforms and self-government. This he did at great personal risk. Despite imprisonment, inhumane treatment, and frequent British efforts at intimidation, in 1929 he organized an action group known as the Khudai Khidmatgars, or literally the "Servants of God." This group grew out of a suggestion from several youths who attended one of Ghaffar Khan's speeches and asked what more they could do to implement his proposed social reforms. Consistent with their code of honor and Muslim beliefs, they said they were willing to swear before God to give their lives for their people. The idea spontaneously burst forth that they might create an indigenous army. Ghaffar Khan liked the commitment, the discipline, and the courage of soldiers. Although most Pashtuns were fighters of one sort of another, those few who joined a modern army fought for the British. Ghaffar Khan felt the Pashtuns needed more soldiers but not more bloodshed. He was convinced that the pervasive violence of his society was responsible for its inability to uplift itself. Yet to transform a politically inert people, he felt they needed recruits for their cause. An army of nonviolent soldiers could be drilled, disciplined, and pledged to fight, not with guns but with their lives. Therefore he decided to create an organization specifically committed to using only nonviolent action to achieve political, social, and economic reforms. As far as Ghaffar Khan knew, such an army had never been created.[15]

Ghaffar Khan reports that he did not at first intend the Servants of God to focus on politics. Their purpose was to uplift their people through social reform. But the oppression of the British and their refusal to allow the Pashtuns even the same modest degree of representative institutions that the British had established elsewhere on the subcontinent led the group soon to focus on home rule.[16] After several months they numbered about 500 people, drawn heavily from the graduates of the schools that Ghaffar Khan had established earlier. Even observers critical of Abdul Ghaffar's nonviolent commitment acknowledged that the nonviolent approach became rapidly popular and that "while the world watched in bewilderment," he "converted hundreds of thousands . . . to this creed." After being involved in hundreds of nonviolent actions against the British in the 1930s, the Servants of God numbered more than 100,000.[17]

Of course many Pashtuns and others balked at the idea of an unarmed army, thinking this was a contradiction of Pashtun history, religion, and culture. The prevailing moral code emphasized Islamic beliefs justifying violence in defense of the faith. In addition, when some of the more vengeful traditional customs came into conflict with Islam, the former often prevailed, leading to feuds that a more profound understanding of Islam might not have condoned. Ghaffar Khan's father, also a devout Muslim, apparently did not condone these blood feuds. Ghaffar Khan felt that the Pashtuns' sense of honor could be employed not only to feud and kill but also to face a hostile army with courage and without arms. For him this was a higher form of honor. Because he knew that many people would see his plan as an insult to the idea of *badal* (the Pashtun code of revenge to maintain honor), Ghaffar Khan deliberately employed this code's emphasis on willingness to fight no matter what the cost. Only a people prepared to fight, he said, could prove the virtue of not fighting. After some initial surprising successes in recruiting people for the Khudai Khidmatgars, Ghaffar Khan gained confidence in advancing his ideas more widely. He told people:

I am going to give you such a weapon that the police and the army will not be able to stand against it. It is the weapon of the Prophet, but you are not aware of it. That weapon is patience and righteousness. No power on earth can stand against it. . . . When you go back to your villages, tell your brethren that there is an army of God, and its weapon is patience. Ask your brethren to join the army of God. Endure all hardships. If you exercise patience, victory will be yours.[18]

The Pashtuns' Commitment to Nonviolence

Despite the persistent violent rebelliousness of many Pashtuns, it was not their ability to inflict violence that finally succeeded in achieving reforms and driving out the British. No matter how successful Pashtun sniper and guerrilla tactics seemed to be, superior British firepower could always be brought in to punish the Pashtuns further. A radically different Pashtun strategy—nonviolent organization and resistance by the Servants of God coupled with the Indian independence movement—finally enabled the Pashtuns to triumph over the British.

They disclosed the nature of their organization in this oath taken by recruits:

I am a Servant of God, and as God needs no service, but serving his creation is serving him, I promise to serve humanity in the name of God.
I promise to refrain from violence and from taking revenge.
I promise to forgive those who oppress me or treat me with cruelty.
I promise to refrain from taking part in feuds and quarrels and from creating enmity.
I promise to treat every Pathan as my brother and friend.
I promise to refrain from antisocial customs and practices.
I promise to live a simple life, to practice virtue and to refrain from evil.
I promise to practice good manners and good behavior and not to lead a life of idleness.
I promise to devote at least two hours a day to social work. I shall expect no reward for my services.
I shall be fearless and be prepared for any sacrifice.[19]

In its earliest formulation, members signed this ten-point pledge:

1. I put forth my name in honesty and truthfulness to become a true Servant of God.
2. I will sacrifice my wealth, life, and comfort for the liberty of my nation and people.
3. I will never be a party to factions, hatred, or jealousies with my people; and will side with the oppressed against the oppressor.
4. I will not become a member of any other rival organization, nor will I stand in an army.
5. I will faithfully obey all legitimate orders of all my officers all the time.
6. I will live in accordance with the principles of nonviolence [adam tashaddud].
7. I will serve all God's creatures alike; and my object shall be the attainment of

the freedom of my country and my religion.

8. I will always see to it that I do what is right and good.

9. I will never desire any reward whatever for my service.

10. All my efforts shall be to please God, and not for any show or gain.[20]

A Pashtun could not take such an oath lightly because one's word could not be broken without losing one's integrity. An oath committed a person to honor it with his or her life.

Ghaffar Khan and other organizers entrenched all of the organization's main attributes in the ten-point pledge. First and most important, the organization's name decreed that their purpose was explicitly religious. As Servants of God, members founded their movement on peoples' Islamic faith. Years earlier, Ghaffar Khan personally had pledged himself to social reform because of a religious calling. Similarly, this pledge called people to serve God by serving other people. As one might expect of devout Muslims, the organizers emphasized that members' commitment should be directly to God, not to any symbol of or competitor to God, not to an organization or a human leader. Their monotheistic tradition led to a singular commitment, a respect for discipline, an obedience to leaders who acted in accordance with God's will, and an uncompromising willingness to sacrifice in the service of God's will.

Second, members dedicated themselves to social reform in which they explicitly sided with the oppressed and to attitudinal change in which they emphasized sacrifice and relinquishment of hatred, jealously, and personal reward for service. The volunteers opened schools, worked on local development projects, promoted hygiene and sanitation, and maintained order at public meetings. Considering the education of the people a sacred duty, Ghaffar Khan also founded the Pashtun Youth League to implement a program of educational and social reform. He started a journal, soon banned by the British and forced underground, written in Pakhtu to disseminate articles on Islamic law, hygiene, and social issues.

Third, every member unequivocally promised not to engage in any violence. This commitment was the most astonishing and demanding part of the pledge. Significantly, Servants of God did not simply vow to use nonviolence in a crusade to oust the British. They vowed to eliminate violence in their relations with other Pashtuns as well as with anyone else. Their pledge was designed to change their way of life. Ghaffar Khan and his coworkers sought to help people win self-respect and human dignity through human solidarity—a solidarity with others that would hinge on refusing to use violence against another person. "I should like to make it clear that the nonviolence I have believed in and preached to my brethren of the Khudai Khidmatgars," explained Ghaffar Khan, "affects all our life, and only that has permanent value." In his view, "the Khudai Khidmatgars must . . . be what our name implies—pure servants of God and humanity—by laying down our own lives and never taking any life."[21]

In this regard the Servants of God adopted a more comprehensive and strict commitment to nonviolence than did the Congress movement in India, which of course was heavily influenced by Mohandas Gandhi and became the main political force in obtaining independence from British rule. Although the Congress Party adopted nonviolence as a strategy because it was Gandhi's chosen method for struggling to achieve independence, the Congress (and the Muslim League, which frequently was at odds with Ghaffar Khan's movement) refused to endorse nonviolence in principle and as a way of life. (Of course the Congress Party deliberately chose to avoid any religious foundation because it sought to appeal to people of different faiths. The Servants of God were explicitly Muslim and required complete devotion to their purposes, whereas the Congress Party was a much larger, looser organization.)

Training the Servants of God

Ghaffar Khan established an officer corps, organized members in platoons, and taught recruits basic army discipline that was not associated with the use of arms. They drilled in military fashion and were required to obey their commanders, as long as officers' orders were "legitimate." Membership in the army of God was voluntary; even officers gave their services without compensation. Women were also recruited and played an important role. The discipline on nonviolence was absolute; leaders did not allow any mixing of violent and nonviolent tactics. Persons found to violate any aspect of the pledge were dismissed at once.

In addition to the officer corps, Ghaffar Khan established a network of committees called *jirgahs*, modeled after the traditional tribal councils that had maintained Pashtun law for centuries. These were elected and centered in a provincial *jirga* that served as an unofficial parliament of Pashtuns. Officers in the nonviolent army were not elected because Ghaffar Khan wanted to avoid infighting and competition among the leaders.

The Servants' training also included religious instruction. But rather than being hardened to hate their opponents, Ghaffar Khan and other leaders taught forgiveness, tolerance, and patience, drawing examples from Islamic history. They emphasized the Qur'anic injunction: "He who forgives and is reconciled, his reward is with God" (Qur'an, 42:39).

Ghaffar Khan taught that nonviolence was the "weapon of the Prophet." He emphasized that *sabr*, which is often inadequately translated as patience or endurance, is counseled repeatedly in the chapters of the Qur'an that were revealed during the early years of the Prophet's teaching in Mecca. At that time Mohammed had no political or military power, faced ridicule, and encountered harsh persecution. Only after he and his followers fled to Medina and acquired more political power did God's revelations endorse war in defense of the faith. Ghaffar Khan noted, with historical accuracy, that the early stance taken by Mohammed and his relatively few followers was to hold firmly to truth without retreating or retaliating violently, the literal meaning of *satyagraha* (discussed below). They took this stance in submission to God, the literal meaning of "Islam." Ghaffar Khan extended the meaning of *sabr* to the renunciation of all violent retaliation.[22] This became a key element in his religious faith and political practice.

When people expressed surprise over Ghaffar Khan's nonviolence, he said "there is nothing surprising in a Muslim or a Pathan like me subscribing to the creed of nonviolence. It is not a new creed. It was followed fourteen hundred years ago by the Prophet all the time he was in Mecca, and it has since been followed by all those who wanted to throw off an oppressor's yoke." Ghaffar Khan emphasized that a Muslim "never hurts anyone by word or deed," but instead "works for the benefit and happiness of God's creatures. Belief in God is to love one's fellowmen." Relatively late in his life, Ghaffar Khan wrote: "It is my inmost conviction that Islam is *amal, yakeen, muhabat* [work, faith, and love]. . . . The Koran makes it absolutely clear that faith in One God without a second, and good works, are enough to secure a man his salvation."[23]

Although Ghaffar Khan's independent spirit and aversion to violence predated contact with Mohandas Gandhi, Ghaffar Khan's belief in nonviolence and commitment to social reform were strongly buttressed and further inspired by Gandhi. Ghaffar Khan's rejection of violence was at least as deeply rooted in his Muslim religious faith as was Gandhi's in his Hindu tradition. Speaking of Ghaffar Khan and his brother who had been jailed together at one point and transferred to a prison in Bihar, Gandhi wrote that he was "struck by their transparent sincerity, frankness and utmost simplicity. . . . They had come to believe in truth and nonviolence not as a policy but as a creed." Gandhi remarked that Ghaffar Khan "was consumed with deep religious fervor." Yet Ghaffar Khan did not practice "a narrow creed. I found him," said Gandhi, "to be a universalist. His politics, if he had any, were derived from his religion."[24] Gandhi's comment on Ghaffar Khan's politics, "if he had any," underscores the extent to which politics and religion were as inseparable for Ghaffar Khan as the two are now for most devout Muslims. All Ghaffar Khan's activities sprang from and were unified in his faith. Because of his principled integrity, much of what he saw in politics he did not like: egocentric people manipulating others to gain power.

Writing about Ghaffar Khan, Mahadev Desai, Gandhi's secretary, said "the greatest thing in him is . . . his spirituality—or better still, the true spirit of Islam—submission to God." Ghaffar Khan "has measured Gandhiji's life all through with this yardstick and his clinging to Gandhiji can be explained on no other ground." According to Desai, it was "not Gandhiji's name and fame that have attracted him to Gandhiji, nor his political work, nor his spirit of rebellion and revolution. It is his pure and ascetic life and his insistence on self-purification that have had the greatest appeal for him." Desai reported that Ghaffar Khan's life "has been one sustained effort for self-purification."[25]

Ghaffar Khan of course strongly agreed with Gandhi's emphasis that nonviolence did not mean meek submission to the will of the powerful. Instead, it meant "the pitting of one's whole soul against the will of the tyrant." Ghaffar Khan subscribed to the understanding of *satyagraha* developed by Gandhi, combining *satya*, meaning truth, and *agraha*, meaning firmness.[26] The Servants of God used force born of truth expressed through nonviolence. This combination amounted in practice to a much more powerful psychological dynamic than a rational appraisal may convey. Those who practiced *satyagraha* developed a spirit of resistance that frequently armed them with an indomitable will to persevere, to accept suffering, and to avoid inflicting suffering on their opponents. Civil disobedience appealed to the psyche of the Pashtuns and their "defiant instincts" against foreign occupation.[27]

Because of Ghaffar Khan's religious concern about the role of women in society, he urged them to come out from behind the veil and to become active in the movement for social reform and political independence. His own sisters and many other women did so, which showed daring in those days (and still today) in that region of the world. Ghaffar Khan emphasized that "God makes no distinction between men and women." He said that as soon as the motherland was liberated, women should obtain equal rights. "In the Holy Koran," he told women, "you have an equal share with men. You are today oppressed because we men have ignored the commands of God and the Prophet. Today we are the followers of custom and we oppress you." He believed that if the women of the subcontinent became engaged in change, no power on earth could oppress India.[28]

Ghaffar Khan rooted his beliefs and actions in his own understanding of the Qur'an. Although he had no formal higher education, he had a strong sense of confidence in his own ability, through study, meditation, and prayer, to find the most faithful path for him and others who might follow his lead. His independent mind, devout faith in God, and understanding of the Qur'an posed a challenge to the authority of Muslim clergy and their traditional religious interpretations.[29] Of all traditional strands of Islam, his views seem most congenial to Sufi mystic traditions, but there is no evidence that they may have influenced his thought. He apparently did not rely on the institutionalized roles of the mullahs, the educated clergy (*ulama*), or those of holy descent (*sayyid*).

The Activities of the Servants of God

During the 1930s and early 1940s, Muslim activists in the Servants of God refused to cooperate with the British and remained resolutely nonviolent in the face of recurrent British provocation and violence, even though they endured humiliations, jail, flogging, destruction of their homes, and mass shootings. They courageously refused to abandon their freedom even though their persistence meant dying in large numbers. There is no evidence of any Servant of God killing an adversary, despite the organization's large membership and repeated provocations by the British. Ghaffar Khan himself spent fifteen years in British prisons during these years, often in solitary confinement. In effect, he was imprisoned one day for every day that he was free during this period of his life.

Despite the repeated risk of arrest because the British had outlawed the Servants of God and banned public gatherings, Ghaffar Khan toured hundreds of villages, constantly on the move when not in prison. This was essential for communication because the villagers were illiterate. The Servants staged dramas to instruct people in nonviolence. Ghaffar Khan faced resistance not only from the British, but also from many of the Muslim mullahs and from large land-owners who felt that social and democratic reforms threatened their economic interests and political power. The British, of course, often protected the privi-leges of the privileged as long as the latter could be used against popular unrest over British rule. Twice Ghaffar Khan narrowly escaped assassination plots. Perhaps the most dramatic example of nonviolent courage occurred in Peshawar in 1930, at a time even before the Khudai Khidmatgars decided to affiliate with the Indian Congress Party.[30]

During a speech in Utmanzai on April 23, 1930, Ghaffar Khan urged civilian resistance against British occupation. On the way back to Peshawar, he was arrested at Naki. In response, almost all local townspeople immediately declared themselves Khudai Khidmatgars and subsequently took the oath of membership. Ghaffar Khan's well-established reputation for uncompromising integrity and nonviolence was crucial in stimulating this massive outpouring of support. Because of the Servants' pledge of nonviolence, thousands of people who sur-rounded the jail refrained from acting violently even as the British decided to move Ghaffar Khan out of town to imprison him elsewhere. In Peshawar, other leaders of the Servants of God were also arrested. A spontaneous general strike occurred. Again, the integrity and nonviolence of the leadership was critical for the public to respond with such unified and firm support. Crowds gathered in Kissa Ghaffar Khani Bazaar to protest the arrests. British troops began to move in. Although the crowd was loud, it was nonviolent. Two or three armored cars approached the square at great speed and drove into the crowd, killing several people and injuring others. The crowd was not armed, even with stones, and showed great restraint in collecting the wounded and dead. Nonetheless nervous British officers ordered their troops to fire upon the crowd, which they did. The crowd then expressed willingness to disperse if they were allowed to collect the dead and injured and if British troops and armored cars would also leave the square. But British authorities refused to remove their troops. As a result, the people also refused to leave. Willingly they faced bullets as the troops repeatedly fired on the crowds. To give themselves courage against armed opponents, they repeated the refrain "God is Great." Many clutched the Qur'an as they went to their deaths. Reports about the number of casualties remain controversial, but several hundred were killed, and many more were wounded.[31]

At one point, a regiment of the Garhwal Rifles refused to obey orders when commanded to fire on the crowds of unarmed demonstrators. A British civil servant noted their refusal "to do their duty in face of the mob." He also noted that "hardly any regiment of the Indian Army won greater glory in the Great

War [World War I] than the Garhwal Rifles, and the defection of part of the regiment sent a shock through India, of apprehension to some, of exultation to others." The entire platoon was arrested, and seventeen men were court-martialed and given long prison sentences.[32]

In Peshawar, Utmanzai, and elsewhere, the Khudai Khidmatgars suffered some of the most severe repressions of the entire Indian independence movement. This was at least in part because, as Ghaffar Khan later wrote, the British thought a nonviolent Pashtun was more dangerous than a violent Pashtun. As a result the British wanted to provoke them to commit violent acts. Because a nonviolent Pashtun in British minds seemed a fraud, Ghaffar Khan and his nonviolent activists became targets of savage repression. At times the entire province was sealed off from the eyes of the outside world to leave military forces a free hand to destroy the movement in any way they could. In 1931, London ordered its police and military to crush the Servants of God. All leaders, including Ghaffar Khan's three sons, were arrested again. Troops went to the villages where the Servants were strong, rounded up people, and despoiled the villages. There were repeated instances of mass firings on unarmed groups, with scores, and in some cases, hundreds of casualties. The British frequently arrested and flogged members of the Servants of God, (more than 10,000 were locked in Haripur prison alone in 1932), herded them into icy streams in winter, forced them at gunpoint to remove their clothes in public, confiscated property, burned fields before time of harvest, poured oil on wheat in storage for the residents' winter food supply, and sacked whole villages.[33] Even though in the following years the Khudai Khidmatgars suffered without retaliating violently, "the Pathans, notwithstanding the fact that they had been brought up in an atmosphere of violence and bloodshed," writes Yunus, "stood unmoved by such provocations and died peacefully in large numbers for the attainment of their goal."[34]

Outside of the Northwest Frontier Province, British officials and journalists attacked Ghaffar Khan's character. Some British and American writers tried to associate Ghaffar Khan with violent uprisings that occurred elsewhere in the Frontier Province to impugn the nonviolence of his movement. Ghaffar Khan was described as a "fanatical, bitterly anti-British Pathan" who "preached war against the British.[35] Yet the incidents of violence among hill tribes occurred in areas where Ghaffar Khan throughout his life had been prohibited by the British from traveling and establishing his movement. Other British insinuated a Bolshevik influence on the Servants of God, and claimed that they were armed by Russians who, because of Russian interest in Afghanistan, sought to loosen Britain's hold on India. In any case, the British military dealt far more easily with the tribal hill violence than with the nonviolence of the Khudai Khidmatgars.

Despite their efforts after the Peshawar massacre, the British could not prevent Ghaffar Khan's nonviolent movement from expanding even more rapidly. Although the Servants of God remained outlawed and their offices were repeatedly sacked by British expeditions, they increased in popularity, reaching well over 100,000 at their peak.[36] No less significant than withstanding hostile fire, the Khudai Khidmatgars also succeeded in establishing a parallel government against the opposition of the civil police, the British-led frontier constabulary, an entire division of troops, a detachment of the Air Force stationed at Risalpur, and the imposition of martial law. To press their case for home rule, the Servants of God continued to protest British taxes and efforts to collect revenues from Pashtuns by controlling the water supply for agricultural regions dependent on irregation canals. The Servants of God succeeded in establishing their own revenue offices and in keeping order in Peshawar and various other towns for brief periods after disturbances. By 1932 the Servants of God had gained significant political concessions, including political parity with the rest of British India and an indigenous minister as head of the regional government.

Many people, including other Indians, were surprised at the strength of the motivation and discipline of the Servants of God. Jawaharlal Nehru, who later became India's first prime minister, expressed astonishment that the Pashtun "who loved his gun better than his child or brother, who valued life cheaply and cared nothing for death, who avenged the slightest insult with the thrust of a dagger, had suddenly become the bravest and most enduring of India's soldiers." Gandhi said that for such men, "who would have killed a human being with no more thought than they would kill a sheep or a hen," to "have laid down their arms and accepted nonviolence as the superior weapon sounds almost like a fairy tale." Pashtun peasants and tribespeople exploded "the myth that nonviolence works only for those who are already peaceful." These people who preferred death to dishonor had usually demonstrated their courage through violence. But they learned they could also express it through nonviolence.[37]

Postindependence Activity

After World War II ended and a postwar British government finally promised self-government for India, rioting broke out between Hindus and Muslims. Gandhi and Ghaffar Khan traveled together trying to stop it, achieving only mixed results at best. Ghaffar Khan returned to the Northwest Frontier Province to address the problem there among his own people. Although the Khudai Khidmatgars movement had been explicitly, intensely Islamic, the leaders had also kept it noncommunal. One of its objectives always had been the promotion of Hindu-Muslim unity. On one occasion, when Hindus in Ghaffar Khan's home region of Peshawar were threatened, his brother called in ten thousand Khudai Khidmatgars. All were Muslim, armed only with faith and courage, yet they were able to protect Hindus and Sikhs against rioters and to restore peace in the city.[38]

Ghaffar Khan deplored the communal violence that erupted between Muslims and Hindus. He also opposed partitioning India into two countries, a predominantly Muslim Pakistan and a predominantly Hindu India, because he thought the result would contribute to violence rather than end it. Unlike most Muslim groups, members of the Khudai Khidmatgars strongly opposed partition. When it came, Ghaffar Khan felt deserted by the Congress, which until the last moment had vigorously opposed partition. He faced particular difficulty because partition placed the Pashtun' Frontier Province within a larger Pakistan under the governance of leaders of the Muslim League. The League had opposed Ghaffar Khan, the Khudai Khidmatgars, and their commitment to nonviolence for many years. Many in the League resented Ghaffar Khan's program of social reforms, the effectiveness of his nonviolent methods, his popularity and influence, and his support for the Congress movement against the British. Yet when partition came, Ghaffar Khan chose to live among his people in Pakistan, even though it meant he and his movement would be governed by those from the Muslim League.

Of course Ghaffar Khan and Gandhi's strong commitments to nonviolent action for social justice did not always succeed in eliciting nonviolent action or even goodwill from others even within their own respective religious traditions. Within a year of Indian independence, Gandhi had been assassinated by a fellow Hindu who thought he was too pro-Muslim, and Ghaffar Khan had been imprisoned by Muslim officials in an Islamic Pakistan because they claimed that Ghaffar Khan was pro-Hindu and insufficiently loyal to the Pakistani government.[39] During the first thirty years of Pakistan's existence, Ghaffar Khan was forced to spend fifteen more years in prison and seven years in exile.[40] Two of India's leading politico-religious leaders were sacrificed by people of their own faith in the name of faithfulness.

After independence the Pakistani government sought to eliminate totally the power of the Kudai Khidmatgars. It feared Indian-Afghan diplomatic support for Pashtun autonomy, possible collaboration between Indians in Kashmir and Pashtuns in Pakistan, and the pre-1947 independent strength of Ghaffar Khan and his supporters. The Pakistani government imprisoned or killed at least several thousand Kudai Khidmatgars, confiscated their property, burned their main offices, and employed Muslim mullahs to discredit Ghaffar Khan and those who supported Khudai Khidmatgars.[41] The mullahs insinuated that Ghaffar Khan was not a loyal Pakistani or a good Muslim because he had been too influenced by the Congress movement, Gandhi, and Hindu beliefs. They claimed that Pashtun nonviolence was not consistent with their history or with Islamic beliefs. From prison or exile Gaffar Khan continued to work for autonomy for the Pashtuns and for more democracy within Pakistan but achieved little success in the face of ruthless repression of his movement.

Although much more work is needed to explain adequately the demise of the powerful nonviolent movments led by both Gandhi and Ghaffur Khan, understanding the sources of the effectiveness and power of the Servants of God during their most fruitful years can shed some light on ingredients that contribute to successful nonviolent movements.

Religion as an Agent of Militancy
and an Antidote to Violence

This case study suggests the following tentative conclusions about how people rooted in a traditional Islamic culture may be inspired by their religious tradition to act boldly yet nonviolently for justice and peace:

1. Islamic religious identity *provided an effective basis for recruiting people to join the Servants of God, for motivating them to bold action, and for nurturing a strong identity and discipline among members,* even though previously they had been politically inert and had acquiesced in unsatisfactory social and political conditions. This religious identity served them well when they faced enormous stress and personal risk while engaged in nonviolent direct action. Bonds of comradeship enabled them to act courageously, much as small groups of soldiers do while protecting comrades in the heat of battle.

2. Islamic religious values *provided an influential foundation for defining activists' purposes to serve others and to implement broad social, economic, and political reforms.* The emphasis on a locally rooted, distinctive Muslim version of nonviolence *enabled people to transform their lifestyle and society,* not merely to alter their military and political strategies. Many of the most faithful embraced nonviolence not only as an organizing tactic but also as a way of life, choosing to live more fully in harmony with human compassion. After visiting the Frontier Province and studying the Khudai Khidmatgars, Turkish scholar Halide Edib concluded that the "psychological aspect of the movement was more interesting than its political significance." The movement among the Pashtuns disclosed a "new" and "very unexpected" interpretation of force. With understatement she noted that for many Pashtuns to conclude that nonviolence, rather than violence, "is the only form of force which can have a lasting effect on the life of society . . . , coming from strong and fearless men, is worthy of study." Bondurant reported that the overall effects of the Khudai Khidmatgars were so sweeping as to be "incalculable."[42] They not only changed attitudes toward nonviolence and mobilized tens of thousands of people to work for social reform, they also brought women into political action in a stunningly unique context and time in history. Furthermore, they posed a challenge to indigenous social and economic institutions that were based on dubious yet time-honored inequities including unfair landlord-peasant relationships. Wherever the Khudai Khidmatgars saw injustice, they initiated action.

In using nonviolent action to achieve their goals, the Servants did not let the means become an end in itself. Nonetheless, the selection of nonviolent means shaped the ends they sought and the degree of success they achieved, especially in working subsequently with others with whom they disagreed during an action. The Khudai Khidmatgars achieved "nothing less than the reversal in attitude and habit of a people steeped in factious violence." In place of violent competition the Khudai Khidmatgars substituted constructive action. They "achieved a discipline for hot-tempered discontents and directed it into political action."[43] These achievements demonstrated clearly that strategic nonviolent sanctions need not be limited to people of ascetic traditions.

3. Muslim religious teachings and Ghaffar Khan's reinterpretation of religious values, although springing from what has been perceived as a nonpacifist tradition, *provided a clear antidote to violent conflict, encouraged activists to avoid intolerance toward other people, and enabled them to overcome their time-honored inclination to use violence against adversaries, both in interpersonal and intergroup conflicts.* Indeed, religious values *laid the foundation for encouraging people to choose nonviolence in principle.* Contemporary political leaders should note the enormous significance that nonviolent direct action "could be, and was, adopted by a people to whom the concepts of *ahimsa* [non-injury or nonviolence], *tapasya* [sacrifice or religious penance], and *satya* [truth] were unfamiliar."[44] In showing that Islamic scripture could support a Pashtun version of *satyagraha*, Ghaffar Khan encouraged a reinterpretation of many teachings that led to a fundamental transformation of people's social and political lives.

Ghaffar Khan's "interpretation of [Islamic faith] was so universal," Halide Edib has noted, "that instead of separating the Muslims from the rest of the world, he tried to make them so that they could cooperate with their fellowmen for the good of all." Ghaffar Khan's "supreme importance lies in his having brought the simplest and truest conception of Islam into the lives of a most elemental people."[45]

Perhaps the best explanation for how some Pashtuns, frequently described as warlike, could conduct a successful nonviolent campaign in the face of repeated violent provocations and humiliations lies in what anthropologists call "cultural reversals," in which traditional symbols are embraced yet employed in new ways to elicit additional power and legitimacy from the obvious rejection of former forms of behavior and the acceptance of new behavior as virtuous. New attitudes helped the Servants of God to identify not only with other Pashtuns, but also to extend a line of identity, modest though it may have been, across group boundaries to former adversaries. This reorientation enabled them to break some cycles of fear and violence that otherwise might have occurred—and in fact *did* occur in their society both before and after the period of the Kudai Khidmatgars' nonviolent successes.[46]

4. Nonviolent action *enabled many Muslims to be politically more effective than they had been when using violent tactics.* Eschewing violence provided some strategic advantages in waging conflict. Previously, both the British and the Pashtuns had associated effectiveness with willingness to use violence, whether employed by British or Pashtuns. Many Pashtuns (and British) believed that the British had never been able to pacify the peoples of the Frontier province because of the latter's violent character. In addition, the Pashtuns' violent rebelliousness provided the justification, in British minds, for decades of military rule, rather than for giving Pashtuns more autonomy or at least for

instituting colonial government in the more accommodating form they had established elsewhere. Yet it was Pashtun organization and courage, uncoupled from violent means and instead linked to nonviolent direct action, that motivated indigenous social reform, that led at first to British concessions, and that later, in tandem with the Indian independence movement, unseated the British entirely.

Mass nonviolent action proved more effective than violence in calling into question the rulers' purposes and legitimacy.[47] It reduced the rulers' capacity to delude themselves and convince others that their violent imperialist repression made good sense. A British civil servant once told the House of Commons that "every Englishman in India" held the "cherished conviction . . . that he belongs to a race which God has destined to govern and to subdue."[48] Whereas Pashtun violence had once enabled the British to believe that they held the high moral ground, Pashtun nonviolent action undermined this conviction. Similarly, in a more modern setting, to the extent that the Palestinian *intifada* avoided military or terrorist activities, it elevated the Palestinians' moral position in the minds of many observers above the position previously held by Israeli security forces. The *intifada* also increased the influence of West Bank Palestinians within the circle of the aging and somewhat distant PLO leadership.

5. Muslim religious teachings and discourse provided a basis for *enabling people to contest the meaning of their own tradition* in contemporary life. Ghaffar Khan creatively used traditional Islamic precepts to communicate to his people about the need for changes in their tradition. This strategy provided a bridge between the old consciousness and the radically new one they successfully employed. Ghaffar Khan's strategy aimed to revitalize religion, rather than marginalize it, a lesson of profound relevance for those now seeking ways of relating creatively to contemporary Islamic militancy. To draw upon, learn from, and revitalize religion may succeed in implementing humanitarian values where secular liberal opposition to religious fundamentalism fails. Ghaffar Khan and other Servants of God did not allow the debate over strategy within the pluralistic Muslim community to be framed as a contest between secular activism and religious faithfulness (as some mullahs sought to portray it). The Servants framed the debate as one between two forms of religious faithfulness.[49] More widespread knowledge of this case and others could enable people elsewhere to recognize that the highest values of Islam may be compatible with a militant nonviolence that has power to liberate and to resolve previously intractable conflicts.

6. Muslim religious commitment *sustained the determination and courage of the leadership* of the Khudai Khidmatgars movement. Although it is clear that many people may use nonviolence effectively as a tactic even if they do not embrace nonviolence in principle, this case strengthens the significance of the observation that astute leaders are drawn to nonviolence and maintain commitment to it because of their religious beliefs. Remarkably, after spending more than thirty years of his life in prisons and suffering a multitude of humiliations, deprivations, and threats to his life, Ghaffar Khan stood by his principles of

compassion and nonviolent service to all of humanity. These were accompanied by a strong commitment to tolerance, freedom from bondage for all people, and the reconciliation of diverse creeds, ethnicities, and races. Ghaffar Khan made a mixed religious, national, and rational appeal to his colleagues and followers, yet religious faith was the bedrock of his own commitment and determination. This faith not only created space within his mind for employing nonviolence in unprecedented ways, it also reduced the moral space within which he considered violence to be legitimate. His religious tradition gave him strength day by day, and courage in crisis after crisis, to sustain his sense of justice and compassion despite opposition from every quarter. Throughout his life, Ghaffar Khan strove to remain a devout Muslim and servant of God by being compassionate, patient, forgiving, resilient, and firm.

Implications

This case study suggests some additional speculation about how the politics of knowledge discriminates against understanding the relative utilities of violence and nonviolence and impedes the liberation of oppressed peoples. On the one hand, scholars and political leaders widely recognize that religious beliefs may contribute to peace by encouraging people to accept things as they are, to maintain social stability, and to seek salvation in an otherworldly context. But such beliefs do not contribute to positive social change. On the other hand, people widely understand that religious identities may function in connection with national identities to ignite rather than quell violence during intense conflicts, whether domestic or international. But people seldom seriously consider a third alternative—politically bold, religiously motivated action that remains nonviolent—because political and religious leaders do not often highlight it.[50] As a result, because of ignorance about what many people acting together could do, they often mistakenly assume that to be nonviolent means being inactive or, even worse, a traitor to the cause of one's group. The present case study contradicts this assumption, demonstrating that a commitment to radical change and bold deeds can generate effective nonviolent action. If nonviolent direct action could succeed among the Pashtuns living in the unfavorable social, economic, and political conditions described in this case, it should be able to achieve some positive results in almost any context.

Yet if such action holds substantial promise, why is it not more frequently embraced, especially by religious nationalists who seek radical change? The answer lies in the lack of courage and imagination on the part of religious and political leaders and their tendency to focus on advancing their own power positions (most are unlike Ghaffar Khan). These leaders, who may be found in any of the major religions, usually see no gain and perhaps political losses for themselves in acknowledging the religious themes that call people to transcend their own group boundaries. Indeed, to the discredit of many religious leaders, they frequently join hands with self-seeking political authorities, as the intermingling of religious and political symbols of legitimation in all cultures has demonstrated over many centuries, in encouraging prejudice against out-groups, as we have painfully witnessed in the genocide blessed by religious authorities among South Slavs in the former Yugoslavia. These leaders generally dismiss and encourage others to dismiss new forms of action that do not depend upon leadership exercised through the traditional institutional channels that have become comfortable for politicians and religious leaders. Yet effective forms of citizen organization and nonviolent action are possible; the Khudai Khidmatgars did indeed succeed for nearly two decades, and as Kenneth Boulding often reminded us: "Whatever exists is possible." Political and religious leaders interested in maintaining their own power take no interest in reminding people that the Khudai Khidmatgars existed, because if enough people knew about their successful deeds against the odds, similar deeds might happen again: People might be faithful to a new understanding of their religious tradition, act boldly for liberation, reject the violent modes of action and leadership that benefit the elite while injuring common people, and transcend narrow identities that both political leadership and institutionalized religion have frequently encouraged.

More dedicated and imaginative leadership, such as Ghaffar Khan provided, would understand that they could benefit from peace and liberation in the long run, that their own interests, insofar as they were legitimate, would not be handicapped by educating their followership about a third course of action that, although certainly no panacea, holds as much promise as doing nothing or attempting socially self-destructive bombings and shootings. They could to this by drawing on the compassionate elements of major religious traditions to encourage themselves and others to adopt boundary-crossing group identities. Some aspects of this approach have been at work in contemporary South Africa in moving to majority government.

To develop a third path between politically inactive, otherworldly religiosity and fanatically religious political violence, political, religious, and educational leaders need to address the harsh political consequences of contemporary group identities. Despite its potential, nonviolent direct action probably is not employed more frequently because it invites, even if it does not always require, those who embrace it to form an identity that crosses traditional group boundaries to acknowledge the humanity of one's adversary. Many people cannot accept this invitation because they have not had positive experiences with crossing identity boundaries of class, nationality, race, religion, or ethnicity. Because of their experience and previous conditioning, people often assume that such boundaries are uncrossable, or they may feel compromised, contaminated, or emotionally devastated when faced with the prospect of trying to cross such boundaries. These emotions intensify peoples' resistance to change and often produce frozen, hostile responses toward out-groups—unless leadership or a trusted community helps people experience their fearful emotions against a backdrop of familiar if reinterpreted religious symbols that provide security and grounding during change. Violence erupts so frequently today because the identities of contemporary religious nationalists tend to be rooted more deeply in nationalist than in religious values, particularly those religious values that contain the seeds of transcendence over national identities and prejudices.

When people become politically active in intercultural contexts, if they are to adhere to nonviolent means, they must not extinguish the possibility for developing a more inclusive identity. Yet to move in that direction calls into question narrow identities and could threaten one's sense of self, unless, as in the case examined here, personal identities remain rooted in a familiar although enlarging view of one's tradition. The use of religious values and metaphors both to sustain a sense of personal security in one's past identity and to call for courage and sacrifice to act for justice or peace seemed essential for success—if success is measured, as it was for Ghaffar Khan and Gandhi, in terms of (1) willingness to act boldly for desirable moral purposes (ethical ends), (2) determination to act nonviolently in order to accept ethical limits upon what one is willing to do to one's opponent and to one's own moral integrity (ethical means), and (3) desire to revitalize the universal rather than the national side of religious identity (synthesis of ethical ends and means).

This case study suggests that a successful path, although not necessarily the only path, for persons attempting to move beyond an "identity of particularity" (ethnic, national, or religious identity that excludes expressions of human solidarity) is to emphasize a religious commitment that affirms the unity and sacredness of human life. The utility of this commitment for expanding one's identity, and the difficulty of making one's identity broadly inclusive without a spiritual foundation, is one reason that some of the best-known leaders of nonviolent transformations have been people for whom religious traditions have been personally important: Gandhi, Thich Nhat Hanh, Jesus, Martin Luther King, and Ghaffar Khan, who respectively were rooted in and reinterpreted the Hindu, Buddhist, Jewish, Christian, and Islamic traditions. Of course the decisive test is whether identities move toward and include all people as subjects worthy of respect, rather than excluding people of other traditions as objects to be exploited, killed, or forcibly converted.

Despite practical objections that may be raised against efforts to encourage a universal identity[51] and the tendency of religious nationalists to spurn even saintly people within their own traditions who espouse universal identities, the goal of universal brotherhood and sisterhood still seems to express one of the highest ideals of the major religious traditions. Cases such as that of Ghaffar Khan and the Muslim Servants of God suggest that we should not deny an ideal religious principle the opportunity to grow into the promise of its own logic.

Notes

I thank Lawrence E. Sullivan, Diana Eck, Douglas Bond, and Christopher Kruegler for commenting on an early draft of this article; the Center for the Study of World Religions, the Center for International Studies, and the Program on Nonviolent Sanctions, all at Harvard University, for providing a stimulating and congenial context for conducting research; and the Lilly Endowment for generous support of my research.

1. Samuel P. Huntington, "If Not Civilizations, What?" *Foreign Affairs*, 72, no. 5 (1993): 192.

2. Mark Juergensmeyer, "Why Religious Nationalists Are Not Fundamentalists," *Religion*, 23, no. 1 (1993): 86.

3. Elise Boulding is one of the few who has written about a "peace culture," wisely calling attention to the culture of peace that contests the warrior culture within all major religious traditions. See Boulding, "The Concept of Peace Culture," in *Peace and Conflict Issues After the Cold War*, Asbjorn Eide, ed. (Paris: UNESCO, 1992), 108-111.

4. Several heads of government from Muslim societies, in part to divert criticism from their own governments' inefficiencies and corruptions and to win support in Western capitals, have recently emphasized the threat of a globally linked Islamic fundamentalism. In addition, Israeli Prime Minister Shimon Peres has said that "After the fall of Communism, fundamentalism has become the greatest danger of our time." Newt Gingrich, leader of the new Republican strength in the U.S. House of Representatives, has warned that Congress must appropriate more money for covert action against "totalitarian Islam." In contrast, John Esposito, director of the Center for Muslim-Christian Understanding at Georgetown University, has said that "the demonization of a great religious tradition because of the perverted actions of a minority of dissident voices remains the real threat." See Eliane Sciolino, "The Red Menace is Gone. But Here's Islam," *New York Times*, January 21, 1996, E1, E6.

5. Paula Cooey, William Eakin, and Jay McDaniel have presented an enlightening set of ideas for how religious traditions may be interpreted and reconstructed to move beyond patriarchy and to create a postpatriarchal world. See *After Patriarchy: Feminist Transformations of the World Religions* (Maryknoll, NY: Orbis Books, 1992). Analogously, the present analysis explores how religious traditions can contribute to a world "after war."

6. See Gordon Kaufman, *In Face of Mystery: A Constructive Theology* (Cambridge, MA: Harvard University Press, 1993), ix, xi. Sallie B. King makes a similar point with regard to Asian religious traditions in noting that contemporary Engaged Buddhism is characterized by the "justification of new principles in terms of reinterpreted traditional language." See King, "Thich Nhat Hanh and the Unified Buddhist Church," in *Engaged Buddhism*, Christopher S. Queen and King, eds. (Albany, NY: State University of New York Press, 1996), 343.

7. In other contexts I have addressed some of these issues for my own cultural tradition and offered policy recommendations rooted in a normative assessment of U.S. national security policy measured against universal values of human dignity. See Johansen, *The National Interest and the Human Interest* (Princeton, NJ: Princeton University Press, 1980).

8. Pashtuns now have a semiautonomous standing in Pakistan's tribal area, but their earlier efforts to attain greater autonomy were repressed.

9. People living in the lands of the Northwest Frontier Province at the eastern end of the Khyber Pass, for example, were long ago ruled by the ancient empire of Ghandhara and then forced over the centuries to live successively under Persian, Greek, Indian, Indo-Bactrian, Sakan, Parthian, Kushan, Turkish, Mughal, Afghan, Sikh, and British rule.

10. William Crooke, *The Tribes and Castes of the North-Western Provinces of Oudh*, vol. 4 (Calcutta: Government Printing, 1896), 167-68. A variety of terms and different spellings of the same term have been used to identify these people. "Pathan" is a Hindustani popularization used widely in the past by many authors including Akbar S. Ahmed, an anthropologist from this tradition. Yet, as Ahmed notes, Pathan is not an indigenous term. See Ahmed, *Millennium and Charisma Among Pathans* (London: Routledge & Kegan Paul, 1976). The people refer to themselves as Pashtuns, Pukhtuns or Pakhtuns. The latter term parallels the informal designation, Pakhtunistan, given to the territory in which they live by those seeking political autonomy. Pathan seems to be declining in usage because it is not indigenous. Pushtun is becoming a keyword of preference for conducting library searches in North America. Yet because many authorative sources, such as *The Oxford Encyclopedia of the Modern Islamic World* and the *Encyclopedia Britannica*, as well as many contemporary anthropologists, use Pashtun widely, although not exclusively or consistently, it is the term of choice in this article. The Pashtun language is designated as Pashto, Pushtu, or Pakhtu. To be considered a "true" Pashtun, a person's father and mother must both be native Pashto speakers. See Louis Dupree, "Pushtun," in *Muslim Peoples: A World Ethnographic Survey*, Richard Weekes, ed., vol. 2 (Westport, NC: Greenwood, 1984), 622-630.

11. Mohammed Yunus, *Frontier Speaks* (Bombay: Hind Kitabs, 1947), 75-76.

12. These were commonly called "butcher and bolt" expeditions and were "generally regarded as the simplest, cheapest method of 'pacifying' the Pathans." ("India," *Encyclopedia Britannica*, 1994, 99-100).

13. For example, the Pashtuns were also known for their warm hospitality and loyal friendship.

14. He quite literally believed that educating the people of his region was a "sacred duty." See Abdul Ghaffar Khan, *My Life and Struggle* (Delhi: Hind Pocket Books, 1969), 58.

15. *My Life and Struggle*, 95-96. In Eknath Easwaran's view, the idea of a professionally trained nonviolent army based upon military models "stands as one of the pivotal moments in the history of nonviolence, much as does Gandhi's spontaneous decision on September 11, 1906, to fight discriminatory legislation in South Africa through passive resistance." See Eknath Easwaran, *A Man to Match His Mountains* (Petaluma, CA: Nilgiri, 1984), 209.

16. The last British governor of the Northwest Frontier Province acknowledged that British failure to grant representative institutions created the impetus for Ghaffar Khan's movement. For too long, the "theory of the powder magazine was allowed to rule decisions." See Olaf Caroe, *The Pathans* (London: Oxford University Press, 1976), 430-432.

17. See Muhammad Korejo, *The Frontier Gandhi: His Place in History* (Karachi: Oxford University Press, 1993), 49; Nayar Pyarelal, *Thrown to the Wolves: Abdul Ghaffar* (Calcutta: Eastlight Book House, 1966), 37.

18. Dinanath G. Tendulkar, *Abdul Ghaffar Khan: Faith Is a Battle* (Bombay: Popular Prakashan, 1967), 129.

19. Tendulkar, *Abdul Ghaffar Khan*, 97.

20. Wilfred Cantwell Smith, *Modern Islam in India* (Lahore: Minerva, 1943), 258-59.

21. Dinanath G. Tendulkar, *Mahatma: The Life of Mohandas K. Gandhi* (Bombay: Times of India Press, 1951), 302.

22. The context for *sabr* makes it clear that its meaning is close to Gandhi's concept of *satyagraha*. *Sabr* suggests "tenacity in a righteous cause, cheerful resignation in misfortune, forgiveness, self-control, renunciation, refraining from revenge. . . ." See Easwaran, *A Man to Match His Mountains*, 209-210.

23. See Pyarelal, *Thrown to the Wolves*, 32; Ghaffar Khan, *My Life and Struggle*, 23, 231.

24. Mohandas K. Gandhi, *Collected Works*, vol. 42 (Delhi: Government of India, 1963), i-ii.

25. Mahadev Desai, *Two Servants of God* (Delhi: Hindustan Times Press, 1930), 90.

26. *Satyagraha* was the technique developed by Gandhi for social and political change, commonly defined as "truth-force" and "based on truth, nonviolence, and self-suffering." See Joan V. Bondurant, *Conquest of Violence: The Gandhian Philosophy of Conflict* (Princeton, NJ: Princeton University Press, 1988), 270.

27. Korejo, *The Frontier Gandhi*, 20.

28. Tendulkar, *Abdul Ghaffar Khan*, 101-102.

29. Korejo, *The Frontier Gandhi*, 81.

30. See James W. Spain, *The Pathan Borderland* (The Hague: Moutan, 1963), 167. Ghaffar Khan later aligned the Servants of God with the Congress Party rather than with the Muslim League, to the consternation of the British and the Muslim League, in part because the Muslim League had cooperated with the British since the 1920s. When Ghaffar Khan made this alignment, the British immediately offered to institute the same reforms in the Northwest Frontier that they had implemented in the rest of India, if Ghaffar Khan in turn would resign from his connection with the Congress. Ghaffar Khan refused.

31. Gene Sharp, *Gandhi Wields the Weapons of Moral Power* (Ahmedabad: Navajivan, 1960), 110.

32. See J. Coatman, *Years of Destiny, 1926-1932* (London: Jonathan Cape, 1932), 284.

33. Ghaffar Khan, *My Life and Struggle*, 143-45.

34. Yunus, *Frontier Speaks*, 118.

35. William Barton, *India's North-West Frontier* (London: Murray, 1939), 164.

36. Although the Khudai Khidmatgar membership exceeded 100,000 at its high point, estimates above that level vary considerably. Ghaffar Khan reports that at one point there were 100,000 Khudai Khidmatgars in Kohat district alone. Korejo reports the total membership rose to 300,000. Because of spontaneous commitments by large numbers of people to join the Servants of God after major incidents between the Servants and the British, a precise total number is not known. See Ghaffar Khan, *My Life and Struggle*, 133; Korejo, *The Frontier Gandhi*, 61-62.

37. See Yunus, *Frontier Speaks*, x; Tendulkar, *Mahatma*, 292. For a discussion of other Muslim applications of nonviolent action see Ralph E. Crow, Philip Grant, and Saad E. Ibrahim, *Arab Nonviolent Struggle in the Middle East* (Boulder, CO: Lynne Reinner, 1990).

38. See Ghaffar Khan, *My Life and Struggle*, 117, 202; Korejo, *The Frontier Gandhi*, 108; Tendulkar, *Abdul Ghaffar Khan*, 396-97.

39. Of course they also disliked his call for social reform, democracy, and more autonomy for the Pashtun region.

40. In all, Ghaffar Khan was imprisoned for 30 years during his adult life, roughly half at the hands of the British and half by Pakistani officials.

41. See Ghaffar Khan, *My Life and Struggle*, 207-209. Korejo estimates that about three thousand were still in prison in 1963; *The Frontier Gandhi*, 209.

42. See Halide Edib, *Inside India* (London: Allen & Unwin, 1937), 334-36; Bondurant, *Conquest of Violence*, 140.

43. Bondurant, *Conquest of Violence*, 144.

44. Bondurant, *Conquest of Violence*, 140.

45. Edib, *Inside India*, 338.

46. The primary identity of most people in the Servants of God remained Muslim and Pashtun, but these two sources of identity did not conflict, in Ghaffar Khan's mind, with an overlapping universal identity that recognized the humanity of all people. This overlapping universal identity was the basis for opposing communal prejudice and violence against Hindus and Sikhs, as well as for not using violence in defense against British attacks under circumstances in which most people in any major religous tradition would have considered violence justified. After Indian independence and partition in 1947, the tendency of some in the persecuted remnant of the Servants of God to retreat into a narrowing of focus and identity, clinging to goals primarily for Pashtuns, led to loss of support among non-Pashtun Muslim groups in Pakistan and Afghanistan, Hindus, and Sikhs, as well as to additional conflicts with the Pakistani government.

47. For general discussion of this point, see Peter Ackerman and Christopher Kruegler, *Strategic Nonviolent Conflict* (Westport, CO: Praeger, 1994); Jorgen Haestrup, *Secret Alliance* (Odense: Odense University Press, 1976); Adam Roberts, *Civilian Resistance As a National Defense* (Harmondsworth: Penguin, 1969); and Gene Sharp, *Civilian-Based Defense* (Princeton, NJ: Princeton University Press, 1990).

48. See Lary Collins and Dominique Lapierre, *Freedom at Midnight* (New York: Simon & Schuster, 1975).

49. Ghaffar Khan frequently cautioned Muslims against being misled in the name of Islam; see *My Life and Struggle*, 176.

50. Significantly, there is some tendency, a half dozen years after his death, to resurrect the name of Abdul Ghaffar Khan in parts of Pakistan, but the emphasis is on his nationalism rather than on his nonviolent religious beliefs.

51. Critics may say that the effort to adopt a universal identity is an attempt to move beyond the limits of human nature and, perhaps, to lose identity. They argue that only with a less-than-universal identity does one have identity. This argument is unconvincing because people may have multiple, simultaneously overlapping identities as members of a town, province, state, country, professsion, ideologocial group, and religion. Sufficient transnational species identity should be possible to avert lethal violence between people of different national, ethnic, or religious identities, even as people maintain their less-than-universal identities to some degree. Evidence to support this conclusion is found in multinational states or multireligious societies that enjoy internal peace.

7

Indian Secularlism and Its Critics: Some Reflections

Thomas Pantham

Secularism is one of the deeply problematic issues in contemporary Indian political discourse. The participants in this discourse include the Parliament, political parties, journalists, academics, and, in a special way, the judiciary. They espouse a variety of positions, ranging from antisecularist manifestos to campaigns for positive secularism. This discourse does call for an ethico-political assessment. Unfortunately such an assessment is not available in the writings of Indian social and political theorists. Some of them in fact are engaged in advocating models or conceptions of state-religion relationships that are clouded in ethico-political incoherence. They are a source of confusion or misguidance.

What then are the ethically, or, rather, ethico-politically incoherent or untenable models of state-religion relationship that are being advocated in/for India today? How do they compare with, or depart from, the constitutional vision? Is the latter altogether flawless or does it call for some contemporary revisions? If it does in fact need to be amended and if the ethico-political incoherencies of the presently available reformulations are to be avoided, how may we proceed? This last question may be formulated somewhat differently as: What kind of relationship between the state and the religions of the citizens of India can claim ethico-political justifiability or soundness in its favor—some form of *secular* relationship or some form of *antisecular or desecularized* relationship?

I have used the expression "some form of" advisedly because both secular and nonsecular states assume different forms in different contexts.[1] For instance, secularism in the West is usually taken to be emphasizing the *separation* of state and religion, whereas Indiana secularism stresses the equal tolerance of all religions (*sarva dharma samabhava*), even though it also upholds a certain differentiation or relative separation of the political and religious spheres. I shall return to these specificities of Indian secularism later on.

Meaning(s) of Secularism

A satisfactory answer to the aforementioned set of questions would require a large-scale study. As a step in that direction, I shall, in the present exercise, try to indicate some of the ways in which those questions are addressed, explicitly or implicitly, in the contemporary discourse on secularism in India. But first, I must say a few words about the meaning of "secularism" and "secularization."

Secularism (which is often translated as *dharma-nirapeksata*) has its origins in Europe. When it was first used at the end of the Thirty Years' War in Europe in 1648, "secularization" referred to the transfer of the properties of the church to the princes. Similar transfer of church properties to the state also formed a part of the achievements of the French Revolution. Later, in England, George Holyoake used the term "secularism" to refer to the rationalist movement of protest which he led in 1851.

In its pursuit of the project of Enlightenment and Progress through the replacement of the mythical and religious view of the world with the scientific and technological/industrial approach, Europe brought about a *differentiation or separation* of the political sphere from the religious sphere. This process, by which "sectors of society and culture are removed from the domination of religious institutions and symbols," came to be variously referred to as the "secularization" or desacralization of the world.[2] In addition to this idea of (1) the *separation* of religion and politics, "secularism"/"secularization" also means (2) the diminution of the role of religion; (3) this-worldly orientation rather than orientation towards the supernatural; (4) the replacement of the "sacred" or "mysterious" conception of the world with the view that the world or society is something that can be *rationality manipulated or socially engineered*; and (5) a view of religious beliefs and institutions as *human constructions and responsibilities* rather than as divinely ordained mysteries.[3]

While these are the meanings of "secularism" in the West, its use in India is accompanied by a significant variation. In fact, because of this variant or *sui generis* nature, the term "secularism" was not included in the Constitution until it was added through a 1976 amendment, even though the original Constitution did contain several provisions which left no one in doubt about the *secular* (i.e. nontheocratic and noncommunal) character of the Indian state and which, in 1973, made the full bench of the Indian Supreme Court to rule that "secularism" is a constitutive feature of the *basic structure* of the Constitution.

In the West, as I noted above, secularism usually refers to the state's separation from, or indifference toward, religion. Hence, the Western antonym of "secular" is "religious." In India, by contrast, it is "communal" that is the antonym of "secular." This is so because given the pervasive religiosity of the people and pluralism of religions, an ethico-politically appropriate pattern of relationship between religion and state had to be one that stressed the equal respect and tolerance of all religions, rather than the erection of any insurmountable wall of separation between the state and religion.

However, a secular state, so conceived, had to make interventions *against* such religiously sanctioned social evils as *sati* (widow burning), polygamy, child marriage, untouchability and other caste-based discriminations. The ethico-political justification for such a reformist intervention by the state was provided by the Western post-Enlightenment liberal-secular theory of the person, society and state—a theory which called for or justified the differentiation or relative separation of the political and religious spheres.

Secularism and the Indian Constitution

Instead of blindly copying Western secularism, the framers of the Indian Constitution, as insightfully pointed out by Professor P. K. Tripathi, "contemplated a secularism which is the product of India's social experience and genius."[4] The main articles of the Constitution providing for a "secular state" may be briefly summarized as follows:

1) All persons have equal freedom of conscience and religion.
2) Discrimination by the state against any citizen on grounds of religion is forbidden.
3) Communal electorates are forbidden.
4) The state has the power to regulate through law any "economic, financial or other secular activity" which may be associated with religious practice.
5) The state has the power to provide for "social welfare and reform or the throwing open of Hindu religious institutions of a public character to all classes and sections of Hindus."
6) Untouchability stands outlawed by Article 17.
7) Subject to public order, morality and health, every religious denomination has the right to establish and operate institutions for religious and charitable purposes.
8) All religious minorities have the right to establish and administer educational institutions of their choice, and they cannot be discriminated against by the state in its granting of aid to educational institutions.
9) No citizen can be discriminated against on grounds of religion for employment or office under the state as well as for admission into educational institutions maintained or aided by state funds.
10) Public revenues are not to be used to promote any religion. However, specified

176 Thomas Pantham

amounts of money from the Consolidated Fund of the States of Kerala and Tamil Nadu are to be paid annually to their Devasom Funds for the maintenance of Hindu temples and shrines which have been transferred to them from the state of Travancore-Cochin.

11) No religious instruction is to be provided in educational institutions which are wholly maintained out of state funds, with the exception of those state-run educational institutions whose founding endowments or trusts require such instruction to be provided in them. Moreover, no person attending any educational institution "recognized" or "aided" by the state can be required to take part in any religious instruction or worship that may be conducted in it unless she/he or her/his guardian has given consent to it.

12) By a Constitutional amendment in 1976, all citizens are enjoined to consider it their fundamental duty to "preserve the rich heritage of our composite culture."

This Indian constitutional framework on secularism is premised on an ethico-political philosophy or ideal of the freedom, equality and fraternity of all its citizens. It is from the perspective of that ideal or moral-political philosophy that the Constitution provides for certain state interventions for the reform of the socio-religious traditions and, subject to "public order, morality and health," for the tolerance, by the state, of the religious form of individual or social life which any or all of its citizens may pursue. This secularism is not antireligious. It is also not blind to, or acquiescent in, the social evils and discriminations that are perpetrated in the name of religion.

Contemporary Debates

The most important contemporary challenge to Indian secularism has been mounted by the forces of Hindu nationalism. In its turn, the ideology of Hindu nationalism has received strong criticism in the writings of some very influential academic writers, notably Ashis Nandy, T. N. Madan and Partha Chatterjee who, interestingly, are also severe critics of the theory and practice of the secular state in India. How, then, are the relationships between politics and religion addressed in their writings?

Since the mid-1980s, the BJP (Hindu nationalist party) and the "Sangh Parivar" have been insisting on a distinction between their own "positive secularism" and the "pseudo-secularism" of the Congress. According to them, "positive secularism," which would mean "justice for all and discrimination against none," should replace the prevailing "pseudo-secularism," whereby the word "secularism" is misused to denigrate the Hindu categories and symbols of the majority community and to justify the pampering of the minority communities.[5]

According to T. B. Hansen, the ideology of *Hindutva* and "positive" or "true" secularism amounts to the principle of rule by Hindu majoritarianism. He notes that it is a "peculiar co-articulation of brahminical ideologies of purity, romanticist notions of fullness and authenticity, and quasi-fascist organicism and celebration of strength and masculinity which characterizes the RSS and its affiliated organizations."[6]

The ideology of "positive secularism" is also subjected to serious criticism in the writings of Partha Chatterjee, T. N. Madan and Ashis Nandy, who, as I mentioned above, are also critics of secularism. I now turn to their writings.

According to Nandy, Nehruvian secularism, which separates state and religion and which has been imposed on the Indian people, is part of a larger package of scientific growth, nation-building, national security, modernization, and development. These constitute a "modern demonology, a *tantra* with a built-in code of violence." Whereas secularism demands that members of religious communities dilute their faith so that they can be truly integrated into the nation-state, it "guarantees no protection to them against the sufferings inflicted by the state itself" in the name of its "secular, scientific, amoral" ideology of nation-building, security, development, etc. As a handy adjunct to these "legitimating core concepts," secularism helps the state-elites

> to legitimize themselves as the sole arbiters among traditional communities, to claim for themselves a monopoly on religious and ethnic tolerance and on political rationality. To accept the ideology of secularism is to accept the ideologies of progress and modernity as the new justifications of domination, and the use of violence to achieve and sustain the ideologies as the new opiates of the masses.[7]

This rational-scientific secularism of the Western/Nehruvian variety, Nandy claims, has failed either to eliminate religion from politics or to promote greater religious tolerance. Hence, it can "no longer pretend to guide moral or political action." He writes: "(A)s far as public morality goes, statecraft in India may have something to learn from Hinduism, Islam or Sikhism; but Hinduism, Islam, and Sikhism have very little to learn from the Constitution or from state secular practices."[8] Nandy goes on to declare that he is not a secularist or, rather, that he "can be called an anti-secularist."

By so criticizing secularism, Nandy does not mean to privilege the communalist ideology of either the majority or minority religious communities. To the contrary. These communalist ideologies are, in his view, the pathological by-products of modernity; they are the dialectical "other" or counter-players of modernity's secular state. He notes that the khaki shorts of the RSS cadres are modeled on the uniform of the colonial police. According to him, the ideology of Hindu nationalist revivalism or fundamentalism, with its borrowing of the models of semitic religions and of the modern Western nation-state, is "another form of Westernization" in the sense that it seeks to

> decontaminate Hinduism of its folk elements, turn it into a classical Vedantic faith, and then give it additional teeth with the help of Western technology and secular statecraft, so that the Hindus can take on, and ultimately defeat, all their external and internal enemies, if necessary, by liquidating all forms of ethnic plurality—first within Hinduism and then within India, to equal Western Man as a new *Übermen-*

schen.[9]

Crucial to Nandy's analysis is a distinction he makes between two conceptions of religion, namely: (1) religions as tolerant and accommodative faiths or folk ways of life; and (2) religions as politically constructed monolithic, communalist ideologies of sectarianism and intolerance. The former, he says, characterized the premodern and preliberal way of life in India, whereas the latter is a product of modernity's nationalism and statecraft.

The next move in Nandy's argument is to suggest that given the constitutive role of modern nationalism and its statecraft in generating and nourishing religious communalism, the ideology of the secular or nonreligious nation-state is resorted to as an instrument to combat the sectarianisms of communalist organizations. This counterposing of the tyranny of the modern secular state and the violence of modern communal organizations is, in Nandy's view, nothing but the internal dialectics of modernity's nation-state paradigm.

By this reasoning, both communalism, be it the majoritarian or the minoritarian variety, and the secular state stand condemned as the perverse gifts or, rather, the inevitable products of Western modernity. In Nandy's view, the ethico-politically appropriate alternative to them lies in the nonmodern, presecular conception of religions as accommodative, tolerant faiths or ways of life practiced, in exemplary manner, by Asoka, Akbar, and Gandhi. They, he reminds us, derived their religious tolerance not from secular politics but from Buddhism, Islam, and Hinduism, respectively. "Gandhi's religious tolerance," he writes, "came from his anti-secularism, which in turn came from his unconditional rejection of modernity."[10]

Like Nandy, T. N. Madan maintains that religious zealots, who contribute to fundamentalism or fanaticism by reducing religion to mere political bickering, are provoked to do so by the secularists who deny the very legitimacy of religion in social life.[11] According to him, because it denies the immense importance of religion in the lives of the peoples of South Asia, secularism is in this region an impossible credo, an impracticable basis for state action and an impotent remedy against fundamentalism or fanaticism. Ruling out the establishment of a Hindu state as an utterly unworkable proposition, Madan concludes that "the only way secularism in South Asia, understood as interreligious understanding, may succeed would be for us to take both religion and secularism seriously and not reject the former as superstition and reduce the latter to a mask for communalism or mere expediency."[12] He commends Gandhi not only for emphasizing the inseparability of religion and politics but also for opening up avenues of interreligious understanding and "of a spiritually justified limitation of the role of religious institutions and symbols in certain areas of contemporary life."[13]

Somewhat like Nandy and Madan, Partha Chatterjee too finds that the ideology of secularism is not an adequate or appropriate political perspective for meeting the challenge of the religious communalism of either the majority or minority communities. In his view, the conventional or official model of Indian secularism and the present campaign for setting up a "positively" secular state have brought India to a "potentially disastrous political impasse."[14]

According to Chatterjee, the project of the nation-state in India has, since its birth, been implicated "in a contradictory movement with regard to the modernist mission of secularization." One part of this nationalist-modernist project was the bringing about of a rational reform of the socio-religious sphere, while another part or task was the secularization of the public-political sphere by separating it from religion. Describing the contradiction between these two parts of the project of modernist secularization, Chatterjee writes that the interventionist violation, by the state, of secularism's principle of the separation of state and religion "was justified by the desire to secularize." Thus, according to him, the enormous powers vested in the Tamil Nadu Government's Commissioner for Hindu Religious Endowments is an instance of the anomalies in the operation of the secular principle of the separation of state and religion. As another such anomaly or contradiction he mentions the fact that the principle of the equality of religions is compromised by the exclusion of persons professing certain religions from the benefits of positive discrimination given to the scheduled castes.

Turning to the recent shift in the ideological articulation of Hindu nationalism, Chatterjee points out that its present championing of "positive secularism" is meant not only to deflect accusations of its being antisecular but also to rationalize, in a sophisticated way, its campaign for intolerant interventions by a modern, positively secular state against the religious, cultural or ethnic minorities in the name of "national culture" and a homogenized notion of citizenship. "In this role," writes Chatterjee, "the Hindu Right in fact seeks to project itself as a principled modernist critic of Islamic or Sikh fundamentalism and to accuse the 'pseudo-secularists' of preaching tolerance for religious obscurantism and bigotry."[15]

The quandaries generated by the career of the democratic state in India and the potentially disastrous nature of the new politics of "positive secularism" lead Chatterjee to the conclusion that the theory and practice of the secular state cannot bring about the needed toleration of religious, ethnic and cultural differences. In so denouncing secularism, Chatterjee is in agreement with Nandy. However, they differ from each other in what they take to be the desirable and feasible alternative to the standard and positive versions of secularism. While Nandy's "antisecularist manifesto," as we noted above, is couched in terms of the nonmodern, preliberal philosophy, symbolism, and theology of tolerance in the everyday faiths of Hinduism, Islam, Buddhism, and Sikhism, Chatterjee's search is for a "political" conception of tolerance "from within the domain of the modern state institutions as they now exist in India." Chatterjee's intellectual efforts are directed not to secularize the state but to highlight "the duty of the democratic state to ensure policies of religious toleration."

Chatterjee seems to me to be saying that for a proper conception of toleration of religious, ethnic, and cultural differences, we need to go beyond the "state sovereignty vs. individual rights" discourse of liberalism. Adopting some of Foucault's ideas on the nature of power in modern societies, he sees religious, cultural, and ethnic communities as well as the secular state as institutional sites of power or as strategic locations of the politics of identity and difference. This being so, according to him, arguments for a universal framework of governance based on so-called pure secular-rational grounds are just "pious homilies" in that they ignore its strategic context of power-political struggles over issues of identity and difference. In other words, the conflict between the claims of secular-rational universalism and the claims for the autonomy of, and respect for, religious or ethnic minorities is not a simple conflict between reason and faith; it is a form of power-political conflict over issues of identity and difference.

On what grounds, then, can a minority group claim autonomy of, and tolerance for, its way of life and way of thought? According to Chatterjee, the ground for such autonomy and tolerance can only be the principle of respect for persons. He writes:

Toleration here would require one to accept that there will be political contexts where a group could insist on its right not to give reasons for doing things differently provided it explains itself adequately in its own chosen forum. In other words, toleration here would be premised on autonomy and respect for persons, but it would be sensitive to the varying political salience of the institutional context in which reasons are debated.[16]

In Chatterjee's view, this approach to religious toleration by the state does not call "for any axiomatic approval of a uniform civil code for all citizens." It would, however, mean that when a religious community insists "that the validity of its practices can only be discussed and judged in its own forums, those institutions must have the same degree of publicity and representativeness that is demanded of all public institutions having regulatory functions." In other words, if a religious community seeks to gain or preserve its autonomy and respect from other persons or from the state, it must conduct its own affairs through representative public institutions in so far as those affairs are not confined to simple matters of innocent beliefs or holy rituals. If a religious group is intolerant towards its own members and shows inadequate respect for persons, it cannot claim tolerance from others. Moreover, if a group or community refuses to enter into a reasonable dialogue with others on the validity of its own practices, it cannot claim respect for its ways.

Critique of Critics

In many of these critical writings on secularism in India, what is being denounced is not only the idea of the secular political institutions but also the ideas of progress, modernity, science, state, and development. Without meaning to deny their "dark side," I feel it is necessary for us to recognize their "bright side" as well. With special reference to the issue of secular political institutions and policies, it cannot be denied that these have served, in India, to emancipate several categories of victims of religiously sanctioned social evils, such as untouchability, *sati*, etc. That Indian citizens such as Shah Bano seek (and are able to secure) secular interventions by the state in their behalf undermines the sweeping condemnation of secularism by the critics whose views have been considered above. As rightly pointed out by Upendra Baxi: "We do not need to exuberantly enfeeble the state and law, in their meandering attainments of 'secularism,' in order to deactivate enmity, and activate mutual toleration, in civil society."[17]

Nandy, it may be recalled, makes a sweeping denunciation of development, science, state, etc. It may also be recalled that Madan finds secularism to be inapplicable to India because its people remain attached to religions. Let me apply Madan's logic to Nandy's reasoning about the utterly oppressive nature of development, state, science, etc. What do we make of that conclusion if we take it that there is an ever-increasing clamor for development, modernization, science, etc. from the part of the people in even the remotest villages of India?

Almost all the critics of Indian secularism, including Nandy and Chatterjee, maintain that given the pervasive role of religion in the lives of the Indian people, secularism defined as a *strictly or absolutely rational* separation of politics or the state from religion would only be an intolerable imposition of an alien ideology on the Indian society. I do not wish to contest either this judgment or its premise about the persuasiveness of religion in people's lives. I do, however, feel that it is wrong to assume, as most critics tend to do, that the Indian constitutional vision of, and provisions for, secularism means such a conception of secularism, namely, the complete or absolute separation of politics/state from religion. I shall return to this point shortly.

Some of the critics, notably Nandy and Madan, find the contemporary Indian model of secularism to be wanting from a so-called Gandhian standpoint. I, too, feel that the presently operating Indian model of secularism is vastly different from the Gandhian conception of the relationship between religion and politics. I cannot, however, agree with the way in which the Gandhian model is claimed by these critics to be different. In my view, they mistake the Gandhian model or perspective as either, a la Chatterjee, a probourgeois one or, a la Nandy, a premodern, preliberal and antisecular one. To me Gandhi seems to have inaugurated a postliberal, ethical-secular trajectory of relationship between politics and religion in which their relative autonomy from each other is used in moral-political experiments or campaigns for the reconstruction of both the religious traditions and the modern state.[18] So understood, the Gandhian approach seems to me to be serving as a critical standard or ideal which brings into bold relief the ethico-political deficiency or limits of the operative and "positive" models of secularism as well as of the alternative models of Nandy, Madan, and Chatterjee.

The foregoing interpretation, given by the critics, of the Gandhian conception of the politics-religion relationship as being premodern, preliberal and antisecular, and their assumption that secularism means the strict separation of state and religion, need to be further examined. In what follows, I shall take a step in that direction by outlining an alternative interpretation of these two aspects of their line of thinking.

Let me begin with the common charge against Indian/Nehruvian secularism, namely, that it seeks to bring about a rigid or complete separation of state and religion. True, the atheists and agnostics, including Nehru at several stages in the evolution of his thought, did hold such a view of secular politics. But that view was *not* made the basis of either the Constitution or the political institutions founded on it. The secular political institutions which Nehru helped to found have been envisaged or designed not to be antireligious but to be governed by the principle of *sarva dharma samabhava*. Acknowledging this, he wrote in 1961:

> We talk about a secular state in India. It is perhaps not very easy even to find a good word in Hindi for 'secular.' Some people think it means something opposed to religion. That obviously is not correct. . . . It is a state which honors all faiths equally and gives them equal opportunities.

Thus, the Constitution, as repeatedly clarified in the adjudicatory discourse of the Supreme Court, envisions and upholds a *sui generis* Indian model of secularism entailing a *nonabsolutist or relative* separation of politics and religion—a model that is clearly different from both the theocratic and fundamentalist models of the state and from the "wall of separation" models of secularism in some Western countries. Far from being antireligious, the Indian state is envisaged by the Constitution to be *equally tolerant* of all religions.

This activity or policy of giving equal tolerance to all religions is not a strictly religious activity or policy. It is a *moral-political* activity or policy which is predicated on a *relative separation* of the political from the religious. It assumes that political institutions and political policies can be constructed and operated in *different ways and for different purposes* from those of religious institutions or religious doctrines.

Despite its variant or *sui generis* character, Indian secularism cannot be said to be situated entirely outside the problematic and thematic of the Western discourse on secularism. The problematic relationship between religion and politics in the West had its analogies in India too. Despite important philosophical or metaphysical differences between them, both European Christianity and Indian religions rationalized, in their own ways, a feudal order of social inequalities prevailing during the medieval period. In India, Hinduism and the other religions were, in different ways and different degrees, complicit in the "social construction" of the social evils mentioned above, namely, *sati*, untouchability, etc. Hence, an ethico-political reform of the socio-religious sphere constituted an integral part of the Indian Freedom Movement. Both the moderate and extremist wings of the Indian National Congress were committed to, and engaged in, wide-ranging programs of socio-religious reform, which gave primacy to the individual's fundamental rights over the collective rights of religious communities.

There was, however, a significant difference between the perspectives and approaches of the moderates and the extremists even though both of them assigned an interventionist role to the state. While the moderates and, in a special sense, Nehru thought of socio-religious reforms on the basis of secular-scientific reason, the extremists maintained that the Hindu religious vision contained an ethical or *dharmic* dimension or level which can be reinterpreted to justify social reform and *religious tolerance* as opposed to *communalism or sectarianism*.

Gandhi went beyond the moderates and the extremists in two respects. Firstly, he maintained that not only Hinduism but all other religions have within them an inherent quest or yearning for a universal ethics of toleration, a yearning that can be an emancipatory resource in moral-political struggles against the untruth or political immorality of communal hatred and violence. Gandhi, in other words, maintained that interreligious harmony can be secured without requiring the people to give up their religiosity or ethicality. Secondly, Gandhi held the view that the modern state itself needed to be "civilized" by integrating it with spirituality or morality, which he believed can be obtained through democratic-political engagements with the basic teachings of the different religions.

For Gandhi, in other words, the Indian quest for an ethico-politically appropriate pattern of relationship between state and religion had as its relevant "background" factors not only the pervasive religiosity of the Indian people and the social evils sanctioned by religions traditions but also the fact of the morally flawed, utilitarian, materialist, imperialist character of the modern state that was already operating in India under colonialism. Hence the political intervention for the reform of the socio-religious sphere had to have as its seamy side some form of ethical or moral intervention for transforming the modern state. Accordingly, the Gandhian vision of Indian secularism, as it seems to me, entails a relative autonomy of the political and the "religious" (*qua* ethical or spiritual or moral) such that they can engage each other in a reconstructive way. In other words, the Gandhian vision of the Indian quest for *purna swaraj* (complete self-rule) or *sarvodaya* through Parliamentary *swaraj* entails not only the principle of reformist moral-political intervention in the socio-religious sphere but also a program of moral-political experiments to integrate political institutions and practices with the principles of *satya* (truth) and *ahimsa* (nonviolence). The significance of this latter part of the Gandhian vision of the politics-religion relationship or, rather, politics-ethics relationship is not grasped adequately or properly by the contemporary critics and redefiners of Indian secularism.

Notes

1. For a convenient classification, see S. K. Mitra, "Desecularizing the State: Religion and Politics in India after Independence," *Comparative Studies in Society and History*, 32 (1991).

2. See P. L. Berger, *The Social Reality of Religion* (London: Allen Lane, 1973), 113.

3. See Upendra Baxi, "The 'Struggle' for the Redefinition of Secularism in India: Some Preliminary Reflections," *Social Action*, January-March 1994, 17.

4. P. K. Tripathi, "Secularism: Constitutional Provisions and Judicial Review," in *Secularism: Its Implications for Law and Life in India*, G. S. Sharma, ed. (Bombay: N. M. Tripathi Pvt. Ltd. 1966), 193.

5. See Nana Deshmukh, *Our Secularism Needs Rethinking* (Delhi: Deendayal Research Institute, 1990).

6. T. B. Hansen, "Globilization and Nationalist Imaginations: Hindutva's Promise of Equality Through Difference," *Economic and Political Weekly*, March 9, 1996, 608. For a critical review of the literature on the ideology of Hindu nationalism, see Thomas Pantham, *Political Theories and Social Reconstruction: A Critical Survey of the Literature on India* (New Delhi: Sage Publications, 1995). The RSS is a wing of the Hindu nationalist movement.

7. Ashis Nandy, "The Politics of Secularism and the Recovery of Religious Tolerance," 13 *Alternatives* (1988): 192.

8. Nandy, 185-86.

9. Nandy, 187.

10. Nandy, 192.

11. T. N. Madan, "Secularism in its Place," *Journal of Asian Studies*, November 1987.

12. Madan, 758.

13. Madan, 757.

14. Partha Chatterjee, "Secularism and Toleration," *Economic and Political Weekly*, July 9, 1994.

15. Chatterjee, 1768.

16. Chatterjee, 1775.

17. Upendra Baki, 28.

18. See Thomas Pantham, "Post-Relativism in Emancipatory Thought: Gandhi's Swaraj and Satyagraha," in *The Multiverse of Democracy*, D.L. Sheth and Ashis Nandy, eds. (New Delhi: Sage, 1996).

8

Confucianism and Communitarianism in a Liberal Democratic World

Russell Arben Fox

Introduction

Nearly twenty years ago, John Dunn suggested that "democratic theory is the public cant of the modern world"; that, in this late day and age, "a democracy is what [it] is virtuous for a state to be."[1] The headlines bear this out. One need not turn to Francis Fukuyama or Samuel Huntington—though their writings can certainly help[2]—to realize the absolute high ground to which the ideal (if not the practice) of democracy has ascended with the collapse of its more collectivist rivals. Fred Dallmayr's observation that "the near-providential advance of liberal democracy, apprehended only dimly by Tocqueville over a century ago, seems to have reached in our time its destined goal and global fulfillment,"[3] could have no finer confirmation than that of the story of Wang Zhenyao, a little-known bureaucrat for the Ministry of Civil Affairs in the People's Republic of China. A tireless exponent of an as-yet "experimental" village democracy program, he has visited over one thousand small rural villages in ten years time, teaching election basics such as voter privacy to often doubtful party officials. Included in his intellectual arsenal is a thorough background in agricultural policy, a strong trust in the common sense of the people, and a Chinese translation of Tocqueville's classic, *Democracy in America*.[4]

How much does the near ubiquitous presence of democratic claims and aspirations on the world stage really mean? In the realm of political theory, it raises as many questions as it lays to rest. For instance, David Held argues that the "uncritical affirmation of liberal democracy essentially leaves unanalyzed the whole meaning of democracy and its possible variants"[5]—and despite the mutuality of sources, the variations between Wang Zhenyao (who sees democracy first and foremost as a way to increase the Communist Party's legitimacy) and most Western exponents of the Tocquevillian tradition (one thinks of Robert Bellah) are great indeed. This problem of difference, in fact, has come to be central to any discussion of democracy's global future. Can the innumerable differences between peoples—religious, cultural, linguistic, historical, and so forth—equally accept and, when necessary, submit to the "institutions of liberal democracy, capitalist free enterprise, and the spread of rational technologies," as David Hall defines the "Modern Age,"[6] or will these differences give rise to resentments toward what Benjamin Schwartz calls the "incorrigibly Western" aspects of our modern democratic world,[7] and thereby inaugurate a new round of conflict, between both states and "civilizations"?[8]

The effort to consider politics within and through non-Western philosophical models is an initial but still important part of engaging this problem. This essay, in what is hopefully a spirit conducive to Wang's good work, takes up a major thread in contemporary democratic thought—communitarianism—and posits it alongside the Confucian heritage of East Asia. In recent years these terms have been too often casually combined or contrasted, to the detriment of both. The similarities between communitarian and Confucian theory deserve deep consideration, both because of what each can teach the other, and because of what they together may contribute to democracy's ongoing march.

Was Confucius a Communitarian?

There are two main reactions to the juxtaposition of classical Confucianism[9] and communitarianism: that it is obvious, and that it is absurd. On the one hand, it is widely (though not universally) assumed that the societies of "Confucian Asia"[10] hold to a set of values fundamentally opposed to those of the West. The label "communitarian" has been frequently used to describe this orientation: In a debate in *Foreign Policy* five years ago, Bilahari Kausikan defended the "communitarian traditions of Asia" as superior to the "adversarial institutions of the West"; Aryeh Neier responded that Kausikan's communitarianism was a "consensus imposing" that it served to mask "authoritarian systems" of government.[11] There has been little moderation in these positions since: for many, a vulgar Confucian-style communitarianism, often traveling under the banner of "soft" authoritarianism, is accepted as the primary obstacle to the liberalization of East Asia.[12]

At the same time, equating Confucianism with contemporary communitarianism is somewhat ridiculous. Confucius was not struggling against a fiercely individualistic and legalistic polity or a materialistic, socially atomized culture. His world—the declining years of the Easter Chou dynasty, two and a half millennia ago—was marked by the near total collapse of internal order and frequent wars between rival warlords. Confucius's audience was not, to borrow descriptions common to the communitarian analysis of liberal citizens, an alienated and discontented population; rather, he spoke to an educated few who were attempting to preserve and promote some sort of civilization in the midst of decades of vicious civil conflict.

To avoid either a polemical or a historically simpleminded equivocation of communitarian and Confucian political theory, it is necessary to move beyond most existing political categories. The election of Kim Dae Jung as South Korea's president provides a fine example in this regard. Kim's election is certainly a meaningful triumph for democracy in Confucian Asia; in his long career as an activist he has often argued against intimately associating Asian culture with authoritarianism, and has recently claimed that much of his nation's financial difficulty lies with past leaders' devotion to a corrupt "Asian-style democracy."[13] But alongside his long admiration for and residence-in-exile in the United States, Kim can still speak of communal "civic frugality campaigns" and other moral endeavors in a manner quite different from any modern Western democrat.[14] What Kim Dae Jung and (in their own way) Wang Zhenyao and other democrats scattered throughout Confucian Asia represent is the move towards a new political formulation, one which challenges both the easy liberalism of classic "modernization theory" as well as the defiant authoritarianism of Lee Kuan Yew.

One recent analysis of this still-developing formulation claims that those East Asian nations which have begun to adapt to the political expectations of the "Modern Age" have indeed modernized, but *not* in the direction of liberal democracy. Instead, it is argued, these nations are developing "illiberal" democratic structures so as to protect and promote "communitarian ways of life," in particular those economic and civic resources seen as supportive of both a strong, active family life and the preservation of moral authority.[15] This suggestion—that East Asia's Confucian heritage points toward a particular theory of communitarian democracy—is an intriguing one. For sure, the basic Confucian texts rarely speak directly on any political matters, much less democratic ones. But Confucianism *does* speak clearly to many theoretical concerns which adumbrate the foundations of the communitarian critique of liberal democracy. In Tu Wei-ming's view, "Confucian communitarianism, far from being a romantic utopian assertion . . . takes as its theoretical and practical basis the natural order of things in human society: the family, neighborhood, kinship, clan, state and world."[16] A similar emphasis on the constitutive power of associations natural to human society, whether they be "a family or tribe or city or class or nation or people," lies at the heart of contemporary communitarian writings.[17]

The proper question, then, is not whether Confucius was a communitarian, but in what way classical Confucianism can serve communitarian ends in what appears for the moment to be a relentlessly modernizing and democratizing world. Such an inquiry need not only benefit thinkers in Confucian Asia struggling with the lure of liberal modernity. Classical Confucianism itself may contribute to communitarian thinking in the West. John Wallach complained over ten years ago that "despite wide-ranging claims about the political bearings of their works, [communitarians] make virtually no comments" about the sort of community the liberal democratic world "desperately needs and foolishly ignores,"[18] and in this he was being prescient. Communitarians have usually been better at analyzing the history of liberalism and the theoretical foundations of community than at actually asking how modern communities actually should be organized, and for that reason many communitarian claims against liberalism have seemed speculative, at best.[19]

Classical Confucianism, on the other hand, provides a system of constitutive practices and principles that shape communities both practically and theoretically. Institutional Confucianism, to be sure, is a thing of the past, but Confucianism's political contributions need not be restricted to such forms. As Lujun Yin suggests, the language of Confucianism must undergo a "philosophical reconstruction," since Confucian culture in the modern world "can rely for its formulation and life *only upon our creative interpretation* of it."[20] By considering the parallels between certain aspects of Confucian thought and the contemporary communitarian critique of liberalism, the interpretive possibilities of Confucianism can be expanded far beyond their traditional conservative, monarchial associations; they may even be understood as a contribution to East Asia's haphazard embrace of liberal democracy, and an example to communitarians who hope to prevent that embrace from being an overly trusting one.

Communitarian Criticisms of Liberalism

Contemporary communitarian theory draws upon many different sources: Aristotle's *polis*, Rousseau's general will, Hegel's *Sittlichkeit*, Arendt's *vita activa*, and many more have provided grounds for challenging the character of liberal modernity. Some versions of communitarian thought focus primarily upon self-government, others on human virtue or the importance of religious institutions. Whatever their theoretical approach, however, their dominant theme is the "failure of liberal society to foster a sense of community among its citizens." H. N. Hirsch, who wrote critically of the communitarian movement, called this claim "a weariness with the politics of interest" that seeks instead "the politics of love."[21] While it is probably too much to say that most communitarians are searching for love in their writings, their worry over the influence of individual interest in society is unquestionable.

The most powerful basic argument against self-interested politics is that a society ruled by such claims a degree of neutrality which it cannot philosophically defend. To say that person A and person B may both pursue what they perceive to be in their best interest, and should only be limited in their pursuits when said interests lead them to interfere with each others' pursuits, is to say that the pursuit of individual interest is always superior to *any other value*—including normative values that may suggest minimizing or abandoning certain pursuits, or collectively focusing on others. Of course, that very claim to impartiality between interests is in itself *normative*, and thus the interests-first definition of politics it articulates is fundamentally confused. Liberalism, or at least this bare skeleton of it, can never justify its own neutrality, for to defend self-interest on anything other than idiosyncratic terms would require an appeal to something larger than the self, and it is exactly that ill-defined "largeness" which a politics of individual interest is designed to ignore.[22]

More important than the philosophical argument, however, has been the civic one: that this failure of justification leaves us with only weak utilitarian supports for our choices, and such supports are insufficient to sustain either the sense of fraternity and common purpose most individuals crave, or the sacrifice and devotion that human existence occasionally demands. What communitarians emphasize is that to distrust any larger idea of expectation or mutuality, even for the best reasons,[23] is ultimately reductionist; it "denies the need for collective concepts or depicts them as the result of aggregations of individual trans-actions."[24] Such an atomized vision of human existence precludes thinking in terms of roles or responsibilities, which results in individuals (and societies) unable to address the possibility that certain normative issues may be funda-mental to their being. In the end, it becomes difficult for a purely liberal polity to promote activities and sentiments which are necessary to the survival of liberal freedom and self-government in the first place.[25]

Moving beyond self-interest and reviving a sense of common aspiration towards the good life requires a reemphasis on our collective existence. Charles Taylor approaches this issue by way of language: a dialogic relationship between person A and person B introduces them to interests that are not just individual creations but rather collective goods. The rituals of language bring people not only into contact with one another but with diverse ways of understanding which shape particular opinions and ideas, both past and present. In orienting oneself to these alternative approaches to the subject at hand, the "monological mind-state" cannot hold; what were individual meanings become *our* meanings, and the contest over those meanings therefore becomes all the more important. It becomes possible to articulate something greater than mere aggregate interest, to introduce a common, moral force to what previously had been indistinguish-able from simple preference. "The move from the for-me-for-you to the for-us," Taylor writes, "the move into public space, is one of the most important things we bring about in language, and any theory of language has to take account of this."[26]

Of course, to emphasize the bonds within a common language will involve an inevitable devaluation of other languages. Yet in a pluralistic society there are a variety of tongues. Isn't it better, many liberals argue, to allow for undisci-plined, even exclusive and self-interested conversations, so to prevent anyone from being silenced? This concern involves two related issues. First, given a multicultural society—one with multiple voices, languages, and norms—the liberal values that most communitarians, as products of the West, generally share suggest a need to establish at least some critical distance between the individual and community, so as to allow for protest and prevent extremes of oppression. In short, community norms should recognize some "overarching values."[27] How these values are to be expressed, and how to justify them, is perhaps the greatest challenge facing those who would argue for a politics which can discuss the common good. The issue of establishing a fundamental ground that can accommodate a pluralistic community begs an second issue, however: community-building. Even allowing for a general theory of community norms, how is a community to be constructed that will allow such norms to be articulated?

Most theorizing of community structure runs along a "spectrum" between two poles. Roughly speaking, collective ties arise from either the mutual acceptance of a common authority by various individuals, the mutual participation in a common activity by those same individuals, or some combination of the two. In both forms of community, individuals "tend to" a certain shared conception of the good, whether embodied in an authoritative text, person, or body of thought (as in many religious communities), or in a historically developed set of practices (as in most civic organizations).[28] Many societies, of course, involve elements of both, but speaking theoretically it is not misleading to characterize communities as organized around rituals of *authority* or *activity*. Contemporary thinkers associated (not always by themselves) with communitarianism range between these poles, with theorists such as Michael Walzer, Benjamin Barber, and Sheldon Wolin, and possibly Hannah Arendt, emphasizing strong, direct, and intimate civic practices, and others, such as Alasdair MacIntyre, William Galston, Charles Taylor, and Michael Sandel, emphasizing the importance of allowing society to operate in light of authoritative and constitutive traditions and purposes (though the methodological approaches and preferred traditions of this latter group vary greatly).[29] Of course, both of these forms of ordering are seen by liberals as possible sources of communitarian extremism. George Kateb fears that the communitarian search for activity may replace democracy with docility and even incipient fascism, while Will Kymlicka contends that the development of any authoritative common good or language perpetuates the antidemocratic exclusion of marginalized groups.[30]

And classical Confucianism? In a surprising way, the thought of the early Confucians develops an approach to community order that involves *both* poles. Confucian ritual suggests standards of authority and activity which merge in ways unusual in Western experience. To inquire after the theoretical character of this ritual community is a relatively new task; whereas many philosophers have approached classical Confucianism with the aim of developing theories of virtue and justification, which would provide the aforementioned moral ground upon which communities may be built, few have tried to "think through" the actual theory and practice of Confucian community itself.[31] That task will be the focus of the remainder of this paper.

Confucian Forms of Community Order

In order to understand how forms of authority and activity work together to create a Confucian community one must first establish what its basic theoretical elements are. David Hall and Roger Ames list several subjects essential to "Confucian political theory": "the cultivation of personal life, ritual activity (*li*) as the foundation of penal law (*fa*), social roles and institutions, the ordering of names, the official as model, and so forth." To say the least, this list suggests a politics of a "distinctly different coloration" from the Western tradition.[32] Not all of these elements can be considered in the space of this essay, but taking three of them—the relationship between ritual activity and law and order, the importance of historically informed social roles, and the idea of personal cultivation—through a hermeneutic reconstruction should serve to demonstrate 1) the relationship between community-ordering activity and authority in classical Confucianism, and 2) how that relationship can be seen to support a uniquely powerful communitarian vision, one which parallels many of communitarianism's complaints with modernity while avoiding falling into any antidemocratic extremes.

An Ontological Difference

The idea that penal judgments should be premised upon traditional ritual practices rather than on codified laws may sound strange to Western ears, especially in the context of a discussion of democracy. The idea of a "transcendental natural law [or] a contract with mutual obligations enforceable by an independent judiciary" is basic to Western democratic thought; yet such notions of "legal right" are absent from classical Confucianism.[33] Confucius was distrustful of relying on what he called "guiding the people by edicts, and keeping them in line with punishments"—that is, depending upon specific laws—as a grounding for the social order, because law does not respect the need for virtue (*Analects* 2/3). This is not to say that he was a moral absolutist who rejected the rule of law entirely; indeed, Confucius contrasted favorably the man who has "respect for the law" with one who always seeks "special treatment" (*Analects* 4/11). Mencius expanded on Confucius's views well when he said that "Virtue alone is not sufficient for government, but law unaided cannot make the government move" (*Mencius* 4/A/1). In general, Confucius believed that a reign of virtue should depend more upon contexts of moral persuasion and social shame than on universally applicable penal laws.[34] Virtue here (the Confucian term is *te*) essentially means "that which embraces the Way (*tao*)"—a concept which served as the morally validating touchstone of most ancient East Asian thought.

Of this concept, Wing-tsit Chan wrote:

We are likely to describe [it] as the absolute, *noumenon*, transcendental; but it is
not. It is the Chinese Way, the Way of existence, the process of being. It is not to
be equated with something which bifurcates subject and object. No! It is the subject
itself; the way is the thing. . . . This is the philosophy of immanence, the way of
things, the way *in* things. Sometimes we assume a dichotomy, that transcendence
and immanence are two different things. That must not hold in the Chinese way of
thought. We do not distinguish between the human and the nonhuman.[35]

Chan's reference to the "human and the nonhuman" is intriguing. Was
Confucius a pantheist as the West understands the term? Possibly—but theology
of any sort is far from Confucius's mind in the *Analects* ("If you are not yet
able to serve man, how can you serve the spirits?"—11/12). Another interpretation of the concern for the "nonhuman" is that the *tao* is literally all things
under Heaven (*t'ien*), given, uncreated. The earliest Chinese religious
beliefs—of the Shang and early Chou—developed an awareness of the world that
bespoke, simultaneously, a timelessness and immediacy; they had no creation
ex nihilo, no natural eschatology.[36] The *tao* was an "onto-cosmological
reality," a constant immanent process of "presenting" the universe.[37] The early
Chinese saw themselves as neither strangers to nor the culmination of this
universe, but simply one more set of participants within it.

As participants, however, it was acknowledged that there was a superior—a
moral—way of living and participating in the world which could be known and
would be made manifest through ritual activity. These *li*, which included
different creative arts, music and poetry, various standards of decorum, and acts
of reverence and propriety, were centuries old by Confucius's time.[38]
Depending on the social role one inhabited—father, son, ruler, minister, and so
forth—a different set of rituals would be appropriate. But Confucius saw these
ritual acts not as merely rites of worship or filial piety, but as suggestions
of—even invitations to—an intimate connection between the person performing
the rite and the immanent order of things itself, one portion of which was *t'ien*,
the "supreme moral will" from which the power of the rituals emanated, though
it did not formally "ordain" the rules of the rituals themselves. In Benjamin
Schwartz's description, "the entire body of *li* itself, even when it involves
strictly human transactions, [also] involves a sacred dimension."[39]

These ancient rituals, which defined, through historical tradition, the different
ways of being in the world, were for Confucius literally "magical." They held
a transformative power; not unlike Charles Taylor's depiction of dialogue
transforming one's moral awareness, *li* took "the explicit and detailed pattern of
that great ceremony which is social intercourse," and makes it part of an
immanent moral world.[40] Activity—of the right sort—became moral in itself,
absent an objective moral end. Such a life would need no strained self-definition
or self-analysis, for the individual would in a peculiar sense recede: an

immanent sociality, not the sovereign individual, would be the root of things. This is not to say that the individual, as an involved, interested and even occasionally defiant self, had no place in Confucian thought—Confucius is quoted as having said that "if one determines one's heart to be right, one goes forward even against men in the tens of thousands" (*Mencius* 2/A/2). But Confucius also felt that the occasions for such vigorous affirmation should be rare. Deference is an important virtue in the *Analects*; Confucius feared that too much talking (that is, self-regard) could lead a person to forget their relationship with *t'ien* through *li*. Indeed, it is deference to tradition which enables a person to participate in, as opposed to merely react to, the immanent order of the world in the first place. Confucius himself once contemplated giving up speech; when his disciples pleaded with him not to, he replied, perhaps mocking them, "What does Heaven ever say? Yet there are the four seasons going round and there are the hundred things coming into being. What does Heaven ever say?" (*Analects* 17/19) Divine power was revealed in, through, and by human action. Thus could the orthodox Confucian very literally say, "*T'ien* is the author of the *te* that is in me" (*Analects* 7/23).

Human Roles and Human Authority

But what does this moral ontology mean for law and politics? Does it mean that an individual in a Confucian community would have only his "ritual virtue" to protect himself against possibly abusive authorities? There is the fear that while the *li* "may be useful in restoring a sense of community . . . [they] simply do not serve the same antimajoritarian role as rights. They [cannot] protect the individual and minorities against the majority, the community, the state."[41] Perhaps—but that is not the whole story. First, Confucianism and human rights are not necessarily *obviously* incompatible; the actual question is more complicated.[42] Second, and more importantly, this fear does not consider the character of authority in Confucian society. Confucius's position was that *all* forms of authority, rather than be centered in legal constructions, should rest upon that *te* which exists in conjunction with one's communal, ritual relationship with *t'ien*. *Li* did not just bind the individual to the power of *t'ien*, but they bound every member of society, and all their respective responsibilities, to each other in a manifest moral order. The idea of the world revealing a moral order in which we participate is an old one in Western culture, but not one that has survived modernity very well. In *li*, on the other hand, there is a sense of "showing forth"; ignoring ritual priorities left one "ill-equipped to take a stand" (*Analects* 16/13). To take a stand is a public act, involving not just a private, inner ordering, but a creating of social meanings as well. This resulted in a uniting of one's personal and public life—the "ritualistic and social," in Karyn Lai's words.[43] Through Confucius "the *li* themselves came to be regarded less as modes of hieratic action than as paradigms of human relations,"[44] which suggests that all individuals would be dependent upon every other individual to "carry out their responsibilities appropriately according to their particular places in the social structure."[45] The exercise of authority, in other words, required the cooperation of all.

Part and parcel to this was what has been called the "autonomous moral sense of the people," and everyone's equal responsibility to their own ritual place in the social order.[46] Does this mean that Confucius saw all men as equal? Not quite—he probably would have regarded the imposition of a universal equality of persons as madness. But there was a "parity" amongst all participants in the social order; as Steven Walker describes it, "Confucian equality is . . . fully relational, involving reciprocity based on societal and familial roles."[47] This notion of reciprocity (*shu*) plays a significant role in the *Analects*, and points toward an understanding of Confucian "parity." Obviously not all roles are equal; the famous *Wu Lun* or "Five Relationships" of Confucian orthodoxy (father/son, older brother/younger brother, ruler/minister, husband/wife and friend/friend) are, with one exception, between unequals. But such inequality is hardly an invitation to domination: the "golden rule" of Confucianism ("do not impose on others what you yourself do not desire"—*Analects* 12/2) is still in operation. Moreover, all unequal relationships shift over time: sons become fathers, students become learned, young women become mothers, and so forth. Those responsibilities—and hence opportunities for exercising (and submitting to) various forms of authority—specific to particular social roles change over the course of time and across social space. There is in Confucianism, as in other systems of ancient East Asian thought, a *yin-yang* heuristic which describes an ultimate balance, a parity, in and through such change. The "line" which distinguishes one role from another never divides irrevocably; there is, instead a "symmetrical relatedness," in which one part of the Confucian cosmos is always "becoming" another.[48] In short, authority becomes diffused and ultimately reciprocal in Confucian society, giving Confucianism a sort of "moral equality."

Of course, this parity between roles is both potential and developmental, but that does not mean that the only recourse when suffering abuse in a Confucian community is to simply endure it. Mencius wrote that there are times when dissent and even revolution are nothing less than a duty on the part of those who desire to be virtuous.[49] Moreover, the aforementioned diffusion of authority is not a methodical process; rather, in a deeply aesthetic sense, authority arises almost spontaneously, without mediating structures, through ritual activity. "If a man is correct in his own comportment, then no commands will be necessary" (*Analects* 13/6). There is not, in Confucian communities, what might be called the "line of authority"; rather, there is a plurality of authorities, each taking on an authoritative character particular to their social role and their *li*. In an argument in some ways similar to MacIntyre's, "authoritative" actions are particular to specific times, places, and traditions, not embodied with supposed neutral procedures. Accepting the possibility of a meaningful moral structure in the world makes it possible for an individual to become an "author" of her own personal narrative, thus supporting and perpetuating the creation of those moral structures.[50] A farmer may be virtuous in his farming and thus speak as an "authoritative" farmer; later, as a virtuous father, he may have authority in that role. Authority is "disclosed" through creative, contextual, and personal acts of *li* and thus is constantly in flux. Roger Ames writes that in a "ritual-ordered community, particular persons stand in relationships defined by creativity rather than power. This distinction between power and creativity is essential" to classical Confucianism.[51]

With authority perceived as more tied to human artistry than power, there is a "transformation of all social relationships into personal relationships."[52] This elevation of personal creativity makes the exercise of authority, and the performance of *li*, an extremely intimate affair. Individuals come to be understood as tightly bound to a common good, not merely tolerating each other within a constructed neutral space. The absence of such a space, however, may appear to pose a contradiction. While an intimate, ritually ordered moral world discounts both the possibility of and need for more empirical or rational concentrations of power, it in some ways also challenges the very idea of creativity. If activity only retrenches the actor in a closely defined ritual and traditional role, where is that "space" which gives room for creativity in the first place?

Far more than any concern with authoritarianism, this is probably the most difficult element of classical Confucianism for many Westerners to understand. Confucius's insistence that individual human beings are not puppets but active and, to a degree, independent *participants* in the Way ("It is man who is capable of broadening the *tao*, not the *tao* which is capable of broadening man"— *Analects* 15/29) is difficult for devotees of the idea of autonomy to reconcile with the influence of tradition in Confucian thought. To this there are two responses. The first is one best made by Hans-Georg Gadamer: Like it or not, we are *all* the creation of our own historical traditions, both in our acceptance and our rejection of them. The "prejudices" of history is what gives us a world within which we may think, act, judge, critique, and commit to one or another direction or set of beliefs; without a linguistic and historical fore-structuring, creative *and* critical thought would be an impossibility. The retrenching that our daily reinterpretation of the world at hand results in is the only way we can have any picture of the world at all—otherwise it would be a mass of information, meaningless. Without a living sense of historical tradition, our ability to even *recognize* issues of conformity and difference, much less judge between them, is greatly restricted.[53]

Secondly, one might say there is a misunderstanding here. One's given place in life—one's role as a son, an American, a mother, a doctor, a student, etc.—do not stymie creativity, because they are not self-conscious "performances" that are required of one's "performing self." One can be a good daughter, surely, but not by choosing to "submit" one's own abstract being to the task of "acting good." Creativity is a much more collective enterprise, in which social signification and meaning—and not just social ends—are created. The classical Confucian concept of finding *te* in one's immanent place collapses some (though not all) of the distinction between what one is and what one *does,* for one does nothing alone. Henry Rosemont writes:

> For the early Confucians there can be no "me" in isolation, to be considered abstractly: I am the totality of the roles I live in relation to specific others. Moreover, these roles are interconnected in that the relations in which I stand to some people affect directly the relations in which I stand with others, to the extent that it would be misleading to say that I "play" or "perform" these roles; on the contrary, for Confucius I *am* my roles. . . . It should become clear that in an important sense I do not achieve my own identity, am not solely responsible for becoming who I am. Of course, a great deal of personal effort is required to become a good person. But nevertheless, much of who and what I am is determined by the others with whom I interact, just as my efforts determine in part who and what they are at the same time. Personhood, identity, in this sense, is basically conferred on us, just as we basically contribute to conferring it on others. Again, the point is obvious, but the Confucian perspective requires us to state it in another tone of voice: my life as a teacher can only be made significant by my students; in order to *be* a friend, I must *have* a friend; my life as a husband is only made meaningful by my wife, my life as a scholar only by other scholars.[54]

This then is the basic connection between authority and activity: in a morally immanent universe, where meaning and identity are created through activity rather than discovered through inquiry, meaningful actions—those which complement one's own self and one's community—bind not only through collective participation (as varied as the styles of participation may be), but through the authority credited to the particular inhabitants of those roles. In doing so, additional sources of moral authority are developed, as activity leads to activity and individuals develop different understandings of their place in the community. A Westerner, however, perhaps suspicious of allowing community authority to be distributed in so unregulated a manner, might still ask about the possibility of abuse. What is to prevent the pursuit of advantage and self-interest, whatever the role or "level of authority" one inhabits? Confucius's writings demonstrate that this was his greatest concern—that *li* would not be properly understood, and the authority given to each in their different times and places would become unreliable and untrustworthy. He recognized that engaging in one's *li* while avoiding the lures of profit or fame required "overcoming the self" (*Analects* 12/1). This overcoming, which is crucial to the whole Confucian notion of authority, involved the personal cultivation of "benevolence,"or *jen.*

Personal Cultivation as Community Ordering

Jen plays the central role in the *Analects*—which does not mean it is easily understood. It has been variously translated as "benevolence," "humanity," "generosity," and even "love." It may be that part of the problem in understanding *jen* arises from translators' tendencies to express it in psychological terms. This is not to say that "benevolence" is not a legitimate translation, but there are other meanings of *jen* in addition to the inner one. One may also think about *jen* as representing particular human beings. Peter Boodberg observed:

> *Jen* (仁), "humanity," is not only a derivative, but is actually the same word, though in a distinct graphic form, as the common vocable *jen* (人), "man," *homo*. That is no mere pun . . . the consubstantiality of the two terms is part and parcel of the fundamental stratum of Chinese linguistic consciousness, and must be reflected in the translation.[55]

Both *jen* (仁) and *jen* (人) mean "person," but persons of qualitatively different types. There are "moral" people and the "people at large."[56] But the gulf between the two is not unbridgeable. Through an education in *li* specific to one's role, one gains learning, and thus becomes *jen* (仁), whatever one's place in society. This explains the enormous importance that Confucius attached to a humanistic education—learning of one's *li* through a study of the classics allowed a person to perceive the mutual immanence of all things, and develop an appropriate sense of awe for the moral history of the world. An educated person goes beyond the "letter" of their *li*: "Unless a man has the spirit of the rites, in being respectful he will wear himself out, in being careful he will become timid, in having courage he will become unruly, and in being forthright he will become intolerant" (*Analects* 8/2). Without a proper education in the tradition, living a ritually ordered life may become stifling, and could make one suspicious and demanding. Such was exactly what Confucius wanted to avoid; he recommended that individuals "inquire earnestly and reflect on what is at hand," for in so doing there "would be no need to look for *jen* (仁) elsewhere" (*Analects* 19/6).

Identifying benevolent human existence as something particular and spontaneously related to what is "at hand" suggests once again that the moral authority of *jen* is inherent in one's own sphere of activity. "What might be *jen* (仁) under one set of circumstance is not necessarily *jen* under another."[57] And, perhaps more importantly, not all benevolent or authoritative humans are the same; in Confucian communities there is "a respect for individual styles of life, deemed as polymorphous expressions of a common culture."[58] Or as Mencius put it, the (always unfolding) pursuit of *jen* may involve many "different paths" (*Mencius* 6/B/6). Whatever their path though, Confucius makes it clear that it is these educated, virtuous individuals, the *jen* (仁), who have authority. Such benevolent, authoritative persons had a special role—their own ritual and social activity—in a community that saw itself as intimately bound together. Surely those in certain positions had more and greater responsibility to show forth authority than those in other roles. But this was not a caste system—Confucius rejected dividing anyone into different "categories" (*Analects*

15/39). Education is not to be reserved for any elite—no matter how poor or lowly a person (*jen* 人), becoming *jen* (仁) remained a possibility. Confucius's argument is simply an acknowledgment that within a community, authority will and should be divided, and one's understanding of and dedication of the common good will play a crucial part in determining to what extent that authority is respected.

Simply put, community in classical Confucianism is a *horizontal* concept. Through ritual activity, everyone holds to their roles, and everyone, in different times and places, has the potential to show forth, through their participation in community activities, the sort of authority which binds the community together. The ultimate result is what has been called a "fiduciary community," described by Fred Dallmayr as one wherein the participants, "without being blandly homogenized, maintain their distinct role[s] through mutual responsiveness and faith-keeping."[59] The fact that Confucianism has over the centuries supported hierarchical governments that have ignored this ethical and moral perspective is tragic but beside the point of what Confucius and his disciples actually wrote.[60] Abusive authority—authority that seeks to amass power behind individual interests—is no longer authority at all, and by extension, any ruler (or father, or older brother) who acts without benevolence or mutuality corrupts their own ability to be part of the cooperative, ritual relationship with *t'ien* which grounds the immanence of the Confucian system. The practical upshot of this, in Benjamin Schwartz's opinion, is that classical Confucianism "represented an age-long sustained resistance to a tendency toward *Gesellschaftlichkeit* in the nature of the state."[61]

On a related point, Confucius asserted that the self-interested, expansive attitude which claims "I do not enjoy being a ruler, except for the fact that no one goes against what I say" would likely lead a state to ruin (*Analects* 13/15). Hall and Ames observe that "superiors [within a community] have an . . . interest in the people. Given that personal, social, and political realization [in Confucian communities] are coextensive, the possibilities for those above are very much a function of the richness" of the lives of those beneath them.[62] But there is a distinction to be made here, between having an "interest in the people" and having "interests." The institution of a general moral vision of tradition and ritual in no way suggests that all members of the community need to submit to one objective truth. Such an assumption is a mistake that arises from assuming that transcendent, teleological verities are at the heart of any quest for moral order. But this ignores the common East Asian "assumption that order is immanent in and inseparable from a spontaneously changing world."[63] Embracing a moral order surely involves shaming those who are "immoral," but it does not necessarily involve coercive instruction of the wayward. One's devotion to *jen*—or lack thereof—will be manifest in one's work within one's tradition: a practical judgment of whether or not one is, in one's one realm of proper authoritative action, complementing the community. Such an act of judgment is described in the *Analects* in terms reminiscent of Aristotelian *phronesis*—it is prudent, respectful of tradition and history, but concerned foremost with the cultivation of the self. Consider:

> Confucius said, "A ceremonial cap of linen is what is prescribed by the rites. Today black silk is used instead. This is more frugal and I follow the majority. To prostrate oneself before ascending the steps is what is prescribed by the rites. Today one does so after having ascended them. This is casual and, though going against the majority, I bow before ascending." (*Analects* 9/3)

Such a practical approach toward tradition exemplifies the Confucian awareness of *ch'uan*, or the need for "moral discretion" or expediency in particular circumstances. Antonio Cua suggests, referring to Confucius's refusal to hold "preconceptions about the permissible or impermissible," that there will always be a need to exercise "judgment in dealing with uncertain, exigent situations . . . it is important for the adherent of the Confucian tradition not to favor any one doctrine of interpretation."[64] All this points toward an ideal of authority, of any sort, being exercised not just in light of an immanent morality but with a sense of judiciousness, pragmatism, and reserve. If anything, in explicitly political terms a Confucian community is relatively decentralized and makes few demands;[65] its leaders, however arrived at, are too concerned with *their* moral, ritual roles, not the particular activities of every member of the community. Edward Shils suggests, on the basis of *Analects* 15/5 (which describes the emperor Shun, "who achieved order without taking action"), that Confucius believed that leaders should be "disinterested" in their subjects.[66] And Roger Ames adds:

> Since in Confucian ethical theory morality is entirely natural and intrinsic, it is not necessary for the ruler actively to augment the character of his subordinates in order to achieve social and political order. Rather, it is a matter of his participating with them in the realization of the incipient virtue which is already theirs by nature. Both the ruler and the subordinate pursue the consummation of their natural possibilities in dialogue. . . . In the ideal relationship . . . neither imposes on the other or elicits from him anything which is inconsistent with his own natural development.[67]

Authoritative individuals in this way become "models" around which assessments of praise and shame could be articulated.[68] Obviously therefore, those in authority, whatever their sphere, must put their "interest" in the natural immanence of their given roles over their own "interested" participation in said roles. It is the difference between a selfish farmer, who wants to maximize produce for personal profit, and an authoritative farmer, who cares about good farming (i.e., the sort which complements the moral needs and traditions of the community as ritually understood—see *Analects* 4/16). There is a horror here of allowing instrumental concerns to trouble the cultivation of *jen,* the absence of which would empty ritual activity of its transformative, community-ordering power. For Confucius, neither person nor society should be

> subordinated as an instrumental means to serve the realization of the other. Rather,
> they stand as mutually implicatory ends. Any and all semblance of order in society
> and the state is ultimately traceable to and is an integral feature of the personal
> ordering of its constituents. . . . Sociopolitical order itself is traceable to the
> concerted achievement of personal order amongst the people. Confucius on
> numerous occasions moves to underscore the interdependence of sociopolitical
> order and the ordering of the particular person. . . . The pursuit of social and
> political harmony must always begin from personal cultivation.[69]

The ordering discussed here is ultimately a creative concept. The governing
of society would be a natural outgrowth of the ordering of the inner man, as
reflected in the outer community. When one properly sees this artistic bent to
Confucius, one can better understand his attitude towards pluralism. Confucius's
writings show a respect for harmony, and his attitude towards *li* was far from
restrictive: "With the rites, it is better to err on the side of frugality than on the
side of extravagance; in mourning, it is better to err on the side of grief than on
the side of formality" *(Analects* 3/4). To Confucius, one who was *jen* (仁)
would seek consensus in a way that respected difference and did not expect
uniformity *(Analects* 13/23). Such a respect for difference, when understood in
conjunction with Confucius's statements of deference, suggests an almost
postmodern attitude regarding language: "Confucian language . : . appeals to
present praxis *and* to the repository of significances realized in the traditional
past in such a manner as to set up deferential relationships between [the
speaker], his communicants, and authoritative texts invoked."[70] The charges
of metaphysical determinacy and uniformity, which have plagued liberal
modernity, are simply inapplicable in the Confucian context; as was said of
Confucius, he refused to be "inflexible or to insist on certainty" *(Analects* 9/4).

In all this, one finds an emphasis on consensus, on fitting in with one another.
Our mutually involved relationships with the immanent moral world are creative
and communal, not power-centered or competitive. Certainly belonging to a
group circumscribes possibilities, but that act of normative "closure" is what
transforms an open plain into a particular space, and the goods of ordered
communities only exist in such spaces. The Western artist is often depicted as
creating through rebellion; for Confucius, what the artist creates "makes new"
through joining together. Such an artist is less a self-conscious critic or an
autonomy-demanding rebel than a selfless "friend of the world."[71] In a sense
then, this returns us to Hirsch's complaint, and we find he may have been right:
the classical Confucian community, at least, is one that disavows interest, and
makes politics a place for fellowship, perhaps even love.

Communitarianism and
"Postmodern Confucian Democracy"

In sum then, does classical Confucianism lend itself to the communitarian critique of liberalism? It does in several ways, both practical and theoretical:

The Idea of Immanence

Classical Confucianism embraced a view of the world which avoids what Robert Solomon called the "transcendental pretense"—the idea of abstract objective knowing as a privileging and empowering concept. The Confucian thought cannot accommodate a materialistic or atomistic worldview; its whole perspective embraces social interdependence. While the Western world is far from being as "enchanted" as the world of Confucius, the notion of an immanent morality is not absent from the Western tradition. And as Taylor points out, any republican or communitarian regime "requires an ontology different from atomism."[72]

An Acceptance of Authoritative Roles, Rituals, and Traditions

Liberal modernity tends to reduce the idea of roles to "stereotypes" that are to be shattered by individuals through a process of education and general enlightenment. And without doubt, many traditional practices are demeaning, even oppressive. Still, to challenge authority simply on the basis of the fact that it complicates human autonomy is to reduce all activity to questions of dominion, ignoring the possibility that roles, duties, and practices may help unify or complement human existence, even direct it toward a particular good. Both communitarians and Confucians argue that human existence is an "embedded" phenomenon, depending far more on communal, inherited meanings than individualistic ones. Confucius would fully agree with the claim that "individuals . . . are able to be virtuous largely *because of* the authoritative obligations and expectations that inhere in the customs and practices of public life."[73]

A Belief in the Transforming Power of Public Activity

While few communitarians would refer to public rituals—whether political, religious or otherwise—as "magical," they recognize that outside the binding actions of social existence, including those developed within the historically given associations of one's everyday life, the meaningfulness of *any* sort of social responsibility—self-government, public accountability, etc.—can be greatly truncated. To preserve a level of civility in society (and thus those values basic to a free society), the private and public worlds, manifest in and through one's personal and social activities, must be seen as having a relationship that is both mutually enriching and, at times, circumscribing and obliging.[74]

A Sense of Disinterestedness and Devotion to the Community

In Confucian thought, the natural immanence of human existence makes indulgence in particular interests an affront to the *tao*; he emphasized a vision of human society wherein those who were *jen* (仁) would serve all the community through their own spheres of action. Similarly, for communitarians like Wolin, citizens "have to acquire a perspective of commonality, to think integrally and comprehensively rather than exclusively."[75]

These are some primary similarities; other intersections between Confucian and communitarian thought include emphasizing change through collective action rather than procedural mechanisms, understanding the power of shame, emphasizing civic and moral education, and so on. No doubt the list could be expanded even further. But classical Confucianism does not support *all* communitarian arguments. On one end of the aforementioned community "spectrum," while the immanent ontology of Confucian culture may save Confucian communities from abstract, procedural thinking, it also prevents authoritative appeals to transcendent beliefs: the religious community, as it is understood in the West, is not compatible with the classical Confucian worldview, and that is in some ways a troubling prospect.[76] On the other end, classical Confucianism, for all the value it places on ritual participation and activity, does not really enjoin individuals to a true *agon* over their future; the willingness to make politics central to one's life, and the struggle against others and oneself to transform that life when necessary, is basically absent from the Confucian sense of creative continuity.[77]

Can classical Confucianism support a theory of communitarian democracy that combines elements of both authority and activity, rather than wholly embracing either? As was said at the beginning of this essay, the democrats of Confucian Asia are necessarily reaching across categories. The reconstruction of the Confucian heritage presented here suggests that moral authority can be aesthetic instead of transcendent, and political activity can be pragmatic rather than procedural. A democratic formulation which followed these lines would be something wholly new, but that does not mean it would not be a democracy.

The very reason this inquiry is a pressing one is that "each of the concrete activities and institutions most associated with modernization," including "liberal individualism and the democratic institutions that uphold it," are "sustained by modalities of modern consciousness which are currently in crisis."[78] In an increasingly postmodern world, the meanings of Confucian Asia's premodern heritage hold great promise, for both the worried liberals of the West and the Wang Zhenyaos and Kim Dae Jungs of the East. But nothing could be further from the careful reconstruction of Confucian political theory attempted here than to insist, in some blandly postmodern vein, that liberal democracy's time is past and done. Liberal democracy would not have such global appeal if it did not continue to solve basic problems of legitimacy, and fill basic longings for liberty. Seung-hwan Lee expressed this concern well when he wrote that suggesting communitarian responses to certain postmodern dilemmas facing Confucian Asia "may not only be inappropriate, [it] may obstruct the recognition of the desperate need for revision" in their traditional practices and politics.[79]

David Hall and Roger Ames characterize our current situation as a "modernizing" Confucian Asia in dialogue with a "postmodernizing" West, a dialogue not likely to produce any winners.[80] But nonetheless the dialogue will continue, if only because economic necessity (and desire) continues to shrink the distances—and consequently highlight the differences—between us. Finding a place for those differences amidst the current hegemony of liberal democracy is the point of presenting classical Confucianism's uniquely composite approach to community. At the same time, students of classical Confucianism cannot ignore how it transforms the relationship between what one is and what one does; in the communitarian democracies Confucian Asia may be reaching toward, the personal may be much more public. Tu Wei-ming agrees that the "lack of clear boundaries between public and private in East Asian societies, occasioned by the pervasive influence of politics in all segments of the lifeworld, may not conform to the Western model" of democracy. But perhaps even divergence from the liberal democratic heritage can be negotiated. In the hypothetical "postmodern Confucian democracy" presented here, the substance of the relationship between public and private would indeed be subject to certain moral "authorities," but the source of that authority would be the collective attachments built up by *all* the participants in the political community. Such attachments, in focusing attention on family integrity, the relationship between group and personal activity, and the "indigenous categories" of civil society, may amount to a wholly "alternative vision of modernity," one which escapes current dichotomies.[81]

In times of cultural conflict and change, a breadth of vision is important. It allows one to notice, among other things, that the theoretical character of both liberal democracy and classical Confucianism may be subject to distortion. There is such a thing, after all, as liberal virtues, and classical Confucianism's idea of community never denied the possibility of disagreements regarding the common good, or even organized partisanship on behalf of different interpretations of it (though such combinations would need to be creations of common principle, not interest).[82] Moreover, in learning from and adapting to liberal modernity, Confucian Asia may find answers to liberal democracy's difficulties substantially similar to the West's, only differing in methodology. For instance, David Wong suggests that the immanent moral project manifest through Confucian *li* might serve the same purpose that notions of "civility" once did in the West: to make possible a respectful arbitration between differences, a way of addressing "the tension between community and diversity" without legalistically pronouncing against one or the other.[83] Even Francis Fukuyama has suggested that

Confucian democracies might have "communitarian social habits" capable of counterbalancing the modern world's "atomizing tendencies."[84]

Surely no Asian state would want to unreflectively accept the identification of political Confucianism with a communitarian form of democracy. To do so would ignore both complexities within the Confucian tradition and unresolved issues within contemporary communitarianism, and would likely end in the sort of authoritarianism individuals that Lee Kwan Yew so blithely endorses today. However, as this essay has hopefully shown, a careful reconstruction of classical Confucian thought supports many communitarian criticisms of liberalism, while rarely challenging those central premises of modernity which make liberal democracy such a powerfully attractive ideology in the first place.

Notes

1. John Dunn, *Western Political Theory in the Face of the Future* (Cambridge: Cambridge University Press, 1979), 11.

2. For example, Francis Fukuyama, *The End of History and the Last Man* (New York: Free Press, 1992), and Samuel Huntington, "Democracy's Third Wave," *Journal of Democracy* 2 (1991).

3. Fred Dallmayr, "Justice and Global Democracy," in *Justice and Democracy: Cross-Cultural Perspectives*, Ron Bontekoe and Marietta Stepaniants, eds. (Honolulu: University of Hawaii Press, 1997), 443.

4. Steven Mufson, "A Quiet Bureaucrat, Promoting the Vote One Village at a Time," *The Washington Post*, 14 June 1998, A1, A24-25.

5. David Held, ed., *Prospects for Democracy: North, South, East, West* (Cambridge, MA: Polity Press, 1993), 14.

6. David L. Hall, "Modern China and the Postmodern West," in *Culture and Modernity: East-West Philosophic Perspectives*, Eliot Deutsch, ed. (Honolulu: University of Hawaii Press, 1991), 50.

7. Benjamin Schwartz, "Culture, Modernity, and Nationalism—Further Reflections," *Daedalus* (Summer 1993): 207.

8. See Samuel Huntington, "The Clash of Civilizations?" *Foreign Affairs* 72 (Summer 1993): 22-49.

9. In this essay "classical Confucianism" refers to principles taught in the *Lun Yu* (the *Analects,* or selected sayings, of K'ung Fu Tzu or Confucius) and, to a lesser degree, in the *Meng Tzu* (the *Mencius,* a collection of sayings attributed to an early Confucian scholar of that name). Unless otherwise stated, all quotations from the *Analects* and the *Mencius* will be based on the translations of D. C. Lau; see *The Analects* and *Mencius,* ed. and trans. D. C. Lau (London: Penguin Group, 1979 and 1970, respectively). Confucian concepts and texts will be referred to in English by their common (if somewhat inaccurate) Wide-Giles transliterations.

It is admittedly difficult to isolate a single strain of Confucian thought which deserves the label "classical." Over the centuries there have been numerous interpretations of Confucius's writings, and many rival schools of Confucian and Neo-Confucian thought. This paper will attempt to stay close to the historical Confucius, turning to Mencius only when his comments are directly pertinent to subjects already brought up in the *Analects.*

The use of Mencius, as opposed to other early interpreters of Confucius, is a reflection of his close association with Confucius's original writings through the centuries, during which the two works have been joined together in the *Ssu Shu* (the *Four Books*), long the basis of an orthodox Confucian education. Over the last thirty years many authors have contributed to a revival of the "classical" Confucian message; their work, which will often be referred to in this essay, has been significant enough that one Confucian scholar has suggested that we may be on the verge of new "epoch" of Confucian humanism. See Tu Wei-ming, "Towards a Third Epoch of Confucian Humanism," in *Way, Learning, and Politics: Essays on the Confucian Intellectual* (Albany: State University of New York Press, 1993), 141-159.

10. Most scholars include China, Taiwan, North and South Korea, Singapore, Japan and sometimes Vietnam in this region. Some useful texts which treat this area as a whole include *Confucian Traditions in East Asian Modernity,* Tu Wei-ming, ed. (Cambridge, MA: Harvard University Press, 1996); *The East Asian Region: Confucian Heritage and Its Modern Adaptation,* Gilbert Rozman, ed. (Princeton: Princeton University Press, 1991) and Peter Moody, Jr., *Political Opposition in Post-Confucian Societies* (New York: Praeger, 1988). Moody uses "post-Confucian" to indicate the political transformation of institutional Confucian regimes, not the end of the influence of the classical Confucian tradition itself.

11. See Bilahari Kausikan, "Asia's Different Standard," and Aryeh Neier, "Asia's Unacceptable Standard," both in *Foreign Policy* 92 (Fall 1993): 35, 43.

12. The oft-made association between the "communitarian values [which] constitute the persistent and dominant social and political understandings in East Asia" and authoritarianism is noted and criticized in Daniel Bell, "A Communitarian Critique of Authoritarianism: The Case of Singapore," *Political Theory* 25 (February 1997): 6-32, see esp. 7 and 26, 5.

13. Kevin Sullivan, "South Korea's Kim Blames 'Lies' For Turmoil," *The Washington Post*, 9 January 1998, A1, A26; see also Kim Dae Jung, "Is Culture Destiny? The Myth of Asia's Anti-Democratic Values," *Foreign Affairs* 73 (November/December 1994): 189-194.

14. Kim Dae Jung, "Korea and the Future of the Pacific Basin," speech delivered at The Georgetown University School of Foreign Service, April 8, 1997, photocopy in possession of author.

15. Daniel Bell, David Brown, Kanishka Jayasuriya, David Martin Jones, *Towards Illiberal Democracy in Pacific Asia* (New York: St. Martin's Press, 1995), 1-16, 36-40.

16. Tu Wei-ming, "Embodying the Universe: A Note on Confucian Self-Realization" in *Self as Person in Asian Theory and Practice,* Roger T. Ames, Wimal Dissanayake, and Thomas P. Kasulis, eds. (Albany: State University of New York Press, 1994), 181.

17. Michael Sandel, *Liberalism and the Limits of Justice* (Cambridge: Cambridge University Press, 1982), 174.

18. John R. Wallach, "Liberals, Communitarians, and the Tasks of Political Theory," *Political Theory* 15 (November 1987): 593.

19. Communitarianism has long been faced with accusations of nostalgia or irrelevancy. Partly this is unavoidable: as Michael Walzer has argued, at the present time communitarianism mostly functions as a periodic correction, reminding modernity of its worst qualities and reinforcing its better ones, without ever actually being able—or willing—to propose an alternative way of life. See Walzer, "The Communitarian Critique of Liberalism," in *New Communitarian Thinking: Persons, Virtues, Institutions, and Communities*, Amitai Etzioni, ed. (Charlottesville: University Press of Virginia, 1995), 52-70. But some writers *have* attempted to make alternatives seem plausible. Michael Sandel's *Democracy's Discontent: America in Search of a Public Philosophy* (Cambridge, MA: Harvard University Press, 1996), goes a fair distance toward arguing for a more republican vision of modern society, drawing upon neglected aspects of American economic and legal history. An even better example is Alan Ehrenhalt's *The Lost City: Discovering the Forgotten Virtues of Community in the Chicago of the 1950s* (New York: Basic Books, 1995), which very plainly sets out the requirements for a more communitarian way of life: more respect for authority, more civic involvement, and a willingness to accept fewer material and social choices.

20. Lujun Yin, "The Crisis of Hermeneutical Consciousness in Modern China," *Journal of Chinese Philosophy* 17 (May 1990): 420, 423, emphasis added.

21. H. N. Hirsch, "The Threnody of Liberalism," *Political Theory* 14 (August 1986): 423.

22. See Sandel, *Liberalism and the Limits of Justice*, esp. chapter 3.

23. There are, of course, very good reasons to distrust "larger ideas." Some may be grand and inspiring, but others may be hateful and murderous. Whereas liberal thought began in the West at least in part because of a deeply moral and humane, even religious, trust in the sovereignty and wisdom of the individual, liberal democracy today is probably more motivated, and not unreasonably so, by a sense of fear—a fear of cruelty, of physical deprivation and abuse, at the hands of people allowed to gain too much authority and power. See Judith Shklar's powerful essay "The Liberalism of Fear," in *Liberalism and the Moral Life*, Nancy L. Rosenblum, ed. (Cambridge, MA: Harvard University Press, 1989), 21-38.

24. Amitai Etzioni, "A Moderate Communitarian Proposal," *Political Theory* 24 (May 1996): 168n4.

25. The point that democracy requires a stronger sense of public life and common good than modern liberal neutrality permits has been exhaustively made from a variety of perspectives. For a succinct, passionate case for creating a robust civil society which can and will involve itself in the search for public good, see Jean Bethke Elshtain, *Democracy on Trial* (New York: Basic Books, 1995).

26. Charles Taylor, "Cross-Purposes: The Liberal-Communitarian Debate," in *Liberalism and the Moral Life*, 167-168; see also several essays in Taylor, *Human Agency and Language: Philosophical Papers 1* (Cambridge: Cambridge University Press, 1985).

27. Etzioni, "A Moderate Communitarian Proposal," 163. Few communitarians are so opposed to the notion of individual rights and political liberty as to suggest abandoning liberal modernity's most basic "universal principles." In reference to the attempt to recognize the normative claims of diverse communities without falling into relativism and xenophobia, Charles Taylor wrote: "There must be something midway between the inauthentic and homogenizing demand for recognition of equal worth . . . and self-immurement within ethnocentric standards." Taylor, "The Politics of Recognition,"

in *Multiculturalism: Examining the Politics of Recognition*, Amy Gutmann, ed. (Princeton: Princeton University Press, 1994), 72. Much communitarian literature is taken up with attempts to develop overarching standards that embrace that midway point.

28. The notion of "tending" is taken from Sheldon S. Wolin, "Tending and Intending a Constitution," in *The Presence of the Past* (Baltimore: Johns Hopkins University, 1989).

29. Sandel, MacIntyre, Taylor, and Walzer, at least, have regularly been labeled communitarians, though all have expressed doubts at different times about the term, MacIntyre especially. Wolin and Barber have a much more marginal, though real, connection to communitarian theory; Galston, on the other hand, has long been intimately associated with various self-described communitarian publications, proclamations and organizations. The degree to which Arendt would comfortably consider herself a communitarian is uncertain; she died in 1975, before the term took on its contemporary relevance. Some have seen Arendt as nothing less than a "patron saint of communitarianism," while others have used Arendt to criticize communitarian writers like Sandel. See Bruce Frohnen, *The New Communitarians and the Crisis of Modern Liberalism* (Lawrence: University Press of Kansas, 1996), 201; and Bonnie Honig, *Political Theory and the Displacement of Politics* (Ithaca: Cornell University Press, 1993), 162-199.

30. George Kateb, *The Inner Ocean: Individualism and Democratic Culture* (Ithaca: Cornell University Press, 1992), 229-232; Will Kymlicka, *Liberalism, Community and Culture* (Oxford: Clarendon Press, 1989), 82-87.

31. The reference is to David L. Hall and Rover T. Ames, *Thinking Through Confucius* (Albany: State University of New York Press, 1987), an excellent and influential example of philosophical engagement with Confucian thought.

32. Hall and Ames, *Thinking Through Confucius*, 131.

33. Daniel Bell et al., *Towards Illiberal Democracy*, 75.

34. A view summarized in Roger T. Ames, *The Art of Rulership: A Study in Ancient Chinese Political Thought* (Albany: State University of New York Press, 1994), 115-120.

35. Wing-tsit Chan, "Influence of Taoist Classics on Chinese Philosophy," in *Literature on Belief: Sacred Scripture and Religious Experience,* Neal Lambert, ed. (Provo, UT: Brigham Young University Press, 1981). 143. In many ways the best route toward a language that can communicate the differences in these traditions is a Heideggerian one. For a review of the distinctive characteristics of an immanent ontological view, see *Heidegger and Asian Thought*, Graham Parkes, ed. (Honolulu: University of Hawaii Press, 1987), esp. the essays by Otto Pöggeler, Joan Stambaugh, Graham Parkes, and Hwa Yol Jung.

36. See Robert C. Neville, "From Nothing to Being: The Notion of Creation in Chinese and Western Thought," *Philosophy East & West* 30 (January 1980): 21-34.

37. Chung-Ying Cheng, "Chinese Metaphysics as Non-metaphysics: Confucian and Taoist Insights into the Nature of Reality," in *Understanding the Chinese Mind: The Philosophical Roots*, Robert E. Allinson, ed. (Oxford: Oxford University Press, 1989), 175.

38. These ceremonial sacrifices, funeral practices, and other rituals of speech, action, and social intercourse, as well as traditions in literature and genealogy, originated with the cult surrounding the Shang and early Chou emperors, but had spread by Confucius's time to all levels of Chinese society. The basic texts of these activities and traditions were called the *Wu Ching* (Five Classics) and included the *Shu Ching* (Book of History, or Documents), the *Shih Ching* (Book of Poetry, or Songs), the *Li Chi* (Record of Rites), the notorious *I Ching* (Book of Changes) and, perhaps most important, the *Ch'un Ch'iu* (Spring and Autumn Annals), a compilation often attributed to Confucius himself.

39. Benjamin I. Schwartz, *The World of Thought in Ancient China* (Cambridge, MA: Harvard University Press, 1985), 48-50, 67 and *passim*.

40. Herbert Fingarette, *Confucius—The Secular As Sacred* (New York: Harper & Row, 1972), 3, 20. Fingarette expands on his idea of "transformative magic" as follows:

By "magic" I mean the power of a specific person to accomplish his will directly and effortlessly through ritual, gesture and incantation. The user of magic does not work by strategies and devices as a means to an end: he does not use coercion or physical forces. He simply wills the end in the proper ritual setting and with the proper ritual gesture and word.

This is not to make Confucius out to be a mystic, but to emphasize that in Confucianism there was no understanding of seeking advantage or popular or social achievement through the rituals. The rites were about one's fundamental relationship with the world; by doing what one should do, what should be will come to pass. For good reason did Fingarette call the *li* "holy."

41. Randall Peerenboom, "Confucian Harmony and Freedom of Thought: The Right to Think Versus Right Thinking," in *Confucianism and Human Rights*, Wm. Theodore de Bary and Tu Weiming, eds. (New York: Columbia University Press, 1998), 249-250.

42. See the essays by Sumner B. Twiss, Julia Ching, Chung-ying Cheng, and others in *Confucianism and Human Rights*.

43. Karyn L. Lai, "Confucian Moral Thinking," *Philosophy East and West* 45 (April 1995): 255.

44. Robert M. Gimello, "The Civil Status of *li* in Classical Confucianism," *Philosophy East and West* 22 (1972): 204.

45. Lai, "Confucian Moral Thinking," 253.

46. Schwartz, *The World of Thought in Ancient China,* 107.

47. Steven Walker, "Confucianism in America," *Journal of Chinese Philosophy* 20 (1993): 499, 2.

48. Hall and Ames, *Thinking Through Confucius,* 17.

49. Consider this coy comment, involving the tyrannical monarchs Chieh and Tchou:

King Hsuan asked, "Is it true that Tang banished Chieh and Wu marched against Tchou?" "It is so recorded," answered Mencius. "Is regicide permissible?" "A man who mutilates benevolence is a mutilator, while one who cripples rightness is a crippler. He who is both a mutilator and a crippler is an outcast. I have indeed heard of the punishment of the 'outcast Tchou,' but I have not heard of any regicide." (*Mencius* 1/B/8)

50. See MacIntyre, *After Virtue* (Notre Dame: University of Notre Dame Press, 1981), esp. chapter 15. The notion that Confucianism suggests that individuals, through rituals which put them in an immanent relationship with *t'ien*, makes everyone an "author" of their own lives has been commented on in Hall and Ames, *Thinking Through Confucius*, 244: "In the interaction between the human being and *t'ien*, a person becomes an 'authority' in his deference to and embodiment of existing meanings . . . he becomes an 'author' in his creative disposition."

51. Roger T. Ames, "Rites and Rights: The Confucian Alternative," in *Human Rights and the World's Religions,* Leroy S. Rouner, ed. (Notre Dame: University of Notre Dame Press, 1988), 201. For a thorough consideration of the issue of creativity from a Confucian perspective, see Antonio S. Cua, *Dimensions of Moral Creativity: Paradigms, Principles, and Ideals* (University Park: Pennsylvania State University Press, 1978).

52. Antonio S. Cua, "Confucian Vision and Human Community," *Journal of Chinese Philosophy* 11 (1984): 227.

53. Hans-Georg Gadamer, *Truth and Method.* 2nd ed., trans. Joel Weinsheimer and Donald G. Marshall (New York: Crossroad Publishing Company, 1990), esp. 265-307. Gadamer's "interpretive politics" have been directly compared to the communitarian arguments about history and hermeneutics made by Alasdair MacIntyre and Charles Taylor. See Georgia Warnke, *Justice and Interpretation* (Cambridge, MA: MIT Press, 1992), chapter 6.

54. Henry Rosemont, Jr., *A Chinese Mirror: Moral Reflections on Political Economy and Society* (La Salle, IL: Open Court Publishing Company, 1991), 72-73.

55. Peter Boodberg, "The Semasiology of Some Primary Confucian Concepts," *Philosophy East and West* 3 (1953): 328.

56. W. Theodore de Bary writes that "*jen* may also be understood as the people, referring to humanity in the most universal sense, embracing all peoples." De Bary, *The Trouble with Confucianism* (Cambridge, MA: Harvard University Press, 1991), 19.

57. Hall and Ames, *Thinking Through Confucius,* 115.

58. Antonio S. Cua, "Competence, Concern, and the Role of Paradigmatic Individuals (*chun tzu*) in Moral Education," *Philosophy East and West* 42 (January 1992): 54.

59. Fred Dallmayr, "Humanity and Humanization: Comments on Confucianism," in *Alternative Visions: Paths in the Global Village* (Lanham, MD: Rowman & Littlefield, 1998), 138. The phrase "fiduciary community" is Tu Wei-ming's.

60. One might consider here a statement from John C. H. Wu, "The Status of the Individual in the Political Traditions of Old and New China," in *The Chinese Mind: Essentials of Chinese Philosophy and Culture,* Charles A. Moore, ed. (Honolulu: University of Hawaii Press, 1968), 344:

It is true that Confucius laid great stress on the rites and the rules of propriety, but his attention was focused on the underlying spirit rather than on the formalities and the letter of specific rules . . . It is most regrettable that his moral teachings became distorted beyond recognition and rigidified into an official system since the period of the Han [dynasty], when Confucianism . . . lost its original rationality, purity and flexibility.

61. Benjamin Schwartz, "Chinese Culture and the Concept of Community," in *On Community*, Leroy S. Rouner, ed. (Notre Dame: University of Notre Dame Press, 1991), 126.

62. Hall and Ames, *Thinking Through Confucius,* 144-145.

63. David L. Hall and Roger T. Ames, *Anticipating China: Thinking Through the Narratives of Chinese and Western Culture* (Albany: State University of New York Press, 1994), 146.

64. Antonio S. Cua, "The Idea of Confucian Tradition," *Review of Metaphysics* 45 (June 1992): 827, 830; Cua quotes *Analects* 18/8. The translation of *ch'uan* as "moral discretion" is D. C. Lau's; see *Analects* 9/30.

65. Mencius writes that a benevolent government will "reduce punishments and taxation," whereas tyrannical governments "take the people away from their own work" (*Mencius* 1/A/5).

66. Edward Shils, "Reflections on Civil Society and Civility in the Chinese Intellectual Tradition," in *Confucian Traditions,* 46.

67. Ames, *The Art of Rulership,* 29.

68. Several scholars of Confucianism have gone so far as to suggest that those individuals who were *jen* served as "prophets," speaking against unvirtuous rulers on behalf of *t'ien.* See de Bary, *The Trouble With Confucianism,* chapters 1 and 6; also Julia Ching, *Confucianism and Christianity: A Comparative Study* (New York: Kodansha International, 1977), 102 and *passim.*

69. Hall and Ames, *Thinking Through Confucius,* 159-60.

70. Hall, "Modern China and the Postmodern West," 66.

71. A Heideggerian term whose applicability to Confucius was suggested in Fred Dallmayr, *The Other Heidegger* (Ithaca: Cornell University Press, 1993), 195-197.

72. Taylor, "Cross-Purposes," 170. See Robert C. Solomon, *Continental Philosophy Since 1750: The Rise and Fall of the Self* (Oxford: Oxford University Press, 1988), 1-7.

73. William M. Sullivan, "Institutions as the Infrastructure of Democracy," in *The New Communitarian Thinking,* 175.

74. A little-known but provocative argument in favor of community obligation is found in Andrew Oldenquist, *The Non-Suicidal Society* (Bloomington: Indiana University Press, 1986), 157 and *passim.*

75. Sheldon S. Wolin, "What Revolutionary Action Means Today," *Democracy* 2 (Fall 1982): 27.

76. Alexis de Tocqueville emphasized the centrality of religious belief to balancing political freedom with community virtues; see Tocqueville, *Democracy in America,* trans. George Lawrence, ed. J. P. Mayer (New York: Harper & Row, 1969), 442-449; see also Glenn Tinder's powerful essay, "Can We Be Good without God?" *Atlantic Monthly,* December 1989, 68-85.

77. Hannah Arendt maintained that this "revolutionary spirit" was the only source of virtue that free societies can appeal to, and hence we must strive to preserve it in our everyday political activity. See Arendt, *The Human Condition* (Chicago: University of Chicago Press, 1958) and the essays in *On Revolution* (New York: Viking Penguin, 1963); see also Benjamin Barber, *Strong Democracy: Participatory Politics for a New Age* (Berkeley: University of California Press, 1984) for suggestions on how one might create a more Arendtian democratic community.

78. Hall, "Modern China and the Postmodern West," 56.

79. Seung-hwan Lee, "Was There a Concept of Rights in Confucian Virtue-Based Morality?" *Journal of Chinese Philosophy* 19 (1992): 257.

80. David L. Hall and Roger T. Ames, "Dewey, China, and the Democracy of the Dead," in *Justice and Democracy,* 276.

81. Tu Wei-ming, "Introduction," in *Confucian Traditions*, 7-8.

82. See William A. Galston, "Liberal Virtues," *American Political Science Review* 82 (December 1988): 1277-1289; and Peter R. Moody, Jr., "The Political Culture of Chinese Students and Intellectuals: A Historical Examination," *Asian Survey* 28 (November 1988): 1140-1160.

83. David B. Wong, "Community, Diversity, and Confucianism," in *In the Company of Others: Perspectives on Community, Family and Culture*, Nancy E. Snow, ed. (Lanham, MD: Rowman & Littlefield, 1996): 32-33.

84. Francis Fukuyama, "Confucianism and Democracy," *Journal of Democracy* 6 (April 1995): 30-33.

9

Confucianism with a Liberal Face: Democratic Politics in Postcolonial Taiwan

L. H. M. Ling and Chih-yu Shih

Introduction

Many today consider Taiwan a democratizing, if not democratic, state. It held its first presidential election in March 1996, has several thriving, openly contentious opposition parties, upholds the free-market norms of individualism and private property, and no longer imprisons citizens for making "seditious" statements such as advocating independence for Taiwan. Yet these procedural developments obscure how democratic values have penetrated a society nurtured on U.S. liberalism since World War II but conceived in Confucian hegemony at least since the Ming Dynasty (1368-1628). Indeed, how do we account for the apparent synthesis in Taiwan of two radically different political traditions and philosophies? Liberalism and Confucianism clash, in particular, on a concept pivotal to democratic politics: i.e., governance. Confucianism views governance from above: it analogizes the relationship between leaders and led as that of parent to child. The relationship may be loving but it is also decidedly top-down, instructional, and, if necessary, punitive. The Confucian canons also refer to the relationship between rulers and subjects as one of "drivers" to "mules," "vases" to "water," or "shelter" to hapless, cowering "victims" seeking refuge from raging storms.[1] In each case, the people look up to and follow a sage (*xian ren*) who will deliver them from suffering to happiness, from poverty to prosperity, from chaos to order. Liberalism, in contrast, frames governance as a social contract between equal parties distinguished by their public and private interests. It emphasizes individual rights, limited government, legal adjudication, freedom of speech and property. Given these contending notions of governance in Taiwan, what does it mean to have a liberal politics of democracy in a neo-Confucian, postcolonial context?

Our paper aims to unpack this question. It focuses on a variety of sources that inform political action and debate in Taiwan: e.g., parliamentary transcripts, scholarly critiques, newspaper reports and editorials. This textual approach offers insight into how local political actors themselves understand democratic politics, with its confluence of Chinese, Japanese, American, and local Taiwanese legacies. As such, this recognition of local authorial agency differs from conventional treatments of democratization in comparative context.[2] These tend to view local renditions of democratization as a "deviation" from the Western liberal norm. Consequently, their prescriptions for democratization invariably begin with external intervention couched as institutional reforms ("liberalization") or resorts to local traditions that claim a democratic potential ("Asian-style democracy"). Still others simply concede that East Asia remains irremediably antidemocratic, focused primarily on economic problem-solving rather than political representation ("illiberal democracy"). Both stances—West-as-norm or anti-West-as-norm—ironically turn "democratization" into an externally-directed, elite-imposed project of hegemony.

The literature on East Asian development and democratization usually categorizes Taiwan as a "capitalist developmental state" (CDS).[3] It refers to East Asia's Confucian-capitalist states as institutionally and ideologically committed to rapid economic growth achieved mostly during the 1960s and 1970s.[4] Common to the CDS is a high level of centralized political decision-making characterized by single-party rule and a political culture intolerant of popular dissent. Many consider Japan to be the sole exception with its multiparty representation, parliamentary elections, and formally free press. Feminists and other dissidents, however, dispute this claim given the patriarchal nature of Japan's corporatist state.[5] Scholars of the CDS often refer to its history of "Oriental despotism." They cite the Confucian literati of old as today's technocratic elite, finely attuned to and masters of global capitalist competition. Accordingly, they identify a variety of "strong" states in East Asia: e.g., "catch-up" fascism in prewar and "administrative guidance" in postwar Japan;[6] "bureaucratic authoritarianism" in Korea;[7] "soft authoritarianism" in Singapore;[8] *etatisme* in Taiwan;[9] and now suggestions of "neo-authoritarianism" in an economically capitalist though ideologically still Marxist China.[10]

Conversionism: Institutionalist and Internationalist Varieties

Within this developmental context, analyses of and prescriptions for democratization in the CDS fall into four paradigmatic approaches. Two reflect institutional and internationalist perspectives; together, they comprise what we call conversionism. It proposes that, to democratize, local traditions, institutions, practices, and norms must be replaced with liberal capitalist ones.[11] Institutionalists see capitalist market practices, in particular, as underpinning the social and political institutions needed for democracy: e.g., a "revolutionary" middle class, active civil society, rational pursuit of individual interest that leads to self-censoring collective action, and so on.[12] As Mancur Olson observes, "the same court system, independent judiciary, and respect for law and individual rights that are needed for a lasting democracy are also required for security of property and contract rights."[13] Lucian Pye's argument that Asians need to Westernize along individualist, capitalist lines exemplifies this institutionalist approach.[14]

Internationalists view liberalization as a necessary political accommodation to capitalist globalization. They contend that an emerging transnational, transpatial, and transcultural liberal infrastructure now embeds democracy "in the depths of people's hearts and minds."[15] To them, the fall of socialist governments in the former Soviet Union and Eastern Europe further affirms liberal capitalism as a transnationalized ideology of development.[16] It preaches "untrammelled international competition, celebration of the market, of wealth and self, anti-communism and anti-unionism."[17] The question before East Asia's "neoautocracies," Minxin Pei concludes, "is not whether [to democratize], but when and how."[18] Indeed, Francis Fukuyama may bemoan an end to history but concedes that all peoples now realize that they need to tread the path of Western liberal capitalism to reach their full social, political, and economic potential.[19]

Conversionism, however, is empirically and conceptually problematic. It presumes that the installation of liberal institutions necessarily replaces traditional norms and practices with a new liberal ethic. That is, conversionists believe that liberalism gives birth to all brave new democracies whose features bear striking resemblance to those of the "founding fathers" in the West. Conversionists regard this institutional paternity with pride yet dismiss outrightly any suggestions of forcible reproduction.[20] Moreover, conversionists fail to acknowledge that postcolonial societies already exhibit a high degree of local-global integration—and not necessarily for liberatory ends. In East Asia, for example, Confucian hierarchy locks easily with capitalist competition in the name of national reconstruction to produce a state authoritarianism sanctioned by both state and society—even when it undermines due process and political representation for the latter.[21] In short, the very idea of an externally imposed liberal conversion renders democratization into "a bitter self-mockery."[22]

Asian-Style Democracy

One response from within Asia to the demands of democratization is a call for an "Asian-style democracy."[23] Clark Neher, a critic of this local approach, associates it with "patron-client communitarianism, personalism, deference to authority, dominant political parties, and strong interventionist states."[24] Advocates of Asian-style democracy may agree with this characterization but view it as a particularly local (Confucian) response to global (democratic) needs. Traditional concepts like the Mandate of Heaven, they point out, validate the right of the people to rebel if the state violates their trust. They also refer to classical texts like the *Minben Zhengzhi* ("People-Based Governance") to indicate an indigenous tradition of democratic governance.[25] It teaches six central principles: (1) the people are the "main body" (*zhuti*) of politics (*zhengzhi*); (2) the prince (*jun*) achieves lordly power only through the consent (*tongyi*) of the people (*renmin*); (3) the most important mission of the prince is to protect the people (*baomin*) and ensure their livelihood (*yangmin*); (4) the prince must uphold the public interest (*gong yi*) over private gain (*si li*); (5) proper governance excoriates rule of force (*wangba*); and (6) the prince and his ministers (*chen*) are but instruments of governance whose purpose is to serve the people.[26] According to Kim Dae Jung, this Confucian approach to governance offers the potential for developing democracy "even beyond the level of the West."[27]

Asian-style democracy, however, begs the question of how authoritarianism came to be privileged in the first place. That is, Confucian societies tend toward authoritarianism precisely because the canons valorize elite interpretations of the norm.[28] For example, advocates of Asian-style democracy claim that they offer the "correct" version of the canons, thereby fostering democracy. But how does this method introduce and legitimate contending interpretations integral to democratic debate? Put differently, what guarantees do Asian-style democrats provide against monopolizing the public forum, even in the interest of democracy? Indeed, *minben* governance historically represents a "gentlemen's agreement" that ruling elites would fulfill the people's wishes by deciding what is best for them rather than consulting their needs, desires, ambitions, or aspirations.[29] Accordingly, *minben* governance continues to cast the people as *objects* of elite rule.

Equally disturbing in Asian-style democracy is the pretension that East Asia's capitalist economies operate in a culturally-pristine environment divorced from a larger, systemic context. Advocates seek to wish away the fact that their societies are already deeply embedded in multicultural forces, most recently from Western liberal capitalism but previously from other civilizational sources as well: e.g., Islam, Buddhism, Taoism, Legalism, and so on. Even a cursory look at Lee's Singapore or Mahathir's Malaysia confirms how much the West is now a part of Asia. Hence, both conversionists and Asian-style democrats commit the same ecological fallacy: just as conversionists presume that one set of cultural values (Western liberalism) can replace another (Confucian authoritarianism), so Asian-style democrats believe that the same cultural systems may synergize into effective developmental regimes for economic competition but remain normatively and intellectually immune from each other for political governance.

Illiberal Democracy

A fourth, emerging approach to democratization in East Asia is "illiberal democracy." It begins with a premise that Asian and Western democracies are inherently different. Contemporary politics in capitalist Asia, in fact, represents "a grafting of democratic practices and institutions on to societies with an alternative cultural baggage, with different ways of organizing their economic life, and with distinctive answers to the question of who counts as 'we the people.'"[30] They note, for instance, that democratization in East Asia, instead of being locally generated, proceeds primarily as a top-down, state-to-society process. "Therefore, political liberalization in these states is manifested in the changing architecture of the state with civil society remaining both limited and circumscribed."[31] Indeed, illiberal democracy bears three distinctive character-istics: (1) a non-neutral (i.e., interventionist) state, (2) a rationalistic and legalistic technocracy, and (3) a government-managed public space and civil society.[32] These institutional adjustments reflect, respectively, contending demands from both liberalism and Confucianism: e.g., self-government vs. elite rule, free speech vs. benevolent hegemony, minority rights vs. moral consensus. Given the classic struggle between liberal individualism and Confucian hier-archy, illiberal democracy introduces a method of top-down mobilization that reconciles the two. This is most evident, for instance, in the state's drive for economic development. One consequence, though, is a politically defanged middle class. Neither revolutionary (conversionist) nor emancipatory (Asian-style democracy), the middle class, instead, is complicit. After all, only the state can ensure its economic security and prosperity.[33]

Table A (see page 218) summarizes this comparison between illiberal demo-cracy, liberalism, and Confucianism. Proponents of illiberal democracy conclude that it "is primarily about problem solving rather than the accommodation of a plurality of interests. Therefore, in East and Southeast Asia, a technocratic and managerial approach to politics appears in the guise of political liberali-zation."[34]

The notion of an illiberal democracy begins to overcome the either-or fundamentalism of previous approaches. In contrast to conversionism, it does not force the square peg of Western liberalism into the round hole of local democratization efforts. Nor does illiberal democracy (like advocates of Asian-style democracy) pretend that local traditions like Confucianism are more liberal than they really are. Rather, illiberal democracy acknowledges that democratic politics in East Asia is a mixed product. It may borrow certain institutional and even normative features of Western liberal democracy—such as multiparty representation, free elections, an unfettered press, and a capitalist economy—but democratic politics in East Asia, especially in the CDS, operates within a different historical-ethical context (e.g., state-led welfare) with different means (e.g., technocratic problem-solving) and through different venues (e.g., managed civil discourse).

Table A:

Illiberal Democracy Compared with Liberalism and Confucianism

Liberalism	Confucianism	Illiberal Democracy
individual equality	social hierarchy	top-down, mobilized citizenry
freedom/autonomy to self-government	duties/obligations to elders and subordinates	rational, legalistic technocracy
free and open speech	benevolent rule	interventionist state
individual rights against tyranny of majority	substantive moral consensus against diversity	managed public space

Nonetheless, this notion of illiberal democracy seems overly static, resolved, and managed. It underestimates the impact of systemic conflicts caused by the very normative incompatibilities that illiberal democracy itself signifies. That is, are the core contentions between liberalism and local traditions (like Confucianism) all under control such that CDS technocrats have little left to do but problem-solve? Theorists of illiberal democracy imply that such issues have been worked out, smoothed over, or somehow eliminated in the process of successful state-led economic development. Yet we see in the history and daily lives of East Asians that they are constantly and heroically grappling with these conflicts. These may range from personal dilemmas (e.g., should grown children live with their parents to fulfill the demands of filial piety or should they move on as autonomous adults competing in a capitalist economy?) to more public, institutional ones (e.g., to what extent is critical political discourse a trans-gression against loyalty to the state?)[35] Additionally, the term illiberal democracy suggests a residual Western bias. It defines democratization in East Asia as a negation of (or perhaps even failure from?) the Western liberal democratic ideal. This oppositional stance denies the very hybridity that underlies illiberal democracy.

We offer an alternative model of democratization in East Asia. In part, it builds upon the findings of illiberal democracy that the CDS has an interventionist state, technocratic bureaucracy, and circumscribed public space. What our model emphasizes, though, is that the process of politics in the CDS is unevenly interactive, normatively contentious, and organically open-ended such that neither the state, bureaucracy, nor public space can operate in a singular, preorchestrated domain. Instead, democratization in a postcolonial context encompasses multiple practices, ideals, and institutions that shade into, clash against, and spill over conventional boundaries between "liberalism" and "Confucianism," "dissent" and "loyalty," "representation" and "reality," "democracy" and "authoritarianism."

Confucian Democracy in a Postcolonial Order

The term postcolonial evokes three related though distinct usages: an historical experience with colonialism now past, a structural ("Third World") location within the capitalist world economy, and/or a socio-cultural dynamic between colonizer and colonized that produces third, unanticipated systemic outcomes. We use postcoloniality primarily in the third sense although the first two definitions apply implicitly as well. Postcolonial theory surfaces most prominently in cultural and literary studies where evidence of such inter-cultural dynamism is more easily traced.[36] But its insights for social science pertain equally, if not more so, to issues of imperialism, Orientalism, and culture.[37]

Postcolonial theorists underscore that absolute categorizations of "us vs. them" dissolve in face of the "carnivalesque" and "contrapuntal" effects of global life. The very act of colonialism and imperialism, they claim, forces interactions that result in hybridity, simulacra, and mimicry. Accordingly, postcoloniality signals a systemic open-endedness and unorderliness that resist attempts at control or prediction. "The native intellectual," cautions Homi Bhabha, "who identifies the people with the 'true national culture' will be disappointed. The people are now the very principle of 'dialectical reorganization' and they construct their culture from the national text translated into modern Western forms of information technology, language, and dress."[38]

Taiwan, in particular, exemplifies postcoloniality. Colonized by Han Chinese into a province of the Middle Kingdom in 1885, it was later occupied by an expansionist Imperial Japan from 1895-1945, only to find itself once again under external rule when Chiang Kai-shek's Kuomintang (KMT) retreated to the island in 1949. Chiang Ching-kuo officially inherited his father's political mantle in 1978 and reconstructed the KMT regime into one of benevolent dictatorship.[39] He first instituted political reforms with the Third Plenum of the Twelfth Party Congress in 1986. But many regard the first anti-KMT riot of 1977 in Chungli as the beginning of political reform in Taiwan. During the 1970s and 1980s, Chiang *fils* raised the standard of living, subsidized massive infrastructure-building, extended public education, privatized several public enterprises, and promoted a thriving consumer economy. In 1986, he legalized the Democratic Progressive Party (DPP), a vocal critic of the KMT. A year later, he permitted direct dialogue with the Chinese Communist Party (CCP) on the mainland. With Chiang's death in 1988, Lee Teng-hui, a native Taiwanese, assumed the helm of the ruling party. Lee himself personnifies Taiwan's multicultural, postcolonial history: born and raised during the Japanese occupation, Lee is more at home speaking Japanese and Taiwanese than Mandarin, Taiwan's official language. Lee's nativist sentiments surface most prominently in his dealings with China. He has refused, for instance, to facilitate trade and investment between Taiwan and the mainland—much to the chagrin of Taiwan's economic elites such as Wang Yung-ching, himself a native Taiwanese. Lee is also well-acquainted with American society and politics given his years as a doctoral student at Cornell University in the 1960s. Note, for example, Lee's masterful lobbying of the U.S. Congress and president in 1996 ostensibly to attend a Cornell reunion. Once in the U.S., he campaigned openly and unapologetically as the presidential incumbent of "the Republic of China," despite vocal objections from the CCP government in Beijing.

In contrast, most analyses of democratization in Taiwan focus on its institutional or structural changes.[40] For example, they probe into bureaucratic responses to societal pressures for greater liberalization, the impact of international political and economic developments on political reform, factional disputes among legislators, and the role of the press/intelligentsia/students in democratization. These studies provide important information on the hard-nosed basics of politics: i.e., "who gets what, when, and how?"[41] But they overlook the meaning of democratic politics—that is, "why?" and "so what?"—particularly as it is assigned and practiced by local political actors. Some discern the importance of this inquiry when faced with an apparent paradox in illiberal democracies: i.e., the middle class, though trained in "(liberal) rules, procedures, institutions, and constitutions," still searches for a "(Confucian) certainty."[42] To this, the island-state of Taiwan adds a third consideration: a rising nativist-nationalist sensibility directed against China.

Two recent events exemplify the location of Taiwanese politics at the interstices of these three normative domains: liberal political institutions, Confucian rationales for power, and Taiwanese nationalist sensibilities. In 1996, Lee Teng-hui attempted to expand the powers of the presidency through an *ad hoc* committee called the National Development Council (NDC or *guofahui*). At the end of the year, Taiwan's governor, James C. Y. Soong, abruptly resigned in protest against another Lee-backed plan: the elimination of Taiwan's provincial status. Both events highlight the continued salience of Confucian (selfless) moral leadership in Taiwanese politics. Contending camps vie for Confucian moral credibility even while making arguments framed in terms of liberal political institutions (e.g., the Constitution, the five branches of government, the Supreme Court) and Taiwan's distinction from China. Politicians may hinge their moral leadership on appearance more than fact, rhetoric more than action. But mass and elite alike demand a ritualized demonstration of selflessness for the common good as the critical standard for public office. Liberal political institutions, by extension, turn into administrative instruments to consolidate Confucian moral leadership.

Expanding the Powers of the Presidency

In December 1996, Lee created the NDC to evaluate and prescribe policy for Taiwan's developmental future. Members of the committee came from the island-state's three main political parties—the KMT, the DPP, and a KMT-splinter group, the New Party.[43] The KMT and DPP (widely believed to be pro-Lee despite its vocal advocacy of Taiwan's independence) proposed to grant the presidency the power to nominate the premier without prior approval from the legislature (as currently required by the Constitution). In fact, this motion would allow the president to dissolve the legislature at will. Clearly, this proposal would strengthen the power of presidency.[44] But supporters claimed that President Lee would be "selflessly" giving up power by sacrificing his authority to chair cabinet meetings and the ability to transfer impeachment power from the independent Control Yuan to the Legislative Yuan.[45] Taiwan's Constitution currently stipulates that the premier heads the national administration and chairs the Executive Yuan. The NDC initially proposed to have the president chair the Executive Yuan's "routine meetings." But with its broader objectives in mind (i.e., presidential nomination of the premier without legislative approval and possible dissolution of the legislature at will), the NDC dropped this proposition as a show of compromise. According to Tsai Cheng-wen, who drafted this proposal, there is "almost no expansion of the presidential power at all."[46]

Not all members of the NDC agreed. The New Party (representing 13 percent of the voting population and advocating a Chinese nationalism) protested that the NDC was an extra-institutional (*tizhiwai*) organization that violated the principle of "checks and balances" in government. When neither the KMT nor DPP would compromise, the New Party walked out of the NDC in protest, thereby provoking widespread public condemnation. The morning after, the *Liberal Times* compared it to Lin Biao's betrayal of Mao in 1971. An editorial in the *Central Daily News* derided the New Party as out of date and out of the mainstream.[47] The *Liberal Times* accused the New Party of deliberately destroying consensus in Taiwan to sabotage its future; therefore, no one should welcome its continued participation in the NDC.[48] One columnist vilified members of the New Party as "supporters of totalitarianism" because they obstructed "democratic negotiations organized by President Lee"; it was better, he concluded, to "let them go."[49] This same columnist added in a later editorial that the New Party hated Taiwan because China remains its ideological and national fixation:

The New Party people embrace the Great China (*da zhongguo*) idea and cannot tolerate Taiwan's progress. . . . The Great China idea can no longer sell in Taiwan.

Any argument which does not recognize Taiwan as sovereign territory would be swept eventually into the dustbin of history. These previously anti-communist jerks who used to cheat to get their food and drinks are now thinking of colluding with China and oppressing Taiwan. The people of Taiwan would spit on them. . . . Once seeing through their ruse, the people of Taiwan should celebrate [their withdrawal].[50]

In contrast, those who expected to benefit from the NDC's proposed reforms cast their position in nonpartisan, even nonindividualist terms. Note this statement from Hsiao Wan-chang, a supporter of the NDC proposal:

When I do things or handle human relations, I do not appreciate being labelled. In Taiwan's politics, we should never categorize factions, we all belong to one life community. . . . Please do not consider my personal stakes. We each work in a temporary position but the institution is long-term. . . . I take my own fame or position very lightly. I feel obliged to the President, my superior and my party who have nurtured my career and to my constituency in Chiayi. I devote all my time to work and only hope to do things well.[51]

Note, also, the public-interest terms in which Tian Hong-mao justified his drafting of this constitutional amendment:

Tian Hong-mao [referring to himself] who represented academia in the NDC was also a participant of the (1990) National Affairs Council (NAC or *guoshihui*).[52] He had an unusual thought: the NDC has an educational role to play. Participation in the unique process of the NDC testifies to a democratic institution with our national characteristics which is not the same as the British or American representative system. We provide new access to the process of policy and institutional debates along with popularly elected officials in the delegate system.[53]

Debates in the Legislative Yuan

Debates in Taiwan's Legislative Yuan, the institution under siege, interestingly endorsed these sentiments both before and after the NDC. Even as some legislators demanded, in accordance with the Constitution, that Premier Lien Chan resign from the Legislative Yuan, given his newly elected status as vice president, they also called for, in the next breath, an application of Confucian morality to politics. Indeed, these debates demonstrate a discursive and normative shift at work. They reconstruct classic liberal themes of individual self-interest, ordered preferences, and constituency-based politics into Confucian rationales for collectivism, governmental benevolence, and a pro-Taiwan, anti-China ethno-nationalism. Note the following excerpts from a session of the Legislative Yuan held on March 26, 1996:[54]

I sincerely urge Premier Lien not to embroil the office of the Premiership in controversy [and] avoid a situation of chaos with the constitutional order. [He] should resign immediately and allow the new Premier to report on new policies and directions for the budget. . . . The New Party would never automatically oppose any policies by a Premier nominated by the President or even if the Cabinet were dominated by KMT members only. Rather, the New Party would use the following three criteria to evaluate the new cabinet: . . . the new Premier's personal ethics (*gerende daode*), professional integrity (*cao shou*), and self presentation (*xin xiang*). (Representative Yao Li-min)

Premier Lien should realize that each vote is for democracy, not for personal power mongering. . . . Premier Lien should reform his attitude and ask: what do the people want (*min zhi suo yu*)? [The answer:] to build the big picture (*da ge ju*) and [develop] an overall direction (*da fang xiang*). (Representative Yan Ching-fu)

As the election comes to a close, we hope that the government will expand its horizons to solicit views from all walks of life and make use of the best and brightest (*jing ying*) from all sectors, so that our country would walk on the path towards internationalization and thereby pave a better future [for the nation]. (Representative Tu Cheng-rong)

Through voting, the Taiwanese people have put all their hopes in Lee Teng-hui. Accordingly, the election of President Lee and Premier Lien is not an affirmation of their personal honor (*geren de rongyu*) but a reflection of the Taiwanese people's "conscious (emotional) commitment" (*you yishide tou she*) [in their leadership]. (Representative Wang Tuo)

Sprinkled throughout are exhortations to regain ethics in government. They urge Lee and Lien to reform government from "black gold politics" (*heijing zhengzhi*), otherwise known as mafia (*cai tuan*) influence. These calls for proper governance may echo those in the U.S. Congress that decry the corrupting influence of political action committees (PAC) and "donations" from organized interests (both domestic and foreign). But where U.S. legislators see the problem as legally defined, Taiwan's regard it as a moral failing.

More significantly, legislators are less concerned about the constitutionality of the president's move than with the international implications of Taiwan's democratization. To many, democratization validates Taiwan as a legitimate member of the international community in contrast to China's "rogue" status. A democratic Taiwan, President Lee has remarked, signals its membership in the "family of democracies."[55] It also shores up a newfound anti-China identity in Taiwan. Though based on liberal notions of electoral democracy and local self-determination, it draws on an older tradition of anti-imperialist, Chinese nationalism. Again, note these speeches made in the Legislative Yuan on March 26, 1996:

Given that we have used voting to clearly announce to the Chinese Communists and the whole world that we want to walk on the great road to democracy—democracy is truly the biggest winner today. (Representative Hong T'ung-kwei)

President Lee, just because you've won an election with a high voter turn-out doesn't mean you can become arrogant and forget who you are! . . . Now that you have 54% of the vote, the only thing you could do with pride is to say loudly to China: "Taiwan is Taiwan, China is China, each with its own household and head. [Only with] one China and one Taiwan could [we have] happiness!" (Representative Cheng Chao-ming)

Recently, the Chinese Communists have again and again utilized "military exercises" to threaten the people of Taiwan. This is outrageous but our government apparently cannot find a policy to deal with this. When the Thousand Island (*qiandaohu*) incident first occurred and Taiwanese people were being killed by mainland Chinese, [we could not even] bring their bodies home. Aside from Lee Teng-hui cursing [the CCP] as "bandits," the government stood by and did nothing. When this regime of "bullying crows" (*yaba zhengquan*) forces us to allow marriage between Taiwanese and mainlanders (*tonghun, hehun*), what on earth do you think our will government do? (Representative Hsieh Ching-chuan)[56]

The people's will (*min yi*) is like water, it can float a boat just as well as sink it. . . . So don't forget that the popular will that you represent comes from many years of hard work put in by many people [so that at last] we have achieved Taiwan's first presidential election . . . Taiwan has implemented a democracy. It is a polity that is capable of self-determination, independence, pragmatic diplomacy and national defense . . . Whether we call it the Republic of China, or the state of Taiwan, it is a country with independent sovereignty. (Representative Lin Feng-hsi)

China is the biggest loser. The success of Taiwan's presidential election creates a political threat to China. At the same time, it offers our 1.2 billion mainland brothers and sisters hope for freedom. (Representative Hsu Shao-ping)

Resignation of Taiwan's Governor

A second event that rocked Taiwan in 1996-1997 involved another controversial DPP proposal legitimized by the NDC: to eliminate Taiwan's provincial status (*feisheng*). Ostensibly, removal of rendundancies between the national and provincial governments would increase the island's administrative efficiency. What this rationale fails to account for—and which everyone privately acknowledges—is that the same administrative system must remain in place whether it is called "national" or "provincial." Hence, this attempt to redefine Taiwan's legal status became a public secret: its real motivation was to pave way for Taiwan's eventual declaration of independent sovereignty vis-à-vis China.

One obstacle to President Lee's plan was his hand-picked governor of Taiwan, James C. Y. Soong. A long-time ally of Lee's, Soong enjoys general public support for his many years as a "loyal public servant." (Among his many posts, Soong had served as secretary-general of the KMT and head of the government's news and information office.) Himself a mainlander, Soong won a landslide victory in Taiwan's gubernatorial race in 1994 in large part due to Lee's active support, especially in Taiwan's rural south where constituents are almost entirely native Taiwanese. Two years later, Soong returned the favor by campaigning avidly for Lee's bid for the presidency. Rumors have long circulated that Soong may succeed Lee in the next presidential election despite his mainland background. (Soong's wife, though, is Taiwanese.)

On New Year's Day of 1997, Soong shocked the island with a dual resignation: from the governorship of Taiwan and his seat on the Central Standing Committee, the KMT's policy-making organ. He prefaced his resignation with a statement of support for President Lee's constitutional, administrative, and democratic reforms. But he outlined four main reasons for this drastic action. We excerpt portions below:[57]

Chu-yu [referring to himself][58] may not have been born here, but [he] grew up eating Taiwanese rice, drinking Taiwanese water. . . . As its first [democratically elected] governor, how can I accept requests to . . . "freeze" [the island's] provincial status (*dongsheng*)?[59]

As governor, how can I tolerate accusations of "inefficiency" (*xiaolu bu zhang*) against my sincere, hardworking colleagues who have devoted their working lives to the provincial government?

Preserving or eliminating Taiwan's provincial status remains a policy change of the utmost importance. As its first officer, I cannot take this matter lightly.

It is only through Taiwan's democratization that we have an elected governorship to represent the Taiwanese people's "true spirit" (*zhenzhengde jingshen*). The learned ones used to refer to it as an "outspoken patriotism" (*i shi e e*). . . . Taiwan's governor does not need sympathy. [Instead] what is needed is [for others to recognize] the dignity (*zunyan*) and Herculean spirit (*dingtian lidi de fengge*) of the Taiwanese people.

In framing his resignation as an act of moral outrage on behalf of his constituency (rather than his own political survival), Soong's words stirred the nation. Thousands of citizens, especially government employees, gathered in front of his house and the governor's office to offer their support of and thanks for his leadership. A subordinate, with Buddhist prayer beads in hand, choked with tears when interviewed on television about when the governor might return. The governor himself disappeared from view, inciting a media frenzy as to his whereabouts and future plans. He emerged three days later to meet with the vice president and premier, Lien Chan, who urged him to stay and ask for a sick leave if necessary. President Lee refrained from comment for ten days until he finally met with Soong. Lee issued a statement that he "would not let you [Soong] go" (*buhui rang ni zou*). Soong responded that he would respect the president's wishes but would not rescind his resignation. As a compromise,

Soong accepted Premier Lien Chan's suggestion of a sick leave. If Governor Soong needs some rest and recuperation due to the awful burdens of his office, Premier Lien intoned, he should be able to do so.

One week after his resignation, Soong analogized himself to an historical figure, Jie Zhitui. Jie was a loyal minister who escaped to the mountains with his defeated prince during China's Spring and Autumn period (771-484 B.C.). Life in the mountains was hard. Legend recalls Jie slicing flesh from his leg to feed his starving prince. One day, the prince regained his throne and sent for Jie to serve as minister. Being a "pure" and "noble" man without rank political ambitions, Jie refused. Instead of confronting his prince directly, however, Jie returned to the mountains for refuge. Infuriated, the prince ordered his men to smoke out the fugitive. But Jie was determined to the end, refusing to give up even at the risk of death. His charred corpse was discovered days later, tightly bound to a broken, smoldering tree.

Jie Zhitui symbolizes a government official who is too loyal to criticize his prince directly but who is also too principled to submit to unjust policies. Hence, he resorts to a traditional and powerful means of protest by embodying his own dissent. In the same way, Soong used his (physical) withdrawal from the governorship and the KMT to convey his moral outrage at President Lee's actions while maintaining the stance of a loyal, incorruptible minister.

Liberal Politics under Confucian Moral Rectification

Politics under Confucian governance means moral rectification: i.e., it is morally wrong to articulate one's own interests in public. The *Analects* (*lunyu*) notes that "politics is rectification" (*zhengzhi zheng ye*). It adds, "If naming is inaccurate (*min bu zheng*), then speech stutters (*ze yan bu shun*), then matters fall apart (*ze shi bu cheng*), then rituals and music become inadequate (*ze liyue bu xing*), then punishments mismatch crimes (*ze xingfa bu zhong*), then the people become inactive (*ze min wusuo cuo shou zu*)." Not only does voicing one's self-interest undermine social harmony but, more egregiously, it opens opportunities for atomistic hedonism. This, the ancients believed, would destroy society as a whole.[60]

Given this normative constraint, candidates in an election cannot promote themselves (as do candidates in the United States, for example). To do so would tar them as "selfish" or "self-centered," thereby rendering them unqualified for public office. Nor can a candidate take sides on a policy issue whose advocates divide into distinctly opposite camps such as pro-life vs. pro-choice, or the National Rifle Association (NRA) vs. the Brady Bill. Instead, a candidate (usually male), seeks to assure voters that he is the "right" leader (as signified by the extent of his public mindedness and educational training) to make the best decisions on their behalf. Campaign slogans in the 1996 presidential election proclaimed that President Lee offers "dignity, valor, and Great Taiwan"— especially in face of China's military threat at the time. Another example comes from that year's mayoral election for Taipei. One candidate declared that his administration would bring "happiness and hope."

Citizens, in turn, expect government officials to protect, rather than represent, their interests. Accordingly, they would not participate directly in liberal democratic politics, lest it expose their self-interest. Not only would this deprive them of any public (moral) legitimacy, it would also jeopardize any real material interests they may have. For this reason, Confucian democratic politics does not coalesce around interest groups, especially if they are economically-based. The public reveals its support for or protest against particular leaders and their policies only through top-down, state-initiated mobilizations.

For citizens in Taiwan as well as China, the purpose of democracy is not limited government. Rather, they support democracy as the most popular (and internationally accepted) means of installing virtuous, benevolent elite rule. For this, society willingly cedes to the reigning leader almost unlimited social power to match his high moral status and also to show its submission to his moral order.[61] Attempts to limit governmental power, conversely, are seen as a lack (or loss) of public trust in the nation's leaders. Huang Hui-cheng, director of *Central Daily News*, once asked his readers to see President Lee Teng-hui as a mediator between opposing political forces, rather than a direct participant.[62] This characterization suits both Huang's and Taiwan society's conception of the president as a moral figure who stands above the fracas and fray of party politics. An editorial in the *Central Daily News* once suggested that the best present to President Lee on the second anniversary of his inauguration would be for all factions of society to "unite together [and] follow the decision of the Party."[63]

This call for public unity naturally concentrates more power for those already in charge. Indeed, few are fooled. Taiwan's citizens understand the hypocrisy that often lies behind such rhetoric, dismissing it as routine to political life. What they accept, rather, is the ritual of political unity: it affirms social harmony, which demonstrates national strength, which vindicates Taiwan's precarious international standing regarding China, specifically, and the world community at large.

For this reason, Taiwan's public blames the New Party's withdrawal from the NDC more than President Lee's naked pursuit of greater presidential power. Similarly, Governor Soong could not frame his resignation in personal terms. Instead, he speaks on behalf of those whom he represents—the people of Taiwan, provincial government employees—and what they stand for—loyalty to the state, democratization, and the entire two-thousand-year legacy of Chinese culture. The public accepts this rhetoric—and is, in fact, clearly moved by it—despite widespread recognition that these politicians are maneuvering to secure or increase their power. To deflect such speculations, both men gesture towards Confucian selflessness: Lee claims to rise above factional politics while Soong appears to defer to his superiors without rescinding his resignation. For his part, Premier Lien Chan, himself an aspirant for the presidency, also played a political sleight of hand: he transmuted Soong's resignation, with its full moral implications, into a mundane, legal matter—i.e., sick leave—over which the premier has full and obligatory jurisdiction.

Later developments in the Soong-Lee-Lien drama in 1997 further demonstrate the salience of Confucian morality in Taiwan's politics. On May 14, Soong returned to the KMT's Standing Central Committee, although he continued to boycott the NDC. The KMT needed Soong's return precisely for his newfound moral stature to counter an implicit censure of the government when another political figure, renowned for his incorruptibility, resigned.[64] When Soong rejoined the Standing Central Committee, President Lee reminded everyone of the importance of being faithful and selfless, especially for the common good. Soong, in turn, squelched rumors that he has accepted President Lee's offer to become the next premier. Indeed, he proclaimed his intention to stay with his provincial constituency until the end of his term. With such selflessness and honesty affirmed, Soong's popularity in the polls rose to 84 percent, far beyond any other cabinet member.

Public Trust vs. Limited Government

The central conflict that these examples reveal is a clash in public trust between Taiwan's liberal institutions and its Confucian ethic. Liberal institutions inherently impute distrust on its politicians (hence, the need for "limited government"). But Confucian ethics demand that both leaders and led share a sense of moral certitude in government.

Leaders in a Confucian democracy face a dilemma: If they remain within the (abstract) confines of liberal institutions, they may honor the law but forgo the privilege of (real) moral power. But if they ignore the state's liberal institutions, they may consolidate short-term power but undermine a long-term effectiveness with the public since respect for the state's political institutions contributes to their moral credibility. For this reason, political leaders in a Confucian democracy sometimes must step outside of institutional bounds with *ad hoc* committees and the like. As validation, politicians either declare the ethical efficacy of such extra-institutional (*tizhiwai*) organizations and/or use electoral success to rationalize greater aggrandizement of power. An electoral victory, placed within the context of Confucian politics, signifies the public's willingness to entrust power in a particular individual. Note, for example, President Lee's justification of *ad hoc* decision-making when he established the NAC:

> From a position filled with a sense of mission and open-mindedness, each of you should jettison all stereotyped partisan or personal perspectives and faithfully act upon a sincere devotion to the country so as to concentrate on the issues through an overall and thorough discussion. . . . I would see to it that all of your recommendations would later become realities through institutional and legal procedures.[65]

In short, the public, rather than institutions or politicians, now provide the checks and balances in Confucian democratic governance. Institutionally, a liberal democracy cannot deliver the moral legitimacy that a Confucian leader needs. But democratic elections provide him with an instrument for accruing such moral legitimacy in the form of public affirmation. With this kind of mass mobilization, no one inside or out of government would dare oppose the virtuous leader. Conversely, all efforts are made to readjust legal institutions to reflect this moral consensus. Taiwan's Grand Justice, for instance, has refused to rule against President Lee's move to expand the powers of the presidency. Huang Chu-wen, former head of the KMT's Policy Institute, lauded this decision as a better reflection of "reality."[66] He cited as evidence President Lee's electoral landslide, which confirms the public's wish that he wield supreme power.

Conclusion

Democracy in Taiwan is not and can never be a derivative of Western liberal democracy. Given that Chinese political culture requires the nation's top leader to serve as moral icon, elections matter only when they serve as occasional mechanisms for demonstrating public trust or to revive, periodically, the leader's moral conscience. The Confucian public participates in voting only through various kinds of group-based inducements such as negative campaigning, vote buying, factional mobilization, and/or ethnic politics. Thus a Confucian democracy could still be authoritarian in political action (e.g., mass mobilizations) even while liberal in institutional structure.[67]

Accordingly, neither conversionism nor localism captures the nature of democratization in postcolonial societies. Though these approaches differ in methods, assumptions, and implications, both commit a common ecological fallacy: i.e., social systems in our postcolonial, globalized world are monolithic and pristine in nature. As Taiwan's case demonstrates, we need to understand and appreciate democratization as a set of political negotiations across unstable, contentious normative domains where institutions, norms, and sensibilities may not coincide. This grab-bag atmosphere may seem to "distort" the democratic process, as suggested by the authors of illiberal democracy. Indeed, this observation may be accurate and even justify laments of despair.[68] But it is precisely the uneven, unwieldy nature of politics in postcolonial Taiwan that, conversely, offers a ray of hope: in destabilizing the political environment, it pushes society to consider more (and possibly alternative) understandings of the common good. Confucian democracy may still incline towards a normative authoritarianism, but at least the management of public space is no longer as certain or tried. In this sense, democratization acts as a hermeneutic to social and political decision-making, rather than a didactic imposition.

Notes

We thank the research assistance of Kuo An-min, Department of Political Science, and Lin Wei-zen, Department of Geography, both of Syracuse University. We are also grateful to four anonymous reviewers from the *Review of Politics* for their insightful and constructive comments. Lastly, we extend special thanks to Fred Dallmayr and Peter R. Moody, Jr. for their encouragement and support.

1. See, for example, *Zhiguo gujian* (Classics of Governance), G. Q. Tian, ed. (Chengdu: Sichuan University Press, 1991).

2. For a more detailed review of this literature, see L. H. M. Ling, "Democratization under Internationalization: Media Reconstructions of Gender Identity in Shanghai," *Democratization* 3 (Summer 1996): 140-157.

3. East Asia's other CDS include Japan, Singapore, and South Korea. Hong Kong before its handover to China qualified only conditionally as a CDS given its formal status as a British colony. But since July 1997, Hong Kong has joined the region's latest CDS, China.

4. For a more detailed review of this literature, see P. Deans, "The Capitalist Developmental State in East Asia," in *State Strategies in the Global Economy*, R. Palan and J. Abbott with P. Deans, eds. (London: Pinter, 1996), 78-102; and J. Henderson, "Against the Economic Orthodoxy: On the Making of the East Asian Miracle," *Economy and Society* 22 (1993): 200-217.

5. See, for example, H. Fukui, "The Japanese State and Economic Development: A Profile of a Nationalist-Paternalist Capitalist State," in *States and Development in the Asian Pacific Rim*, R. P. Appelbaum and J. Henderson, eds. (New York: Sage Publications, 1992), 199-226; M. Osawa, "Bye-bye Corporate Warriors: The Formation of a Corporate-Centered Society and Gender-Biased Social Policies in Japan," *Annals of the Institute of Social Science* 35 (1993): 157-194; and Y. Mikanagi, "Understanding Japan's 'Undemocracy': A Study on Equal Employment Opportunity Law," paper presented at the conference on "Gender and Global Restructuring: Shifting Sites and Sightings," May 12-13, 1995, University of Amsterdam, Netherlands.

6. D. S. Landes, "Japan and Europe: Contrasts in Industrialization," in *The State and Economic Enterprise in Japan*, W. W. Lockwood, ed. (New Jersey: Princeton University Press, 1965), 93-182; and C. Johnson, *MITI and the Japanese Miracle, 1925-1975* (Palo Alto, CA: Stanford University Press, 1982).

7. H. B. Im, "The Rise of Bureaucratic Authoritarianism in South Korea," *World Politics* 39 (1987): 231-257.

8. R. Denny, "Singapore, China, and the 'Soft Authoritarian' Challenge," *Asian Survey* 34 (1994): 231-242; and E. Jones, "Asia's Fate: A Response to the Singapore School," *National Interest* 35 (1994): 18-28.

9. T. B. Gold, *State and Society in the Taiwan Miracle* (New York: M. E. Sharpe, 1986); A. Amsden, "The State and Taiwan's Economic Development," in *Bringing the State Back In*, P. B. Evans, D. Rueschemeyer, and T. Skocpol, eds. (London: Cambridge University Press, 1985), 78-106; and A. Amsden, "Taiwan's Economic History: A Case of Etatisme and Challenge to Dependency Theory," *Modern China* 5 (1979): 341-380.

10. M. P. Petracca and M. Xiong, "The Concept of Chinese Neo-Authoritarianism," *Asian Survey* 30 (1990): 1099-1117. For a comparison of East Asian capitalist authoritarianism with other types of repressive regimes in the Third World, see H. Feith, "Repressive-Developmentalist Regimes in Asia," *Alternatives* 7 (1981): 491-605.

11. See, for example, C. Y. Shih, "Public Citizens, Private Voters: The Meaning of Election for Chinese Peasants," in *PRC Tomorrow: Development under the Ninth Five-Year Plan*, C. P. Lin, ed. (Kaohsiung: National Sun Yat-sen University, 1996), 145-171.

12. H. S. Rowen, "The Tide Underneath the 'Third Wave,'" *Journal of Democracy* 6 (1995): 52-64.

13. M. Olson, "Dictatorship, Democracy, and Development," *American Political Science Review* 87 (1993): 572.

14. L. W. Pye, *Asian Power and Politics* (Cambridge: Harvard University Press, 1985) and "The State and the Individual: An Overview Interpretation," *China Quarterly* 127 (1991): 443-466.

15. Y. Sakamoto, "Introduction: The Global Context of Democratization," *Alternatives* 16 (1991): 122.

16. See, for example, Olson, "Dictatorship"; R. Rose, "Toward a Civil Economy," *Problems of Postcommunism* 3 (1992): 13-26; N. Genov, "The Transition to Democracy in Eastern Europe: Trends and Paradoxes of Social Rationalization," *International Social Science Journal* 128 (1991): 331-341; and D. Held, "Democracy and Globalization," *Alternatives* 16 (1991): 201-208.

17. H. Overbeek and K. van der Pijl, "Restructuring Capital and Restructuring Hegemony," in *Restructuring Hegemony in the Global Political Economy*, H. Overbeek, ed. (London: Routledge, 1993), 1.

18. M. Pei, "The Puzzle of East Asian Exceptionalism," *Journal of Democracy* 5 (1994): 102.

19. F. Fukuyama, "The End of History?" *National Interest* 30 (Summer 1989): 3-18. In a later essay, Fukuyama modifies this statement to acknowledge that not all democratic polities need converge in form even while they embrace a common developmental program in content. Specifically, he notes a possible compatibility between Confucianism and democracy. But he spends the rest of the essay highlighting their differences only to conclude that "Confucian values might work well in a liberal society (as they clearly do for many Asian immigrants to the United States), where they can serve as a counter-balance to the larger society's atomizing tendencies." See, F. Fukuyama, "Confucianism and Democracy," *Journal of Democracy* 6 (1995): 32-33. Casting East Asia's struggles with Confucianism and democracy in terms of the Asian diaspora in America not only short-changes both historical experiences. It also underscores the Western bias that this paper critiques.

20. Note, for example, the rapist imagery underlying this nineteenth-century justification of colonialism, the historical precursor to twentieth-century liberalism as global ideology: "Colonization is the expansive force of a people; it is its power of reproduction; it is its enlargement and its multiplication through space; it is the subjection of the universe or a vast part of it to that people's language, customs, ideas, and laws." French philosopher Leroy-Beaulieu quoted in Edward Said, *Orientalism* (New York: Vintage Books, 1979), 219.

21. See, for example, J. Han and L. H. M. Ling, "Authoritarianism in the Hypermasculinized State: Hybridity, Patriarchy, and Capitalism in Korea," *International Studies Quarterly* 42 (March 1998): 53-78.

22. Ling, "Democratization," 145.

23. Foremost among its advocates are political leaders in the region, such as Lee Kuan Yew of Singapore, Mahathir Mohammad of Malaysia, Suharto of Indonesia, and Roh Tae Woo of South Korea.

24. C. D. Neher, "Asian Style Democracy," *Asian Survey* 34 (1994): 961.

25. This concept first appeared in a pre-Confucian source, the *Shangshu*. It stipulated that "heaven hears what the people hear, heaven sees what the people see." Subsequently, Mengzi (Mencius) incorporated this notion to conclude that the "people's heart" (*minxin*) should function as the ultimate arbiter of a regime's legitimacy. The people, Mengzi claimed, came first because they are the most noble, next comes the country, last is the prince. See, S. K. Lao, *Zhongguo zhixue shi* (The History of Chinese Political Philosophy, 4th ed.) (Taipei: Sanmin, 1988).

26. See Y. C. Chin, *Zhongguo minbengsixiangshi* (Intellectual History of China's People-as-Essence) (Taipei: Shangwu Publishing Co. Ltd., 1993). Sun Yatsen sought to converge *minben* governance with Lincoln's democracy triad but ended up modifying the latter instead. Chinese nationalism, Sun claimed, instantiates government "of the people" (*minyou*) by permitting Chinese from all walks of life to participate in government. Ruling the country and evaluating their own performance thus constitutes government "by the people" (*minzhi*). Lastly, maximizing "the people's livelihood" (*minxiang*) exemplifies government "for the people." See Y. Chou, *Zhongshan sixiang xin quan* (A New Anthology of the Thought of Sun Yatsen) (Taipei: Sanmin, 1990).

27. D. J. Kim, "Is Culture Destiny? The Myth of Asia's Anti-Democratic Values," *Foreign Affairs* 73 (1994): 191.

28. See, for example, L. H. M. Ling, "Rationalizations for State Violence in Chinese Politics: The Hegemony of Parental Governance," *Journal of Peace Research* 31 (November 1994): 393-405.

29. M. W. Sa, *Rujia zhenglun yanyi* (The Legacy of Confucian Political Thought) (Taipei: Tongta, 1982).

30. D. Bell and K. Jayasuriya, "Understanding Illiberal Democracy: A Framework," in *Towards Illiberal Democracy in Pacific Asia*, D. A. Bell, D. Brown, K. Jayasuriya, and D. M. Jones, eds. (New York: St. Martin's Press, 1995), 2.

31. Bell and Jayasuriya, "Understanding Illiberal Democracy," 14.

32. D. M. Jones, K. Jayasuriya, D. A. Bell, and D. Brown, "Towards A Model of Illiberal Democracy," *Towards Illiberal Democracy*, 163-167.

33. D. Brown and D. M. Jones, "Democratization and the Myth of the Liberalizing Middle Classes," *Towards Illiberal Democracy*, 78-106; C. H. Nam, "South Korea's Big Business Clientelism in Democratic Reform," *Asian Survey* 35 (1995): 357-366; and H. Koo, "The Interplay of State, Social Class, and World System in East Asian Development: The Cases of South Korea and Taiwan," in *The Political Economy of the New Asian Industrialism*, F. C. Deyo, ed. (Ithaca: Cornell University Press, 1987), 165-181.

34. Bell and Jayasuriya, "Understanding Illiberal Democracy," 13.

35. Confucian political thought requires both filial piety (*xiao*) and loyalty (*zhong*) for the polity, seen as family relations writ large, whereas Lockean liberalism celebrates the right of the individual to mature and live a life marked largely by contractual relations with both family and state. See, for example, Ling, "Rationalizations for State Violence."

36. See, for example, *The Post-Colonial Studies Reader*, B. Ashcroft, G. Griffiths, H. Tiffin, eds. (London: Routledge, 1995).

37. See, for example, F. Buell, *National Culture and the New Global System* (Baltimore: Johns Hopkins University Press, 1994); P. Darby and A. J. Paolini, "Bridging International Relations and Postcolonialism," *Alternatives* 19 (1994): 371-397; and S. Hall, "The Local and the Global: Globalization and Ethnicity," in *Culture, Globalization and the World System*, A. D. King, ed. (Binghamton: Department of Art and Art History, State University of New York at Binghamton, 1991), 19-40.

38. H. Bhabha, "Cultural Diversity and Cultural Differences," in *The Post-Colonial Studies Reader*, 209.

39. After his father's death in 1975, Chiang Ching-kuo served as premier for three years under President Yen Chia-kan. Informally, though, Chiang gripped the reins of power.

40. See, for example, C. L. Chiou, *Democratizing Oriental Despotism* (New York: St. Martin's Press, 1995); J. J. Wu, *Taiwan's Democratization* (Hong Kong: Oxford University Press, 1995); L. Chao and R. H. Myers, "The First Chinese Democracy," *Asian Survey* 34 (1994): 213-30; S. C. Leng and C. Y. Lin, "Political Change on Taiwan: Transition to Democracy?" *China Quarterly* 136 (1993): 805-39; J. Domes, "Taiwan in 1992: On the Verge of Democracy," *Asian Survey* 33 (1993): 54-60; P. R. Moody, Jr., *Political Change on Taiwan* (New York: Praeger, 1992); T. J. Cheng, "Democratizing the Quasi-Leninist Regime in Taiwan," *World Politics* 41 (1989): 471-499; E. A. Winckler, "Institutionalization and Participation on Taiwan: From Hard to Soft Authoritarianism?" *China Quarterly* 99 (1984): 481-499.

41. H. Lasswell, *Politics: Who Gets What, When, How?* (New York: Meridian, 1958).

42. Brown and Jones, "Democratization," 97.

43. Since assuming the chairmanship of the KMT, Lee has subtly and irreversibly transformed Chiang Kai-shek's party into one that is pro-Taiwan rather than pro-China. For this reason, the KMT split into two: the "old new guard" of Lee supporters remains under the KMT banner while a "new new guard" of second-generation KMT loyalists-cum-intellectuals forms the New Party.

44. The National Assembly no longer elects the president but retains the authority to approve the president's nomination of the head of the Control, Justice, and Examination Yuans as well as their council members. The NDC proposal, in effect, would remove the premier, who chairs the Executive Yuan, from the Legislative Yuan's jurisdiction and shift his political allegiance completely to the president. Additionally, this proposal would allow President Lee to send the premier's cabinet to the National Assembly, thereby installing a *de facto* presidential caucus.

45. Meng Rong-hua, *Central Daily News*, December 28, 1996, 2.

46. *Central Daily News*, December 30, 1996, 4.

47. December 27, 1996, 2.

48. *Hu Wenhui*, December 27, 1996, 2.

49. December 28, 1996, 2.

50. Hsu Wen-pin, *Liberal Times*, December 29, 1996, 7.

51. *Central Daily News*, December 30, 1996, 2.

52. The NAC sought popular support to terminate the incumbent National Assembly, the Control Yuan, and the Legislative Yuan by electing new representatives for each of these institutions.

53. *Liberal Times*, December 29, 1996, 3.

54. *Public Records of the Legislative Yuan* (*Lifa gongbao*) 85 (12), 287-296.

55. *United Daily*, December 30, 1996, 6.

56. The Thousand Island Incident occurred in April 1994 when three mainland Chinese robbed and burned twenty-four Taiwanese tourists along with their eight mainland crew members on a yacht touring the area. Embarassed by the event, local mainland authorities stalled requests by Taiwanese families to retrieve the bodies of their loved ones and to see the burned yacht. For the implications of this event for mainland-Taiwan relations, see C. Y. Shih, "Human Rights as Identities: Difference and Discrimination in Taiwan's China Policy," a paper presented at the annual meeting of the Western Political Science Association, March 18-20, 1995, Portland, Oregon.

57. *Central Daily News*, January 1, 1997, 3.

58. This form of self-address invokes traditional Confucian protocol for scholar-officials.

59. The term "freeze" (*dong*) was used to avoid the impression that Taiwan's provincial status was being eliminated even though that, in effect, would be the result.

60. Xunzi, Mengzi, and the Four Books (*si shu*) all targeted individual "desire" as a source of social disintegration. See Sa, *Rujia zhenglun yanyi*.

61. C. Y. Shih, "The Decline of China's Moral Regime," *Comparative Political Studies* 27 (1994): 272-301.

62. *China Times*, September 21, 1991, 4.

63. May 20, 1991, 2.

64. Former Minister of Justice (*sifabu*) Ma Ying-jiou (now Taipei's newly elected mayor) resigned when thousands of demonstrators demanded government action to restore public order when the seventeen-year-old daughter of a well-known actress was kidnapped and killed for ransom. This incident followed two other highly publicized murders, one committed against a DPP feminist in a taxicab and another with eight victims killed in the home of a KMT party member. These murders remain unsolved, thereby escalating public hysteria about law and order in Taiwan.

65. *Records of the National Affairs Council*, 226.

66. *Central Daily News*, December 30, 1996, 4.

67. F. Hu, *Zhengzhi wenhua de yihan yu guancha* (Connotations and Observations of Political Culture) (Tianjin: Tianjin People's Publishing, 1995).

68. K. K. Huang, for instance, lambasts politics in Taiwan for failing to approximate the Western liberal democratic ideal by: (1) not functioning as a democracy but delivering a form of populism that is a "distorted product" (*guai wu*) of Oriental despotism and Western democracy; (2) failing to govern by tolerating personal power mongering; and (3) deluding the public that money politics (*jingqian zhengzhi*) is really techno-industrial development and that mafia politics (*heidao zhengzhi*) constitutes a kind of family values. But he blames these structural/institutional problems on a single individual leader, Lee Teng-hui, and his moral character. See K. K. Huang, *Mincuiwang-tailun* (On the Annihilation of Taiwan through Populism) (Taipei: Choushang Wenhua Co. Ltd., 1995). This application of Confucian morality to liberal politics is ultimately self-contradictory and self-defeating. Logically, it implies that Taiwan needs another

individual (most likely male) imbued with the moral "right stuff" to lead it to democracy. How, then, is this democratic?

10

Beyond "East and West": Nishida's Universalism and Postcolonial Critique

Yoko Arisaka

Eurocentrism and Japanese Philosophy

For a century, Asian intellectual and cultural life has been inordinately preoccupied with the meanings and implications of "Westernization" and "modernization." Japan sidestepped this problem during its long years of isolation,[1] but finally in 1853 Commodore Perry and his cannon-wielding "black ships" came to the shores of Yokohama and demanded the opening of the country. At that point the country faced two alternatives—either become a victim of Western expansionism, or modernize in order to protect itself. Japan chose the latter path, and with the Meiji Restoration of 1868, it inaugurated an era of daunting modernization in all aspects of life: social, intellectual, technological, political, economic, religious, aesthetic, and, of course, popular culture.

It is not an exaggeration to say that the history of post-Meiji Japan has been a history of the struggle with the notions of westernization and modernization. At first, aversion to the "barbarians" caused public outcry against any foreign influence. However, as the political leaders of the new government actively promoted the idea of building a new, modern country and getting rid of old feudal ways, people in the cosmopolitan centers began to embrace the new way of life with enthusiasm. Soon infatuation with things Western became extreme; for instance, one group of reformers proposed to convert the Japanese emperor to Christianity, since that was the religion under which science had developed in the West. Beef-eating became popular, and the local authorities issued a public notice "recommending this unorthodox diet on the ground that it would create energy for the performance of patriotic duties and strengthen the national physique."[2] "*Perry kawara-ban*," an ornamental tile depicting the "beautiful" black ships, became a sought-after *objet d'art* among the fashionable. "Red Hair" prints, depicting northern Europeans and their lifestyles and technologies, became popular as well. Western style dance halls became the craze among the forward-looking modern types.

Viewing the world in terms of "East vs. West" (*toyo vs. seiyo*) became a deeply ingrained practice in almost all aspects of life; it was the framework people used to understand their rapidly changing and often chaotic lives. Cutting across class and gender lines, people became keenly aware of their "non-Western" way of life vis-à-vis what they imagined to be "the Western," the "foreign," the "new" way of life. The process of negotiating with the West manifested itself in myriad ways: Political elites debated how to construct a modern nation-state called Japan; education reformers had to reconsider the balance between the traditional and the scientific so as to cope with the bombardment of new knowledge; women and men alike were suddenly faced with the problem of self-presentation—clothing, hairstyle, and possessions were transparent markers of their stake in the cultural transformation, both to others and to themselves.[3] The initial shock of "difference" established a long-standing paradigm of "Japan as the other of the West."

While some thinkers, such as Yukichi Fukuzawa, fully embraced the Western notions of liberalism and democracy, the rapid process of modernization/westernization also provoked a strong traditionalist reaction. Although Japan was already cut off from its premodern past (represented as "Eastern"), cultural conservatives actively promoted traditions that they had to put together from remnants of the old way of life. For example, Takamori Saigo, a major political figure in the Meiji Restoration, was known for his antiforeign beliefs and his praise of the "spirit of the samurai." He eventually led a tradition-centered rebellion against the very modernizing regime he had helped to create. Japanese calligraphy, using the traditional brush, which had been chased from the educational curriculum as outmoded, was reintroduced in order to "preserve the spirit of Japanese style and thinking." Buddhism was reformed and modernized, and new martial arts such as judo were constructed from traditional elements. The result of this modernization process was a peculiar combination of rapid westernization and a rather artificial return to imagined origins. The hopeful intellectuals echoed the sentiment epitomized in Shozan Sakuma's slogan: "Eastern morality and Western techniques."

Japanese philosophy was born in this general cultural milieu, and it was by no means an exception to this trend. What came to be identified as "philosophy" in Japan—"Western" philosophy as opposed to Confucianism and Buddhism, which were increasingly regarded as feudalistic—was introduced around the time of the Meiji Restoration.[4] At first Japanese thinkers concentrated on exegesis and commentary on Western philosophers. However, as they became more aware of the fruitful tension between "Western rationality" and "traditional Japanese values," philosophy became a site in which Japanese intellectuals negotiated their relation to European intellectual trends.

In the European consciousness of the time, the "West" represented the "universal"; the age-old quest of philosophy has been to find the "truth" which speaks to *the* human mind, just as scientific knowledge is considered "universal."[5] Moreover, as exemplified by Hegel, the dominant view of history is represented as a temporally linear "progress," from the premodern past to the modern present, culminating in the techno-scientific culture of Europe and America.[6] Since both philosophy and science developed chiefly in Europe, the notions of "truth," "universality," "modernity," and "being Western" often came to be conflated in the minds of philosophers, both Japanese and Western. In this framework, what was "non-Western" was either simply "false," or due to a particular "time lag" within the universal scheme of things. The central reference point remained the West—hence, the familiar problem of "Eurocentrism."

As is well-known, American intellectuals have recently begun to criticize their own Eurocentric representation of intellectual history and to pay closer attention to the different voices at the margins of this intellectual mapping. The critique of Eurocentrism has gone along with a new appreciation of "multiculturalism" and a wider self-understanding in the context of global history. However, despite such efforts, Eurocentrism does remain a persistent reality, both in the United States and elsewhere, Western as well as non-Western. As Dipesh Chakrabarty laments, "That Europe works as a silent referent in historical knowledge itself becomes obvious in a highly ordinary way. . . . Third-world historians feel a need to refer to works in European history; historians of Europe do not feel any need to reciprocate."[7]

What is significant about Japanese *philosophy* in this context is its self-positioning vis-à-vis Western universalism. The idea was that Japan, as a non-Western nation, could provide something "universal" of its own, the truth of which the West could recognize. As Kitaro Nishida optimistically claimed:

> Up to now Westerners thought that their culture was superior to all others, and that human culture advances toward their own form. Other peoples, such as Easterners, are said to be behind and if they advance, they too will acquire the same form. There are even some Japanese who think like this. However . . . I believe there is something fundamentally different about the East. They [East and West] must complement each other and . . . achieve the eventual realization of a complete humanity. It is the task of Japanese culture to find such a principle.[8]

Japanese philosophy could not be reduced to Eastern spirituality, a mere particularity, since it too could validate itself in terms of rational universality. In Nishida's words, "To become global Oriental culture must not stop at its own specificity but rather it must shed a new light on Western culture and a new world culture must be created,"[9] and further, "Today's Japan is no longer a closed society, an island in the East. It is a Japan in the world. The principle of the formation of Japan should reflect the principle of the formation of the world."[10] The West no longer had a monopoly on universal culture. Japanese philosophy exemplified the claim that history does not "culminate" in European civilization; instead history would have to recognize multiple centers, all of which had claims to being just as valid as the West. Hence, Nishida's thought gave voice to the cultural ambivalence people felt at the time, that somehow Japan was "different" but not thereby "worse" than or "behind" the West. Japanese philosophy represented one of the earliest formulations of anti-Eurocentrism.

Universalism and Nationalism:
Kitaro Nishida's Case

Japanese philosophy is said to find its own voice with the publication of Kitaro Nishida's *Zen no Kenkyu* (*An Inquiry into the Good*, 1911).[11] Influenced by William James's concept of "pure experience," Nishida initially attempted to articulate an experiential ontology of immediate experience[12] partially inspired by Zen Buddhism.[13] He presented his early philosophy as a "synthesis of Western and Eastern thinking." What was "Western" was his method; he deliberately chose the language of Western philosophy, borrowing from Aristotle, neo-Kantianism, German idealism, and in his later writings, Hegelian Marxism. What was "Eastern" was his inclusion of the concept of "absolute nothingness" (*zettai-mu*) derived from Buddhist metaphysics. This hybrid trope became standard in the "Kyoto School,"[14] which established itself as the dominant philosophical school after the 1920s. All major thinkers after that time either belonged to the Kyoto School, or as in the case of Marxists and neo-Kantians, responded polemically to it. What is known as Japanese philosophy today in the West largely represents the legacy of the Kyoto School.

Despite its initial, seemingly apolitical, philosophical stance, the Kyoto School became entangled in politics during the 1930s and 1940s when a wave of nationalist sentiment swept the country. Then the critique of Eurocentrism took a distinctively nationalist turn. The chief concern of Japanese intellectuals at the time was to theorize a specifically Japanese form of modernity that would remedy the defects of a Euro-American model driven by rationalism, material-ism, technocentrism, and the will to domination. Japan was supposed to be uniquely suited to develop such an alternative modernity, since it was the only nation in Asia to modernize successfully while retaining the spirit of the East. Several series of roundtable discussions and symposia on this theme were held in the early 1940s, the most infamous of which was the "Overcoming Modernity" (*kindai no chokoku*) debate of 1942[15] in which some of Nishida's students participated. Iwao Koyama, for instance, developed a "philosophy of

world history" based on Nishida's thought, as an answer to Western imperialism. In order to fight Western domination, Japan had to offer some non-
Eurocentric "principle" which could unify Asia and establish a new world
order.[16] As such, it was Japan's responsibility to "free Asia from Western
colonial powers" so that it could develop a modern global culture equal to or
even better than the model hitherto established by the West. As anyone familiar
with the nationalist discourse of the day can easily recognize, this rhetoric
coincided with the slogans of the imperialist regime.

After the war, progressive leftists harshly criticized the debate for its
reactionary agenda, its complicity with nationalism, and its justification of the
Greater East Asia Co-Prosperity Sphere. The debate was cast into oblivion, at
least during the years following the war, and the Kyoto School acquired an
unsavory imperialist image. During the postwar period, just the mention of
"Nishida" or the Kyoto School would have made one appear complicit with
imperialism, and the intellectual community shunned their philosophy as
politically evil. However, the followers of the Kyoto School continued to maintain its tradition of religious philosophy somewhat in isolation. They believed
that their philosophy was not inherently nationalist despite its problematic
associations, and that it was the only original thought ever to appear in Japanese
philosophy, and as such, still worth pursuing.

The assessment of Nishida's own role in this debate is far from clear. He did
not participate in the debate nor did he explicitly support the nationalist regime,
but his philosophy is held accountable for many of the politically problematic
concepts his students employed. However, Nishida did not explicitly state his
political views but rather buried them in complicated philosophical theories, so
the evaluation of his politics has given rise to an intense controversy in the
postwar years. His writings were so coded and cryptic that interpreters used
them to support politically opposing views.[17]

Nishida developed his metaphysical theories during the late 1920s and 1930s,
when Japanese military and political leaders were mobilizing the whole nation
with full-blown nationalism. He was by then a well-known figure, and his books
were widely read. However, until he began to write on history during the mid-
1930s, he had concentrated primarily on abstract metaphysical theory with little
reference to politics. As a result, his philosophy was attacked by Marxists for
lacking real historical significance. For instance, Nishida's Marxist student, Jun
Tosaka, denounced his teacher's philosophy as an "academic, bourgeois philosophy of idealism" that is "trans-historical, formalistic, romantic, and
phenomenological."[18] Nishida's letters indicate that he began to write on
politics in the late 1930s, partly in response to such criticism, and partly to show
his concern for the issues of the day. His writings soon touched on such subjects
as the Imperial House, the project of World War II, Japanese National Polity
(*kokutai*), and the role of the Greater East Asia Co-Prosperity Sphere.[19]

According to his many postwar critics,[20] Nishida is guilty of complicity with
imperialism or ultranationalism because not only did he employ the nationalist

discourse of the time, but he also gave it philosophical meaning in essays such as "The Principle of the New World Order" (1942) and "The Problem of Japanese Culture" (1940).[21] For example, regarding the concept of "*hakko iu*" (Eight corners, one world),[22] a wartime slogan, Nishida claims:

> Each nation/people lives its own unique historical life and at the same time joins in a united global world through carrying out a world-historical mission. This is the ultimate Idea [principle] of human historical development, and this is the principle of the New World Order that should be sought in the current world war. It seems that our country's principle, "Eight corners, one world," expresses this idea. I humbly believe that this view is also expressed by the imperial statement proclaiming that all nations should understand this principle.[23]

Pierre Lavalle points out that ideas such as this put Nishida squarely in the camp of the ultranationalists, in their justification of the self-appointed leadership of Japan in Asia.[24] The language of "respecting the historical lives of each nation," while it sounds good, was itself a part of imperialist discourse.[25] Nishida further comments on the Japanese national polity (*kokutai*) and the Imperial Way (*kodo*):

> Japan's national polity is not merely totalitarianism. The Imperial House is the beginning and the end of the world, as the absolute present that embraces the past and the future. The quintessence of the unbroken line of our national polity consists in the completion of the historical world itself with the Imperial House as its center.[26]

In light of such blatantly nationalist ideas, it seems hardly possible to defend Nishida. However, others insist on more nuanced analyses of these passages in a wider philosophical and historical context, especially since his letters and diaries clearly demonstrate his anti-imperialist sentiments.[27] Moderates in the debate, such as Jan Van Bragt, hold that while there is evidence of theoretical complicity, nationalism was not the fundamental inspiration of Nishida and other figures of the Kyoto School.[28] John Maraldo also argues that Nishida did not intend to support state nationalism, although he was complicit "more by effect than intention" and thus should still be held responsible.[29] Andrew Feenberg examines the application of his "dialectic of place" to history and acknowledges that it has strong cosmopolitan implications,[30] a point Nishida's defenders emphasize.

For these defenders, Nishida's cosmopolitanism derives from a universalistic philosophy which excludes nationalism on principle despite his concessions to the regime.[31] Hence, they argue that the accusation that Nishida was complicit with ultranationalism is unwarranted. What I argue in the last section is that the chief claim of the defenders—that Nishida's philosophical "universalism" is incompatible with nationalist ideology—fails because universalist discourse was used both as a tool of liberation *and* oppression in Japan's case. How does

Nishida apply his universalistic philosophy of place to history?

Nishida's signature theory of "place" ("*basho*") is a system of "concrete universals," which explains the "conditions" of abstract thought.[32] All of the categories which appear in this system are universals, such as "judgment," "consciousness," "action," "historical world," and "absolute nothingness." The theory is modelled after Hegel's logic, which is meant to be a universal system of reality as such and not the expression of a *particular* nation. What makes this theory distinctively non-Western, despite its universal form, is the last stage of absolute nothingness (*zettai mu*). If the whole history of Western philosophy is a history of objectified Being, then absolute nothingness is the "place" of such Being. This utterly nonobjectifiable "place" is the ultimate nonreifiable "that in which" all beings manifest themselves; it cannot be objectified, for if it were, it would simply be another "being" and not the "place" of being. As such, it does not appear in the (Western) system of metaphysics. Insofar as the place of nothingness "encompasses" the metaphysics of Being, it is an ultimate universal under which all categories are subsumed.

Nishida applies his concept of absolute nothingness historically. At the ultimate historical stage, absolute nothingness appears not as the goal of a temporal progression ordered in terms of premodern to modern, but as a spatialized realization of all of cultures in a global "place." All cultures interact to create their own identity vis-à-vis each other in his dialectical theory of "the identity of contradictions." Nishida opposes the "undialectical" conception of national self-determination of nineteenth-century Western imperialism: "Each nation considered that its historical mission was to strengthen itself by subjugating others."[33] He contrasts this view with his own dialectical "formative global-ism," which calls for the self-realization and self-transcendence of nations/ peoples. In this view, "each nation develops itself, yet at the same time it must negate itself and reach beyond itself to participate in building a global world."[34] Each nation must have a "world historical mission," which seeks the preservation of the identity of the nation *and* forms a global community through mutual codetermination and self-negation.

In this view, the West is not a privileged center of world culture, but just another particular site in which certain forms of civilization developed. By "spatializing" global history, that is, by treating the world as the place of nations' historical codetermination and self-transcendence, Nishida includes non-European spheres as full participants in the realization of global history. All other cultures have different ways of participating in world culture which are no less valid than the European forms. The "new world order," therefore, must involve all nations coming to a dialectical self-understanding in these global terms, and the historical mission of Japan is to further that process. This theory is "postmodern" to the extent that it destablizes the Eurocentric conception of history and culture and makes each cultural formation and identity a matter of interaction and codetermination rather than assuming essentialized entities.[35] If cultural identities are formed through *difference,* i.e., through the identity of contradictions, then there cannot be any "center" which would dominate others. But if so, Japanese nationalism itself would be excluded.

In fact, Nishida explicitly opposed the ethnocentric and totalitarian interpretation of the official policy. For example, he states:

> What is most deplorable is to subjectivize Japan. That merely militarizes the Imperial Way and transforms it into imperialism. . . . In contrast we must contribute to the world by discovering our own principle of self-formation in the depth of our historical development; that principle is the identity of contradictions. This is the authentic Imperial Way and the true meaning of "Eight corners, one world.[36]

In "The Principle of the New World Order," Nishida further states that "mere racialism, which lacks true globalism and envisions the world only from its own self-centered perspective, is ethnic egoism; only expansionism and imperialism can result from it."[37] These passages may indicate that he was distancing his own philosophical position from state nationalist ideology.

To explain Nishida's embarrasing references to such imperialist notions as "hakko iu" and the Great East Asia Co-Prosperity Sphere, the defenders claim that Nishida used the language of the day in the hopes that the political leaders would be influenced by his own anti-imperialist interpretation of it.[38] Moreover, even with respect to Nishida's claim that Japan (in particular the Imperial House [kôshitsu]) offers the paradigm of cultural codetermination (which contradicts his own "no-center" view), the defenders argue that in his theory the words "Japan" or the "Imperial House" cannot refer to a particular entity, a "being," since they represent his philosophical concept of "absolute nothingness" as the "field" or "place" [basho] in which all nations coexist dialectically. In other words, Japan is not one of these nations which interact, but is in fact an empty "scene" in which all others work out their mutual existence. It is truly "universal" since it is not in any sense a "particular"; it enfolds all being. If so, Japanese nationalism is again impossible, since the Imperial House is not an "entity" which could exert a force on others. The defenders thus claim that Nishida was not a nationalist, neither as a person nor as a philosopher, since his philosophy cannot theoretically accomodate nationalism. If every nation followed his thought, no nation could fall into the sort of nationalism which embraces expansionism.

Nishida, Orientalism, and Postcolonialism

The notion of "absolute nothingness" in the theory of place is conveniently invoked to undercut the claim that the Japanese Imperial House is an "entity" which dominates the rest of the world. Strange as this theory sounds today, the idea that a particular nation may be the bearer of a universal principle, such as freedom or democracy, and that, therefore, its actions in history serve a higher end, should be familiar from recent American experience. However, leaving aside historical parallels, there is obviously a problem with this theory given the *actual* imperialist expansion of Japan into East Asia. I would like to address this issue in the context of Nishida's "orientalism" and its relation to postcolonial critique.

Since its publication in 1978, Edward Said's *Orientalism* profoundly changed the way the issues related to "East and West" are discussed. Said's main thesis is that the very category of the "Orient" was a European invention produced in order to "contain difference"[39] in the era of colonial expansion. Either by way of rejection or exoticism, the category "Orient" served as a tool for Europeans to bring under control the hitherto unknown "other" of Europe; it is by definition a part of European imperialism. The "Orient" was a sweeping category applied to Asiatic cultures regardless of the differences among them. So despite its apparent anti-Eurocentrism, boosting the "Orient" (and likewise the "East") is in fact very much parasitic on Eurocentrism, and the whole framework only reinscribes the fact that the point of reference still remains Europe. What is called for, in Said's view, is to put to rest these very categories: "if it [his discussion] eliminates the 'Orient' and 'Occident' altogether, then we shall have advanced a little in the process of what Raymond Williams has called the 'unlearning' of 'the inherent dominative mode.'"[40] By contrast, in confronting the West, Japan "reverse-orientalized" itself in order to assert its identity as the "other," thus retaining the Western reference point.

Seen from this perspective, Nishida's theory is orientalist in that he had a vision of creating a "Japanese" philosophy which would offer something unique to the world. However, as we noted, what appealed to Nishida about philosophy was its ability to speak a universal language. It was precisely against the backdrop of this philosophical universalism that Nishida was able to assert the specificity of Japanese philosophy vis-à-vis the West.[41] Yet, he wanted Japan's contribution to share in the universality of Western thought. He thus had to adopt the language of Western philosophy, precisely because Japanese thought could not have been *recognized* by the West as of universal significance if it did not "speak their language." Given the choice between "speaking a purely Japanese philosophical language and being ignored" and "speaking in a universal philosophical language and being recognized," Nishida chose the latter.

Moreover, the very drive for universality which Nishida maintained throughout is itself a product of the Western metaphysics which postmodernism criticizes so harshly. The "grand narrative" is the phantasmic child of modernism. According to this view, Nishida's "logic of place" is as Western as Hegel's system, regardless of its "non-Western" flavor. But all this would have been fairly innocuous had it remained just a theoretical issue. The problem is that Nishida's universalist theory became unintentionally implicated in Japanese imperialism, thereby ominously betokening the most pernicious aspect of Eurocentrism—the problem of colonialism. This is not to suggest that colonialism is inherently European; but Japanese imperialism was certainly modelled after and motivated by the modern colonial empires of the European nations (in particular the British, French, and Dutch endeavors in Asia). What I would like to address is the particular way in which Nishida's philosophy became entangled with this brand of colonialism.

Recent studies in postcolonial critique have analyzed the relation between the colonized consciousness and its oppressor, the European colonizing consciousness. Postcolonial critique may be traced back to Frantz Fanon's books, *Black Skin, White Masks* (1952) and *The Wretched of the Earth* (1961), which thematized the ways in which European imperialism systematically enslaved the culture and consciousness of the colonized. But the full blown postcolonial critique began in 1982 with a group of Indian intellectuals who established the journal, *Subaltern Studies*, and theorized their colonized subjectivities vis-à-vis their colonizer, Great Britain.[42]

Some of the main theoretical concerns of this group were to understand how the colonizing power, despite its "good intentions" of "modernizing India," systematically warped the thinking of the colonized sujects to the advantage of the imperialist administration. The way this often worked was by convincing the colonized that, since modernity liberates nations and their peoples, the British ruled them "for their own good." Many Indians were convinced and began to see their own culture as "backwards" and the "new" and "European" form of life as "better" and more "cosmopolitan." The real power of colonization is to achieve this willing participation by transforming the colonized subjects' own point of reference from the native culture to the Western one. But what this process did was to rob Indians of their own voice. The point of the critique, then, is to save the "subaltern," the oppressed subjects under British imperialism, by theoretically empowering them, using Marxism, post-structuralism, deconstruction, and an analysis of power based on Foucault, exposing the ways in which their own thinking was systematically subjugated by imperialism.[43]

Postcolonialism opened a space in which to critique the hegemonic workings of the colonizing power. However, current postcolonial studies primarily focus on the Indian or African cases where the relation between the colonizer and the colonized more or less overlaps with the West/non-West. The case is much more complex in East Asia: all of the Asian nations were threatened by the imperialism of the West; within this solidarity vis-à-vis the West, however, Japan became a colonizer itself; Korea, Taiwan, and other South Asian nations were fully colonized by the Japanese, while China was partially colonized. So "colonized consciousness" in East Asia is not at all a unified experience, and is much more conflicted than the colonized consciousness of India or Africa under Europe.[44] Korean and Taiwanese women in the 1940s, for instance, were triply oppressed by the Japanese, by the West, and by those of their own men who became accomplices of the imperialist power.

It is within this context that I would like to return to Nishida's philosophy of world history and its claim to universality. Here we must look at the two positions Japan occupied in the 1930s and 1940s. First there is Japan's position vis-à-vis the West. While Japan was never colonized by the West, the effect the

West had on Japanese consciousness resembles its effect on a colonized country. What is "Western" becomes the point of reference, even in the creation of an indigenous theory. As we noted, Nishida's theory sought to validate the universality of all non-Western cultures against the domination of the West. It was primarily intended to be a theory of liberation. But to develop such an overarching theory, Nishida necessarily had to adopt Western philosophy, thereby "westernizing" Japanese philosophy. In fact, with respect to human rights, some sort of westernizing universalism has been an essential vehicle in many nations' successful struggle for decolonization. Nishida's cosmopolitan appreciation of the multiplicity of cultures can be seen as emancipating in that light.

At the same time, Japan occupied a very different position vis-a-vis other nations in East Asia. This is the problem: The very universalism which is presented as the vehicle of liberation became a tool of oppression when it was implicated in Japan's own colonizing endeavor in Asia. Just as European modernity was claimed to have liberating power in India because it was believed to raise India to the level of universal (i.e., European) culture, so Nishida optimistically believed that Japanese philosophy could help liberate Asian nations by raising them to universality. In Asia, Japan was the bearer of "truth," because of the unique nondominating metaphysics of "place as nothingness" expressed in the Imperial Way. This belief in theoretical universalism eclipsed the understanding of Japan's historically contingent position and made it impossible for Nishida to evaluate Japan's Asian war realistically. He himself did not endorse colonialism, but his theory nevertheless *functioned* formally in a similar way to the way European universalism was used to convince colonized subjects to submit to imperialism. In fact, the ideologized slogan of Japanese imperialism was precisely to "free Asia from Western imperialism," while the reality was simply just another brutal colonialism. So even though Nishida personally steered clear of the militarist regime, his theory was useful to that regime to the extent that it replayed aspects of the universalist discourse of Western imperialism.

The category of the "East" (or "Asian unity" in the language of the Japanese imperialists) was pernicious precisely because it weakened the perception that Japan was a colonizer, a brutal force *against* other Asian nations, in favor of promoting the perception of unity vis-à-vis the West. Japan appointed itself to be the leader of this Asian unity, since it was, again, the bearer of truth as well as being most "modern." As Nishida claims,

Up to now, East Asian peoples have been oppressed under European imperialism and regarded as colonies. We were robbed of our world-historical mission. It is now time for East Asian peoples to realize our own world-historical mission. . . . We, the people of East Asia, must together assert our principle of East Asian culture and assume our stance world-historically. But in order to build a particular world [of East Asia], a central figure that carries the burden of the project is necessary. In

East Asia today there is no other but Japan.[45]

Here again, the double-edged colonized/colonizing language is at work; Japan is seen as one of the "oppressed," but it can be the leader of the pack in the fight for freedom. This rhetoric even had the advantage of convincing some of the other Asians that Japan could save them from the West, the "real" colonizing power.

Nishida's belief in the universal implications of Japanese philosophy did not stop at the borders of East Asia. His optimism went so far as to claim that "Long ago, the victory of Greece in the Persian War determined the direction of development of European culture up to this day, and in the same way the current East Asian war may determine a direction for world history to come."[46] As Feenberg notes, "from that standpoint Japan's defeat would seem to represent the destruction of a cultural universe, indeed of the very possibility of cultural plurality in the modern world."[47] As such, not just Asia but the whole world awaited a Japanese victory. The full extent of Nishida's ambition for Japan appears in the conclusion of "The Principle of the New World Order," where he writes, "It is fair to say that the principle of our national polity can provide the solution to today's world-historical problems. Not only should the Anglo-American world submit to it, but the Axis powers too will follow it."[48] The apparently harmless idea of Japan's "leadership," infused with the notion of universality, disguises a concrete historical project of world domination.

Japan thus exemplifies two uses of universality—liberatory and oppressive. Japan's failure was to employ the discourse of liberation in order to justify oppression—a standard colonial procedure. Despite his intentions, Nishida's discourse was not sufficiently critical, since it did not take into account the ambivalence inherent in the very notion of universality. As Hegel argues in his critique of the French Revolution, no matter how "universal" a theory, the only way in which it can be *implemented* is through the concrete actions of particular agents. Universality is necessarily particular in its *actual* manifestation; thus even the United States, with its ideals of democracy, market society, and equality, for instance, discovered in Vietnam that it was not the bearer of a "universal" culture it took itself to be. The execution of "universality" (democracy) in Vietnam proved just as "particular" as any earlier colonial adventure. In the Japanese case, too, the universal elements Nishida identified in Japanese culture were transformed into their opposites in the *practice* of empire. He may have personally opposed imperialism, but his theory is still complicit; not only did he naively assume that its cosmopolitanism immunized it against the hazards of concrete political implementation, but his language formally mimicked the colonizing language of universalism.

In sum, postcolonial critique is helpful in seeing how Japanese philosophy's claim of universality became entangled with the imperialist regime. This claim became a disguised form of colonizing ideology, but all this was mediated by Japan's imaginary self- consciousness as the colonized. Coupled with its claim to modernity, the category of "East vs. West" was also utilized to mask the operations of colonial power. The question which remains for us today is this: How do we draw on the resources of modernity without unconsciously serving domination? The language of Asian unity and Japan's possible leading role in it has resurfaced in the economic sphere in recent years. We must not forget what happened in our recent history, and if we are to tell ourselves a responsible story about the intra-Asian relations as well as the relation to other nations, our philosophical discourse must examine the theoretical pitfalls and hopefully avoid them.

Notes

I wish to thank Andrew Feenberg for comments.

1. From 1639 to the mid-1850s, the Tokugawa Shogunate isolated Japan from nearly all foreign contact in order chiefly to control the spread of Christianity; only the strictly controlled port of Nagasaki was open to continue trading with China and Holland. After 1653, no Japanese could travel abroad, and all Japanese who lived abroad were prohibited from returning.

2. G. B. Samsom, *The Western World and Japan* (Tokyo: Charles Tuttle Co., 1984), 383.

3. For instance, women wearing dresses, as opposed to the traditional *kimonos*, were "modern." The choices in daily life—anything from umbrellas, shoes, furniture, eating utensils, hairstyle—reflected one's position in the process of the assimilation of things Western.

4. Funayama Shinichi dates the introduction of Western philosophy to Japan in 1862, when Nishi Amane and Tsuda Mamichi went to Holland and brought back Comte and Mill's utilitarianism. Shinichi Funayama, *Hegeru Tetsugaku to Nishida Tetsugaku* [Hegel's Philosophy and Nishida's Philosophy] (Tokyo: Mirai-sha, 1984), 107. See also Ryosuke Ohashi, *Nihon-teki na mono, Yoroppa-teki na mono* [Things Japanese, Things European] (Tokyo: Shincho-sensho, 1992), chapter 2. Nishi is credited with coining many philosophical terms in Japanese, including the term "*tetsugaku*" (philosophy).

5. Of course, ethnocentric discourse is not limited to Europe. China, for instance, has had a long tradition of understanding itself to be the "center" of the world; however, this consciousness was already eroding with the arrival of the British and the Opium Wars in 1839.

6. Less dominant views of history included, for example, the romantic conception of Rousseau, which represented history not as "progress" but as "decline."

7. Dipesh Chakrabarty, "Postcoloniality and the Artifice of History: Who Speaks for 'Indian' Pasts?" *Representations* 37 (Winter 1992): 25.

8. Nishida's works are collected in *Nishida Kitaro Zenshu* [Collected Works of Nishida], vols. 1-19 (Tokyo: Iwanami Shoten, 1987-1989), which will be abbreviated as *NKZ* and followed by the volume number. This quote is from a lecture, "Nihon Bunka no Mondai" (The Problem of Japanese Culture), *NKZ* 14, 404-405. For a good discussion of Nishida's conception of modernity, see Andrew Feenberg, *Alternative Modernity: The Technical Turn in Philosophy and Social Theory* (Berkeley: University of California Press, 1995), Chapter 8.

9. *NKZ* 14, 407.

10. *NKZ* 12, 341.

11. *Zen no Kenkyu* is *NKZ* 1. For an English translation, see *An Inquiry into the Good*, Masao Abe and Christopher Ives (New Haven: Yale University Press, 1987).

12. For a discussion of the theory of pure experience, see Andrew Feenberg and Yoko Arisaka, "Experiential Ontology: The Origins of the Nishida Philosophy in the Doctrine of Pure Experience," *International Philosophical Quarterly* 30 (1990): 173-205.

13. Robert Sharf argues that the kind of Zen which emphasizes "immediacy," such as D. T. Suzuki's writings, is a post-Meiji construct already driven by nationalism. For analyses see Sharf's "Zen and Japanese Nationalism," *History of Religions* 33 (1993): 1-43, and "Whose Zen? Zen Nationalism Revisited," in *Rude Awakenings: Zen, the Kyoto School, & the Question of Nationalism*, John Maraldo and James Heisig, eds. (Honolulu: University of Hawaii Press, 1995). See also Bernard Faure's critique, "The Kyoto School and Reverse Orientalism," in *Japan in Traditional and Postmodern Perspectives*, Charles Wei-shun Fu and Steven Heine, eds. (Albany: State University of New York Press, 1995).

14. The broad rubric of "Kyoto School" (*Kyoto Gakuha*) includes Nishida and his colleagues and students, such as Hajime Tanabe, Tetsuro Watsuji, Keiji Nishitani, Iwao Koyama, Masaaki Kosaka, Torataro Shimomura, and Shigetaka Suzuki. The term "Kyoto School" was first used by Jun Tosaka, a Marxist student of Nishida's, in order to designate the right-wing thought which developed in the early 1930s.

15. The debate was intially published in *Bungakukai* (Literary World), 1942; for the texts and commentary, see T. Kawakami et al., *Kindai no Chokoku* (Tokyo: Fuzanbo, 1990). For commentary, see also Wataru Hiromatsu, *'Kindai no Chokoku' Ron* (Tokyo: Kodansha, 1989). Discussions in English include H. D. Harootunian, "Visible Discourse/Invisible Ideologies," in *Postmodernism in Japan*, M. Miyoshi and H. D. Harootunian, eds. (Durham: Duke University Press, 1989), 63-92, and Ryoen Minamoto, "The Symposium on 'Overcoming Modernity,'" in *Rude Awakenings*, 197-229.

16. Jeffrey Herf's concept of "reactionary modernism" is useful for understanding Japanese philosophers' reaction to Western rationality from the 1920s to the end of the war. Jeffrey Herf, *Reactinary Modernism: Technology, Culture, and Politics in Weimar and the Third Reich* (Cambridge: Cambridge University Press, 1984). The works of the German reactionary modernists—such as Ernst Juenger, Oswald Spengler, Werner Sombart, and Carl Schmitt—were introduced to the Japanese audience through young Japanese philosophers who went to Germany in the 1920s and 1930s. German nationalists believed that Germany could meaningfully combine technical rationality and spirit, since Germans were supposedly uniquely cultured in a way the Anglo-Americans and French were not. Many promodern Japanese intellectuals were also strongly nationalistic and hoped to create a specifically Asian modernity in Japan. They rejected Western imperialism while trying to co-opt Western rationality for their project.

17. For a more detailed analysis of the debate, see Yoko Arisaka, "The Nishida Enigma: 'The Principle of the New World Order,'" *Monumenta Nipponica* 51 (1996): 81-105. For a collection of essays on the politics of the Kyoto School, see *Rude Awakenings*.

18. Masakatsu Fujita, "Nihon ni Okeru Kenkyushi no Genjo" (An Overview of the History of Research [of Nishida] in Japan), in *Nishida Tetsugaku: Shin Shiryo to Kekyu e no Tebiki*, Y. Kayano and R. Ohashi, eds. (Kyoto: Minerva Shobo, 1987), 118. At that time, Nishida accepted this criticism (see his letter to Tosaka, no. 749, *NKZ* 18, 460).

19. See, for instance, his essay "Sekai Shin Chitsujo no Genri" (The Principle of the New World Order), *NKZ* 12, 426-434.

20. The critics, largely representing the intellectual historians of modern Japan, include H. D. Harootunian, Tetsuo Najita, John Dower, Robert Sharf, Peter Dale, Bernard Faure, and Pierre Lavelle. See especially Lavelle's "The Political Thought of Nishida Kitaro," *Monumenta Nipponica* 49 (1994): 141-162.

21. Excerpts from "The Problem of Japanese Culture" are translated in *Sources of the Japanese Tradition,* vol. 2, W. T. de Bary, ed. and trans. (New York: Columbia University Press, 1958). Both the "New World Order" essay and "The Problem of Japanese Culture" are included in *NKZ* 12.

22. "*Hakko iu,*" or more typically "*hakko ichiu,*" was used to justify Japanese expansionism. The phrase was taken from *Nihon Shoki.* It is also translated as "All the world as one family," or "The universal harmony."

23. *NKZ* 12, 428. Arisaka, "The Nishida Enigma," 102.

24. Lavelle, "The Political Thought," 160.

25. One of the items of the declaration at the Great East Asia Meeting reads: "Each nation of the Great East Asia should respect each other's tradition and each people should promote each other's creativity in order to enhance the culture of Great East Asia." Kenryo Sato, *Dai Towa Senso Kaikoroku* (Tokyo: Tokuma Shoten, 1966), 318. The meeting was held in 1943 in order to strenghthen the coherence of the Greater East Asian Co-Prosperity Sphere under the auspices of Tojo. Nishida's "The Principle of the New World Order" was initially conceived at the request of the Tojo military government in preparation for this meeting. For detailed discussions of the circumstances, see Michiko Yusa, "Fashion and *A-letheia,*" in *Hikaku Shiso Kenkyu* 16 (1990): 281-294; Hikaru Furuta, "'Sekai Shin Chitsujo no Genri' Jiken-ko, I and II," *NKZ* 14 and 19, inserts; and Hisashi Ueda, *Zoku Sofu Nishida Kitaro* (Tokyo: Nansosha, 1983).

26. *NKZ* 12, 430. Arisaka, "The Nishida Enigma," 102.

27. On Nishida's personal writings, see Michiko Yusa, "Fashion and *A-letheia,*" and "Nishida and the Question of Nationalism," *Monumenta Nipponica* 46 (1991): 203-209, and "Nishida and Totalitarianism: A Philosopher's Resistance," in *Rude Awakenings.*

28. Jan Van Bragt, "Kyoto School Philosophy—Intrinsically Nationalist?" in *Rude Awakenings,* 233-254.

29. John Maraldo, "The Problem of World Culture: Towards an Appropriation of Nishida's Philosophy of Nation and Culture," *Eastern Buddhist* 27 (1995): 183-197.

30. Andrew Feenberg, "The Problem of Modernity in the Philosophy of Nishida," in *Rude Awakenings,* 151-173.

31. For the universalist implications of this aspect of Nishida's thought, see Shizuteru Ueda, "Nishida, Nationalism, and the War in Question" and Michiko Yusa, "Nishida and Totalitarianism: A Philosopher's Resistance," both in *Rude Awakenings.* The followers of the Kyoto School today generally agree on the defensive voice represented by these essays.

32. For Nishida's theory of "place," see his works from 1926-1937, primarily *NKZ* 4-7 and other essays. In English, see Feenberg, *Alternative Modernity,* chapter 8; Masao Abe, "Nishida's Philosophy of 'Place,'" *International Philosophical Quarterly* 28 (1988): 355-371; and Robert Wargo, *The Logic of Basho and the Concept of Nothingness in the Philosophy of Nishida Kitaro* (doctoral dissertation, Ann Arbor: The University of Michigan UMI 73-11291, 1972).

33. *NKZ* 12, 427. Arisaka, "The Nishida Enigma," 100.

34. *NKZ* 12, 428. Arisaka, "The Nishida Enigma," 101.

35. For a "postmodern" reading of Nishida, see Kojin Karatani, "The Discursive Space of Modern Japan" in *Japan in the World,* M. Miyoshi and H. D. Harootunian, eds. (Durham: Duke University Press, 1993), and Yujiro Nakamura, *Nishida Tetsugaku no Datsukochiku* (Deconstruction in/of Nishida's Philosophy) (Tokyo: Iwanami Shoten, 1993).

36. *NKZ* 12, 341.

37. *NKZ* 12, 432-433. Arisaka, "The Nishida Enigma," 104.

38. For the discussions of Nishida's "semantic struggle" with the official doctrine, see Ueda and Yusa above in *Rude Awakenings.*

39. See Edward Said, *Orientalism* (New York: Random House, 1978), 1-28.

40. Said, *Orientalism,* 28. For criticisms of Said, see Aijaz Ahmad, *In Theory* (New York: Verso, 1992).

41. As Naoki Sakai observes, "Japan's uniqueness and identity are provided insofar as Japan stands out as a particular object in the universal field of the West. Only when it is integrated into Western universalism does it gain its own identity as a particularity. . . . But this is nothing but the positioning of Japan's identity in Western terms which in return establishes the centrality of the West as the universal point of reference." Naoki Sakai, "Modernity and Its Critique: The Problem of Universalism and Particularism" in *Postmodernism and Japan,* 105.

42. For a brief history of *Subaltern Studies,* see Chakrabarty, and also Gyan Prakash, "Writing Post-Colonialist Histories of the Third World: Perspectives from Indian Historiography," *Comparative Studies in Society and History* 32 (1990): 383-408.

43. For representative thoughts on postcolonialism, see Homi Bhabha's, *The Location of Culture* (New York: Routledge, 1994) and Gayatri Spivak's "Can the Subaltern Speak?" in *The Post-Colonial Reader,* B. G. Ashcroft Griffiths and H. Tiffin, eds. (New York: Routledge, 1995). For a scathing criticism of postcolonialism in general, see Russel Jacoby, "Marginal Returns: The Trouble with Post-Colonial Theory," *Lingua Franca* (September/October 1995): 30-37.

44. The theme of colonialism and postcolonialism in East Asia has been the working project of "Colonialism and Modernity: The Cases of Korea, China, and Japan" (Spring 1995), sponsored by the University of California Humanities Research Institute. I wish to thank the organizers and the members of this group who introduced me to many of the ideas discussed in this paper.

45. *NKZ* 12, 429. Arisaka, "The Nishida Enigma," 102.

46. *NKZ* 12, 429. Arisaka, "The Nishida Enigma," 102.

47. Feenberg, *Alternative Modernity,* 189.

48. *NKZ* 12, 434. Arisaka, "The Nishida Enigma," 105.

11

Taoist Politics: An Other Way?

John J. Clarke

In 1705 Leibniz wrote to a Jesuit correspondent:

> Since [the Chinese] language and character, their way of life, their artifacts and manufactures and even their games differ from ours almost as much as if they were people from another planet, it is impossible for even a bare but accurate description of their practices not to give us very considerable enlightenment.[1]

The question I wish to raise in this chapter is whether we can hope to gain any "enlightenment" by addressing ourselves to the sharply contrasting philosophies of the ancient wisdom traditions of the East and those of modern Western politics. There are some historical precedents to encourage us here. Since Leibniz's day, Oriental enthusiasts have frequently made use of contrasts between East and West for serious critical purpose. In the eighteenth century, for example, Voltaire, Quesnay, and many other thinkers paraded China as an ideal polity with which to cast illumination on the benighted state of the European political and social order. In the nineteenth century, Buddhism, seemingly remote from Western rationalist traditions, was recruited into campaigns on behalf of a more progressive, even positivistic, approach to the understanding of both human and natural worlds. And in the twentieth century Eastern attitudes towards the human/nature relationship have been used to challenge underlying economic and political assumptions.[2]

This methodology of exploiting the very otherness of an "alien" culture to instigate a fundamental critique of one's own assumptions has interesting and complex echoes and ramifications in the context of mounting opposition to the universalizing compulsions of modernity. Recent attempts to rethink the social and the political realms in pluralistic and global terms, and to problematize the ideas of identity and culture in the language of otherness, have gained much of their momentum through the resuscitation of supposedly moribund worldviews and the engagement with alternative ideologies, in particular those of non-European origin. The new cultural politics of difference, in its embracing of such movements as subaltern empowerment, feminism, postcolonial literature, black politics, and radical ecology, has exploited to considerable effect the heuristic power of cultural diversity, and so, by offering the ancient wisdom traditions of the East as further exemplification of the recovery of the "suppressed other," I believe it is not entirely absurd to ask, in the spirit of Leibniz, whether these "people from another planet" can bring any enlightenment to bear on contemporary issues in political, social, or moral thought.[3]

Clash of Civilizations

China is a useful place to begin, for it has often appeared in Western eyes as a locus, even a paradigm, of otherness, of all that is strange and alien, yet perennially fascinating. When Jorge Luis Borges wished to characterize the elusiveness of methods of classification he chose as his model a fictional Chinese encyclopedia in which bizarre categories collide in bemused cognitive dissonance. This imagined eccentricity of the Chinese mind has usually been twinned with China's reputed cultural ossification. As Michel Foucault pointed out in his now famous discussion of this Borgesian conceit, China has appeared to the Western gaze as "the most meticulous, the most rigidly ordered, the one most deaf to temporal events . . . spread and frozen, over the entire surface of a continent surrounded by walls."[4] According to Marx, Ranke, Mill, and many others it was "a nation of eternal standstill," contrasting conspicuously with the dynamic, progressive West, an "embalmed mummy," as Herder had earlier described it. "What can be a better sign of the Other," in the words of a modern Chinese writer, "than a fictionalized space of China? What can furnish the West with a better reservoir for its dreams, fantasies, and utopias?"[5]

Yet are we not now awakening from these dreams, and beginning to reflect critically, if only in the bleary light of dawn, on such fantasies? Certainly we have witnessed in recent years a strong movement towards the displacement of Western civilization from its position of historical and cultural authority. Through the writings of Edward Said and others we have become aware of the ideological deceptions that have ensnared Westerners in their quest for Oriental enlightenment, and of the way in which Western knowledge of Asia has often involved the construction of the "Orient," not only as an intellectual distortion, but as a means of enhancing its power over Asian peoples. Said has traced out important links between the discourse of orientalism and imperialism, making use of Foucault's discourse analysis whereby the strategies of orientalists are seen as embedded in the whole process of discipline and control by Western colonial power. Orientalism, in its affirmation of the ideological fiction of the "West versus the Rest," has, according to Said, played a role in creating a Western "nexus of knowledge and power" whereby "European culture gained in strength and identity by setting itself off against the Orient."[6] Furthermore, we are beginning to free ourselves from the linear, progressive notion of history which for so long has distorted our perception of non-European cultures, and in our postcolonial, post-Saidian world there is evidence of a recognition that, instead of all "emerging" societies being necessarily and desirably assimilated into European models of thought and practice, the cultures of the non-European world have their own self-legitimating identity.

Yet, even though we may like to believe that we have outgrown orientalism, its illusions and stereotypes mostly purged, we may still find it useful to compose ancient China and the modern West in some kind of counterpoint with each other, not in order to create a new hierarchy of dominance, nor even a comforting harmony of complementary opposites, but in order that the thematic contrasts may illuminate each other in critically productive ways. The hermeneutical philosophy of Hans-Georg Gadamer will prove serviceable here, for it is premised on an assumption of a similar kind, namely that it is the very strangeness of the Other which can facilitate an expansion of critical self-understanding. To address a text which is historically and temporally distant is precisely to open up a space in which our own prejudices and assumptions are put into question, and it is in the encounter between apparently distinct horizons of vision that fresh insights become possible.[7] As I hinted above, orientalism has in the past often taken on the role of critic and even subverter of Western beliefs and values, affording us the opportunity to experience ourselves afresh from another's perspective. By virtue of its very cultural remoteness and difference, the traditional East has often been seen to pose an especially sharp contrast with indigenous Western traditions, and in particular with those that we have come to title "modern."

This distance, which can of course supply the occasion for mystification and for all kinds of racist and colonialist projections, may also facilitate a post-colonial discourse in which ethnocentric and Eurocentric assumptions can be critically examined, and where the West's cultural hegemony can be challenged. The East's role as a kind of gadfly—for example, as a reminder of the historical contingency of our own world-views and social practices—is one which, as I suggested earlier, has a long history in orientalist discourse. One of the remarkable features associated with the West's imperialist expansion over the past few centuries has been the way in which Western intellectuals have sought, not only to study and appropriate, but energetically to advocate and privilege, non-European systems of thought. It is not simply that imperial expansion has brought about awareness of a greater sense of cultural relativism and sensitivity towards otherness, but that this in turn has given stimulus to bouts of critical self-analysis on the part of the West. From this point of view, the "clash of civilizations," often seen as a battleground of mutual animosity and incomprehension between East and West, can become the construction site for the creation both of an enhanced moral empathy and of a productive reflection on the adequacy of our own thinking.[8]

As an historian of ideas I want to give some substance to these reflections by outlining some of the ways in which the wisdom traditions of Asia have entered into contemporary moral and political discourse. A major conduit of these traditions into modern Western discourse has, of course, been the work of orientalist scholars, but these represent only one end of an ever-widening spectrum of thinkers from a variety of disciplines who have begun to engage in serious conversation with Eastern thinkers. I will try to show how ideas from these sources have begun to articulate a contrapuntal voice whereby, through the setting up of a hermeneutical exchange with non-European traditions, our modern Western worldviews are being placed within a wider frame of comparative and critical reference. Specifically, I have chosen *Taoism* as my Oriental partner in dialogue. This might seem an unlikely, even perverse, choice. There has for some time been a lively and productive discourse on Buddhism within the Western intellectual tradition which has impinged on ethical questions *inter alia*, and Confucianism has once again, following its earlier celebrity in the Enlightenment period, entered into contemporary political consideration.

By contrast, Taoism, with its paradoxical teachings and its occultist practices, has featured less conspicously in "serious" intellectual debates.[9] It is a common perception that this philosophy is a vague, if harmless, nature-loving mysticism, one which has typically been "written off wholesale as nothing more than superstition . . . interpreted as purely religious mysticism and poetry," its more worldly aspects largely overlooked.[10] As a philosophical system—even granting that such a term is appropriate—Taoism is surely little more than a form of quietism, characterized by the search for inner peace at the expense of useful social and political precept or practical moral code. Is it not notorious for pursuing a way (*tao*) of mystical harmony with nature, backed up by "wordless" doctrines on such esoteric matters as "the void" and "the uncarved block," and following a path of studied nonaction (*wu-wei*), a philosophy suitable only for those who have retired from life? As a religious practice is it not associated with a number of fanciful activities such as flying though the air, living on dew, indefinitely prolonged orgasm, and the search for the elixir of immortality? Among its chief oracles, did not Lao-tzu speak in riddles and confront Confucius's sensible social teachings with mystical nonsense? And did not Chuang-tzu advocate self-cultivation at the expense of public service, and teach anarchic individualism rather than social reform? In brief, is not Taoism the very archetype of the impenetrable Oriental Other, embalmed in its own historical mausoleum, with little to offer a world facing severe social, political, and economic crises?

There is undoubtedly a grain of truth in these conventional opinions. Since its early historical development Taoism has been seen as diverging sharply from the social philosophy of Confucianism, has frequently encouraged the virtues of yielding and passivity, and has engaged in esoteric magical and alchemical practices. It has maintained a conspicuously undogmatic and nonprescriptive stance on moral and metaphysical matters, and even in its more widely influential form as a Taoist "church," it has often refrained from providing explicitly moral, let alone political, leadership.[11] Nevertheless it is important to recognize that commonly dismissive opinions of Taoism are to some extent a legacy of Western projection and willful misperception. As ideological distortions these opinions can be traced back several hundred years. In the seventeenth century Jesuit missionaries, in their attempt to forge an alliance with Confucianism in order to further their proselytizing ambitions, saw in Taoism and Buddhism their most dangerous rivals, and portrayed Taoism in particular as a religion of ignorance and superstition, a putrid and poisonous brew of myth and magic. Hegel, in pursuit of an even more explicitly Eurocentric project, gave philosophical substance to this attitude by subordinating the religions of Asia to the Western Christian tradition, describing Taoism as a religion of magic which had yet to attain the level of rational self-consciousness of Christianity. And in the nineteenth and twentieth centuries, an epoch characterized by visions of progress through scientific rationalism, Taoist religion has often been seen as mired in mystical beliefs and superstitious practices and hence as one of the factors responsible for China's inability to confront the demands of the modern world. Moreover, during the same period Chinese intelligentsia, steered by a modernizing agenda, have themselves looked upon Taoism as an embarrassment and as a mark of China's underdevelopment in relation to the West. Indeed, even after the ending of the Cultural Revolution and the reemergence of more tolerant policies towards religions in China, Taoism has continued to be designated as a "feudal superstition."[12]

This assemblage of myths has recently been subject to increasing interrogation and has begun to give way to more informed and critical judgments. In the first place, orientalist scholarship has itself undergone a complete revolution in recent decades leading to a reworked and historically more adequate assessment of Taoism and its role in Chinese cultural and political history.[13] And beyond this in wider intellectual circles there is evidence of a much greater readiness to engage in sympathetic and productive ways with the Taoist tradition. There have been some well-known examples of this more expansive encounter, associated with names such as C. G. Jung and Fritjof Capra. However, the specific foci of these examples—psychology and science—are still far removed from social and political concerns, and get us little closer to addressing our opening question. Arthur Danto, one of the earliest philosophers of the postwar Anglo-American tradition to take Oriental thought seriously, summed up this apparent social irrelevance of Taoism in his remark that its worldview

pictures the person as a wanderer in the void, and perceives his happiness to lie in drifting with the stream, unanchored by the network of demands and responsibilities. . . . [It] seems to dissolve any relations we may have with one another and to replace them with the relationship we have to the universe at large.[14]

Nevertheless, attitudes have changed since Danto wrote these words, and there is a strongly growing body of evidence which points more encouragingly to the possibility of bridging the historical chasm that has seemed to divide the Taoists' world from our current social and political preoccupations. This transformation has brought into prominence several facets relevant to our present inquiry. In the first place it has led to a blurring of the long-established distinction, encouraged in the West from the time of early Jesuit missionaries, between a "pure" pristine philosophical Taoism (*Tao-chia*) and its "corrupt" religious manifestation (*Tao-chiao*), a distinction which has encouraged Westerners to think of Taoism as marginal to social and political concerns. This change has pointed the way in turn, not only to a timely recognition of the complex interactions between these two strands of Taoism, but more significantly to a deepening of respect for the cultural richness and sophistication of the religious traditions associated with Taoist belief.[15] In consequence of this there is growing awareness, not only of the pervasive influence of the "basic" philosophical teachings of Lao-tzu, Chuang-tzu, and Lieh-tzu, but also of the degree to which Taoist values have penetrated into the whole fabric of Chinese life.

In recent years scholars such as Kristofer Schipper have argued compellingly for Taoism's inseparability from the traditional practices and activities of everyday life in China, and have studied in detail the ways in which, even in its surviving form in Taiwan, Taoism remains in touch with its ancient philosophical roots.[16] The stereotypical picture of Taoism as essentially apolitical, to be identified with an individualistic reaction against Confucian social practice, a way of "dropping out" from social and political obligation, is one that is increasingly being questioned, therefore. It is certainly true that Taoists and Confucians have often been at loggerheads with one another, that Taoists have often identified themselves by way of contrast with Confucianist orthodoxy, and that the former have offered in certain respects a more individualistic philosophy than the latter. But Taoist and Confucian concerns have historically intersected and complemented each other at a number of points. Taoists have frequently been participants in the processes of government, have given advice to emperors, and have constituted a significant factor in political argument in China for over two thousand years.[17] The *Tao Te Ching* itself (the *ur*-text of Taoism) has long been recognized as having, in common with most early Chinese philosophical writings, important political implications, and as suggesting in broad outline a distinctive political philosophy; but what is relatively new is the realization that its philosophy played an especially significant role in political debates in the subsequent history of China.[18]

An Alternative Politics?

What sort of politics, then, can we discern in the Taoist tradition? In spite of the fact that at various times over its long history Taoists and Taoist principles have entered into alliance with Confucianism and have penetrated the inner sanctum of imperial power, its origins betray a distinctly recalcitrant, even subversive, quality. It often stood apart from and in opposition to the state, displaying a model of knowing and behaving which was centered outside the main sites of metropolitan knowledge and power, and was distrusted by the Confucian establishment as a religion of rebels, visionaries, and protest movements. As one historian of Chinese political thought puts it, the early Taoist philosophers "adduced an ideal of a free society of a kind that had never existed in history," and hence one which at times ran counter to state power and orthodoxy.[19] From the fourth century B.C.E. onward Taoists were closely associated with opposition to feudal society, and later to the bureaucratic and economic centralism that followed the unification of the empire in 221 B.C.E., harking back to an earlier mythical society of frugal simplicity, social equality, and spontaneous collectivism, a characteristic which "continued to cling to the Taoists all through Chinese history."[20] And while the *Tao Te Ching* may be addressed to the concerns of rulers and their advisors, the writings of Chuang-tzu, which have often in the West been seen as those of a lonely, defeatist recluse, "have constantly been favorites of rebels, social outcasts, and those whose worldly ambitions were failed."[21] The philosophical attitude of the early Taoists became politically activated with the rise in the second century C.E. of Taoist religious sects which not only installed Taoism as a popular force beyond the privileged sphere of the literati, but which also helped to provide a focus for the articulation of the voices of the disempowered masses. There was present in Taoism as an organized religion a messianic element which helped to instigate popular uprisings against authority, and, as the sinologist Norman Girardot comments, Taoism served "essentially as the 'official' legitimation of the 'non-official' world of the people of the land, those who were traditionally the flesh and blood of the 'real country' of China."[22]

This observation is especially relevant to the period up to the fifth century C.E. when several Taoist-inspired rebellions erupted with the aim of establishing the reign of the "Way of Great Peace," a dream of a return to a society free from oppressive state interference and economic exploitation, recreating a condition believed to have prevailed before the coming of civilization. Its connection with philosophical Taoism is not a simple one, but can be discerned in the latter's suspicion of the restrictive and manipulative force of linguistic and social convention, and in its belief in the possibility of personal transformation as a way toward a more harmonious life in common. Amongst these insurrectionist movements the most important was the so-called "Yellow Turban" rebellion of 182 C.E. which, though suppressed after spreading through many provinces of China, helped to weaken the Han Dynasty, and which established a number of autonomous, self-governing, quasi-democratic communities.[23] In the centuries that followed, right up to the turbulent final years of the Celestial Empire, Taoists for the most part sought accommodation with official centers of power, supporting a largely conformist moral outlook, and advocating responsibilities towards family, community, state, and gods, for "as we would expect of any major world religion, the establishment of ethical standards and their justification and enforcement were a central element of Taoism from its inception."[24] Nevertheless, at various times Taoist ideas also provided an inspiration to dissent and were often "associated with the forces of opposition, protest, and rebellion in Chinese society," for example in the Mongol Yüan Dynasty (1260-1367) when Taoists provided a nucleus of passive resistance to foreign occupation.[25] In more recent centuries groups with Taoist leanings engaged in seditious activities directed against the Manchus (1644-1911), another foreign dynasty, and in the Boxer Rebellion (1900-01) the Taoist image of perfect government, Taoist-inspired secret societies, martial arts, and "magical" techniques of invulnerability all played a part in encouraging radical ideas and anti-imperial insurgency.[26]

In the light of this historical sketch it is not surprising that Taoism has been drawn into the orbit of Western *anarchist* discourse. Ever since Lao-tzu became known in the West, anarchists have claimed him as one of themselves, and indeed it has become almost commonplace to identify the two; as one writer puts it, the *Tao Te Ching* "is one of the great anarchist classics," and according to another, Taoism as a purely secular and social vision "anticipated [Western] anarchism in many ways."[27] Nevertheless, this comparison has proved contentious and has given rise to some interesting debates, the distancing between the Taoist and Western notions providing a useful means for examining the underlying assumptions of Western anarchist thinking, while at the same time raising some more general moral and political issues.

Let us begin by looking at some recent discussion of the standard coupling of Taoism and Western anarchist theory. These studies suggest that this association, while correctly indicating some specific convergences, involves an uncritical projection of Western libertarian ideas without sufficient regard for certain fundamental differences between them, and especially for the metaphysical basis on which Taoist thinking rests. The latter, according to the philosopher Roger Ames, involves a distinctively organicist metaphysics, which, by contrast, is not a significant feature of Western anarchism, and he points out that the concept of the person in Taoist thought is not that of "the autonomous, discrete, and discontinuous 'atomistic' individual characteristic of the Western liberal tradition," but rather of an element or process within "a matrix of relationships which can only be expressed by reference to the organismic whole."[28] This has important implications for the notion of freedom in the two traditions, for, it is argued, while Western anarchism has often (in the cases of Bakunin and Stirner, for example) been premised on the ideas of rational self-determination and freedom of action, the Taoist notion entails a nonegoistic conception of self-actualization through harmony with the community and with nature.[29] Views such as this are evidently of more than antiquarian interest at a time when Enlightenment humanistic assumptions are under question, and when the relationship between the human and the natural worlds has come to a prominent place in the political agenda. Such considerations enter into the thinking of another philosopher, David Hall, who argues that, in devising its own form of anarchism in the context of a distinctive cosmological and metaphysical theory, Taoism offers a view which is not anthropecentric but "polycentric" in that it gives no privileged status to humans, let alone to any class of humans. It presupposes a sense of cosmic harmony which arises spontaneously, a "harmony of self-creative events," which is quite at variance with the Western tradition, going back to Plato, of a harmony imposed from outside.[30]

There are further suggestive differences which concern the relationship between government and citizen. The ideal society for Western anarchists is one in which the role of government is reduced to a minimum or abolished altogether, whereas a Taoist is concerned only to remove those supposedly artificial hindrances to the spontaneous and natural workings of the political/ social apparatus. The *Tao Te Ching* itself is, in part at least, a treatise on statecraft and, far from advocating the eradication of the state, is full of advice and exhortations directed towards the behavior of rulers. Moreover, contrary to the conception of abstract citizens' rights in the Western Enlightenment tradition, which could be enlisted to challenge state power and legitimacy, Taoist thinkers stressed a more conservative approach to statecraft, which encouraged the refinement of harmonious attitudes, whether in rulers or ruled, and which saw political authority, not in terms of power and manipulation but rather of example and ritual. Thus, confrontation on the Western model between autonomous citizen and arbitrarily imposed authority is to be compared with the Taoist differentiation between a society in which authority becomes authoritarian by overreaching its natural boundaries, and one in which all functions, whether of ruler or ruled, are harmoniously integrated. This integration was for the Taoist a spontaneous order which implied the absence of the need for coercive state action, which, in their view, was the cause of and not the remedy for social disorder. One of the consequences of this outlook was that, while rebellions were frequently inspired by Taoist ideals, revolutions in the European sense were not. Early Taoist uprisings rarely took an ideological stance in opposition to the imperial regime as such, or sought to overthrow the state, but might turn against a particular emperor if he was seen to have forfeited his "mandate" through misrule.[31]

In one sense, then, Taoist political thinking could be said to encourage a *laissez-faire* attitude towards politics. However, it is interesting to note that this term was an eighteenth-century translation of the Taoist concept of *wu-wei*, which, while meaning literally "nonaction," might be better translated as "acting naturally" as distinct from simply not acting at all. This serves to underline once again the important contrast with Western emphasis on the fundamental principle of individual freedom. Taoism is a form of anarchism which is in effect completely lacking in a vision of individual freedom in the modern Western sense, and is a politics of *laissez-faire* which needs to be distinguished from its Western counterpart, and which certainly has nothing to do with economic free enterprise. The Taoist attitude was one which encouraged self-cultivation and self-fulfilment rather than a libertarian ideal of unfettered rational agency, and the distinctive characteristic that emerges from Taoism is not that of the absolute value of the individual, which underlies Western anarchism, but a kind of "paternalistic anarchism," which advocates an ideal of self-realization within the compass of a harmonious and natural whole.[32] This "whole" embraces, as we have noted, the order of the cosmos at large, but it is also seen as having implications for the ideal role of the individual within the social order. Undoubtedly one of the richest veins of modern anarchism is communitarianism, and it is in this context that Taoism is sometimes seen to make its most important contribution to anarchist theory.[33] Civilization is typically perceived by Taoism as artificial and stultifying, reducing the capacity for self-realization, and the aim is, therefore, not simply the abolition of constraints on freedom, but rather the encouragement of a more simple society with reduced wants, small human groupings, and a central government which interferes little and encourages local autonomy. For historian of religions Julia Ching it represents a recovery of important values and lost ways of life, a "back to nature romanticism" which envisages "a small, pacifist village state with minimal government."[34]

While some might dismiss such views as having little purchase on contemporary reality, this "Fourierist" view of Taoism, with its antipathy towards the inflationary and centralizing tendencies of civilization, has found an important champion in Joseph Needham. The author of a monumental work on the history of Chinese science and technology, Needham ascribes to Taoism a vital role in the emergence of this once-neglected dimension of Chinese thought, and ties it in with his antimechanistic crusade and with his espousal of a Whiteheadian organicism. In his endeavor to demystify the standard interpretations of Taoism, and to subvert the common conception of Taoists as "milk-and-water mystics delivering the 'Wisdom of the East,'"[35] he has been at pains to emphasize its political, as well as, and indeed in conjunction with, its scientific contributions. The Taoist political ideal, as he sees it, is a kind of agrarian collectivism, a cooperative society which mirrors the image of Tao as "feminine, tolerant, yielding, permissive," a model which he compares to the manifestoes of the Levellers and Diggers of seventeenth-century England.[36] It involves, in his view, a reaction against Confucianism whose "social-ethical thought-complex was masculine, managing, hard, dominating, aggressive," and implies, not libertarian individualism, but a return to a mythical primitive communism based on egalitarian, nonaggressive, and cooperative principles, and on a close relationship with the land, "an undifferentiated 'natural' condition of life, before the institution of private property, before the appearance of . . . feudalism . . .

prior to the development of classes."[37] Important for Needham, too, is the Taoist emphasis on practical skills, on craftsmanship, agricultural techniques, and on the physical processes associated with alchemy and the production of medicines, activities which he sees as arising out of an extremely close contact with nature, in marked contrast to the Confucians who disdained manual labor and who relied exclusively on book-learning.[38]

Doing Nothing?

What further implications does this Taoist way of thinking have? In the first place the passages just quoted reveal a pacifist tendency within Taoism, one which was alluded to earlier in the utopian ideal of "The Way of Great Peace," and which has been remarked on by a number of commentators in addition to Needham.[39] Certainly Chinese Taoism has little in common with the nihilist-inspired terrorism or the aggressive confrontationalism associated with certain strands of nineteenth-century European anarchism, and early Taoist scriptures tended to echo the Buddhist ideal of universal compassion and its interdictions against the harming of sentient beings. The intimation of military strategies in the *Tao Te Ching*, not to mention the development of martial arts within Taoist circles, might seem to counter this claim. It would be erroneous to maintain that Taoists have never been involved in warfare, but it is important to note that the concern with military and pugilistic methods was based on a recognition of the inevitability of violence rather than its desirability, and was associated with the attempt to formulate means of dealing with conflict in the least destructive of ways, and on the refinement of defensive techniques which minimize the use of force.

On this question Lao-tzu and his successors advocated the doctrine of *wu-wei*, a notion which is central to the whole of Taoist teaching. As we have already indicated, this often misunderstood term does not mean precisely doing nothing or meekly submitting to aggression, but rather, in this context, the adoption of something akin to the "Fabian tactic" of allowing one's enemies or opponents to defeat themselves, a view typically expressed in epithets such as "weapons of war are wont to rebound," and "the softest thing in the world [ie water] overcomes the hardest." The glorification of war, of fighting, of military prowess, and combat play no part in Taoist thinking and practice, and indeed in Chinese culture generally the military virtues have ranked far less eminently than in European traditions. It must be emphasized that this attitude, and the con-comitant rejection by Taoists of capital pushishment, is not based on any absolute precept of nonviolence, or on any principle concerning the right to or sacredness of life, but rather on the belief that violence has a way of producing more violence, and so never achieves the end intended, and hence that "To impose order by force only results in disorder."[40] Furthermore, the privileging of nonviolent activities and attitudes in Taoist traditions is not based on a high estimation of the virtues of meekness and humility, but rather on a belief that violence is a form of weakness, not of strength, and that the "*yin* power of passivity is more enduring than the *yang* force of direct action."[41]

This quasi-pacifist attitude of yielding, combined with the idea of close association with the rhythms of nature, and emphasis on small-scale communitarian politics, inevitably leads to comparisons with contemporary environmentalist thinking. An apparent congruence between Taoism and radical ecology has been found especially suggestive, and Taoist philosophy has in a number of ways attracted attention through its potential as a fundamental critique of Enlightenment anthropocentrism, indeed in one writer's view as "the most fertile soil for the growth of a genuinely ecological sensibility . . . the philosophical foundations for a genuinely ecological society."[42] Taoism, with its sense of a deep correlation between humanity and the world of nature, and its distaste for masculine assertiveness, has been seen as offering a way of thinking which is more in keeping with contemporary environmental needs than traditional Western modes of thought, and which can therefore provide a useful resource in constructing "an alternative set of categories for rethinking some of the issues of environmental ethics."[43]

Comparative discussions of these issues often key in on the concept of "dualism." It is frequently argued that, where the West has tended to draw sharp distinctions between matter and spirit, and between God and nature, Taoism (like other Oriental systems of thought) sees the world of nature as a continuum in which all things, spiritual as well as material, human as well as nonhuman, are inextricably intertwined. The classic Taoist polarity between *yin* and *yang* implies, not mutual opposition and exclusiveness, but "a holographic interpretation of the world . . . characterized by interconnectedness, interdependence, openness, [and] mutuality," an approach which offers the possibility of finding "new integrative and moral paradigms by means of which to establish a more harmonious and mutually fulfilling and beneficial relationship of man to nature."[44] The crucial point here is that in Taoist philosophy the order of things, at all levels, arises, not out of the imposition of superordinate authority, but from the mutual interaction of the elements that go to make up the whole.[45] In cosmological terms this implies a sense of order which arises spontaneously out of chaos without the need to postulate preexistent Platonic archetypes or a transcendent *Logos*. In the social and political sphere it implies a nonmanipulative politics in which power and authority are seen to reside in the interactions among people rather than in the action of power from above. In the economic sphere it implies a critique of the idea of limitless economic growth and its accompanying cult of consumerism and the multiplication of unsatisfiable needs. And ecologically it points to a nonmanipulative attitude towards the natural world, an ethos in which the ideal of dominating nature is replaced with one of mutuality and cooperation, of "man as . . . the participant in nature rather than as a predator of nature." In this way, according to the philosopher J. B. Callicott, Taoism supports "an ecological ethic of non-coercive or cooperative action, expressed in the more recent environmental concept of 'sustainable livelihood' through appropriate technology."[46]

The holistic quality of Taoist thinking, with its sense of the rootedness of the human in the natural world and its emphasis on cooperation rather than contest, has occasioned close links to be drawn with modern feminist concerns, and a number of writers have given voice in various ways to this connection. Sinologist A. C. Graham, for example, points out that, just as the familiar ranking of strength and hardness above passivity and yielding is reversed in Taoist thought, so too in the case of the male/female polarity where Taoist texts typically give precedence to the latter over the former. Going beyond this, Graham suggests "a modern parallel in Jacques Derrida's project of deconstructing the chains of oppositions underlying the logocentric tradition of the West."[47] Several other writers have emphasized the complementary roles of the feminine and masculine principles in Taoist thinking, the way in which "the masculine and the feminine gender traits are integrated in harmonious and balanced relationship."[48] This is seen to entail, for example, an insistence on the need to transcend "agonistic dualisms" and "sharp divisions and separations" typical of the West, and the endorsement of the contrasting values of "integration, interrelatedness . . . caring and love" which can be drawn from Eastern traditions such as Taoism.[49]

Some have gone further than this and insisted on the *superior* role that the feminine plays in Taoist thinking, drawing attention to those passages in the *Tao Te Ching* where the Tao is portrayed as the "mother of all things," and where, according to Kristofer Schipper, the earth itself is identified with the female body as "the only one able to accomplish . . . the work of the Tao."[50] Needham, too, offers a strongly "feminine" interpretation of Taoism, and argues that in Taoist thought and practice women play an important role, in marked contrast to "the paternal, repressive austerity of Confucianism . . . or the chilling other-worldliness of Buddhism."[51] Many feminists would no doubt want to point out that in practice Chinese society remained firmly patriarchal, though they might take some comfort from the relative equality of women and men in the Taoist church, which ordained both sexes on equal terms, and offered women a socially acceptable alternative to marriage, with opportunities for them to engage in the sorts of spiritual practice that have usually been associated exclusively with men.[52]

Beyond Morality?

It is difficult to distill out of all of this a clearly definable moral-political philosophy. Indeed, recalling the words of the *Tao Te Ching*, "The Way is eternally nameless," and "Those who know do not say; and those who say do not know," it may be that the very absence of definition constitutes a fundamental characteristic of Taoism. According to critics such as Danto, writing at a time when Taoism was beginning to be associated with the counterculture movement of the 1960s; it offered an individualist ethic which gave little moral guidance beyond the injunction to "do your own thing." Some would argue that, with its notoriously relativistic outlook, it offers no morality at all, or even that it is dangerously immoral, the baneful outcome of the tragic defeat of Reason.[53]

However, in the context of postmodernist debates Taoism's somewhat nonprescriptive and distinctly relativistic outlook, hitherto a justification for its exclusion from respectable philosophical company, is now seen by some to be its most seductive feature in that it implies a radical questioning of the foundations of Western ethical traditions, even a Nietzschean transcendence of good and evil. The absence of any precise set of moral codes or principles and the rejection of any attempt to provide rational justification for morality or social conduct, but rather a reliance as we saw above on a naturalist-inspired spontaneity, is no longer seen as a license to "do your own thing," even less a green light to moral depravity. As I indicated earlier, Taoism has at times taken on a counterestablishment role, but this has been impelled by a high sense of moral purpose, not a craving for self-indulgence, escape, or riotous chaos, and indeed the pursuit of the Way by Taoist adepts has always been seen as premised on a morally pure life and the practice of good works. Taoist sexual yoga is a case in point, one which has attracted some attention of late in the West. With its techniques for the enhancement of erotic pleasure it has in the past been seen as an affront to standard Western Christian moral sensibilities, and indeed in its more orgiastic forms incurred official censure in China itself. But in this regard the Taoist approach has come to be viewed in fresh light, and to be seen, not as an encouragement to immorality, but rather as an alternative approach to sexual mores, and a powerful critique of traditional Western attitudes concerning sex and the body, one which demonstrates a liberating awareness of the central position of sexuality in life and nature, and which, in the absence of any doctrine of original sin, views sexual union as "beautiful, good for health, and right."[54]

In more philosophical terms, Taoism is sometimes seen as implying criticism of the very notion of a highly prescriptive moral code founded on logocentric principles, and as a rejection of the emphasis on outward conformity to rules rather than self-knowledge and self-cultivation. In the writings of Chuang-tzu, for example, we find no moral prescriptions and no search for foundational principles, but rather a serious, if mordantly ironic, questioning of traditional moral language and categories, leading to a "transformation in how one thinks and feels about the world."[55] Indeed there are those who argue that, contrary to the standard view, Chuang-tzu did not teach moral skepticism or relativism at all but rather a kind of Nietzschean tactic of unravelling the closely woven fabric of delusions and deceptions that clothe our standard values. Some commentators have come to see Chuang-tzu as offering a clear moral vision, but one based not on rules or conceptual knowledge, but on naturally arising human skills, and that Taoist ethics is best understood, not in terms of theoretical knowledge, but, by analogy with the mastering of certain practical techniques such as engraving or archery, as a skill, aimed at the cultivation of equanimity, spontaneity, and a sense of being in harmony with the world.[56] In a similar vein the writings of Chuang-tzu and other Taoists can be interpreted as aiming to shock us, not out of behaving morally, but out of our Kantian moralism with its strenuous pursuit of absolute, rigid, universal principles, and by contrast as encouraging us to return to a spontaneous feeling of affinity with others and with the natural world.[57] According to the modern Chinese scholar Chang Chung-yuan, it was because of the artificiality and coldness of the Confucian ideal of *jen* (benevolence), with its strongly ritualistic and prescriptive character, "that the Taoists often declared that they would banish *jen* so that people could once again love one another," and indeed Chuang-tzu went so far as to claim that it was "necessary to get rid of *jen* so that virtue might flourish."[58]

By contrast, then, with the Western religious and philosophical traditions, Taoism offers no absolute set of objective ideals nor any morally transcendent reality from which eternal moral principles could be derived. Instead of providing a deontological platform on which to erect a structure of moral prescriptions concerning duties or rights, it rather recommended a way of self-actualization or transcendence of the egoistic self. This in turn may be seen as a way in which social and political harmony might be established, not on the basis of absolute moral laws, but on an inner transmutation wrought with the aid of an image of the ideal human being, whether as ruler or ruled.[59] On this view neither the central Christian ethic of caring for others, nor the Enlightenment principle of equal rights, is abandoned but rather reformulated, no longer in terms of rules that need to be validated by means of some kind of rationally attested authority, but rather in terms of a lessening of egoic demands through a transformation of one's perception of oneself and of one's ontological status vis-à-vis other persons. From this it is arguable that Taoism is not by implication an amoral teaching but rather that its moral attitude rests on exhortations on how to *be* rather than on what to *do*, and that, having seen through the superficiality and uselessness of moral rules, it points the way towards a path of self-transformation. From this perspective the intellectualizing of morality, which the Taoists identified with Confucianism, misses the point that moral prescriptions are only effective in so far as they are supported by a change of heart, indeed a change of being.[60] Moreover, to bring about this change requires the appropriate method, not primarily one of rational comprehension but rather of meditative concentration, a kind of technique so often perceived in the West as implying a retreat from the world into a trancelike state of indifference, but in the present context is increasingly seen as a highly practical way of bringing about a refigured perception of oneself and the world.

"Considerable Enlightenment"?

Has Taoism, then, any useful contributions to make to political or social thought and action in the modern world—whether Eastern or Western? For some, even amongst its more sympathetic critics, it remains "too philosophically remote to yield any obvious practical lessons,"[61] or at any rate would need to be "demythologized (or remythologized) to test whether it contains contemporary wisdom."[62] Its vague and minimal—some would continue to say mystical—cognitive content still leads many to conclude that Taoism does not provide "a basis for very positive action," and hence from a moral point of view "is completely indifferent."[63] Its supposed quietism as evidenced in what some see as its "inactivist attitude towards nature"[64] is certainly a stumbling block, particularly in the field of green politics where urgent problems appear to demand a more activist philosophy. And Taoist moral relativism, while contributing to contemporary philosophical debates, may be seen as a further encouragement to a dangerous amoralist attitude which can open the way to fascist and racist ideologies. This danger is reinforced by a self-transformative conception of morality which appears to transmute moral discourse into a kind of aesthetics and thereby to leave us without the rational means of distinguishing between those transformed selves which are good and those which are evil.

Such misgivings will leave many with a reconfirmed sense of the foreignness and strangeness of Taoism, at best an amusing curiosity "from another planet" in Leibniz's phrase. Yet from the standpoint of critical hermeneutics it is this very eccentricity that seems to offer a provocative external reference point from which to think productively about our contemporary global concerns. From this perspective the East may no longer seem an exotic other, a romanticized elsewhere on which our fantasies can be projected, but rather a coherent alternative discourse that confronts and challenges our own. In such a way its very otherness and distance can give us the opportunity to see ourselves anew from a contrasting perspective, and thereby serve as a point of departure for a renewed self-understanding. As Richard Bernstein put it at an East-West Philosophers' Conference, "it is only through an engaged encounter with the Other, with the otherness of the Other, that one comes to a more informed, textured understanding of the traditions to which 'we' belong."[65] From this hermeneutical perspective it becomes evident that comparative East-West studies are not necessarily conducted, as some have wished, in order to discover an alternative worldview, nor to secure new and more reassuring foundations, nor even to celebrate a worldview which matches our currently favored paradigm, but rather to set our entrenched ideas and vocabularies into a wider, more critical, and hence more enriching context. It would be wildly implausible to suggest that ancient Taoist ideas have the potential to meet all the challenges of the modern world, but this leaves open the possibility that they may offer conceptual resources with which to supplement and redeploy our own.

Is this whole approach—as the language of "resources" might suggest—simply another form of orientalism, a manipulation and expropriation of ideas as part of the West's will-to-power, yet another example of Europe's "epistemic overpowering of the other"?[66] I do not think so. The balance of power between East and West has altered significantly by comparison with the colonial situation that Edward Said confronted in *Orientalism*, and the revolutions in our thinking about the Orient, led by advances in orientalist scholarship, have moved us beyond the ideas associated with a West-versus-the-Rest mentality. This does not mean that we have now reached a detached and objective "view from nowhere," or have coupled ourselves to Rortyan "skyhooks" which enable us to swing clear of our history, but rather that we now have the tools to become critically aware of our prejudices and fore-understandings, and stake out a reflexive distance in order to illuminate those issues which currently concern us. Sinologist A. C. Graham draws his own studies of Taoism into this hermeneutical circle when he comments that "we fully engage with the thought [of an other] when we relate it to our own problems," and that the study of Chinese thought "constantly involves one in important contemporary issues in moral philosophy . . . [and] the deconstruction of established conceptual schemes."[67]

Philosophers have not always been eager to take advantage of this particular type of critical instrument. On the whole, Western philosophical thinking has in the past lagged behind both the insights of specialists such as Graham, as well as the bold excursions of more popular writers into the realms of "oriental wisdom." I believe we are now witnessing something of a sea change in which orientalist explorations can be seen as part of a wider search for more ample and inclusive perspectives, appropriate to a world which can no longer be adequately reflected upon from within its traditional narrowly fashioned ethnic or cultural boundaries. Taoism represents only one, indeed a somewhat late, contributer to this "new orientalism," but its—to us—highly idiosyncratic way of thinking seems to me to have a unique capacity to loosen our grip on habitual categories, and to unsettle us from our introverted gaze, thus enabling us to see beyond our mental monoculturalism, and to free up our cultural certainties by the very perversity and unexpectedness of its thinking. Its cultural and historical remoteness from us means, to be sure, that no comprehensive program of reform or ready-made solutions are on offer, yet this very distance provides us with the opportunity to rethink our political values from within.

This "critique of modernity by tradition," as it has been called, has specific reference, in the light of our own discussion of Taoism, to a number of currently contested issues. I have drawn attention to some of these issues in the foregoing exposition, but one issue, running as a uniting filament through many of them, deserves special note by way of conclusion, namely that of power. Questions concerning power were of course central to Said's critique of orientalism, and as we noted earlier he endeavored to show how the history of the West's appropriation of the East must necessarily be understood in terms of configurations of power and of the West's global cultural hegemony. What our own discussion suggests is that, whatever the case in the colonial period of Said's concern, orientalism now provides a means of rethinking the discourse of power in new ways, and of challenging some of modernity's normalizing and totalizing trends. Our exploration of the various routes along which Taoism has been brought into dialogue with debates concerning anarchism, feminism, pacifism, and general ethics, suggests, in broad-brush strokes, ways in which our assumptions about control, power, and violence can be reconceptualized. Against what may be seen as the absolutism and repressiveness of a normative morality, Taoism offers a thoroughgoing critique of all forms of domination, moving out from traditional political issues of government and social order to pressing questions concerning gender, violence, and our relationship with the natural world.

There is about this strange ancient philosophy an air of gentle toleration and a spirit of openness and compromise which contrasts with the aggressive and confrontative dogmatism of so much of contemporary social and political discourse. It encourages a questioning of moral fundamentalisms and totalizing perspectives, a philosophy which fosters different ways of being in the world, and a blossoming of a tolerant pluralism of values. It offers a non-masculinist approach to politics, to laws and rules, and social relationships, a sense of trans-egoistical relatedness. Of course, our moral and political assumptions are not about to be transformed by an infusion of Oriental wisdom, but Taoism's mocking critique of rigid rationalisms, its themes of counter-cultural dissent and of resistance to social normalization, and its sense of harmonious composure and stillness, and of the interconnectedness of things, may help us to discover through dialogue with an apparently alien past the intimations of new and more hopeful ways of thinking about ourselves and our future. This may be an inkling of the "considerable enlightenment" that Leibniz was seeking.

Notes

1. Cited in J. Gernet, *A History of Chinese Civilization* (Cambridge: Cambridge University Press, 1982), 523.

2. I have developed this theme in detail in *Oriental Enlightenment: The Encounter between Asian and Western Thought* (London and New York: Routledge, 1997).

3. Contrast Leibniz's view with that of Heidegger (with reference to "the adoption of Zen Buddhism and the Eastern experience of the world"): "Thinking is transformed only by thinking that has the same origin and destiny," cited in R. May, *Heidegger's Hidden Sources* (London: Routledge, 1996), 8.

4. *The Order of Things: An Archaeology of the Human Sciences* (London: Tavistock, 1970), xix.

5. Zhang Longxi, "The Myth of the Other: China in the Eyes of the West," *Critical Inquiry* 15, no. 1 (1988): 110. For historical studies of Western prejudices concerning China, see for example J. Goody, *The East in the West* (Cambridge: Cambridge Univeristy Press, 1996), and C. Mackerras, *Western Images of China* (Hong Kong: Oxford University Press, 1989). The classic twentieth-century version of the "stagnation" theory is in K. A. Wittfogel, *Oriental Despotism* (New Haven: Yale University Press, 1957).

6. *Orientalism* (Harmondsworth: Penguin, 1995), 3 and 27. The orientalist debate has moved on since this book was first published in 1978; for a summary of post-Saidian arguments, see J. M. MacKenzie, *Orientalism: History, Theory and the Arts* (Manchester: Manchester University Press, 1995); G. Prakash, *"Orientalism Now," History and Theory* 34, no. 3 (1995); and B. S. Turner, *Orientalism, Posmodernism and Globalism* (London: Routledge, 1994). See also Said's Afterword to the 1995 Penguin edition of *Orientalism*.

7. See *Truth and Method* (London: Sheed & Ward, 1975), 264-74.

8. This approach has been powerfully argued by Hans Herbert Kögler in *The Power of Dialogue: Critical Hermeneutics after Gadamer and Foucault* (Cambridge: MIT Press, 1996).

9. Historically in China there are close affinities and significant mutual influences between the teachings of Confucianism and Taoism, but they are sufficiently distinct for us to be able to treat Taoism as a distinct tradition.

10. Joseph Needham, *The Shorter Science and Civilization in China*, vol. 1 (Cambridge: Cambridge University Press, 1978), 86.

11. See H. Welch, *The Parting of the Ways: Lao Tzu and the Taoist Movement* (Boston: Beacon, 1957), 151.

12. See T. H. Haliu, "New Developments Concerning Buddhist and Taoist Monasticism" in *The Turning of the Tide: Religion in China Today*, J. F. Pas, ed. (Hong Kong: University of Hong Kong Press, 1989).

13. Among Western scholars from earlier generations who must be mentioned here are Marcel Granet, Henri Maspero, Max Kaltenmark, Herrlee Creel, Holmes Welch, Joseph Needham, Edward Schafer, Isabelle Robinet, Michel Strickmann, and Angus Graham. There has also been a considerable growth of Taoist scholarship in Japan. Something of the scope and significance of this revolution is conveyed in Anna Seidel's "Chronicle of Taoist Studies 1950-1980," *Cahier d'Extrême Asie* 5 (1989-90). For a more recent bibliographical survey see F. Verellen, "Taoism," *Journal of Asian Studies* 54, no. 2 (1995).

14. *Mysticism and Morality: Oriental Thought and Moral Philosophy* (Harmondsworth: Penguin, 1976), 115 and 119.

15. See for example L. Kohn, *Taoist Mystical Philosophy: The Scripture of the Western Ascension* (Albany: State University of New York Press, 1991), chapter 10, and K. Schipper, *The Taoist Body* (Berkeley: University of California Press, 1993), 192-4.

16. See Schipper, *The Taoist Body*, and also J. Ching, *Chinese Religions* (London: Macmillan, 1993), 217-23.

17. On the role of the Taoist sage as counsellor to emperors, see Seidel, "Chronicle," 273-78, and Verellen, "Taoism," 326-7. On Taoism as a state philosophy in the T'ang Dynasty, see C. Benn, "Religious Aspects of Emperor Hsüan-tsung's Taoist Ideology" in *Buddhist and Taoist Practice in Medieval Chinese Society*, D. W. Chappell, ed. (Honolulu: University of Hawaii Press, 1987).

18. The role of Taoist thinking in political debates is brought out in A. C. Graham, *Disputers of the Tao: Philosophical Argument in Ancient China* (La Salle: Open Court, 1989), and L. Kohn, *Laughing at the Tao: Debates among Buddhists and Taoists in Medieval China* (Princeton: Princeton University Press, 1995).

19. K. C. Hsiao, *A History of Chinese Political Thought*, vol. 1 (Princeton: Princeton University Press, 1979), 20. It is important not to overemphasize the contrast with Confucianism, which was opposed to the excessive imposition of law and punishment, and taught that education and ritual were preferable to compulsion or intimidation.

20. J. Needham, *The Grand Titration: Science and Society in East and West* (London: George Allen & Unwin, 1979), 254.

21. A. C. Graham, *The Book of Lieh Tzu* (London: John Murray, 1960), 10. On Chuang Tzu as a social thinker, see Wu Kuang-ming, *Chuang Tzu: World Philosopher at Play* (New York: Crossroads, 1982).

22. In the Foreword to Schipper, *The Taoist Body*, xv.

23. See *Facets of Taoism*, H. Welch and A. Seidel, eds. (New Haven: Yale University Press, 1979), passim. Mather and Miyakawa, in their articles in this volume, draw interesting parallels with the religious/political dissenters of seventeenth-century England, and with Renaissance utopian movements, as does Needham in *Science and Civilization in China*, vol. 2 (Cambridge: Cambridge University Press, 1956), 89-98.

24. T. Kleeman, "Taoist Ethics," in *A Bibliographic Guide to the Comparative Study of Ethics*, J. Carman and M. Juegensmayer, eds. (Cambridge: Cambridge University Press, 1991), 163.

25. Da Liu, *The Tao in Chinese Culture* (New York: Schocken, 1979), 53. See also Yuji Muramatsu, "Some Themes in Chinese Rebel Ideologies," in *The Confucian Persuasion*, A. C. Wright, ed. (Stanford: Stanford University Press, 1960), which emphasizes the role of Taoism in inspiring mass rebellion in the eighteenth and nineteenth centuries.

26. See H. Welch, *The Parting of the Ways*, 157-8, and Da Liu, *The Tao in Chinese Culture*, 62-5. Though the Taiping Rebellion in the mid-nineteenth century is primarily associated with a Christian-inspired ideology, Taoist writings and practices also had some influence; see W. Franke, *A Century of Chinese Revolution* (Oxford: Blackwell, 1970), 33.

27. J. P. Clark, "On Taoism and Politics," *Journal of Chinese Philosophy* 10:1 (1983): 65, and P. Zarrow, *Anarchism in Chinese Political Culture* (New York: Columbia University Press, 1990), 11. See also, for example, R. T. Ames, "Is Political Taoism Anarchism?" *Journal of Chinese Philosophy* 10:2 (1983); P. Marshall, *Demanding the Impossible: A History of Anarchism* (London: HarperCollins, 1992); and the writings of Paul Goodman.

28. Ames, "Is Political Taoism Anarchism?" 32.

29. It must be noted that there is a strong mutualist tendency in the thinking of Proudhon and Kropotkin, and organicist metaphors perform an important role in the latter's writings, though in both cases libertarian assumptions are pivotal. Furthermore, there has been a significant reaction against individualist assumptions in recent anarchist writings.

30. See D. Hall, "The Metaphysics of Anarchism," *Journal of Chinese Philosophy* 10:2 (1983): 51.

31. Though even the notion of the imperial 'mandate of Heaven' was rejected by some Taoists. For a general historical account of Taoism and anarchism in China, see P. Zarrow, *Anarchism*, and also A. Dirlik, *Anarchism in the Chinese Revolution* (Berkeley: University of California Press, 1991), and M. Gasster, *Chinese Intellectuals in the Revolution of 1911* (Seattle: University of Washington Press, 1969). Both these latter authors argue that anarchist theory in general, and Taoist ideas in particular, played a crucial, if largely unacknowledged, role in the shaping of twentieth-century political thought in China.

32. See Graham, *Disputers of the Tao*, 303. He suggests that in these terms even Confucius could be regarded as an anarchist.

33. See J. P. Clark, "What is Anarchism?" *Nomos* 19 (1978): 23.

34. Ching, *Chinese Religions*, 89-90. Ching notes the danger in such beliefs of a lapse into "political authoritarianism."

35. Needham, *Science and Civilization in China*, 100. Needham avoids the term "anarchism," preferring the phrase "primitive collectivism."

36. See *Facets of Taoism*. There is, however, a difference between the affirmation of the authority of God's justice, compared with the authority of the impersonal natural order, over the human order.

37. *Facets of Taoism*, 59 and 104.

38. *Facets of Taoism*, 122. There is certainly a theme of rural nostalgia in Western anarchist writings, one which earned the contempt of Marx. See the chapter on the "School of Tillers," a peasant utopian movement based on principles of self-sufficiency and local autonomy, in A. C. Graham, *Studies in Chinese Philosophy and Literature* (Singapore: Institute of East Asian Philosophy, 1986). See also Graham, *Disputers of the Tao*, 306-11, which offers a "primitivist" interpretation of Chuang-tzu.

39. See Needham, *Science and Civilization in China*, 105. "The Way of Great Peace," *T'ai-p'ing tao*, was the name of a second-century C.E. Taoist school which derived its name from a highly influential text, the *T'ai-ping ching*.

40. Graham, *Disputers of the Tao*, 308.

41. J. C. Cooper, *Taoism: The Way of the Mystic* (London: Harper Collins, 1990), 40. See also Da Liu, *The Tao in Chinese Culture*, chapter 5. For a comparison between the Taoist concept of *te* (power, virtuality) and Nietzsche's "will to power" see R. T. Ames, "Nietzsche's 'Will to Power' and Chinese 'Virtuality' (*De*): A Comparative Study," in *Nietzsche and Asian Thought*, G. Parkes, ed. (Chicago: University of Chicago Press, 1991). Pacifism has, of course, also played its part in Western anarchist thinking, for example in that of Tolstoy, who was influenced by Taoist ideas; see D. Bodde, *Tolstoy and China* (Princeton: Princeton University Press, 1950). Tolstoy rejected the title "anarchist" because of its association with terrorist violence.

42. P. Marshall, *Nature's Web: An Exploration of Ecological Thinking* (London: Simon & Schuster, 1992), 11 and 23.

43. *Nature in Asian Traditions of Thought*, J. B. Callicott and R. T. Ames, eds. (Albany: State University of New York Press, 1989), 113. See also P. Sloterdijk, *Eurotaoismus: Zur Kritik der politischen Kinetic* (Frankfurt: Suhrkamp Verlag, 1989), which finds in Taoism a heuristic device for counterbalancing the Western tendency to restless activism. This work is discussed by Gerhold Becker in *East-West Encounters in Philosophy and Religion*, N. Smart and B. S. Murthy, eds. (London: Sangam Books, 1996), 344-7. But see G. J. Larson, "'Conceptual Resources' in South Asia for 'Environmental Ethics,' or The Fly is Still Alive and Well in the Bottle," *Philosophy*

East and West, 37, no. 2 (1987), which argues that talk of "exploiting the conceptual resources" of Eastern philosophy is in effect part of the problem it seeks to address in so far as it perpetuates the hegemonic myth of the West's right to expropriate the world's assets.

44. *Nature in Asian Traditions*, 120 and 11.

45. This idea has been discussed at length in comparative terms in D. L. Hall and R. T. Ames, *Anticipating China: Thinking Through the Narratives of Chinese and Western Culture* (Albany: State University of New York Press, 1995).

46. *Earth's Insights: A Survey of Ecological Ethics from the Mediterranean Basin to the Australian Outback* (Berkeley: University of Calfornia Press, 1994), 86. See also Po-Keung Ip, "Taoism and the Foundations of Environmental Ethics," *Environmental Ethics* 5, no. 4 (1983); S. Tominaga, "The Possibility of a Taoist-like Wittgensteinian Environmental Ethics," *Journal of Chinese Philosophy* 21, no. 2 (1994); and M. Tucker, "Ecological Themes in Taoism and Confucianism," in *Worldviews and Ecology*, M. Tucker and J. Grim, eds. (Maryknoll, NY: Orbis, 1994).

47. Graham, *Disputers of the Tao*, 227.

48. R. Ames, "Taoism and the Androgynous Ideal," *Historical Reflections* 8, no. 3 (1981): 43. Ames emphasizes complementarity and rejects the standard view which characterizes Taoism as being predominantly "feminine" in orientation.

49. See *Worldviews and Ecology*, 187.

50. Schipper, *The Taoist Body*, 129.

51. *Science and Civilization in China*, 152. See also L. S. Cahill, *Transcendence and Divine Passion: The Queen Mother in the West in Medieval China* (Stanford: Stanford University Press, 1993), 213-4 and 223-30; J. Ching, *Chinese Religions*, 95; E. Kleinjaus, "The Tao of Women and Men: Chinese Philosophy and the Women's Movement," *Journal of Chinese Philosophy* 17, no. 1 (1990); J. Needham, *Three Masks of Tao* (London: Teilhard Centre for the Future of Man, 1979); and J. Paper, *The Spirits Are Drunk: Comparative Approaches to Chinese Religion* (Albany: State University of New York Press, 1995), 217. For a critique of Needham's views on this, see R. T. Ames, "Taoism and the Androgynous Ideal," *Historical Relfections* 8, no. 3 (1981).

52. See C. D. Benn, *The Cavern-Mystery Transmission: A Taoist Ordination Rite of A.D. 711* (Honolulu: University of Hawaii Press, 1991), Cahill, *Transcendence and Divine Passion*.

53. See for example Arthur Koestler, *The Lotus and the Robot* (London: Hutchinson, 1960), which is concerned with Japanese Zen, a tradition which is in many ways an heir to Taoist thinking, and Murray Bookchin, *Re-enchanting Humanity* (London: Cassell, 1995), which speaks of the lamentable "rhetorical recycling of Taoism . . . into vulgar Californian spiritualism," linked dangerously to the occult and the cultic (100).

54. Schipper, *The Taoist Body*, 145. See 144-55 for a balanced discussion of Taoist views on sexuality. He is critical of R. H. van Gulick's influential but somewhat idealized views contained in *Sexual Life in Ancient China* (Leiden: Brill, 1961). For a more recent discussion, see the Introduction in D. Wile, *Art of the Bedchamber* (Albany: State University of New York Press, 1992).

55. J. Kupperman in *Essays on Skepticism, Relativism, and Ethics in the Zhuangzi*, P. Kjellberg and P. J. Ivanhoe, eds. (Albany: State University of New York Press, 1996), 188.

56. P. Ivanhoe, "Zhuangzi on Skepticism, Skill, and the Ineffable *Dao*," *Journal of the American Academy of Religion* 61, no. 4 (1993). See also Kjellberg and Ivanhoe, *Essays on Skepticism*, chapters 6 and 7.

57. See for example R. M. Smullyan, *The Tao Is Silent* (San Francisco: Harper Collins, 1977), 124ff.

58. *Creativity and Taoism* (London: Wildwood House, 1963), 23.

59. See M. LaFargue, *The Tao Te Ching: A Translation and Commentary* (Albany: State University of New York Press, 1992), 193-4. It should be noted that there has been a perceptible shift of interest among some philosophers in recent years from the Kantian/ liberal emphasis on autonomy, rights, and rules to an Aristotelian discourse of virtues, character formation, and individual flourishing; see, for example, *Virtue*, J. W. Chapman and W. A. Galston, eds. (New York: New York University Press, 1992), and C. Hansen, "Duty and Virtue" in *Chinese Language, Thought, and Culture*, P. J. Ivanhoe, ed. (La Salle: Open Court, 1996).

60. On this see D. Wong, *Moral Relativity* (Berkeley: University of California Press, 1984), which supports a version of Taoist "relativism" while arguing that at the same time it provides an effective basis for social and political cohesion; "It is not obvious," he says, "that we need any moral absolutes by which to live" (175).

61. D. Cooper, *Asian Philosophy* 4, no. 2 (1994): 123.

62. Holmes Rolston III, "Can the East Help the West to Value Nature?" *Philosophy East and West* 37, no. 2 (1987): 181.

63. H. G. Creel, *What is Taoism?* (Chicago: University of Chicago Press, 1970), 3.

64. D. Pepper, *Modern Environmentalism* (London: Routledge, 1996), 19-20.

65. In *Culture and Modernity: East-West Philosophic Perspectives*, E. Deutsch, ed. (Honolulu: East-West Center Press, 1991), 93.

66. This phrase is from Kögler, *The Power of Dialogue*, 218, a work I have found especially useful in this context.

67. Graham, *Disputers of the Tao*, ix-x.

12

Postmodernity, Eurocentrism, and the Future of Political Philosophy

Hwa Yol Jung

The critique of ethnocentrism . . . should be systematically and historically contemporaneous with the destruction of the history of metaphysics. Both belong to a single and same era.

Jacques Derrida

There is not *a* philosophy which contains all philosophies; philosophy as a whole is at certain moments in each philosophy. To take up the celebrated phrase again, philosophy's center is everywhere and its circumference nowhere.

Maurice Merleau-Ponty

There is a Third World in every First World, and vice-versa.

Trinh T. Minh-Ha

There is neither a first word nor a last word. The contexts of dialogue are without limit. They extend into the deepest past and the most distant future. Even meanings born in dialogues of the remotest past will never be finally grasped once and for all, for they will always be reviewed in later dialogues.

Mikhail Bakhtin

I

Postparadigms rule the contemporary world. Among them, postmodernity is the basic mood of intellectual life today, although for some—notably for Jürgen Habermas—modernity itself is still an "unfinished project." Its currency has been accepted as an intellectual medium of the contemporary literati. The basic style of postmodernity pervades philosophy, cultural critique, literary criticism, anthropology, theology, and ecology all in an interdisciplinary way. Because so much has been said about and written on postmodernity, Gianni Vattimo, who is himself a postmodern thinker, is about ready to distance himself from the overused buzzword.[1]

What, then, is postmodernity? It is, in the first place, the irreverent "interruption" or "deconstruction" of modernity which may be defined, for our purpose here, as that condition which is driven by the Faustian ideology of material progress propelled by unblemished faith in "enlightened" reason translated into the iron cage of science and technology as the indomitable and unrepentant will to power over nature and, eventually, humanity itself. Although it initially began as a Western idea, it has now become unstoppably a global phenomenon under the banner of *modernization*, which is the shortened name for the planetary capitalization of Europe as the model of development. It is the last Western adventure of historical teleology or what Francis Fukuyama, following Hegel and Alexandre Kojève, characterizes as "the end of history." Although as an *inter/ruption* it is connected to modernity, postmodernity is unmistakably a *rupture* from the modern past—a new conceptual *institution*, as it were, which is meant to be thoroughly subversive, transgressive, and transformative. Martin Heidegger points principally to "a critical process in which the traditional concepts, which at first must necessarily be employed, are de-constructed down to the sources from which they were drawn."[2] In the second place, postmodernity is a constellation of many splendid ideas; it is a colorful, rainbowlike polygraph. Jean-François Lyotard sets the intellectual tenor for, and defines the parameter of, postmodernity when he writes in *The Postmodern Condition*: "Postmodern knowledge is not simply a tool of the authorities; it refines our sensitivity to differences and reinforces our ability to tolerate the incommensurable. Its principle is not the expert's homology, but the inventory's paralogy."[3]

What modernity is to postmodernity, identity is to difference. The very fact of difference itself makes postmodernity radically discontinuous with modernity. As the cultural politics of identity, Eurocentrism is that disposition or propensity of the modern West (Europe) which willy-nilly legislates or legitimates itself as the privileged or anointed guardian of the historical *telos* of the entire globe.[4] By positioning itself as the teleological temple of the world, Eurocentrism becomes a tribal idolatry. The astute observer of modernity Zygmunt Bauman writes:

> From at least the seventeenth century and well into the twentieth, the writing elite of Western Europe and its footholds on other continents considered its own way of life as a radical break in universal history. Virtually unchallenged faith in the

superiority of its own mode over all alternative forms of life—contemporaneous or past—allowed it to take itself as the reference point for the interpretation of the *telos* of history. . . . Now . . . Europe set the reference point of objective time in motion, attaching it firmly to its own thrust towards colonizing the future in the same way as it has colonized the surrounding space.[5]

Eurocentrism is tantamount to a refusal to recognize or acknowledge the otherness of the non-European Other. As knowledge and power conspire with each other—the fact of which Michel Foucault has amply and conclusively shown in his works throughout his life, the conquest of knowledge leads inevitably to the conquest of power. Speaking of the "conquest of America," Luis Villoro puts it succinctly: "The annihilation of the great American cultures was the inevitable result of the impossibility of one culture to accept [the] otherness [of another culture]. It was *the achievement of a modern mentality.*"[6]

It is no accident, therefore, that heterology has drawn so much academic attention in recent years. Michael Theunissen is unassailable when he comes to the conclusion that "the problem of the Other has certainly never penetrated as deeply as today into the foundations of philosophical thought. It is no longer the simple object of a specific discipline but has already become the topic of first philosophy."[7] Indeed, heterology has become the "first philosophy" of postmodernity. Alterity has been placed at the *altar* of postmodernity, so to speak: what *différance* is to Jacques Derrida, *altarity* is to Mark C. Taylor.[8] Heidegger's formulation of *Unterschied* offers a postmodern alternative to the cultural politics of Eurocentric identity. For *Unterschied* has the double meaning of *difference* and the *between* (*Unter/schied*): it works like a hinge that connects and preserves difference and the relational, that is, difference as dif/ference (*Differenz* as *Unter/schied*).[9] Difference as dif/ference implies a transitive relation that conserves the principle of complementarity. The relational—which may be interhuman or interspecies—is marked by the play of difference and as such promotes pluralism, i.e., diversity, multiplicity, and multiversity. The more difference, the more reciprocity. Without difference, relationality is *unnecessary*. Hannah Arendt contends that human plurality has the twofold character of equality and distinction. If human beings are not equal, there would be no common ground for communicating or acting; if human beings were not distinct, on the other hand, there would again be no need to communicate or act. Distinction—individual differences—thickens the density of human plurality.[10]

Unlike Heidegger's *Unterschied* that conserves difference, Hegel's dialectic that mediates or identifies difference as identity, that is, *converts* difference into rather than *diverts* it from identity (i.e., the dialectical *Aufhebung*) is related to his Orientalism which forever condemns and marginalizes Oriental thought at the edge of truth and philosophy.[11] What really shocks us is the Eurocentric racism professed by two of the guiding philosophers of the modern West: David Hume and Immanuel Kant. Hume is without doubt a Eurocentrist and his professed racism is rampant and uncontained. The offensive and violent subtlety of every word in his essay "Of National Characters" (1742/1758) should be sounded out loud and clear and should not be missed or taken lightly:

> I am apt to suspect the negroes, and in general all the other species of men (for there are four or five different kinds) to be naturally inferior to the whites. There never was a civilized nation of any other complexion than white, nor even any individual eminent either in action or speculation. No ingenious manufactures amongst them, no arts, no sciences. On the other hand, the most rude and barbarous of the whites, such as the ancient *Germans*, the present *Tartars*, have still something eminent about them, in their valour, form of government, or some other particular. Such a uniform and constant difference could not happen, in so many countries and ages, if nature had not made an original distinction betwixt these breeds of men. Not to mention our colonies, there are *Negroe* slaves dispersed all over *Europe*, of which none ever discovered any symptoms of ingenuity; tho' low people, without education, will start up amongst us, and distinguish themselves in every profession. In *Jamaica* indeed they talk of one negroe as a man of parts and learning; but 'tis likely he is admired for very slender accomplishments, like a parrot, who speaks a few words plainly.[12]

Now Kant—who is reputedly the philosophical paragon of the "enlightened" age (*Aufklärung*) of invincible modernity by envisioning it as emancipation from man's "self-incurred tutelage" and championed *human* dignity, obligatory moral integrity, and universal knowledge—tailgated and parrotted mindlessly Hume's racism in *Observations on the Feeling of the Beautiful and Sublime* (1763), the section of four of which was called "Of National Characteristics . . ." In addition to ridiculing the "grotesqueries" of the Indians and Chinese, Kant observed in a singularly unenlightened and prejudicial way:

> The Negroes of Africa have by nature no feeling that rises above the trifling. Mr. Hume challenges anyone to cite a single example in which a Negro has shown talents, and asserts that among the hundreds of thousands of blacks who are transported elsewhere from their countries, although many of them have even been set free, still not a single one was ever found who presented anything great in art or science or any other praiseworthy quality, even though among the whites some continually rise aloft from the lowest rabble, and through superior gifts earn respect in the world. So fundamental is the difference between these two races of man, and it appears to be as great in regard to mental capacities as in color. The religion of fetishes so widespread among them is perhaps a sort of idolatry that sinks as deeply into the trifling as appears to be possible to human nature. A bird feather, a cow's horn, a conch shell, or any other common object, as soon as it becomes conse-crated by a few words, is an object of veneration and of invocation in swearing oaths. The blacks are very vain but in the Negro's way, and so talkative that they must be driven apart from each other with thrashings.[13]

II

Postmodernity dethrones modernity and decenters Eurocentrism. There is indeed an inerasable sign of change, of sea change. The *crisis* of passage from modernity to postmodernity marks a liminal opportunity for the Orient—the shadowy or forgotten "Other" of the Occident—to brighten the new dawn of globalization and forge a new alignment of truth by celebrating its own legacy and heritage, which is not a retreat to nativism. It refuses to remain in the philosophical shadow of the Occident. The Oriental rite of passage to post-modernity is celebrated by reterritorializing its ancient philosophical claims. There is, as Mikhail Bakhtin rightly insists, neither a first nor a last word in history as ongoing dialogue. No word or idea is ever completely exhaustible, that is, finally grasped once and for all. It will always be reviewed in a later dialogue.[14] In this section, I wish to dwell on the Sinitic contribution to the globalization of truth as a momentous event of postmodernity by confining myself to two interconnected or interdependent issues, that is, (1) body politics/carnal hermeneutics and (2) green thought.[15]

II. 1. From the very outset, it should be made clear that Confucius's *Analects*, which has been a seminal document in shaping the Sinitic mindset both intellectual and everyday, may be characterized as the *ethical hermeneutic of proximity*, the systematic exploration of which has by and large escaped the attention of Sinologists.[16] In the *Analects*, Confucius recognized the pluralism of cultural practices when he noted that although humans are by nature nearly alike, they are by practice widely apart. In Confucius's cultural hermeneutics, there is robust and resolute insistence on the inseparability of language and the humanity of the human: As Confucius asserted, it is impossible to know the nature of humanity without knowing the power of words. By the power of words, Confucius meant primarily the heraldry of spoken words as *performatives*. Take a few samplings of what Confucius says in the *Analects*: when the superior man "is heard to speak, his language is firm and decided" (19:9); "the wise err neither in regard to their men nor to their words" (15:7); "the virtuous will be sure to speak *correctly*, but those whose speech is good may not always be virtuous" (14:5); "the superior man is modest in his speech, but exceeds in his actions" (14:29); and friendship with the "glib-tongued" is injurious (16:4).

The motto "I perform, therefore I am" unlocks the inscrutable mystery of Sinism including "Sinograms" whose "performing art" is called calligraphy. It certainly has a family resemblance to Goethe's famous line in *Faust*: "In the beginning was the deed!" (*Im Anfang war die Tat!*) The very concept of performance gives integrity to the verbal or ethical conduct of humanity. Bereft of performance, Sinism is unthinkable: it may be said that thought is the beginning of action, and performance is the completion of thought.

The anatomy of Chinese ideography (logography) points to the centrality of performance in Sinitic culture. Indeed, Chinese ideography (calligraphy in particular) is a kinetic art: it is the kinaesthetic transcription of the human body in graceful motion. No wonder the East Asians—the Chinese, Koreans, and Japanese alike—revere the *art* of calligraphy as much as painting. In very significant measure, Chinese ideography is the choreography of human gestures, it is an anthology of somatemes, of dancing anthropograms. It is, in sum, "pragrammatological." Particularly when calligraphed, it turns into a vortex of corporeal energy—to use the expressive language of Marshall McLuhan who toyed with the idea of writing *The Gutenberg Galaxy* (1962) in tactile ideograms.[17] It is the "corporeal writing" *par excellence*. It was Samuel Beckett who came to the discerning and elegant conclusion that in language as gesture the spoken and the written are identical. As dancing anthropograms, Chinese ideography *performs* well, indeed. Shoshana Felman evokes the psychoanalytic sense of corporeality or the carnality of language when she defines speech (*parole*) as "corporeal promise" (*promesse corporelle*), which beckons the conjugal relation between John Austin's philosophy of language as *speech acts* and Freudian/Lacanian psychotherapeutic discourse as "talking cure."[18] Speaking of Lacan's psychoanalytic dialogue between the therapist and client as "talking bodies" is illocutionary: "fundamentally, the dialogic psychoanalytic discourse is *not so much informative as it is performative*" and thus is by necessity ethical as well.[19]

The ethical principium of Confucian hermeneutics is the "rectification of names" (*cheng ming*)—calling things by their right (rite) names—which may be said to be an ethical analogue to the body's "upright posture" whose four "dignities" are standing, walking, sitting, and lying. The rectification of names is quintessentially an ethical hermeneutic. In the end, it is a *political* concept *par excellence*. It is no mere accident that both ideograms *to govern* and *to rectify* are homonyms (i.e., pronounced *cheng*) and, in Chinese ideographic writing, the former contains the latter as its radical. Although the rectification of names is an influential hermeneutical concept in the Sinitic body politic and the history of Sinitic political thought, it is mentioned explicitly only once—in the *Analects*—in conjunction with the proprietary conduct of the ruler in the affairs of the body politic: the first necessary deed the ruler (of Wei) had to perform in administering the government, Confucius suggested, is "to rectify names," for "if names be not rectified, language is not in accordance with the truth of things. If language is not in accordance with the truth of things, affairs cannot be carried on to success" (*Analects*, 13:3.2-5).[20]

Furthermore, I would single out sincerity (*ch'eng*) as a cardinal moral precept that underpins, motivates, and governs the thought and action of a Sinitic soul. Sincerity means "we mean what we say" or "we perform in action what we promise in words." It spells syntactically *word-performed*. In other words, the word as performed actually embodies an index of moral value. The keyword in translating the concept *sincerity*, I suggest, is *performance*, which has a familiar ring to those of us who read Austin's philosophy of language as "How to Do Things with Words." The idea of performance not only denotes the fulfillment of the spoken word *in* and/or *as* action but also transcends the dualism of mind and body on the one hand and of thought and action on the other, both issues of which have plagued Western philosophy since its inception in ancient Greece and particularly in modern Western philosophy since Descartes. In Confucianism, there is a persistent emphasis on the unity of knowledge and action, that is, the notion that knowledge is the beginning of action and action the consummation of knowledge.

II. 2. It may be said without equivocation that the destruction of the earth, which is the unanticipated but inevitable consequence of the modernist project based on anthropocentrism, is the greatest and ultimate threat to the survival of humanity itself. Where would we earthlings be without a habitable earth? We are in dire need of "geophilosophical" ideas in which the earth is not just one element among other elements but the encompassing element of all elements.[21]

Nature's mutiny called the ecological crisis, whose resolution demands both thought and action (i.e., as the saying goes, "think globally, act locally"), is truly symptomatic of the crisis of modernity couched in the ideological verbiage of infinite progress. Francis Bacon put forth most forcefully the Promethean principles of *Herrschaftswissen*, in which knowledge and power intersect at the crossroads of utility, that is, they denature nature as a pile of use/ful objects. In the womb of nature, according to Bacon, we find secrets of excellent use. As a postmodern paradigm, deep ecology or ecophilosophy, which is concerned holistically with the question of *ethics as if the earth really matters*, subverts the perpetuation, and calls for the end, of anthropocentric humanism embodied in Bacon's "philanthropic" disenchantment of nature.[22]

The (ancient) Orient, in contrast, is rich with "earthwords." Its "Orphic" tradition is thoroughly ecocentric by embracing the interconnectedness of all the earthly elements however small (i.e., "small is beautiful," indeed).[23] By the tradition of Orpheus, I am alluding to the tradition of the legendary Thracian musician in ancient Greece who was capable of making all of nature ("ten thousand things") dance in delight. This legend has been celebrated by Claudio Monteverdi, Christoph W. Gluck, Jacques Offenbach, Franz Liszt, and Igor Stravinsky. Beethoven, who said that "I love a tree more than a man," also composed the Pastoral Symphony (Symphony No. 6) in the spirit of Orpheus. It was Rainer Maria Rilke who, in *Sonnets to Orpheus*, praises the quintessence of the Orphic legend: singing is existence or Being (*Gesang ist Dasein*).[24] In the tradition of Sinism, the Taoist text *Tao Te Ching* contains the most celebrated passage concerning the "Orphic" genesis of nature as "self-thusness" or "spontaneity" and the ecological continuum of Being or Interbeing:

In the universe we have four greatnesses, and man is but one.
Man is in accordance with earth.
Earth is in accordance with heaven.
Heaven is in accordance with Tao.
Tao is in accordance with that which is [*tzu-jan*].[25]

In the *Book of Rites*, Confucius, too, prompted the idea that to fell a tree or kill an animal unseasonably is to violate filial piety. Couched firmly in the Confucian language of compassion and ethical proximity, Chan Tsai—the eleventh-century neo-Confucian patron saint of Chinese deep ecology—wrote the following elegant earthwords:

> Heaven is my father, and Earth is my mother, and even such a small creature as I finds an intimate place in their midst. Therefore that which fills the universe I regard as my body and that which directs the universe I consider as my nature. All people are my brothers and sisters, and all things are my companions.[26]

In the ecological continuum of Being or Interbeing, humans are naturally connected to the land or earth. By way of ancient "eco-art" called geomancy—*feng shui* in Chinese—the East Asians have developed a deeply abiding sense of reverence for living *in harmony with* nature (or "ten thousand things"). Geomancy is but ecophilia, which nurtures human habitation with the land. *Feng shui* is composed of two cosmic elements: "wind" (*feng*) and "water" (*shui*). The two elements—wind and water—emblematize nature to which humans are attuned. It is the Sinitic way of harmonizing the human with his/her natural surroundings with care and reverence. It is an attempt to define our earthly habitat on the land. To think in terms of *feng shui* is to be thankful for the generosity of the earth as a "gift" where we plant our firm foothold of life and to pledge and confirm our inseparable and lasting bond with the earth.

While masculinity symbolizes the death of nature, femininity stands for the rebirth of nature. There is indeed a generic bond between feminism and the green movement, which has come to be known as ecofeminism. As an unhyphenated word, ecofeminism incorporates and valorizes the doubling of the feminine and the natural (earthly). Mary Daly's neologism "gyn/ecology" is the perfect emblem of the interconnectedness of feminism and ecology as a postmodern movement.[27]

Writing the body as social inter(dis)course is a shifting concern of *Écriture féminine*. Gynesis—to appropriate the neologism of Alice A. Jardine—signifies the feminine genesis of things and the valorization of the feminine. In so doing, it erases the false dichotomy between the mind (con/ception) and the body (per/ception), which may be called a "patriarchal bifurcation." Gynesis has emerged, I think, as a keyword in postmodern thinking that is capable of redefining the human as a being-in-the-cosmos. In sum, it rejects phallocentric identity. The "one-sex model" refers to the misplaced notion that "*man* is the measure of all things, and woman does not exist as an ontologically distinct category" in which the male body is the standard of the human body, of physiology itself and its representation.[28] As the female body is the "negative mirror" (Italo Calvino's phrase) of the male body, phallocentric identity refuses to acknowledge feminine *difference*. The influential French feminist Luce Irigaray convincingly argues that femininity—particularly feminine sexuality—is *ontologically distinct* in at least a threefold way. First, feminine sexuality is capable of autoeroticism without male intervention or interdiction because female genitalia are, as she puts it plainly, "formed of two lips in continuous contact" capable of caressing each other.[29] Second, female sexuality, unlike male sexuality whose zone of detumescence is confined to and focused on "one," is multiple or many in that the "geography of her pleasure" is not only diversified but also everywhere, ubiquitous. Third, most importantly I think, feminine difference subverts the panoptic regimes of modernity where phallic sovereignty has reigned.[30] It is tactiliphilic whereas phallic identity is scoptophilic.

It is said that in the universe everything *touches* everything else. Many feminists today hold not only that women speak with a "different voice" but also that femininity is allied with the sense of touch more closely than that of sight. Gynesis exudes the joy (*jouissance*, which is also pronounced *j'ouis sens*) of tactile exuberance, which points to communal intimacy, contact, and proximity of the "body's touch." Feminists contend—rightly, I think—that the hegemony of vision is a peculiarly phallogocentric, patriarchal, and matrophobic institution and the logic of voyeurism is uniquely a male logic. The "participatory" sense of touch valorizes the feminine, whereas "spectatorial" vision glorifies the masculine. To femininize the body politic, therefore, is to valorize the sense of touch and to decenter or de-panopticize the spectre of vision in our thinking and doing.[31] By so doing, we loosen up the global visual grip on, and bring the communal sense of intimacy or proximity to, the oversighted or overtelevised world. Gynesis, when translated into tactility, intervenes and fleshes out masculine ocularcentrism. And *that makes all the difference*, which is also implicated in the dialectical subversion and reversal of what many Westerners call the "feminine East" and the "masculine West." Now we know why ecofeminism is capable of transcending racism, sexism, and speciesism all at once.

III

The Enlightenment, as we have seen in Kant who is its champion, is at best a Pyrric victory for humanity: it is brilliant emancipation from self-incurred immaturity for European humanity but a dark era for the rest. Speaking after the fashion of Heidegger, the ecological crisis, which marks the destructive end or abrupt completion of modernity in enlisting and soliciting the holy trinity of racism, sexism, and speciesism in the allegedly ennobling ideology of enlightened reason and progress, is truly a thought-provoking dénouement. There emerges now the inter/esting convergence of ecophilosophy as a postmodern paradigm and postmodernity as a post-Western phenomenon which openly embraces cultural pluralism and intercultural dialogue by letting a hundred flowers bloom, so to speak.[32] First, multiversity as the cherished condition of postmodernity mirrors the inherent condition of nature's diversity, of biodiversity. Second, postmodernity celebrates the gift of alterity or the otherness of the Other including nature's own heterogeneity. To celebrate

Oriental alterity free from Eurocentrism is, for me personally, also to celebrate a sort of intellectual homecoming. I find a deep solace in Heidegger who questions in an inquisitive way with a somewhat admonishing tone why East Asians (particularly Japanese) have constantly and eagerly been chasing after European thought rather than dwelling in the "venerable" tradition of their own thought.[33] Here Heidegger is hinting at the reverential tradition of East Asia that would be able to resist the planetary domination of Western "calculative thinking" over Eastern "meditative thinking," of Western *Gestell* ("im/posed" closure) over Eastern *Gelassenheit* (letting the Other be in its difference).

The deconstruction of the one-dimensional flatland of modern Western identity in this paper is intended to be provocative and provisional rather than systematic and consummate. The politics of modernization is the politics of one-dimensional identity, of Western identity, not of multidimensional differences. By promoting "monotheistically" the essentializing tendencies of Eurocentrism, it makes any intercultural or transcultural dialogue in(com)possible. Michel Foucault observes that the condition of slavery does not lead to a power relationship. So correlatively it must be said that there can be no relationship of dialogue between the superior and the inferior, that is, between two unequals. By embracing One God, One Reality, One Truth, One Good, and One Culture, the ideology of monotheism refuses to recognize and even silences the otherness of the Other and courts ethnocentric chauvinism.[34] As an invention of human intelligence and ingenuity, it also defies nature's diversity. Likewise, the one-dimensional and uni-directional "newspeak" of modernization has reduced everything we do and think to one totalitarian denominator and standard-bearer, whether it be the modernist ideology of John Locke or Karl Marx: *homo oeconomicus*.[35] Every stream or river of human activity empties itself out into the same vast bottomless ocean of *homo oeconomicus*. Indeed, the politics of modernization is monolithic; it is the politics of westernization pure and simple, of Western homogenization. It is the politics of "gone Western," of a fateful *fait accompli* which measures the "progress" of entire humanity by the lightning rod of *homo oeconomicus*. Without the active intervention of the indigenous voice, the politics of modernization becomes merely an echo or the voice of a ventriloquist. Postmodernity, on the other hand, coincides with the new age of ecology, which brings about a continental shift from *homo oeconomicus* to *homo ecologicus*—the sovereign subject of ecophilosophy as "first philosophy"—to which the Orient has much to contribute. The new age of *homo ecologicus* makes us humbly aware that *homo sapiens* has quickly turned into *homo insapiens*. *Homo sapiens's* "enlightened" intelligence manifested in science and technology in modernity is "a fatal combination" to his nascent appearance on this earth as "an environmental abnormality"—to echo the biophilic voice of Edward O. Wilson.[36] One cannot help but wonder if humanity has reached the pinnacle of its environmental abnormality and perhaps even the point of no return.

What monologue is to modernity, dialogue is to postmodernity. Modern "*uni*versity" gives way to postmodern "*multi*versity," which is capable of tolerating the zone of ambiguity. The virtue of the postmodern is the *ability to think in the plural*, and the deconstruction of Eurocentrism is a "modulation" of the postmodern condition. Not as an echo of modernity but as a novelistic voice, postmodernity seeks the subversion of identity and Ovidian reversals by replacing monologic identity with dialogic difference. The logic of identity is monologic because it reduces the otherness of the Other to the (Self) same and thus is intolerant of difference and multiple realities, whereas the logic of difference is dialogic because it nurtures heterology or the relationships of heterogeneity without which dialogue degenerates into nothing but a monologue or a seriality of monologues, which is to say, it harbors no dialogic and harvests no dialogue. To foster genuine dialogue is to *dissolve*—as Ludwig Wittgenstein was fond of describing the function of philosophy—identity in favor of difference, of hermeneutical autonomy in comparative thought and culture that respects "local knowledge." By challenging the complacency of Eurocentrism, the phenomenologist Maurice Merleau-Ponty judiciously contends that "if Western thought is what it claims to be, it must prove it by understanding all 'life-worlds.'"[37] He understood the diacritical hermeneutics of cultures better than any Western philosophers I know in inoculating, conscripting, and empowering *lateral universals* as the intercultural configuration of truth by defamiliarizing, deprovincializing, decentering, and overturning Eurocentrism. Unlike Hegel, Kant, even Husserl and Habermas, who safeguard themselves jealously against and insulate themselves from "unenlightened" alien ideas, Merleau-Ponty introduced and outlined the *principium* of inscribing cultural intertexts. He had particularly in mind Hegel's totalizing Eurocentrism,[38] which unjustly orphans the Orient from the family of philosophy and wantonly displaces it in the marginalized periphery of truth, when he wrote the following suggestive passage:

> Civilizations lacking our philosophical or economic equipment take on an instructive value. It is not a matter of going in search of truth or salvation in what falls short of science or philosophical awareness, or dragging chunks of mythology as such into our philosophy, but acquiring—in the presence of these variants of humanity that we are so far from—a sense of the theoretical and practical problems our institutions are faced with, and of rediscovering the existential field that they are born in and that their long success has led us to forget. The Orient's "childishness" has something to teach us, if it were nothing more than the narrowness of our adult ideas. The relationship between Orient and Occident, like that between child and adult, is not that of ignorance to knowledge or nonphilosophy to philosophy; it is much more subtle, making room on the part of the Orient for all anticipations and "prematurations." Simply rallying and subordinating "non-philosophy" to true philosophy will not create the unity of the human spirit. It already exists in each culture's lateral relationships to others, in the echoes one awakens in the other.[39]

The seductive question of the One and the Many, of Pan and Proteus, has burdened and overwhelmed the philosophical soul everywhere throughout the ages. It has elevated the postmodern intellectual world to a new plateau. In the context of postmodernity, globalization[40] (or the globalization of truth) acquires and distills a radically new meaning: it is wary of "ethnocentric chauvinism" on the one hand and "faceless universalism" on the other—to borrow the well-chosen and erudite expressions of Cornel West who attempts to map out what he calls "the new cultural politics of difference." It cannot be mistaken for and confused with ethnocentric identification or essentializing totalization. Rather, it subverts and transgresses the Eurocentric *enframing* (Heidegger's *Gestell*) of truth. It interrupts and interdicts any ethnocentric overtone and arrogance whether it be Eurocentric, Sinocentric, Indocentric, or Afrocentric. For it is the result of a cross-cultural intertwinement or chiasm in which one culture can no longer be the "negative mirror" of another.

As differentiation is thoroughly relational, harmony Intercultural hermeneutics in search of lateral or cross-cultural universals must be truly of "cosmopolitan" (cosmopolitical) nature,[41] of the new "Orient of the mind" (Paul Valery's expression), which allows the fusion of horizons both temporal (past/old and present/new) and cultural (Western and non-Western) to take place,[42] i.e., cosmopolitanism or cosmopolitics, which incorporates difference as dif/ference (*Differenz* as *Unterschied*). (Harmonization) itself—like making music together—is not inimical to difference; it *is* rather the play of difference(s), of heterogeneity, not of homogeneity. It accentuates the *eccentricity of difference*. Cosmopolitanism is the question not merely of discovering a Plato, an Aristotle, a Machiavelli, a Descartes, a Kant, or a Hegel in the non-Western world but also of finding a Confucius, a Mencius, a Nishida, a Watsuji, a Hu, a Tagore, or a Radhakrishnan in the West. Globalization in search of lateral universals is, in short, a matter of confluence, of mutual influence in the *recognition* of what Mikhail Bakhtin calls heteroglossia, which makes linguistic or cultural *dialogization* (com)possible.[43] The confluential humanism of postmodernity as the fleshfold of the human spirit exists only in the lateral relationships of all cultures including emerging ones in which the echoes of each awaken and are resonant with the others. For, as Merleau-Ponty alludes to the celebrated idea, truth's center is everywhere and its circumference nowhere.

Notes

1. *The Transparent Society*, trans. David Webb (Baltimore: Johns Hopkins University Press, 1992), 1. For Habermas's own critique of postmodernity in defense of modernity, see *The Philosophical Discourse of Modernity*, trans. Frederick Lawrence (Cambridge, MA: MIT Press, 1987). For a special collection of critical responses to Habermas's contention that modernity is an unfinished project, see *Habermas and the Unfinished Project of Modernity*, Maurizio Passerin d'Entrèves and Seyla Benhabib, eds. (Cambridge, MA: MIT Press, 1997).

2. *The Basic Problems of Phenomenology*, trans. Albert Hofstadter (Bloomington, IN: Indiana University Press, 1982), 23.

3. Trans. Geoff Bennington and Brian Massumi (Minneapolis: University of Minnesota Press, 1984), xxv. For further nuances of what Jean-François Lyotard means by the postmodern, see *The Postmodern Explained*, trans. Don Barry et al., and Julian Pefanis and Morgan Thomas, eds. (Minneapolis: University of Minnesota Press, 1992). Cf. the African-American philosopher Cornel West who writes: "Distinctive features of the new cultural politics of difference are to trash the monolithic and homogeneous in the name of diversity, multiplicity and heterogeneity; to reject the abstract, general and universal in light of the concrete, specific and particular; and to historicize, conceptualize and pluralize by highlighting the contingent, provisional, variable, tentative, shifting and changing." "The New Cultural Politics of Difference," in *Out There*, Russell Ferguson et al., eds. (Cambridge, MA: MIT Press, 1990), 19.

4. Edward W. Said's *Orientalism* (New York: Pantheon Books, 1978) has been a focus of the contemporary academic debate on Eurocentrism. He defines Orientalism as "a Western style for dominating, restructuring, and having authority over the Orient" (3). He has recently written a sequel to it: *Culture and Imperialism* (New York: Alfred A. Knopf, 1993). From a perspective of political theory, we should not forget that a comprehensive and controversial work of Orientalism or Asiaticism is Karl A. Wittfogel's *Oriental Despotism* (New Haven, CT: Yale University Press, 1957). For the marginality of Africa in Eurocentrism, see V. Y. Mudimbe, *The Invention of Africa* (Bloomington, IN: Indiana University Press, 1988), which underscores the Foucauldian leitmotiv that there is no pure system of knowledge independent of power and which shows that many African intellectuals themselves are drowned in the torrent of Europeanization. The theme of "beyond Orientalism" has now gained—rightly so, I might add—intellectual attention. In this regard, the following two sequential works of Fred Dallmayr must be singled out and deserve our serious attention: *Beyond Orientalism: Essays on Cross-Cultural Encounter* (Albany, NY: State University of New York Press, 1996) and *Alternative Visions: Paths in the Global Village* (Lanham, MD: Rowman & Littlefield, 1998). By stepping aside the narcissistic orbit of the conversation of the West with itself and in exiting from Orientalism, he envisions the global *Bildung* of the West and the non-West by way of "dialogical engagement" toward the creation of a global village or cosmopolis.

5. *Legislators and Interpreters* (Cambridge, England: Polity Press, 1987), 110. Speaking of colonizing time and the future in particular, the introduction of Western clocks—those time machines which dissociate time from human events and then nature—by Matteo Ricci to China turned out to be a hub of cultural politics between the Christian West and Confucian China. Western clocks not only embodied the validity of Christianity or God's clockwork but also constituted an assault on the self-esteem of China as the Middle Kingdom, as the center of the world. Chinese scholars readily argued that Western clocks were derived from the Chinese clepsydra. See David S. Landes, *Revolution in Time* (Cambridge, MA: Harvard University Press, 1983), chapter 2, "Why Are the Memorials Late?" 37-52. The cultural politics of time, of objective time, indeed points to the important insight that whoever controls time also controls the world.

6. "The Unacceptable Otherness," trans. Katherine Hagedorn, *Diogenes*, no. 159 (1992): 68 (italics added). A classic work on the subject is Tzvetan Todorov's *The Conquest of America*, trans. Richard Howard (New York: Harper and Row, 1984).

7. *The Other*, trans. Christopher Mccann (Cambridge, MA: MIT Press, 1984), 1. For a classic discussion on the representation of the Other from an anthropological perspective, see Johannes Fabian, *Time and the Other* (New York: Columbia University Press, 1983). Cf. the author's "Editor's Introduction," *Human Studies*, 16 (1933): 1-17, which is a general introduction to a special double issue of *Human Studies* on the topic of "Postmodernity and the Question of the Other."

8. See Mark C. Taylor, *Altarity* (Chicago: University of Chicago Press, 1987).

9. See *Identity and Difference*, trans. Joan Stambaugh (New York: Harper and Row, 1969).

10. *The Human Condition* (Chicago: University of Chicago Press, 1958), 175-76.

11. Mark C. Taylor remarks that "In his search for a reconciling middle ground, Hegel, in keeping with the tendency of Western thought, privileges identity and unity. Hegelian philosophy can be understood as a systematic attempt to secure the *identity* of identity and nonidentity and the *union* of union and nonunion" (*Altarity*, xxiii). Cf. Gianni Vattimo, *The Adventure of Difference*, trans. Cyprian Blamires (Baltimore: John Hopkins University Press, 1993), 160: "It is precisely in the Hegelian dialectic that the history of the notion of identity in the metaphysical tradition is in fact accomplished." Jacques Derrida's deconstruction of Western metaphysics as logocentrism is relevant to my critique of Eurocentrism. "Logocentrism, in its developed philosophical sense," he writes, "is inextricably linked to the Greek and European tradition. As I have attempted to demonstrate elsewhere in some detail, logocentric philosophy is a specifically Western response to a much larger necessity which also occurs in the Far East and other cultures, that is, the phonocentric necessity: the privilege of the voice over writing. The priority of spoken language over written or silent language stems from the fact that when words are spoken the speaker and the listener are supposed to be simultaneously present to one another; they are supposed to be the same, pure unmediated presence. This ideal of perfect self-presence, of the immediate possession of meaning, is what is expressed by the phonocentric necessity. Writing, on the other hand, is considered subversive in so far as it creates a spatial and temporal distance between the author and audience; writing presupposes the absence of the author and so we can never be sure exactly what is meant by a written text; it can have many different meanings as opposed to a single unifying one. But this phonocentric necessity did not develop into a systematic logocentric metaphysics in any non-European culture. Logocentrism is a uniquely Eueopean phenomenon." See Richard Kearney, *Dialogues with Contemporary Continental Thinkers* (Manchester: Manchester University Press, 1984), 115-16.

12. *Essays Moral, Political, and Literary*, T. H. Green and T. H. Grose, eds., 2 vols. (London: Longmans, Green, 1875), I: 252.

13. *Observations on the Feeling of the Beautiful and Sublime*, trans. John T. Goldthwait (Berkeley, CA: University of California Press, 1960), 110-11. *Race and the Enlightenment*, Emmanuel Chukwudi Eze, ed. (Oxford, England: Blackwell Publishers, 1997) documents Kant's racism which is the greatest prejudice as well as blunder of the philosophical paragon of the Enlightenment. A spirited discussion of the future of African philosophy is found in *Postcolonial African Philosophy*, Emmanuel Chukwudi Eze, ed. (Oxford, England: Blackwell Publishers, 1997). I first came upon the reference to Hume and Kant while I was reading Henry Louis Gates, Jr., "Editor's Introduction: Writing 'Race' and the Difference It Makes," in *Race, Writing, and Difference*, Henry Louis Gates, Jr., ed. (Chicago: University of Chicago Press, 1986), 10-11.

14. The contemporary relevance of Confucius and Confucian philosophy is intimated by, for example, the American philosopher Herbert Fingarette in *Confucius—The Secular As Sacred* (New York: Harper and Row, 1972), 7: "When I began to read Confucius, I found him to be a prosaic and parochial moralizer; his collected sayings, the *Analects*, seemed to me an archaic irrelevance. Later, and with increasing force, I found him a thinker with profound insight and with an imaginative vision of man equal in its grandeur to any I know. Increasingly, I have become convinced that Confucius can be a teacher to us today—a major teacher, not one who merely gives us a slightly exotic perspective on the ideas already current. He tells us things not being said elsewhere; things needing to be said. He has a new lesson to teach." Cf. the author's "Confucianism as Political Philosophy: A Postmodern Perspective," *Human Studies* 16 (1993): 213-30.

15. In "Enlightenment and the Question of the Other: A Postmodern Audition," *Human Studies* (forthcoming), I discuss (1) body, (2) woman (3) nature and (4) non-West as the four untouchables of Enlightenment.

16. There is, however, a notable exception in Watsuji Tetsur, *Rinrigaku*, 2 vols. (Tokyo: Iwanami Shoten, 1965). The major portion of this work has recently been translated into English, as *Watsuji Tetsur 's Rinrigaku*, by Yamamoto Seisaku and Robert E. Carter (Albany, NY: State University of New York Press, 1996). The translation of Watsuji's *Rinrigaku* (Ethics) is the long overdue recognition in the West of the importance of his work in ethics. While we are dwelling on the important subject of ethics, it must be said that with the late Emmanuel Levinas, postmodernity made its decisive turn to ethics. In this respect, there is an important affinity between Confucius (or Confucianism) and Levinas despite their difference on the question of alterity. It should be noted that Confucian thought has been sneered at by the Western intellectual circle for too long: it is allegedly less than fully philosophical or nonphilosophical because it is merely social and ethical.

17. For the author's discussion on the subject of reading "Sinograms," see "Misreading the Ideogram: From Fenollosa to Derrida and McLuhan," *Paideuma* 13 (1984): 211-27.

18. *The Literary Speech Act*, trans. Catherine Porter (Ithaca, NY: Cornell University Press, 1983).

19. *Jacques Lacan and the Adventure of Insight* (Cambridge, MA: Harvard University Press, 1987), 118-19 (italics added).

20. Craig Owens describes "de/nomination" as integral to the European conquest of the native inhabitants of South America and comes to the conclusion that the European project of visualizing or panopticizing the (native) Other should be stopped and the Europeans should listen to what the natives may have to say. See *Beyond Recognition*, Scott Bryson et al., eds. (Berkeley, CA: University of California Press, 1992), "Improper Names," 284-97.

21. Cf. Gilles Deleuze and Felix Guattari, *What Is Philosophy?*, trans. Hugh Tomlinson and Graham Burchell (New York: Columbia University Press, 1994), chapter 4, "Geophilosophy," 85-113. See also the author's "The Greening of Postmodern Ethics: The Ethical Question of Reinhabiting the Earth," in *Postmodern Ethics*, Hugh J. Silverman, ed. (New York: Routledge, forthcoming). The Norwegian philosopher Arne Naess began in 1973 to promote deep ecology as an academic inquiry. Deep ecology seeks the intrinsic connection between the practical movements of ecology and philosophy as an encompassing discipline. To quote him: "In so far as ecology movements deserve our attention, they are *ecophilosophical* rather than ecological. Ecology is a *limited* science which makes *use* of scientific methods. Philosophy is the most general forum of

debate on fundamentals, descriptive as well as prescriptive, and political philosophy is one of its subsections. By an *ecosophy* I mean a philosophy of ecological harmony or equilibrium. A philosophy as a kind of *sofia* [or] wisdom is openly normative, it contains *both* norms, rules, postulates, value priority announcements *and* hypotheses concerning the state of affairs in our universe. Wisdom is policy wisdom, prescription, not only scientific description and prediction." "The Shallow and the Deep, Long-Range Ecology Movement: A Summary," *Inquiry* 16 (1973): 99.

22. Lockean "possessive individualism," whose backbone is the labor theory of value, is no less anthropocentric than Bacon's utilitarianism in taking the anti-ecological stance of viewing wilderness or the uncultivated land as "waste" (Locke's own term).

23. See the author's "The Way of Ecopiety: An Essay in Deep Ecology from a Sinitic Perspective," *Asian Philosophy* 1 (1991): 127-40.

24. For the author's discussion of the Orphic legend and ecology, see "The Orphic Voice and Ecology" 3 (1981): 329-40, and (with Petee Jung) "The Way of Ecopiety: A Philosophic Minuet for Ecological Ethics," in *Commonplaces: Essays on the Nature of Place*, David W. Black, Donald Kunze and John Pickles, eds. (Lanham, MD: University Press of America, 1989), 81-99. It is extraordinarily interesting to find that the Japanese legend of Semimaru parallels the legend of Orpheus. Semimaru is an archetype of the performing artist in Japan, and he inspired the composition of many poems, tales, and plays in the history of Japanese literature. As the legend goes, Semimaru was a blind begger lutenist whose gift for music compensates for his blindness. Thus this legendary "composite individual" personifies the spiritual "sight" of the blind.

25. *Tao: A New Way of Thinking*, trans. Chang Chung-yuan (New York: Harper and Row, 1973), 76.

26. *A Source Book in Chinese Philosophy*, trans. Wing-tsit Chan (Princeton, NJ: Princeton University Press, 1963), 497.

27. Modernization or westernization in Oriental societies has miserably failed, I think, to demarginalize women. One of the most scathing critiques of the marginality of women within the Confucian tradition is the French feminist Julia Kristeva's *About Chinese Women*, trans. Anita Barrow (New York: Urizen, 1977).

28. Thomas Laqueur, *Making Sex* (Cambridge, MA: Harvard University Press, 1990), 62.

29. *This Sex Which Is Not One*, trans. Catherine Porter (Ithaca, NY: Cornell University Press, 1985), 24.

30. For modern panopticism, see Martin Jay, "Scopic Regimes of Modernity," in *Vision and Visuality*, Hal Foster, ed. (Seattle, WA: Bay Press, 1988), 3-23.

31. In *The Public and Its Problems* (New York: Holt, 1927), John Dewey asserted that "The connections of the ear with vital and on-going thought and emotion are immensely closer and more varied than those of the eye. Vision is a spectator; hearing is a participator" (218-19).

32. See the author's *The Question of Rationality and the Basic Grammar of Intercultural Texts* (Niigata, Japan: International University of Japan, 1989) and *Rethinking Political Theory: Essays in Phenomenology and the Study of Politics*, Series in Continental Thought, no. 18 (Athens, Ohio: Ohio University Press, 1993), chapter 5, "The Spectre of Ethnocentrism and the Production of Intercultural Texts," 91-110.

33. See *On the Way to Language*, trans. Peter D. Hertz (New York: Harper and Row, 1971), "A Dialogue on Language Between a Japanese and an Inquirer," 1-54. Cf. the author's "Heidegger's Way with Sinitic Thinking," in *Heidegger and Asian Thought*, Graham Parkes, ed. (Honolulu: University of Hawaii Press, 1987), 217-44. For Heidegger and deep ecology, see Hwa Yol Jung and Petee Jung, "To Save the Earth," *Philosophy Today* 19 (1975): 108-117. Asian intellectuals have been asking themselves seriously for some time if Asian societies can join globalization as genuinely Asian societies or merely Western replicas. The British political philosopher John Gray has recently added an unscathing criticism of the Enlightenment project, which is tantamount to the destruction of the whole earth. He comes to the conclusion that "any prospect of cultural recovery from the nihilism that the Enlightenment has spawned may lie with non-Occidental peoples, whose task will then be in part that of protecting themselves from the debris cast up by Western shipwreck. Or it may be that even those non-Occidental cultures which have modernized without wholesale Westernization have nevertheless assimilated too much of the Western nihilist relationship with technology and the earth for a turning in man's relationship with the earth to be any longer a real possibility. If this were to be so, it would be consonant with the sense of releasement invoked in this inquiry, which encompasses an openness to ultimate danger, to the contingency and mortality not only of human cultures and of other living things, but also of the earth itself." See *Enlightenment's Wake: Politics and Culture at the Close of the Modern Age* (New York: Routledge, 1995).

34. It is noteworthy that even the scientific objectivity of political behavioralism is not immune from Eurocentrism. Charles Taylor contends that "the result of ignoring the difference in intersubjective meanings can be disastrous to a science of comparative politics, viz., that we interpret all other societies in the categories of our own. Ironically, this is what seems to have happened to American political science. Having strongly criticized the old institution-focused comparative politics for its ethnocentricity (or Western bias), it proposed to understand the politics of all society in terms of such functions, for instance, as 'interest articulation' and 'interest aggregation' [Gabriel Almond's terms] whose definition is strongly influenced by the bargaining culture of our civilization, but which is far from being guaranteed appropriateness elsewhere. The not surprising result is a theory of political development which places the Atlantic type polity at the summit of human political development." "Interpretation and the Sciences of Man," *The Review of Metaphysics* 25 (1971): 34.

35. For a penetrating critique of *homo faber* in modernity, see Hannah Arendt, *The Human Condition*, chapter 4, "Work," 136-74. The primacy of the economic over the political and thus the eclipse of the political, Sheldon S. Wolin argues, began in modern times with Lockean liberalism. See *Politics and Vision* (Boston: Little, Brown, 1960), chapter 9, "Liberalism and the Decline of Political Philosophy," 287-351. In "Marxism and Deep Ecology in Postmodernity: From *Homo Oeconomicus* to *Homo Ecologicus*," *Thesis Eleven*, no. 28 (1991): 86-99, the author argues against modern *homo oeconomicus* in favor of postmodern *homo ecologicus*. It is indeed a sad intellectual state of affairs when David Gress zealously defends the idea of the West on the question of ecology. He asserts adamantly but naively: "To accuse liberalism and capitalism of environmental destruction overlooked the fact that the more liberal and capitalist a society the less pollution it produced. To accuse the scientific revolution overlooked the fact that environmentalism as a moment depended on science to define and measure pollution and on technology to cure it. Gore's prescriptions for a nonpolluting society

yielded the vision of a Stone Age Soviet Union run by moralistic enforcers who had a monopoly of the means of coercion and propaganda; the very denial of liberalism and economic development, the only historically tested and reliable means to a cleaner environment." See *From Plato to NATO: The Idea of the West and Its Opponents* (New York: Free Press, 1998), 520. As the old saying goes, Gress is barking up a wrong tree! What he should examine closely is modern anthropocentrism in the West as the root cause of earthly devastation. I would submit that the anthropocentric question is "Why do animals cross the roads we build?" while the nonanthropocentric question is "Why do we build roads where animals cross?"

36. In *The Firmament of Time* (New York: Atheneum, 1960), the ecopoet Loren Eiseley describes human arrogance from the very moment of our appearance on this earth: "It is with the coming of man that a vast hole seems to open in nature, a vast black whirlpool spinning faster and faster, consuming flesh, stones, soil, minerals, sucking down the lightning, wrenching power from the atom, until the ancient sounds of nature are drowned in the cacophony of something which is no longer nature, something instead which is loose and knocking at the world's heart, something demonic and no longer planned—escaped, it may be—spewed out of nature, contending in a final giant's game against its master" (123-24).

37. *Signs*, trans. Richard C. McCleary (Evanston, IL: Northwestern University Press, 1964), 138.

38. Hegel's Orientalism triggered and sustained my interest in comparative philosophy. Its primary aim was to show that the Orient, particularly China, indeed has a *philosophy*, despite Hegel's claim to the contrary. The first of my writing in comparative philosophy was "Wang Yang-ming and Existential Phenomenology," *International Philosophical Quarterly* 5 (1965): 612-36. A sequel to it was "The Unity of Knowledge and Action: A Postscript to Wang Yang-ming's Existential Phenomenology," *Journal of Chinese Studies* 3 (1986): 19-38.

39. *Signs*, 319. See also *Continental Philosophy*, I: *Philosophy and Non-Philosophy Since Merleau-Ponty*, Hugh J. Silverman, ed. (New York: Routledge, 1988), chapter 1, Maurice Merleau-Ponty, "Philosophy and Non-Philosophy Since Hegel," 9-83. The structural anthropologist Claude Lévi-Strauss was sensitive to lateral thinking when he paid homage to the "primitive" or "savage" mind in his inaugural lecture at the Collège de France—the homage paid to the preservation of the *lateral continuity* to humanity in the spirit of Merleau-Ponty, who was also his close colleague. See *Structural Anthropology*, vol. 2, trans. Monique Layton (New York: Basic Books, 1976), 32. It is also worth noting that Habermas continues Hegel's Orientalism. In *Studies in the Theory of Ideology* (Berkeley, CA: University of California Press, 1984), John B. Thompson notes that "in fact Habermas's 'reconstruction' of the developmental logic of world-views looks very much like a mere project of Piaget's ontogenetic stages on to the phylogenetic scale; many readers will no doubt balk at what appears to be a continuation of Hegelian ambitions with cognitive-developmental means. One is bound to wonder, moreover, just how Habermas's theory of social evolution can be applied to the developmental course of societies outside of Europe, just how it can avoid the ethnocentrism and oversimplification which characterize so many evolutionary schemes" (298). It should also be pointed out in passing that the idea of "*universal* pragmatics" in Habermas's as well as Karl-Otto Apel's philosophy without any reference to non-Western philosophy is at best unmindful.

40. For a comprehensive analysis of globalization from a sociological perspective, which touches on the issues of modernity vs. postmodernity and universalism vs. particularism, see Roland Robertson, *Globalization: Social Theory and Global Culture* (London: Sage Publications, 1991).

41. The anthropologist Michel-Rolph Trouillot makes the following point: "'We,' here, *is* the West, as in Michael Jackson and Lionel Richie's international hit, 'We Are the World.' This is not 'the West' in a genealogical or territorial sense. The postmodern world has little space left for genealogies, and notions of territoriality are being redefined right before our eyes. . . . It is a world where black American Michael Jackson starts an international tour from Japan and imprints cassettes that mark the rhythm of Haitian peasant families in the Cuban Sierra Maestra; a world where Florida speaks Spanish (once more); where a Socialist prime minister in Greece comes by way of New England and an imam of fundamentalist Iran by way of Paris. It is a world where a political leader in reggae-prone Jamaica traces his roots to Arabia, where United States credit cards are processed in Barbados, and Italian designer shoes made in Hong Kong. It is a world where the Pope is Polish, where the most orthodox Marxists live on the western side of a fallen iron curtain. It is a world where the most enlightened are only part-time citizens of part-time communities of imagination." See "Anthropology and the Savage Slot: The Poetics and Politis of Otherness," in *Recapturing Anthropology*, Richard G. Fox, ed. (Santa Fe, NM: School of American Research Press, 1991), 22. Stephen Toulmin speaks of "an ecological cosmopolis" as a "post-modern" project and of "an ecological model [which] opens up the possibilities for diversity and change, and so can be emancipatory." See *Cosmopolis: The Hidden Agenda of Modernity* (New York: Free Press, 1990), 195. Cf. Anthony Giddens, who considers "the increasing prominence of ecological concerns" as an integral part of the "post-modern" intellectual movement. See *The Consequences of Modernity* (Stanford, CA: Stanford University Press, 1990), 46.

42. Here I am extending Hans-Georg Gadamer's well-known idea of hermeneutics as the fusion of (temporal) horizons (the past and the present) (*Horizontverschmelzung*). See *Truth and Method*, 2nd rev. ed. and rev. trans. Joel Weinsheimer and Donald G. Marshall (New York: Crossroad, 1991). Cf. Vattimo, *The Adventure of Difference*, 153: "The fusion of horizons takes place to the extent to which each of the interlocutors 'renounces' his *own* horizon, not by renouncing the fact of having a horizon, but by renouncing the fact of managing it as his own or disposing of it as he pleases. This phenomenon of permanent 'renunciation' is attested by the modes in which the integration of individual horizons into anonymous suprapersonal horizons (which in turn also stand at the basis of the constitution of individual horizons) actually takes place in society. Gadamer aptly describes these modes in terms of the concept of *play*, emphasizing its *expropriating* dimensions."

43. All along in this section, I have been speaking of the dialogical prose of the Russian literary theorist Mikhail Bakhtin, for whom *dialogization* may be appropriated as the globalization of heteroglossia that leads to the production of intertextuality. For Bakhtin's dialogism, see *The Dialogic Imagination*, ed. Michael Holquist, trans. Caryl Emerson and Michael Holquist (Austin, TX: University of Texas Press, 1981). In Bakhtin's dialogism, there is another cue: as dominance breeds resistance, carnivalization is a recalcitrant and oppositional intellectual toolkit to dethrone or deterritorialize "officialdom"—the "officialdom" of Eurocentrism in my argument here. In *Multiculturalism and "the Politics of Recognition"* (Princeton, NJ: Princeton University Press, 1992), which was the inaugural lecture for the opening of the University Center for

Human Values at Princeton University, Charles Taylor discusses the long-standing problematical question of recognition and cultural pluralism. Moreover, he invokes Bakhtin's dialogism and writes that "Human beings are constituted in conversation; and hence what gets internalized in the mature subject is not the reaction of the other, but the whole conversation, with the interanimation of its voices. Only a theory of this kind can do justice to the dialogical nature of the self." "The Dialogical Self," in *The Interpretive Turn*, David R. Hiley, James F. Bohman, and Richard Shusterman, eds. (Ithaca, NY: Cornell University Press, 1991), 314. The author's discussion of Bakhtin's carnal dialogism is found in "Bakhtin's Dialogical Body Politics," in *Bakhtin and the Human Sciences*, Michael Mayerfeld Bell and Michael Gardiner, eds. (London: Sage Publications, 1998), 95-111.

Index

'Abduh, Muhammad, 3, 14, 16-19, 22
Abdulhamic II, Sultan, 91, 93
Abraham, 82
absolute nothingness concept, 243, 244
absolutism, 28, 30
Abu-Lughod, Leila, 4, 46-49, 53, 58n30
accountability, public, 201-2
Adorno, Theodor, 36n66
Al-Afghani, 94, 113n11
Afghanistan, 95
agency: expression of, 54-55; individual, 50; sexual, 49; veiling and, 43-44; women's, 51
Ahmad, Ilyas, 115n27
Ahmed, Leila, 40, 43-44, 54-55
Ali Abd ur-Razik, 96
Ali, Imam, 129, 134
Aligarh College, 93
Alishan, Leonardo, 135
alterity, 279, 285-86
Amane, Nishi, 249n4
Ames, Roger, 191, 195, 198-99, 203, 260
Analects, 191-94, 197-201, 204-5n9, 281
anarchism, 260-62, 272n29

anthropocentric humanism, 283, 292n22
anthropocentrism, 264, 283, 294n35
antimodernism, 12
Apel, Karl-Otto, 294-95n39
Appleby, R. Scott, 31n12
al-Aqsa, Masjid, 104
Arendt, Hannah, 36n62, 190, 207n29, 210n77
Arisaka, Yoko, 8, 237-52, 397
art, nature and, 284
artists, 130, 200-201
asceticism, 129-33, 140-41n13
Ashura rituals, 127-28, 139
Asia: communitarianism and, 186-88; democracy, Asian-style, 216-17
Astarabadi, Fadl Allah, 128
authenticity, 35n59
authoritarianism, 187, 215-16
authority; abusive, 198; acceptance of, 201; activity and, 196, 202; communitarian structure and, 190; Confucianism and, 193-95; Taoism and, 264-65
autonomy, 24, 46-49, 180, 195
Ayoub, Mahmoud, 124
Ayyubi, Salahaddin, 114n24

Bacon, Francis, 283

ABOUT THE CONTRIBUTORS

Yoko Arisaka is assistant professor of philosophy at the University of San Francisco. She received her Ph.D. in philosophy from the University of California at Riverside in 1996. Her fields of research include modern Japanese philosophy and Asian philosophy, nineteenth- and twentieth-century continental philosophy, and political philosophy. She is a coeditor of *Nishida and the Question of Modernity* (forthcoming) and is currently working on her book, *Philosophy and Imperialism: Asian Modernism in Prewar Japan*.

A graduate from London University, **John J. Clarke** is currently Reader in the History of Ideas at Kingston University, United Kingdom. His publications include: *In Search of Jung: Historical and Philosophical Enquiries* (Routledge, 1992), *Jung and Eastern Thought: A Dialogue with the Orient* (Routledge, 1994), and *Oriental Enlightenment: The Encounter between Asian and Western Thought* (Routledge 1997). He is currently working on the relationship between Daoism and Western thought and completing a book titled *A Way for the West: Daoism and Western Thought*, to be published by Routledge in 2000.

Fred Dallmayr is Packey J. Dee Professor of Government at the University of Notre Dame, specializing in political theory with a focus on late modern and contemporary political thought. A graduate from the University of Munich and Duke University, he has been teaching at Notre Dame since 1978. Among his publications are: *Twilight of Subjectivity* (1981); *Language and Politics* (1984); *Critical Encounters* (1987); *Between Freiburg and Frankfurt* (1991); *Hegel: Modernity and Politics* (1993); *The Other Heidegger* (1993); *Beyond Orientalism* (1996); and *Alternative Visions: Paths in the Global Village* (1998).

Ahmet Davutoglu is associate professor of political science at Marmara University, Istanbul, Turkey. He is chairman of the Foundation for Science and Arts in Istanbul. His publications include *Alternative Paradigms: The Impact* *of Islamic and Western Weltanschauungs on Political Theory* (University Press of America, 1994) and *Civilizational Transformation and the Muslim World* (Kuala Lumpur: Quill, 1994). He also has published many scholarly articles and research papers in several languages on international relations, political thought, and comparative civilizational studies.

Manochehr Dorraj is associate professor of political science at Texas Christian University. Among his publications are: *From Zarathustra to Khomeini: Populism and Dissent in Iran* (Lynne Rienner Publishers, 1990); *The Changing Political Economy of the Third World* (Lynne Rienner Publishers, 1995); *Middle East at the Crossroads: The Changing Political Dynamics and the Foreign Policy Challenges* (University Press of America, 1999).

Roxanne L. Euben is assistant professor of political science at Wellesley College. She is the author of a forthcoming book on comparative political theory, *Enemy in the Mirror: Islamic Fundamentalism and the Limits of Modern Rationalism* (Princeton University Press, 1999), as well as several articles on the relationship between Western and non-Western political thought.

Russell Arben Fox is a doctoral candidate at the Catholic University of America, where he is writing a dissertation on J. G. Herder, Charles Taylor, and the moral theory of contemporary communitarianism. He has published articles in the *Review of Politics* and *Polity*.

Azizah Y. al-Hibri is a professor of law at the University of Richmond, where she teaches corporate law and Islamic jurisprudence. She is founder and current president of KARAMAH: Muslim Women Lawyers for Human Rights, and member of the board of directors of The Interfaith Alliance Foundation. She has authored, edited, and contributed to several books, including *Deontic Logic* (1978), *Women and Islam* (1981), and *Religious and Ethical Perspectives on Population Issues* (1993). She is also founding editor of *Hypatia: A Journal of Feminist Philosophy*, and an associate editor.

Nancy J. Hirschmann is associate professor of government at Cornell University, and a fellow at the Institute for Advanced Study in Princeton for the 1998-99 academic year. She is the author of *Rethinking Obligation: A Feminist Method for Political Theory* (Cornell University Press, 1992), coeditor with Christine Di Stefano of *Revisioning the Political: Feminist Reconstructions of Traditional Concepts in Western Political Theory* (Westview Press, 1996), and coeditor with Ulrike Liebert of *Between the Cradle and the Grave: Feminist Theoretical and Empirical Perspectives on the Social Welfare State* (Rutgers University Press, forthcoming).

Robert C. Johansen is professor of government and international studies at the University of Notre Dame and acting Regan director of the Joan B. Kroc Institute for International Peace Studies. He is author of *The National Interest and the Human Interest: An Analysis of U.S. Foreign Policy* (Princeton University Press, 1980) and coeditor of *The Constitutional Foundations of World Peace* (State University of New York Press, 1993). He has published articles on security issues in numerous professional and popular journals. He is the founding editor in chief of *World Policy Journal* and past president of the World Policy Institute.

Hwa Yol Jung is professor of political science at Moravian College where he teaches political theory with a focus on phenomenology, existential philosophy, hermeneutics, comparative philosophy, environmental philosophy, and post-modernism. Among his publications are *The Question of Rationality and the Basic Grammar of Intercultural Texts* (1989) and *Rethinking Political Theory* (1993). He has recently been working on the publication of a collection of his essays in comparative philosophy.

L. H. M. Ling is senior lecturer of international studies at the Institute of Social Studies (ISS) in the Hague, the Netherlands. Her research covers international relations theory and international political economy with East Asia as a geocultural focus. Specifically, she examines issues of democratization in nonliberal societies, hegemony and identity in world politics. Her book, *Conquest and Desire: Postcolonial Learning between Asia and the West*, is forthcoming from MacMillan Press in London and St. Martin's Press in New York.

Thomas Pantham is professor of political science at the M.S. University of Baroda, India, where he has been teaching since 1966. He has been a visiting research scholar at the universities of Cambridge, Princeton, McGill, and Heidelberg. In addition to numerous journal articles, he has published *Political Parties and Democratic Consensus* (1976) and *Political Theories and Social Reconstruction* (1995) and has coedited *Political Discourse: Explorations in Indian and Western Political Thought* (1987) and *Political Thought in Modern India* (1986).

Chih-yu Shih is professor of political science at National Taiwan University where he teaches Chinese politics, political psychology, and feminism. His two most recent English publications are *Collective Democracy: Political and Legal Reform in China* (Chinese University Press of Hong Kong, 1999) and *State and Society in China's Political Economy* (Lynne Rienner, 1995). His recent research focuses on civic culture of minorities in China and Taiwan.